Illustrated by Joann Lane Traeger

Prentice-Hall, Inc.
Englewood Cliffs, New Jersey

Prentice-Hall Psychology Series
Arthur T. Jersild, Editor

Understanding Human Development

Howard Lane and Mary Beauchamp

Fourth printing . . . January, 1962

Designed by Walter Behnke

Preface

How a cell becomes a personality is the theme of this book. It is written for young people in the early stages of their preparation for teaching.

To those who pause to look and reflect upon it no phenomenon in nature approaches the wonder of the growth of a human being from a single cell through ever-changing postures, proportions, capacities, interests, needs, circumstances. Babies Noah, Socrates, Michelangelo, Napoleon, Bach, Lincoln, Hitler, Einstein were very much alike. They cooed and howled in their cradles, walked at about age one. What factors cause one cell to develop into a thoughtful, creative, altruistic member of the human race and another to become a talented demon who terrifies the world is the problem posed, and not fully answered, by this book.

During the lifetime of the authors, teaching has changed from imposing a set of classroom chores upon reluctant pupils to a profession nurturing and guiding the development of masses of varied potentialities into whole, unique, cooperating personalities. The rearing of young human beings is ever and always the most meaningful and productive enterprise of a people. To be a professional in this process is unparalleled in opportunity and responsibility. A vocation becomes a profession when it is based upon a body of principles and special knowledge and directed to socially valuable outcomes. The basic principles and knowledge of teaching are concerned with the growth of human beings as evidenced in their developing behavior; the social outcome is the development of persons able to live well in the worlds of which they are a part and to participate in the continuous creation of these worlds.

The worlds of individuals consist not of toys, planes, mountains, shores, buildings, machines, and gadgets but of the behavior of people and the relationships among them. Our nations and cities are not mere locations of buildings and streets; they are the relationships, values, and ways of the lives of people. In the middle of this Twentieth Century people seem anxious and confused. Are our child-rearing ways producing anxious and confused persons? Do our anxiety and confusion result from failure to nurture the intelligence, stability of personality, and character necessary to living in the worlds we inhabit?

This is written for teachers who believe in the democratic way of life. It is intended as a guide for nurturing the infinite capacities of human beings so that they may flower into self-respecting, dignified, freedom-loving people who can live and prosper in an interdependent culture. It is not a guide for developing slaves, or subjects, or docile followers.

We offer relatively few isolated facts. We offer instead some meanings, interpretations, and applications of some of the more relevant facts and principles that have been derived from careful studies and from the insights of wise and thoughtful scholars. Readers who wish to study more deeply and widely will find reference to many studies and materials which the authors have found to be of much worth to them and to their students.

The materials in this book have stemmed largely from the concerns of classroom teachers. For several years the writers have conducted a course entitled "Child Study for Teachers." In small groups over a period of several months teachers studied and discussed real, live, non-problem boys and girls. Their goal was, not to find faults needful of correction, but to see each individual as a unique human being in order to discern the teacher's role in his life. No person can be understood apart from the groups in which he functions. Much emphasis was given, therefore, to the study of children and adolescents in varieties of group situations. As these groups of teachers considered together the individuals they were studying, they found more and more need for more and more kinds of knowledge about human behavior. They felt a need to gain an understanding of the lives of their pupils and to acquire many skills and techniques for working with young people. They moved farther and farther away from conceiving the teacher as one who molds clay into predetermined shapes, tossing aside the imperfect ones. In their study, the teachers soon realized the need for deepened self-knowledge.

In their own living and teaching and in helping teachers see purposes and ways of understanding children, the authors have come to some well-defined beliefs:

> In this complex world, the rearing of children cannot be left to chance. Education of all children is an urgent function of a people.
>
> No teacher can teach well without knowledge and appreciation of the meaning of the complete span of human development from conception to the natural end of life. For high-school teachers to study only adolescents, or primary teachers to study only young children is to perpetuate folly. Appreciation of the importance of the quality of living in the early years is essential to all teachers. Age is an extremely rough measure of ability, interests, concerns.
>
> Individuals and cultures tend to develop habits and firm attitudes in the realm of child-rearing. A profession must constantly subject these to the scrutiny of intelligence in the light of emerging knowledge, values, and conditions. We look neither to Socrates nor to John Harvard for authority on the education of a child. We respect the authority of our own intelligence, of our perceptions of contemporary circumstances, and of our estimate of probabilities and expectations. We urge that teaching become more and more a highly intelligent profession—not continue as a set of habits and prescribed standardized procedures.
>
> Teachers are not purveyors of privilege and advantage. Every child has the right to live in dignity, self-respect, and worth regardless of the quality and status of his parents, his ability to make a spectacular touchdown, his skill in the three R's, or his IQ. The school is not a gigantic mental test.
>
> No man can understand another without understanding himself. If a teacher is to guide the immature toward maturity, he must seek his own maturity through continued efforts to know himself.

The authors offer this book in full knowledge and appreciation of the fact that any man can know but little of what man knows.

Howard Lane
Mary Beauchamp

Contents

Understanding
Human Development

The Foundations of Human Behavior

The earth today is shaking beneath the feet of many human beings just as surely as it did in San Francisco in 1906. Boundaries that have been fixed for many centuries are blurred; many of them are erased. Time and space have truly become infinite. Loyalties once held inviolate are being rejected by millions of people. Our old securities are loosening; the foundations of our physical and psychological world seem shaken and trembling.

How can we build a foundation of security in the world of 1960 and beyond? We believe we can do this only by looking within ourselves, by coming to understand more completely the inner springs of every man's behavior as he seeks to relate to other human beings. His deep wants must be recognized and satisfied.

We recall a story of a winsome urchin who sat down next to a kindlylooking woman on a streetcar. As she got nearer her stop, she changed her seat to get near the exit. The urchin moved with her, again nestling near her as he took his seat. When she got off the car, the small boy followed her. She became curious and gently said to him, "Why do you stay so close to me?" His answer was, "I was just pretendin' I belonged to someone." Many are the humans today who are pretending to belong to someone and to be important.

3

This section is designed to help you understand more fully some of the reasons why mankind seeks security and belongingness and how the teacher's task is complicated by the culture of our day. If our inner foundations are strongly built, we have faith that by common endeavor teachers will enhance the dignity and worth of those they teach.

1

The Importance of Understanding Humans

Ellen (age nine) has the oldest parents of anyone in her class. Her father is nearing sixty, and her mother is in her fifties. Last year her father had two successive heart attacks and had to be hospitalized. Ellen didn't see her father for a long time. She began to worry about him and kept asking to see him. Her anxieties came to school with her. I noticed that she was not the same little girl. I see Ellen reading and biting her nails—one as an escape from reality; the other a physical manifestation of her frustrations. Her father is in Palm Springs for a rest and she misses him.

A very vivid imagination and memory are among Bob's (age ten) endowments. When I see him staring into space, I know that he is watching people and places that are as real to him as the class blackboard and desks. Because of this, Bob will often withdraw from the people and events that surround him to investigate with interest and curiosity that rich world of pictures, thoughts, and feelings that lie within. I wonder what I ought to do about this. How much should I allow him to withdraw into his fantasy world without disturbing him?

Barbara, in grade seven, was very quiet most of this week and it would have been easy to overlook her altogether. She seemed more moody than usual and disturbed about something. She didn't seem interested in her work and had trouble concentrating. Barbara recently has taken to wearing lipstick. On several occasions this week she has returned from the girls' room with her lips painted a bright shade of red. Barbara visibly lacks the necessary skill to apply the lipstick properly and it is often smeared over the corners of her mouth and on her cheeks. This week I saw Mrs. G., Barbara's foster mother. As she talked there was a note of desperation in her voice. She said she was concerned with Barbara's relationships with boys. She said, "Barbara has always liked the boys. I've tried to watch her very closely. I knew her mother very well, and I don't want Barbara to be like her mother. Barbara had a bad experience with sex a few years ago. I hope you'll keep your eye on her around school. She will obey me because she knows I will punish her."

Jack (age fifteen) is an isolate. He lives on the other side of the tracks. I cannot help but feel that part of the reason for the group's non-acceptance of him is his socio-economic status. It is difficult to state specific instances which make me feel this. My opinions are based on a word I hear dropped by one of the boys now and then. "My father *owns* such and such," or "I am going to be a big shot like my dad." There is a very strong feeling of family superiority among these kids. They know they are wealthy and they just don't seem to see Jack. And Jack seems to try to make himself inconspicuous as he hunches over in his seat.

Hanya's (age four) doing quality, her ease with materials, her ever-widening curiosity seem to me to stem from her wonderful body control. Hanya does not attempt anything unless she knows she can do it, and consequently she performs all skills well and efficiently. I have never seen her fall, spill anything, or mistake how far she can jump, reach, or expand in any way. I believe that Hanya's precision and carefulness are related to this quality of putting her energy to work efficiently. Hanya has a wide range of interests: painting, clay modeling, music, large muscle activities, imaginative play with other children. In everything she is active, concentrated, definite, focused, and purposeful. There are hints of aggressiveness in her as she slaps other children, grabs toys and materials when she wants them, but this is a four-year-old's way.

I became attracted to Jane (age eight) because of her irresistible personality. She has a most infectious laugh, a sort of happy gurgling sound which is recognizable even when one's eyes are closed. She is a real antidote for gloom. I feel a certain closeness with Jane that I do not share with the others. Perhaps it is because I recognize certain characteristics which seem vaguely familiar to me. I can remember when I was in school doing things very much like Jane. I, too, loved to eat candy, act, and be funny. As a matter of fact, I find myself an adult edition of her. Jane seems a restless sort of girl, constantly on the go. She is either chatting with friends, drawing pictures, biting her fingernails, or else engaged in her favorite pastime of eating candy. You can always depend on Jane for being well-stocked in the candy department. I have noticed, however, that when Jane's interest is aroused, she is completely absorbed in what is going on. She no longer exhibits this nervous energy, becomes placid, and won't even bat an eyelash. Jane is such a normal, happy, well-adjusted youngster that I want to find out how she "got that way."

These are descriptions of real children written by real teachers. Suppose you were teaching these boys and girls—would you wonder how to relate to each of them? How would you feel about Barbara's problems with boys, Ellen's anxiety, Bob's daydreaming, and Jane's exuberance? Would you know what Hanya needs in her school experience? Would you be able to define the role you play in the life of each of these individual children?

This is a mere handful of vignettes of young humans that our students have studied. Each one of these individuals is unique, as is every other human being. In all the world no person is a carbon copy of another. What makes each of these individuals tick? Which of his experiences have significant meaning for him—meanings of joy or grief, of fear or assurance, of feeling wanted or rejected, of being a part of or apart from? These are some of the probings and soundings that we use in an attempt to understand human behavior. In this quest we are not alone. The world's great thinkers, today and in the past, have long been trying to understand why humans behave as they do. Man has always been curious about himself, about what marks him off from the rest of creation and what unites him with all creation. You, too, have probably wondered and spoken of your wonderings, as indeed each of us has. As the poet Laotzu says:

Existence is beyond the power of words
To define. . .
If name be needed, wonder names them both:

From wonder into wonder
Existence opens.[1]

Our century has seen the opening of new horizons in the field of human development. The intuitive genius of the poets and philosophers and the folk wisdom of former days are now being validated by the studies made in the "baby" disciplines of sociology, anthropology, and psychology. Much, too, of what we formerly believed to be sound knowledge is being discredited as we learn more in these fields. This is the process of learning—to be able to establish a bench mark at any given time on the basis of accepted theory and knowledge and still hold oneself ready to revise, re-evaluate, and reformulate one's understandings as new findings emerge.

What does this mean to us as teachers? It means that we must know present-day thinking in the field of human development as thoroughly as we can. Then, we must apply this thinking to our beliefs and practices and ask ourselves, "Is this belief sound or is it a relic of outmoded thought?" We must be flexible, open-minded, ready to change and reconstruct our thinking as new knowledge comes into focus. New knowledge is bound to emerge. We must guard constantly against the notion that answers in human development are final ones. They cannot be final. Every new discovery in the chemistry of the body, for instance, gives us more data with which to interpret the causes of different behaviors. Every new insight in the functioning of the brain, in the workings of the endocrine glandular system gives us another thread to use in unraveling the mysteries of human behavior. So we call our study a quest; a quest that began for each of us as soon as we began to wonder about ourselves and one that will continue as long as we live.

For teachers this quest has more than the usual significance, for into our hands are entrusted the world's young. While we are searching for meaning for *ourselves*, others are looking to us to give them direction in *their* quest. Thus we are at the same time searchers and guides.

This dual role presents an unusual responsibility and a rare opportunity to the teacher. It means teachers today must be willing to give more than a token of themselves to the children with whom they work. They must be competent, dedicated people who can challenge the young to go that extra mile in attempting to resolve the problems of greed, hate,

---

[1] Witter Bynner, *The Way of Life According to Laotzu* (New York: John Day Company, Inc., 1944), p. 25.

and violence that seem to be securing such a strong grip upon mankind. Teachers must be more concerned about the quality of their teaching than about finding a comfortable niche in life. Teaching is for the rugged, the determined, the zestful ones, the ones who have a shine in their eyes. Teaching is for those who wish to live on the growing edges of their own beings, for that is where children live. We like the expression of one of the great teachers of our day, William Lyon Phelps:

> I do not know that I could make entirely clear to an outsider the pleasure I have in teaching. I had rather earn my living by teaching than in any other way. In my mind, teaching is not merely a lifework, a profession, an occupation, a struggle: it is a passion. I love to teach. I love to teach as a painter loves to paint, as a musician loves to play, as a singer loves to sing, as a strong man rejoices to run a race. Teaching is an art—an art so great and so difficult to master that a man or woman can spend a life at it, without realizing much more than his limitations and mistakes, and his distance from the ideal.[2]

Have you ever considered the fact that the teacher is the only professionally trained adult with whom all children and youth have daily relationships? Some boys and girls are not fortunate enough to have parents who want them or who are wise in dealing with them or to have two living parents. Not all children and youth participate in an activity outside school managed by trained adults. But nearly all youngsters under sixteen years of age *are* in school. In every classroom are some children to whom the teacher is the most important person in the world. In our society the teacher is the "pro" designated to stimulate and guide the development of the young. The teacher is required to hold a certificate. This is his badge of competency. His certificate states that he is qualified to teach certain grades or certain subjects in these grades. In addition, parents assume that the teacher knows how to work with young humans.

[2] William Lyon Phelps, *The Excitement of Teaching*, excerpts from Chapter V, pp. 60-71. (By permission of Liveright Publishers, New York. Copyright: Horace Liveright, Inc., 1931.)

The Roles of the Teacher

The teacher is expected to understand human behavior. He must understand himself before he can hope to understand others. What do we mean by understanding? Literally the word means "to stand under"; as an adjective it means "knowing, intelligent." If we combine these two meanings, we can define an understanding teacher as a *knowing* teacher who *stands under* those he teaches, ready to support them if they need support, ready to help them get up if they fall, ready to bind up wounded egos and bruised shins, ready to do and be what is needed by those who are less mature, less knowing. This is a large order for anyone, a Herculean task when each teacher is expected to understand twenty-five or thirty youngsters, or in some instances—for a teacher of adolescents—125 or more!

Teaching Is Relating

The essence of teaching is *relating* to those one teaches. Relating is significant only to the extent that the qualities of *knowing* and *support* are combined to develop new insights, new comprehensions, and new skills. What is meant by knowing as applied to teaching? It simply means knowing with what we work as we teach. We teach with ourselves. Whatever we are comes through in the relationships that develop between teacher and pupils. The skill of the cabinetmaker is demonstrated by how well he knows the properties of the wood he handles, by how well he knows his own skills, by the methods he uses in combining woods to make a beautiful piece, and by his knowledge of the various tools he employs. In like manner the quality of a teacher is shown by the depth and breadth of understanding he has of himself and of those he teaches. His pupils are the raw materials with which he works. His methods are the ways he contrives to live (work and play) with his pupils so as to secure challenging, constructive, and unique results. His tools are books, films, pictures, paints, music, field trips, sociometry, and the host of other aids that are available.

One difference exists between the work of the cabinetmaker and that of the teacher, however. Like nearly all analogies, there is a fallacy in this one. The cabinetmaker works *on* materials and can throw away his mistakes. His personality becomes a part of his work only in a very limited sense. The teacher, on the other hand, works *with* his materials—his pupils. Any mistakes that he makes must be assimilated by society. His responses become an integral part of the teaching process, for they change the flow of events that occurs between him and his pupils. When the authors were taught to teach, they were trained merely to instruct with the assumption that the pupils would be reluctant to learn. They were taught that emotions and feelings usually interfered with learning and that the teacher's only concern with them was to see that they interfered as little as possible. Only in the past few decades has it become commonly recognized that the teacher must be concerned with the total development of the learner. The authors recognize the teacher's role as one of instrucing; but we see that learning takes place in a human being who is a whole person and that little significant learning results from the mere assigning of lessons.

An experienced teacher, who was participating in a nursery school while doing advanced study, made the discovery that teaching is relating. Listen to her:

> I'm beginning to see children as processes not mere animated objects. I'm beginning to see the wonder and wonderfulness of this. I haven't had the desire to "finish them off" as in the past. I've been able to accept them as they are. It's a good feeling. This has reduced the pressures I formerly felt in teaching.

Self-Knowledge Is Necessary

It is unlikely that a teacher can understand another person better than he understands himself. Only when he learns to anticipate his own responses to an emerging situation and to predict the effects of his responses on the situation can he arrange the most promising circumstances for his pupils' growth. How would you answer these questions·

Do I become anxious when not fully in control of the group?
Am I overconcerned about what other teachers and the principal think about me and my work?
Do I tend to strike or hide when I feel threatened?
Am I afraid to try out things—do I have to be sure I know how something will turn out before I start it?
Do I resent criticism, disapproval?
Am I able to relate to people who have authority over me?

Do I become impatient and irritable when weary? How much sleep do I
need to keep from being irritable at three o'clock?
Am I clinging to childish attitudes and notions as a child clings to his old
rag doll?

Since these are feelings that are shared by those of us who teach, the
important fact is to know and to take into account your own unique
responses to the many complex human relationships with which you are
dealing as you teach. Your study of human growth and development will
fall short of its possibilities if it does not increase your own knowledge
of yourself. As one student wrote:

Throughout the time I was studying this youth, I was beginning to
understand my own shortcomings, personality-wise. All of a sudden I
realized that I was studying myself. I began to understand why I was able
to speak in a small group and was reticent in a large group; why I could
crack jokes and make everyone laugh and be a live wire when I was with
my friends. I began to see that it takes a long time to know people well
enough to feel at ease.

A teacher of some experience states: "My study of human behavior is
helping me find myself in my classroom. I am finding out why I resent
some children and why these children are resentful of me. I am discovering why my breaking point is so easily reached with boys and why I
have more toleration with girls." In Chapter 16 we examine the process
of acquiring self-knowledge.

Self-Perceptions Impaired by Society

The pictures that teachers have of themselves are of vital importance
to the quality of their teaching. So much of teaching has consisted of
judging, of giving special privileges to those who conform to the teacher's standards and demerits to those who don't that the public sees
teachers as not quite human. We are often looked upon as somewhat odd
individuals, around whom children and adults must mind their manners
and their morals. Try to watch some children play "school" and note the
roles in which they cast the teacher.

Our culture neglects teachers and education notoriously; every survey
of education indicates this and yet the neglect continues. Many so-called
"backward countries" are amazed at the low status accorded teachers in
this, the richest country in the world. Unfortunately, we tend to accept

the pictures society has of us as teachers. This accounts in part for the metamorphosis that takes place in many teachers. Frequently, promising young teachers—who enter the profession as bright, enthusiastic, vigorous, colorful individuals—after a few years of teaching can be seen doing their work in the easiest manner, scoffing slightly at the idealistic theories of their training days, pooh-poohing experimentation, and securing their most dynamic satisfactions from that part of their lives which lies outside their work.

Something else happens, too. They cease regarding themselves as human beings who take a significant part in preserving and extending democratic values. They take on the roles of judges, moralizers, manner-correctors, and they treat their pupils as if they were there to be judged (we call it evaluated) rather than instructed and helped to grow. This is one of the major problems that teachers face as they work with the young, for young people tend to accept the evaluation of their teachers. A teacher who labels a child "dumb" makes it easier for that child to behave as if he were dumb. Democracy depends upon citizens who feel good about themselves, who think critically, and who know how to communicate their feelings and thoughts effectively. If teachers are to play a major role in developing these qualities in others, they must first have a chance to realize them to some degree in their own lives. We hope this book will help to combat some of the discouragement and dissatisfaction with education that have been so prevalent in recent years and that it will help prospective teachers to discover for themselves the significant roles they must play in a democratic society.

Why We Study Human Behavior

Today we study human behavior so that we may understand our roles in the lives of our pupils. This requires us to understand ourselves. As the behavioral disciplines have developed, new methods for studying human behavior have emerged; knowledge, insight, and skill have increased. Interpretations given to behavior are different now than they were even a generation ago. An ancient philosopher observed that the most important question one can ask a man is "What do you see when you see a man?" Certainly one important fact about a teacher or a parent is "What does he see when he sees a child?"

Adult Attitudes toward the Young

It is worth while to contemplate the history of adult attitudes toward children and youth because all of these attitudes persist to some degree in current ideas and practices of child-rearing.

CHILDREN AS LITTLE ADULTS. For many centuries the young were perceived and treated as "little adults." An examination of the portraits of children during the Renaissance, for example, shows many of them proportioned like adults. Children's behavior was expected to reach the same standards of perfection as that of adults. What was "good" for adults was likewise considered "good" for children. This belief persists today; we try to impose upon young children as much adult behavior as we can. The polite and considerate six-year-old is cherished in most schools and families; the thirteen-year-old who "just loves to study" and has no time for horseplay and frivolity is highly valued by many grown-ups. By the same logic a tadpole can be made a frog the quicker by snipping off his tail.

CHILDREN AS LITTLE ANGELS. There came a time when children were thought to be angels who could do no wrong. This attitude was eloquently set forth in Rousseau's famed book, *Emile,* in which he urged that children be allowed to live in nature without the restraints and pressures of civilization until age fourteen, at which time they were to be corralled and broken to civilization. At that time the noted French physician, Sequin, learned that a youngster about twelve to fourteen years of age had been found in the woods, apparently without previous human association. The learned doctor exclaimed with joy that he would take this unspoiled child and make of him a fine human. Some time later the doctor threw up his hands in dismay at the sad misfortune that such a child had turned out to be feeble-minded and uneducable.

CHILDREN AS LITTLE DEVILS. There was a time when children were commonly thought to be conceived in sin and born in iniquity. It has always been true that some children have been conceived in quite sinful (unwise) circumstances and born into iniquitous surroundings. When this was held to be true of all children, it seemed sensible to stifle impulses, to train rigorously, to demand prescribed behavior, to punish conduct that was held improper by adults. Even today, many teachers and parents regard training and discipline as concerned largely with making children stop doing things. We continue to *correct* papers. Evaluation at both the elementary- and high-school level seems commonly synonymous with fault-finding.

The gloomy notion of a child's origin came to be translated into belief in being possessed by devils, evil-spirits which must be driven from the bodies of unruly (unadult-like) children. "I'll beat the devil out of you," was once a declaration of specific, literal intent. We still hear this expression being used. Some of you may recall the time when bitter medicine was thought to be better than tasty medicine, when adults believed that a child's body had to experience a certain amount of pain if he were to grow up to be good. Today the idea is prevalent that a child must go through a goodly amount of arduous, distasteful toil in order to become a disciplined personality. Even today numerous adults believe that proper training requires that a child's body shall be struck by those who love him.

The assumption in this doctrine is that if we succeed in identifying and controlling the devil (wicked impulses) the young will become fine, moral adults. The devil is an acceptable symbol for receiving all the *blame* that one wishes to heap upon him. We have learned better today, but we (being human) still must blame something for behaviors that we do not understand. The devil has undergone many metamorphoses during the past generations. When the authors were young, the devil wore the guise of bad tonsils. Any child who was having difficulty in school or who was having trouble physically or socially had his tonsils "snatched out" as a routine matter. Lack of intelligence masqueraded as the devil for a few years. Youngsters who got into trouble with adults were believed to be those with low intelligence. Then along came working mothers to receive the blame for the difficulties that youngsters manifested in growing up. Lately television, motion pictures, and comic books are holding the center of the stage as the major devils of the day.

We seem to have to blame something for whatever behavior is disturbing to us as adults. One of our young students came to this realization and expressed her discovery this way:

> My "fed-upness" interested me, so I began observing *me* along with Carol. It didn't take too long to realize that I only got fed up when she didn't do what I wanted her to do. In fact, then, I didn't want Carol to be like she wanted to be; I wanted her to be like I thought she ought to be. This, of course, revealed an idea that most adults have; namely, that children should attempt to fit the adult's concept of what children are. Carol taught me the error of my thinking. My relationship with her has changed now. Carol is as Carol thinks she ought to be, and I am getting so that I can almost accept her that way. This change is growth and maturation— not Carol's, *mine!*

Today professionals are abandoning their quest for the devil. We recognize that an individual's behavior is purposeful to him and seldom seems negative to the *behaver* at the time it occurs. However another behaves, regardless of its irritating quality, must be accepted by others as the beginning point of relationships. The phrase "What's gotten into that child?" is being replaced by "What is that child trying to do?"

CHILDREN AS PLAYTHINGS. Now and then we are distressed to observe parents and neighbors treating little children as if they were playthings or pets. They dress the children as dolls, teach them tricks, display them, show them off. To some parents, grandparents, aunts, recreation workers, and teachers, a child is a pet, an animated toy, a dress-up doll. The adult trains the child to speak a piece, to do a dance, to play the piano, much as a puppy is taught to do tricks. This seems particularly tempting to teachers of music, dramatics, and physical education. We have the impression that schools today are spoiling many talented children and youth by using them for public display. We believe it is imperative that adults enjoy children, but we must make sure that the child is having hearty enjoyment in the process. A thin line indeed marks off gratification from exploitation.

CHILDREN AS PEOPLE. In recent years we have come to the more mature conception that children are people, that life for them is as sweet as for their elders, that they cherish their dignity and individuality as much as ever they shall. We older people might well read some of the great declarations of human dignity such as *The Bill of Rights, The Declaration of the Rights of Man, The Declaration of Independence* to note that in them age is not mentioned. By the time the individual has finished public school, he has lived more than one-fourth of a normal lifespan. Childhood and youth cannot be viewed merely as a period of preparation for being grown up. We once heard an eight-year-old say to her father, "Daddy, I am not waiting to grow up."

Reasons for Studying Children

In our habits and ways of dealing with children, the persistence of these various pictures can be seen in the culture. Each of us has incorporated quite unconsciously some of these pictures into our concepts of children. Therefore, it is necessary for teachers to evaluate prevailing practices by up-to-date knowledge and insight about human development. We dare not teach in accord with our habits. We must teach in accord with the best that is known about how individuals grow. *Teaching must be a thoughtful process—not a habitual process.*

TO DETERMINE CAUSES FOR MENTAL DEFICIENCY. The pictures we have had of children have affected the purposes for studying young human beings. Originally, the scientific study of children was undertaken in an attempt to find out what was wrong with their mental ability. The assumption was that if one could just discover what was wrong with an individual, it could be fixed in a short time. The children and youth studied were those who deviated so markedly from the norm in intelligence that they were labeled "mentally deficient."

Alfred Binet, a physician, was employed by the French government early in this century to study groups of retarded children in order to identify sooner subnormal children for separation into special classes. Out of his work grew the Binet tests, which were later introduced into America along with a peculiarly American adaptation, the intelligence quotient (IQ). Many educators fastened upon the Binet tests as a handy means for excluding some individuals from regular school classes, and intelligence tests are still used in this manner. The effort to discover what is wrong with a youngster's mental development doubtless has a place in the study of human behavior. Some of the ways in which we have used this knowledge to discriminate against those who do not meet our standards is a matter for the thoughtful consideration of the profession. We discuss the use of intelligence tests at greater length in Chapter 4.

TO PREDICT FUTURE. During World War I tests were developed to classify military personnel. Professional educators became greatly interested in the possibilities of adapting these tests and constructing similar ones for use in determining the educational futures of their pupils. For a decade or so, educators went overboard in their use of all the new tests that quickly became available and profitable. Test makers claimed and publishers proclaimed that a human being's complex range of interests, aptitudes, abilities, and growth potential could be translated by a pencil and paper test into a score that would predict the individual's future achievements, his probable social status, and his occupational possibilities. This emphasis on the use of tests led the profession into some serious errors. Twelve- and thirteen-year-olds were counseled into specific courses of study which had marked influence upon their opportunities for later occupational choice. Performance on tests often became synonymous with worth in the minds of many educators. A test score became more significant than day-by-day acquaintance with a pupil. Those who scored high in areas that indicated an aptitude for the professions often were most valued.

Today we are in grave danger of limiting opportunity for college education to those who make high test scores in early adolescence. The range of interests of a twelve-year-old is likely to be quite limited and unstable. Suspended judgment rather than emphasis should be accorded the predictive value of tests that are given to young adolescents. The commonly used tests *average* a variety of abilities. This hides the peaks and valleys of specific capacities and abilities of individuals. Currently the trend in testing is toward giving pupils the opportunity to reveal their specific strengths.[3]

TO DISCERN ADULT ROLES IN LIVES OF THE YOUNG. Today one of the most significant reasons for studying human behavior is to discern the roles of adults in the lives of the young. In this book we are specifically con-

---

[3] This statement is amplified in Chapter 4, "The Growth and Functioning of Intelligence."

18

cerned with the role of the teacher in the life of the pupil. Much of this book is focused on helping the teacher discern the various roles he needs to play in the life of each of his pupils, recognizing that each individual has a unique configuration of needs, interests, concerns—in short, a unique life experience. Some specific aids are given to help you individualize your approach to each pupil as you work with them in groups.

Instead of lamenting individual differences, we rejoice in them. Democracy depends upon the cultivation of uniqueness. How little this concept is understood as an educational principle is affirmed by the disproportionate emphasis most of our schools place upon standardization, regimentation, and mass approaches to teaching. Even now, as America competes for world leadership, Americans are beginning to realize that they have not cherished creative thought as much as they might have. Almost every day school boards speak of saving money and make elaborate plans to teach larger and larger numbers of pupils in a single setting through the medium of television, thus reducing further the pupil's opportunities for relating to a teacher. Mass approaches to teaching are economical of money, alarmingly expensive in self-realization.

In summing up the challenge to the educational system, Melby states: "Only a great creative education for all our people can give us pre-eminence in science, in art, and in human relations. . . . Human survival depends on an education in human values, one which gives all of us awareness of membership in the human race." [4] If we are to cultivate uniqueness, we must understand that the teacher has a distinct role to play in the pupil's life. He cannot discern that role accurately unless he continuously strives to know each human being with whom he is relating and unless he tries to know that individual's feelings, perceptions of himself, perceptions of adults, attitudes toward authority, and attitudes toward his own age-mates.

This book will be more successful in illuminating the teacher's role in the lives of the young if you bring your own experiences, your thoughts, and your feelings to the book as you read. We hope that you will ask yourself questions such as these:

Am I learning how to accept many varieties of temperament?
How do I show my basic respect for each of the young people with whom
    I am associating?

---

[4] Ernest O. Melby, "Role of Evaluation in Improving Teaching," *Educational Leadership,* January 1958, p. 220.

Am I learning how to help each child develop his own unique personality?

Am I giving myself the chance to try out the premise that "raw behavior" means little unless seen in the context of the total life of the individual?

Am I clarifying, as I work with young people, the extent of my right to control others?

How is my study of human development adding to my own self-understanding?

Am I learning some ways to counterbalance society's neglect of its teachers?

What am I doing as a prospective teacher to build the kind of dedication to teaching that will keep the shine in my eyes when the job gets tough?

Am I learning to discern the roles that are most helpful to the young with whom I am now working?

Am I evaluating what I do with children against a framework of democratic values?

As you read, continue to question. This book will come to have more meaning for you as you test it out in your work with children and youth in the situations in which you find them.

Additional Sources You May Find Helpful

William F. Bruce and A. John Holden, Jr., *The Teacher's Personal Development.* New York: Henry Holt and Company, 1957.

This book was designed to help young people understand themselves as teachers. The human relationships that one has as a teacher and the great opportunities that these relationships bring are discussed wisely. The resources one has to bring to his task are used as an organizing theme.

Arthur T. Jersild, *In Search of Self*. New York: Bureau of Publications, Teachers College, Columbia University, 1952.

————, *When Teachers Face Themselves*. New York: Bureau of Publications, Teachers College, Columbia University, 1955.

These two brief works describe Dr. Jersild's work in exploring the role of the school in promoting self-understanding and the persistent problems teachers have in discovering themselves. They give valuable insights to one in quest of self-understanding.

Daniel A. Prescott, *The Child in the Educative Process*. New York: McGraw-Hill Book Company, Inc., 1957.

This volume is Dr. Prescott's latest book describing the work he has been doing for the past two decades in helping teachers learn how to study human behavior. A student in this field should become acquainted with Prescott's work. He is a pioneer and his contributions have enabled many others to build upon his foundations.

Marie I. Rasey, *This Is Teaching*. New York: Harper and Brothers, 1950.

————, *It Takes Time*. New York: Harper and Brothers, 1953.

These books, along with her other works, are a monument to a great soul in education. This Is Teaching *is a recording of meetings of a college seminar. The book abounds in earthy wisdom and quotable quotes, such as: ". . . it is precisely in the areas of greatest values that we become fiercely defensive or destructive."* It Takes Time *is Dr. Rasey's poignantly told autobiography through which one perceives the continuing development of a great teacher from her girlhood through more than fifty years of growth.*

2

The Meaning of Human Behavior

As we begin our study of human behavior, let's look at the ways in which boys and girls are seen by many of those who work with them. Then we will see if these ways are adequate for the purposes of understanding behavior. We ask our students, experienced teachers, to select a pupil to study, not an unusual or an abnormal or a "problem" child, "but just any youngster you feel you would like to understand better and would like to spend some time each week observing more closely than you observe the group as a whole."

One group of teachers described the individuals they had selected in these ways:

Bobby is three. He is nice, sweet, gentle, and bright.

Gilbert is a bully. He's a big nine-year-old, has a deep voice.

Larry is the best-adjusted one in the group. He functions well for an eleven-year-old. He is sensitive to others, is thoughtful, speaks slowly, and seems well-established.

Gertie is a charming four. She is graceful, has a long pony tail, is friendly, sensitive to adults, bright, and clothes-conscious. She is the smallest in her group.

Mark is changeable, troublesome. He has temper tantrums, does what he wants to do, is aggressive. He is eight and has six brothers and sisters.

Shirley, age eleven, is popular. She's a leader. Children want to be near her. She is bright, diplomatic, graceful, tall, thin, the only Negro child in her class.

Manuel, age seventeen, is creative and sensitive. He wants limits placed upon him. He has high mechanical aptitude, has an after-school job. He prizes the independence that comes from having some money of his own.

George is a non-conformist. This twelve-year-old feels the world should adjust to him. He has a precocious interest in music.

Betsy is a pretty, healthy fifteen-year-old with much talent and little interest in academic work. She sees no point in doing a lesson merely because someone says she should. She is usually quite actively engaged in some enterprise that seems good to her.

Robert wears glasses, has a pixie-like face, is very enthusiastic, has a sense of humor, is a good storyteller. He has a twin sister.

Carol is dynamic, talkative, imaginative. She is very creative. She always plays the mother in the nursery. She doesn't like to be kissed and hugged. She is the product of an interracial marriage.

Hanya, age four, has been in this country only a few months. Her parents are Hungarian. She is expressive, independent, has definite opinions and a nice sense of humor. She is very direct. She picks up after herself.

David is always in a hurry. This seventh-grader is tall, stocky, and aggressively sensitive. He is a happy boy. He relates best to adults.

Stephen is a good-looking blond. He is one of the smallest boys in his ninth grade homeroom. He is imaginative, loves being the center of attention, is bright. He likes to grow things. He's very competitive. He has an older sister.

What do these descriptions tell us? They tell us what the teachers thought was important to say about these individuals in the space of a few words. And what a variety of differences! These descriptions tell us something about the outward manifestations of behavior, quite a bit about the appearance of the individuals, and very little about the dynamics of *why* these children and youth behave as they do. As we discuss human development, our focus will be on the why's of behavior. In this way we will gradually develop some basic principles applicable to human beings in a variety of situations.

As you use this book, we suggest that you select a child or young person to study and observe. As you observe this person in the active process of living, the concepts that we describe and illustrate will come to have real meaning for you. Choose someone in whom you are interested (not a relative, so that you may see him somewhat objectively) and write about him in a free-association manner for twenty or thirty minutes at least once a week. At the end of this chapter and in subsequent ones, we make some suggestions for you to consider as you study this one individual. We suggest this approach because it will make your study of human behavior more alive and dynamic.

In this chapter we introduce you to some of the basic concepts underlying human behavior and indicate how the various fields of knowledge contribute to our understanding. We also draw a portrait of a healthy personality. The rest of the book amplifies these ideas.

What Is Human Behavior?

Human behavior is the body in action. All that we do, all that we are is expressed by our bodies. All our efforts to reach out to others are attempts to get outside our own skins and establish relationships with others. Yet we can never succeed fully in these attempts. We are contained within ourselves and we must recognize this as a primary human characteristic as we seek to understand the behavior of others. We urge caution about assuming that we understand another person merely because we have known him for a long time, have shared many significant experiences with him, or feel close to him. An understanding of the limited way in which we can ever know another person gives a teacher the humility he needs to relate meaningfully to the young with whom he is associated. The essential aloneness of man is the theme of Thomas Wolfe's *Look Homeward Angel* [1] and many other novels and plays. Since the next chapter discusses the body in some

---

[1] Thomas C. Wolfe, *Look Homeward Angel* (New York: The Modern Library, 1934).

detail, we note here only that one must know a great deal about the body in order to understand human behavior.

Human's Unique Capacity to Think

The one quality that makes a human being unique and superior to other creatures is his capacity to think. His large brain and his complex central nervous system enable him to remember and to reflect upon his memories, to imagine and to realize the images he fashions, to plan his choices by using foresight, to use symbols to stand for ideas and to find relationships among them. Man's brain makes it possible for him to adjust to varieties of environment. By thinking and planning, which are qualities of intelligence, man can contrive what he wishes to do and how he may achieve his goals. He does not have to accept himself nor the earth as he finds them. A most important concern of the teacher is cultivating ways to reach goals, foreseeing likely consequences of various courses of action, choosing ways which promise successful achievement as well as gratification to the individual.

Human's Ability to Use His Hands

James Harvey Robinson, distinguished American historian, maintained that man is man quite as much because of his marvelous hands as because of his complex brain. Man's long, prehensile, opposing thumb makes it possible for him to carry out the plans he contrives. With his wondrously constructed hands, he can manipulate materials and thus control his universe. He has learned to extend the use of his hands a hundredfold by the tools he has devised. Man's long history of achievement from the days of crude tracings on cave walls to our present atomic age is a history of brain and hand accomplishment.

The Why's of Human Behavior

It still startles us a bit to reflect that in all man's history there has never been nor never in the world will be a person just like any one of us. To state that each of us is unique is a truism; but to understand the significance of this statement we must delve deeply into many fields of knowledge. Each human being is involved in a never-ending process of becoming the self that others identify as you or me or Sarah or José. While the self is constantly responding to all the forces that are *within us* and those that play *upon us,* enough of each of us persists throughout time so that people recognize us even after a lapse of many years.

All Human Behavior Is Caused

Whatever we are at this moment is the product of all that has happened to us up to this time. Note we said *product, not sum.* The principle involved is that each one of us is the product of his own inborn qualities and the uniqueness of his own culture. To understand another human being then, we must look into his background. More importantly, we must gain some understanding of how that individual has responded to what has happened to him, how he has *felt* about the happenings of his life. As we look for the why's of behavior in children and youth, we find causes. Understanding causes tends to reduce our proneness to blame.

We must remember that the causes of behavior do not remain static. Life flows and eddies. An event does not stop because it is over, for the effects of all events are within us. These effects are altered by new experiences. We are constantly changing, reconstructing, and reinterpreting the past. We do not have to settle for our original feelings and responses to experiences that seem ended. In a real sense no significant experiences are ever finished. This is a promising concept, for it makes possible the development of a mature person. This thought is expressed in the Scriptures: "When I was a child, I spake as a child, I thought as a child; but now that I have become a man, I have put away childish things." [2] This is central to our understanding of human behavior. To illustrate:

In *The Journey,*[3] Lillian Smith tells the story of Marty, who as a child was fearful, unsure of herself, and afraid to face the hurts of life. Marty's little boy lost both arms in an automobile accident, and the mother relived her own painful childhood experiences as she responded to this cruel blow. For many months she withdrew into herself. As Marty tells her own story, "I went to the hospital every day, my body did; but deep down in me I wasn't there. . . . It is a strange thing how you hold on to fear." Through the months that her boy was mending his torn body,

[2] I Corinthians, 13:11.

[3] Lillian Smith, *The Journey* (New York: World Publishing Company, 1954).

Marty was mending her torn soul. She relived all her old childish fears and anxieties. In this process, she brought to her childhood experiences all that had happened since she had grown up: the warmth and security that a happy marriage had produced, and the joy of being a mother. The childhood experiences were reinterpreted. Suddenly one morning she found she could accept life and the burden of this new tragedy. Her past was now different for Marty. She saw it through a clearer prism, felt it in a more realistic manner, and became a different person because she was able to change the past as it related to her and to the present.

Causes Are Multiple and Interdependent

The causes of human behavior are multiple and are so interlaced and interdependent that it is futile to try to untangle them. We must therefore avoid simple, single-factor explanations if we are to avoid error. One teacher remarked that all the adolescents in her school who had been referred to the psychologist for help had working mothers. She concluded that the mothers' working was the cause of the teen-agers' difficulty both inside and outside of school. When asked what else she knew about the youngsters, she had little information. Nor did she know how many of the boys and girls who were getting along satisfactorily had working mothers. To understand why these youngsters were having difficulty in school, one would need to know many factors about them: health, sibling rivalry, parents' expectations, parents' mobility, emotional stability of the home and of the individual, previous school experiences, unexpected happenings in their lives, and as much other data as possible.

Some Causes Are Culturally Oriented

As we try to understand the multi-dimensional quality of the causes of behavior, we draw upon the knowledge of many disciplines to explain why we are who we are. The study of the forces that play *upon us* from the outside is primarily rooted in sociology, economics, and anthropology. We need to know something about the ways in which mores, traditions, taboos, values, and cultural expectations affect the young as they grow. We need to understand what it means to be a child of wealthy parents, or to be one of a large family growing up on the poorest street in town. We need to understand something about the ways in which group structure and organization impinge upon the individual. What does it mean to be part of a culture that segregates its schools on the basis of color, or national origins, or religion, or special competency? These are all culturally oriented forces that push us in certain directions as we grow.

Some Causes Are Individually Oriented

The study of the forces that play *within us*, that cause us to respond as we do to any specific experience, is rooted in the disciplines of physiology, psychology, and psychiatry. Our individual responses are affected greatly by the bodies we have, the genes we inherited, our glandular systems, as well as by all the other more visible systems that constitute the human organism. This is why students of human development need a knowledge of biology and physiology.

The wide stream of human development is made up of many disciplines.

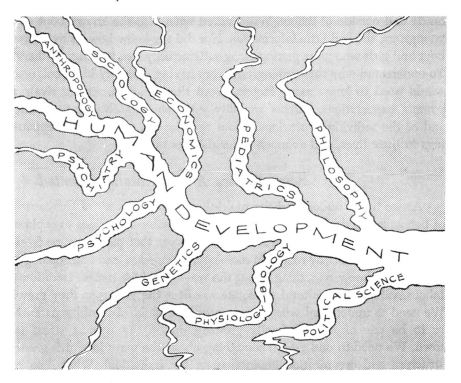

We respond in a certain way because we have learned to select certain stimuli to which to respond. At any given moment the individual is bombarded with many different stimuli, most of which he ignores. As this is written, for example, the noise of a large machine outside the window could draw me away from the desk to investigate. Overhead a child is jumping rope and the thump, thump, thump might distract me so much that I would put my work away. The faucet drips. I may not be disturbed by the drip but by my annoyance that the faucet has not been fixed. A clock ticks loudly; were I timing a soft-boiled egg, this stimulus would have first importance. I can hear a radio in the next room. I do not attend to any of these stimuli. They are not pertinent cues, for I am now writing a book. We select out of our total environment only those things that are pertinent to the task at hand. So I ignore the machine, the child's rope jumping, the dripping faucet, the clock, and the radio; but I respond

to the urge to write. Psychology is concerned with the reasons we select or ignore various stimuli and the interplay between our choices and our process of becoming. When we get into the workings of the subconscious and the more specialized areas of motives and drives, we turn to psychiatry for our explanations.

Some Causes Are Value Oriented

The forces that grow out of established and accepted ways of behaving are known as group standards. As these standards function in our lives, we develop attitudes, beliefs, and values relative to them. When they are organized into some logical system, we recognize them as a philosophy. As we begin our study of human behavior with a willingness to investigate, to evaluate, to try out, and to change preconceived notions, we need to know some of the workable value systems of the present day and of past generations. We need to relate the inferences that we draw from these value systems to the knowledge we gain from the other disciplines mentioned above.

We need to understand the values of the homes and of the communities in which the children grow as well as the values of a democratic culture. One student, teaching in an upper-middle-class community, stated:

> These children, even at the early age of eight, reflect their parents' ambitions for them. Most of them intend to go on to college, and the necessity for being "good" in school has already been impressed upon them. Therefore, the majority of these third graders are concerned about their work; they wish to do well and to take home good reports.

These home values, which children bring to school, are responsible for certain kinds of behavior. In contrast to the parent who wants his child to do well, consider the remarks of a father who was called to school about his son's failing work: "Well, I'm going to get him working papers when he's sixteen. He's had more schoolin' now than I had and I've gotten along all right." Teachers are admonished by some parents to beat their children if they don't mind, while other parents threaten a lawsuit "if you lay a hand on my child."

Education in Nazi Germany was directed to a given set of values. Professional educators employed their knowledge and skills to instill definite values prescribed by Adolph Hitler and his staff. Mann's *School for Barbarians* [4] describes the culture required to grow Nazis. While America does not endorse indoctrination, it is very important for teachers to be consciously aware of their own values so that they may know what they teach, and may evaluate how much their own values influence their teaching. Conflicts in values frequently occur in our schools because a democracy encourages many diverse loyalties. One can be a loyal American citizen and a loyal Republican, a loyal Democrat, a loyal Jew, a loyal Catholic, a loyal Protestant, and a loyal Bing Crosby fan. The possibility of multiple loyalties requires us, as teachers, to think critically and thoughtfully with our pupils about life's goodnesses. If we overemphasize matters such as tidiness, cleanliness, speech patterns, and rowdiness, we may forfeit our chances to influence values in major areas of living.

Thus, to understand the multiple causes of behavior, we must have a speaking acquaintance with many disciplines. You will note that we do not label each contribution as stemming from a particular discipline for we believe that all this stuff must be integrated into a whole in the same way that it functions in the lives of people.

Teacher's Function
Is to Orchestrate Disciplines

The teacher's function is to orchestrate the principles that are significant and relevant from all the behavioral sciences and from the arts in order to understand more fully the dynamics of human behavior. This orchestration of knowledge is one of the most satisfying phases of a teacher's work because it gives to teaching a challenge that makes it worthy to be called a profession. As one orchestrates what he knows, in order to use it more effectively in his teaching, he tends to avoid accepting narrow viewpoints and single-minded explanations, for he discovers that usually two and often more theories are needed to explain the same phenomenon. To make a comparison with physics, we quote Oppenheimer: "... state and orbit, like position and impulse, are complementary notions; where one applies, the other cannot be defined, and for a full description we must be able to use now one, now the other, depending on the observation and the questions that we put." [5] Our goal in teaching is to learn to

---

[4] Erika Mann, *School for Barbarians* (New York: Modern Age Books, 1938).

[5] J. Robert Oppenheimer, *Science and the Common Understanding* (New York: Simon and Schuster, 1953), pp. 62-63.

use "complementary notions" creatively. If we are successful, our descriptions of behavior will be richer, our questions will be more pertinent and we will develop new knowledge.

Some Malfunctioning Personalities

Human beings have an infinite potential for development in an infinite variety of ways. No one ever cultivates all his capacities. Even the most ordinary of us could develop a hundred skills that he doesn't now have, could become expert in a dozen fields now unknown to him, and could, in so doing, become a fuller, richer human being. He could, that is, if his life were long enough and if he had that indefinable something known as *health*. We are speaking of health now in a whole sense, including health of body, mind, and soul. It is interesting to note that Webster's dictionary lists *wholesome* as a synonym for healthy.

Every human body must be nourished to stay alive. If not given the nutrients required for health, the body grows crooked. In the same manner the spirit or personality or soul grows crooked if not given the nutrients that the psyche requires. Man lives not by bread alone. The effects of deprivation of the spirit vary from person to person, but deprivation leads to some kind of malfunctioning. Today, the outbreaks of juvenile delinquency throughout the world, especially in the so-called civilized countries, indicate how deprivation of the spirit has affected young people. Wise heads saw this coming a generation ago, but, as Abe Martin once observed, "Ther seems to be plenty o' money fer ever'thing but necessities. . . . Human life an' turnips remain cheap an' plentiful." [6] This commentary upon our values seems even more true today than when it was said in 1910. We believe the most glaring fault of our age to be the neglect of our young

---

[6] Ken Hubbard, Indiana humorist during the first part of this century, used "Abe Martin" as a pen name.

people. With the deprivations we endure, we grow dull personalities, neurotic personalities, and slugging personalities.[7]

The Dull Personality

Much of what teachers regard to be dullness is learned. Dullness is the opposite of sharpness, as we speak of a "dull" knife. A dull personality expresses slowness in perception and in sensibility. Dullness is often an adjustment to frustration. Unreasonable pressure to do things one cannot do or has no interest in doing may result in dullness. Dullness provides a respectable escape from demands and pressures. Probably each of us has utilized dullness as a means of escaping unpleasant tasks. The man of the house may be quite dull about housekeeping. Women are frequently dull about making minor household repairs. A child who can't read escapes doing homework. As long as one can decide whether or not he wants to be in the situation in which he is dull, such pleading of dullness results in little harm. The experience becomes quite different when one is *compelled* to be in a situation in which one is generally looked upon as dull. We recently interviewed some bright-looking, bright-acting young citizens who said to us in one way or another, "I don't do very well in school. I'm kinda dumb." The acceptance of dullness by a boy or girl—just because he or she can't go through certain academic rituals—results in one of the great wastes of our day for if a child thinks he is dull, he tends to behave in a dull manner. Teachers are coming to realize that effective intelligence consists basically of an attitude toward one's self and one's adequacy to deal with life's problems.

The Neurotic Personality

The neurotic thinks crookedly. To the extent to which he is neurotic, his attitudes and behaviors are out of touch with facts. We hazard a guess that the historians of the future will characterize this age as a dangerously neurotic one. One of the insidious effects of our present-day neurotic thinking is displayed in racial and religious prejudice. One's particular religious affiliation is frequently considered an important qualification for

---

[7] These terms and the description of each kind of personality were developed by Howard Lane in *Shall Children, Too, Be Free?* (New York: Anti-Defamation League of B'nai B'rith, 1949).

political office. Science finds no inherent differences between races that function in human behavior, yet, because of confused motivations and reasoning blurred by cherished beliefs, thousands of young people were denied schooling during the 1958-59 school term.

Another neurotic manifestation that plagues us is disregard for the authority of knowledge. We have, to a dangerous extent, equated authority with power rather than with knowing. This crooked thinking leads us to make decisions that rest on shaky foundations. Too many issues are resolved by the amassing of power in the guise of lobbies, pressure groups, and use of mass media, with almost complete disregard for the knowledge that scholars have accumulated through serious, dedicated, selfless study.

The extent of neurotic behavior among people is manifested by alcoholism and divorce, and other frantic efforts to escape. We would rather be entertained by others than entertain ourselves. These examples, while not exhaustive, indicate the kind of malfunctioning that comes from neurotic adjustment to deprivation of the spirit.

The Slugging Personality

The sluggers are the ones who must have power regardless of the cost to others. As children they are the ones who insist upon having their own way, who fail as they grow to develop empathy for their playmates. The clinical term for the slugger is the aggressive personality. The slugger is a selfish person—power driven and greedy for whatever gives him *control over* others. From the sluggers, who do not hesitate to impose themselves and their wishes upon other people, emerge the dictators, the gang-leaders, the ward bosses as well as the bullies, the overbearing, and the unethical hucksters of our modern day.

In America we have tended to extol aggressiveness as an essential quality of the free, enterprising individual. We still cling to an image of the national hero as a swashbuckling fellow who rides roughshod over the people around him to attain his ends. We frequently fail to distinguish clearly between slugging activities and genuine leadership toward goals which are mutually planned and accepted. Mankind has suffered much from failure to understand the qualities of democratic leadership.

Doubtless the world has need of persons eager to push ahead. It needs also to recognize the danger of deterioration of individuals who are unaware of the feelings and desires of others. The slugging personality is maladjusted for he has not learned to control his aggressiveness. Each aggressive act requires another one more aggressive, more controlling for the slugger to be satisfied. His words, his desires, his wishes are *all* that he recognizes as important.

Man tends to treat others as he himself is treated. The slugging treatment received by the subservient pupil today is likely to be passed on tomorrow by the same pupil to someone weaker than he is. One can almost hear in some authoritarian classrooms the pupils saying, "Wait until I get my turn!"

The Vitamins of Personality

To avoid these warped, malnourished spirits, what is needed? What makes life good? A primary assumption of this book is that we want to learn how to grow *good* people. To do so we must make sure they lead *good* lives. While the men and women who have studied human development thoughtfully have different ways of categorizing people's needs, the essence of their thinking is markedly alike. To know the quality of living of human beings you must know the extent to which the basic needs described in the following pages are supplied, recognizing that none of us finds all his needs satisfied completely. We shall attempt to draw a profile of a healthy, wholesome person which may serve as a usable reference point as you study human development. We like to think of these needs of the spirit as the vitamins of one's psychological diet.

Affection, Friendship

EVERY HUMAN BEING HAS TO BE LIKED. Nature wisely provides that adults readily learn to love the infants for whom they care. Babies can wither and even die for lack of love. But the infant who is loved learns to love those who care for him. As he grows and makes friends, his affection extends beyond the home. Often adults say to children, "A person is known by the company he keeps." What do we know about a child by the company he keeps? We know to whom he must go to find people who like and respect him as he is.

No adult has a higher responsibility than to make certain that the children within the realm of his influence have interesting, dependable friends. Modern life makes the exercise of simple friendship difficult for children. Fault-finding remains a common activity of some parents and teachers. Normal, friendly relationships among children are discouraged in some schools. Older children find their friendships in groups, gangs; modern life provides few facilities for respectable ganging. Children need time and place just to be with their friends. Play space in many cities is limited and inaccessible to large portions of the population. We adults have much to do if we are to meet our responsibility to young humans as they seek the vitamins of affection and friendship.

Self-Respect

THE CEMENT OF MENTAL HEALTH IS SELF-RESPECT. No healthy person is ashamed of himself. The answer to the question, "Aren't you ashamed of yourself?" is "No!" The fundamental treatment of disorders of personality is the rebuilding of self-respect. The adult who undermines a child's respect for himself is assuming a greater responsibility than he has the right or wisdom to assume. At times every child does behave inappropriately, even intolerably. The adult who seeks genuinely to preserve his own integrity and to strengthen the child's self-respect will behave in terms of that wonderful line from Carl Ewald's beautiful book *My Little Boy*. At the point where he and his little boy face the fact that the boy has misappropriated a cent, the father says most earnestly, "What are *we* going to do?" [8]

We adults often make it difficult for a child to be a child and retain his self-respect. This leads children to believe that adults are "sour-pusses" and "kill-joys." Some associate pleasure with defying adult authority and come to disdain all adult values. We must avoid this reaction by planning our homes, our schools, and our neighborhoods so that they accommodate normal childlike behavior in complete respectability. Only in such a com-

---

[8] Carl Ewald, "My Little Boy," in *The Scribner Treasury* (New York: Charles Scribner's Sons, 1953).

prehensive way can we hope to rear a generation of self-respecting human beings.

Freedom

ONE OF THE FIRST URGES A CHILD HAS IS TO BE FREE. He kicks off his blankets; he revels in being released from his diaper. Among the first ideas a child learns to express is, "I will do it myself." One of his first words is "No." Dr. Aldrich [9] maintained that modern culture puts children through the "No! No!" stage of development immediately after they first learn to get around the house.

Press firmly the sole of an infant's foot; he presses back. Turn his head, ever so gently, to the right; he turns it to the left. We are born with a natural resistance to the imposition of outside forces. Homes, schools, neighborhoods must be so managed that a child can exercise his natural disposition for freedom. Following dictatorial orders is no more tolerable to a child in his home and school than to the citizen in his community and nation.

Plato commented, "A slave is one who gets his purposes from somebody else." Most adults could profitably examine their own behavior to detect vestiges of the world's historic acceptance of human slavery. Some of what we call courtesy and respect of children for adults seems to us to be merely the expression of the acceptance of servility—behavior expected of his slaves by the master. Among the most coercive devices of mankind is control through charm or through appeals for loyalty and devotion. All of us have doubtless experienced the sweet command, "You *do* want to take the garbage out, don't you dear?" We shall make few gains in human relationships until children are included as full-fledged, respected members of society who are given as many choices as they can learn to handle competently with adult guidance. The vitamin of freedom is one that children need, quite as much as do adults, in order to grow healthy personalities.

Faith, Respect for Authority

NONE OF US IS SUFFICIENT UNTO HIMSELF ALONE. Man is man only when he is a part of a group. Each of us needs someone upon whom we can

---

[9] C. A. Aldrich was one of the pediatricians who early recognized the importance of gratification to wholesome growth.

rely in complete confidence, and who "won't tell." Happy is the child who finds this person in his home. We adults find him in a husband or wife, a clergyman, a political figure, an old friend, the physician, the bartender, the psychiatrist. Desolate, indeed, is he who has no faith in anyone, anywhere.

Respect for authority is not to be confused with fear. Like love, respect must be earned; it cannot be demanded. A child expresses it in questions such as, "What would you do if you was me?" Many parents, teachers, neighbors unwittingly disqualify themselves as authorities by unjust decisions, foolish and insignificant demands, lack of perspective on manners, cleanliness, friends, play. Adults can hardly expect children to respect their values unless they respect the values of children.

In order to gain respect from the young, we must demonstrate interest, competency, and wisdom in matters that concern them. We cannot hope for genuine respect from those whose interests and behaviors we deplore, nor from those whose wishes we ignore.

Challenge

EACH HUMAN BEING IS BORN WITH THE URGE TO GROW. Stimulation of this urge, which we call challenge, is an important vitamin that the adults in the child's life must provide if they seek to build healthy personalities. Few of life's great moments equal the joy of hearing our first-born child answer our seemingly inane baby-talk. We have been cooing at him for

several weeks, and then—sweet moment!—he coos back. For months we hold out to him our hands, urging, "Come to Daddy," until finally he takes his first hesitant steps. We toss a ball to him many times, and at last see in him talents that assure him success with the Dodgers. This is challenge, an essential factor in the growth of the human personality.

What becomes of challenge when the child is six, ten, sixteen years of age? Challenge is too often displaced by commands and prescribed behavior. If we want our children to use good language, we must use good language ourselves, and treat them so well that they will want to speak as we do. Genuinely good manners are learned only from people who employ them with children and who challenge imitation. Man tends to create himself in the image of the people he likes.

Nature

BEING A PART OF NATURE, MAN NEEDS TO PARTICIPATE IN THE PROCESSES OF NATURE. It is likely that modern man has protected himself too much from wind and weather. Our urge to get close to nature impels us to do strange things at times. These words are written in immediate and joyful anticipation of traveling in a boat to a rocky, bug-infested woods to eat food which will have recently been carried from a clean house, well-screened, and completely equipped for the proper preparation and serving of food. We need to be close to the earth.

The most important aspect of nature for man, however, is his participation in the processes of living. Man needs to influence growth. The amazing, and seemingly illogical preponderance of dogs and cats, ivy and geraniums, in our crowded city neighborhoods is an expression of the common need to help living things live and grow—be they petunias, pups, or babies. Apparently we need, too, to play with basic natural phenomena. We go to great effort to play with water; we like to make and poke a fire. Every child needs continuous opportunities to be close to nature in as many ways as possible. Caring for growing, living plants and animals is a necessary vitamin in the child's life.

Art, Creativeness

MAN IS MADE TO CREATE. We attribute to God great satisfaction as He sat down upon the Seventh Day, surveyed the product of His creation, and called it "good." Our way of putting it would be: "Look! I did this myself."

We have recently come to recognize the importance of the significant and helpful new profession of occupational therapy. Many shattered souls are being made whole by centering attention upon a concrete task and achieving a planned result—a rug, a poem, an ax-handle, a picture, a lovely garden. Mud pies are as essential to growth as milk. Today we have clean "mud" in the form of washed sand and refined clay. Today it is the exceptional person who builds a house, makes a vehicle, fashions a suit, raises a child.

It seems essential that each of us be able to center his whole attention and energies upon some purpose and carry it out. We need to make things happen, to work, and to see beneficial results from our labors. Thus the arts, instead of being fads and boondoggling frills, are fundamentals in the lives of our young and of ourselves. Genuinely artistic—that is creative —experience is attained only in pursuit of one's own purposes or in cooperative pursuit with others. The vitamin of creativeness must be returned if we are to grow completely whole.

Value, Appreciation

WE NEED TO BE NEEDED. The little child plays with pots and pans and carpet sweepers; he demands a place at the family dinner table; he tells tall tales like Daddy's or helps Mother in cleaning the apartment; not in mere imitation, but as a declaration of his demand to play a part in the life about him. Older people need to be needed, too. Who has not seen active, healthy people retire to sit and enjoy a life of leisure—and soon die. We need to be needed, always.

Modern, efficient civilization has no greater task than to find genuine use for youngsters and for the aged. No factor in human life is more degrading than to be a "kept" person, whether by a man, the county, a trust company, one's parents, or one's children. The need to carry one's own weight is at once the great need of mankind and of man. Only slightly less demoralizing to young people is adult imposition of work that does not need to be done. Most modern homes today cannot find adequate, significant work for youngsters. The community then should do so. School should be a place where children's abilities, and talents are employed for the benefit of each other. The talents of a child should be assets to his associates, never claims to distinction from them. Application of this principle would revolutionize school practices; it might save the world.

Fun, Zestful Experience

WE NEED TO HAVE FUN. An essence of wisdom and of morality is the long-time widespread view of human gratification. The busyness of little children astounds their elders. Ever since Noah's boys were little, children have been running, jumping, shouting, wrestling, splashing, throwing things at other things; they have been active, adventuresome. Recently, I beheld a half-dozen boys clinging to the outside of a speeding city bus. I was horrified by their gleeful disdain of extreme danger. Yet I can recall my own childhood pleasure in seizing a heifer's tail, in whipping up the horses to make them race, in swinging from grapevines to drop into deep river pools, in daring to walk on the steep barn roof—much to my father's dismay as he saw cracked shingles, not boyish adventure. Young people have to have fun. Where do they find it in your town?

In many American communities it is becoming increasingly illegal to do childish things. Ball-playing in the streets is unlawful. A boy can't throw anything with all his might unless he is old enough to have a businessman's name printed on his back, or can make the team at school. There are few places where young children can argue about whether they made first-down or first-base without an umpire saying, "Yer out!" Robert P. Smith's *"Where Did You Go?" "Out." "What Did You Do?" "Nothing."* [10] gives an entertaining and informative picture of American childhood in two generations. Smith helps the reader understand how much harder it is today for youngsters to have fun than when he was a boy.

One of the saddest developments in modern civilization is synthetic fun. We get excitement, live dangerously, from bottles, slick magazines, rock n' roll, movies, TV—all without moving from our soft chairs. We go to stadiums to scream invective at umpires from the safety provided by walls and league rules. We crowd Madison Square Gardens to watch hired men work diligently to separate each other from consciousness. The adult world seems compelled to find appropriate, practical excuses for the little fun it has. We golf to exercise, and pay a caddy to take most of the exercise; we play bridge to relax, but woe to the partner who actually relaxes. Seldom do we hear an adult proclaim his intent to do anything simply because he likes it.

---

[10] Robert Paul Smith, *"Where Did You Go?" "Out." "What Did You Do?" "Nothing."* (New York: W. W. Norton and Company, Inc., 1957).

42

These then are the vitamins human beings must have to grow whole-somely. Our job as professionals is to see that the children and youth with whom we work and play have as rich, as satisfying, as well-balanced a diet of these vitamins of personality as we can possibly contrive.

As we study human beings to see if they are functioning in a healthy manner, we watch the trends of behavior, for these trends are more signifi-cant than any present, isolated example of behavior. All growth is in an uneven line. Immediate behavior gives scant clues to personality. The many stages of development which children and youth go through as they mature markedly affect their behaviors. We discuss the meanings of these stages in Section Two (see pages 177-368).

Suggestions for Further Exploration

▶ Write a short description of the individual you have chosen to study. Try to write it in such a way that we can get to know the child or youth. If he were coming to our house for the weekend, what could we expect? After you have written your description, read it over and ask yourself these questions:

What makes this individual unique—different from all others?
What do I need to find out about him to explain how he ticks?
Where would I go to find out these things?
How does his *body in action* express his uniqueness?
How does he express the culture in which he has grown?
In what ways does he express the urges and forces that are within him?
How have you seen him express his values?

As you continue reading, come back to these questions and see how much more fully you can develop them. Discuss your child study with some of your class-mates. Compare the approaches that different ones of you have used in describ-ing your child or youth.

▶ Start compiling a list of words and phrases that you feel need fuller explana-tion, and begin to develop the concepts needed to bring full meaning to your list. Your own lexicon will be invaluable to you as you proceed with your study.

▶ Note some teaching practices that seem to violate the simple rules of friend-ship. How common is the practice of teachers' seeing their pupils outside school?

▶ Find a teacher who is unusually skillful in developing self-respect among his pupils. Study what he does to see how he achieves this end. Also study the atmosphere in this classroom and see what it tells you.

▶ What is your neighborhood doing to make children and youth feel needed?

► View: *Helping Teachers to Understand Children,* Part I, 20 min., sound, (United World Films).[11]

This film presents the methods devised by Daniel Prescott and his associates to help teachers in group situations learn how to study human behavior with clarity and insightfulness. We recommend that you view it as you start your study of a child and again later to refresh your thinking about important phases of development. The film is in two parts. Part I will be more pertinent to your study.

Additional Sources You May Find Helpful

John Dewey, *Human Nature and Conduct.* New York: Random House, The Modern Library, Inc., 1930.
John Dewey's classic presentation of the idea that man is part of nature but has the capacity to go far beyond nature in creating a life good for himself. This is not easy reading but the study of this book is most rewarding in deepening understanding.

Lawrence K. Frank, *Nature and Human Nature.* New Brunswick, N. J.: Rutgers University Press, 1951.
A thoughtful presentation of a wise man seeking to dispel the idea that there is a conflict between human nature and human goodness.

Earl C. Kelley and Marie I. Rasey, *Education and the Nature of Man.* New York: Harper and Brothers, 1952.
In this book two master teachers present in clear language important facts about the human organism as bases of the beliefs about learning and teaching which guide many in the teaching profession.

Sir Charles Sherrington, *Man on His Nature,* 2nd ed. Garden City, N. Y.: Doubleday Anchor Books, 1953.
In this book one of the most learned men of our time discusses many of the imponderables of human behavior. Chapter XII entitled "Altruism," is worth serious study. A difficult book but one most people cherish once they have made it their own.

---

[11] When films are mentioned, consult the most accessible film library for source of distribution of film.

3

The Organic Bases of Behavior

All human behavior is the body in action, whether it is sucking for food, admiring a sunset, rejecting an idea, or accepting a belief. Mankind has suffered much confusion by trying to separate his mind from his body, saying of some behavior "this is the mind," and of other behavior "that is the body." Someone has wisely put it that we should say of ourselves "I am a body," rather than "I have a body."

Many of the ways in which humans behave are yet incompletely

understood. Where in you has been the image of the friend you recognize after years of separation? Where have you kept the old song which "popped into your head" at the song-fest? Physiological explanations of memory have not been made, yet we know that we remember less well when we are fatigued or ill. Elderly people recall events of their early lives more clearly than their recent experiences. We have no physiological explanation of mental imagery, yet we know that individuals differ greatly in its vividness and accuracy. We have used the term *mental* to refer to activities such as remembering, imagining, reflecting, aspiring, and valuing.

We think more clearly when we are aware of the vast variety of behaviors of creative life which range from the sheer physical gratification of the mud puppy that seeks greater depths in slime to the emotional gratification a human receives when he seeks to enhance the happiness of a loved one. Whatever we do, we do it with our bodies.

Each Body Is Unique

It is quite futile to try to understand another person without understanding his body. To understand ourselves we must understand our own bodies, the ways in which they function, and their limitations for carrying out certain functions. We differ much from each other. In all the world, none of us can find another person who looks exactly like himself. Very little of the total functioning of our bodies can be seen by ourselves or by others. In this chapter we shall discuss some of the more important aspects of the body.

Natural Characteristics Are of the Body

Much of the quality of the body is set down in a single cell at conception. At that time it is determined whether we are to be male or female, dark or light complexioned. Also, the ultimate length of the bones, our approximate shapes at age ten, fifty, or ninety are determined. This single cell, resulting from the fertilization of one egg, determines a person's ultimate size, the shape of his features, the rate and patterns of his growth. These qualities we call native. The term *native* is a specific, meaningful term. It refers to the qualities of the body of which we can say "that is natural." One can never say of a person, "He is a natural-born thief," or "He is a natural-born good reader." *Natural* refers to inborn characteristics of the body.

Nature Sets Limits

Nature sets limits of capacities for each of us. We each have an infinite variety of capacities—to lift weights, to run, to leap, to memorize, to discriminate colors, to imagine, to make nice movements, to interpret symbols. How we use these capacities and to what extent they develop depend upon opportunity, challenge, and desire. Nature provides capacities, the culture converts them into abilities. We urge that this distinction be kept in mind: an ability is a cultivated capacity. When we speak of native ability, we really mean the capacity to become able.

Most of our activity is not at the limit of our potential. We do not walk as fast, nor read as rapidly, nor think as carefully as we are able to do. Doubtless the world would turn more smoothly and securely if more of us developed more of our capacities more nearly to the limits. Native capacity limits what we can do; it does not determine what we do.

It is appropriate to note here that in all of life's activities each of us assumes a congenial pace of functioning. We walk, or saunter, or race at highly consistent rates of speed. We read at rates quite below our maximum capacities, but at consistent rates. Slow readers can vastly increase their speed by several months of self-imposed practice in reading simple, interesting material, by consciously striving to read rapidly and to remember.

Body's Uses Are Learned

Our bodies are subject to all nature's laws that affect other creatures. Being human is improving upon nature, going beyond it. It is not defying nor denying nature. Since man has begun to study himself as part of nature, he has pondered much about heredity. Early in the twentieth century came the science of eugenics based upon the idea that if we could rid the social structure of "bad blood," society would achieve goodness, freedom from degradation and wickedness. Then, wise men recommended programs of sterilizing unfit persons to stem streams of "bad blood" flowing through our civilization. We have since learned that man's social problems cannot be resolved by such simple methods. We take no exception to the idea that the body is subject to laws of inheritance. We do insist that human behavior, the way one uses one's body, is largely the result of learning.

The body structure of most human beings is adequate to enable them to function as fine humans if well nurtured. However, characteristics of the body account for specialized capacities and deficiencies. For example, human beings differ markedly in their capacity to make nice movements. When you look at the drawings of children, you see not merely differences in the ideas, you see differences in the niceness of muscular control and sensitivity to color and design. You will find in any second, third, fifth, or tenth grade wide differences in the quality of handwriting. Too often we say to children, "If you would practice like Mabel does, you could write well, too." Usually this is not true. Some people can make quite nice, freely flowing movements which others can scarcely approach.

Many as yet unknown features of the brain are subject to the laws of inheritance. Doubtless some people have more capacity for higher mental processes than others because of the differences in physical qualities of their nervous systems. However, human behavior is so predominantly unfixed, so much the result of learning, premeditation, and deliberate planning, that the individual's family tree can be of scant interest to the teacher.

Likely you have read of the family histories such as that of the Kalikaks. Martin Kalikak, a soldier in the Revolutionary War, made pregnant a tavern girl to whom a son was born. Hundreds of degenerates descended from this illegitimate union. This Kalikak event occurred at a time when illegitimacy was scorned. You may recall the plight of the New England mother and her illegitimate child in Hawthorne's novel, The Scarlet Letter. The fact that Martin Kalikak went back home and married a fine young woman who gave us no recorded improvident descendants has been taken to prove the importance of inheritance. This study could as well be viewed as an illustration of the effects of rejection and of the plight of the illegitimately conceived child, as of the power of heredity.

Teachers are prone to attribute dullness to inheritance. We know that dull children tend to come from dull families. This seems to prove that the quality is inherited. It is quite as reasonable to believe that dull persons provide dulling circumstances for their children. Abundant data show that children who are born to socially inferior people but reared in good homes are not to be distinguished in quality of behavior from children born in the good neighborhoods in which they live. Evidence on the relative importance of nature and nurture is conflicting. Doubtless the next decade or so will yield additional data to clarify our understandings of what is intelligence and how it best can be nurtured. Surely no one can maintain that the quality of nurture makes no difference in the quality of human behavior. We urge you to read Stoddard's *The Meaning of Intelligence* [1] as an early account of efforts to probe this area of human development.

Some Qualities Subject to Inheritance

Let us now consider some qualities of the body that are more subject to the laws of inheritance than others. We have competent agreement that if certain characteristics are found in both father and mother, or in the families of father and mother, we can anticipate them in children. Among these are body proportions, size, color and shape of eyes, softness or hardness and spacing of teeth, length and proportion of bones, brittleness of bones, degree of pigmentation in hair, eyes, and skin. We can help our children by guiding them to see the patterns of development in their own families and accepting these as their own. We might note here that quite often a child is seen to be much like one relative—aunt or uncle, grandparent, or parent. That individual's growth pattern is useful in prediction. In some families, children approach physical adulthood early in their teens, while others attain physical maturity quite late.

Some people with pardonable pride but undue assurance make much point of their ancestry. Numerous Americans are proud to be descendants of Priscilla and John Alden. From how many other

---

[1] George D. Stoddard, *The Meaning of Intelligence* (New York: The Macmillan Company, 1943).

persons do they descend? Each of us has two parents, four grandparents, eight great-grandparents, and so on. Going back ten generations to John Alden's time, we have 2046 ancestors, from each of whom we may have inherited some characteristics. We tend to assume that we inherit only from that male who carries the family name down through the years.

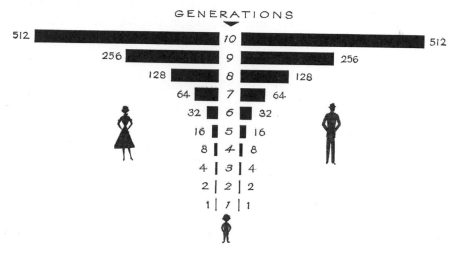

GENERATIONS

Ancestors multiply rapidly. Counting back ten generations to John Alden's time, each of us has 2,046 ancestors.

Sense Organs

One of the more important physical qualities is the sensitivity of sense organs. Has it ever occurred to you that our sense organs are highly specialized feelers? The eye is sensitive to the touch of the light wave, the nostrils to the touch of gases. The ear detects differences in waves of sound; the taste buds react to touches of chemicals in solution. We differ much from each other in the sensitivity of these organs to stimuli. We may say to little Rosa, who can hardly bear the dentist, "Why can't you be brave like Susie?" Susie's teeth hurt hardly at all with the drilling, while Rosa's teeth hurt tremendously. They have different thresholds of pain. Some people can hear tones that are inaudible to other people. Not all ears can enjoy sopranos. A dog responds to a whistle so highly pitched that no human can hear it.

Tissue Strength

The size of muscles and the vigor and strength per unit of muscle are markedly influenced by inheritable factors. An important fact of health is the strength and elasticity of blood vessels. Some children frequently have broken capillaries; some of us have arteries that will age much earlier than those of other people. The rupture of a cerebral blood vessel, which had caused so many deaths in the Mendelssohn family, brought death to young Felix at age thirty-nine.

Stability of Nervous System

The stability of the nervous system tends to be inherited. Some individuals and families can tolerate a great deal of adversity without undue strain. It is well here to warn that we cannot judge nervous stability by outward displays of emotion. When members of some cultural groups do not weep and wail at funerals, their associates assume that they just don't care for the departed. Other cultures would feel quite unhappy to allow their emotions to be displayed in these circumstances. We cannot judge stability of the nervous system by outward behavior.

Maturing Patterns

The patterns of maturing—early maturing and late maturing—tend to run in families. In any school grade of like ages, we see great differences in the degree of being grown-up. In a sixth grade we find shapely women, strong "he-men," and little children. Some children need to be helped and reassured about their own patterns of maturing. Early development does not mean ultimate superiority. Many large men were little boys at age sixteen. Teachers must avoid fostering undue adulation for early growers. This frequently is done by giving approbation to early readers in first grade, by assigning parts in music and dramatics to the more mature students. Favoring the early growers is especially flagrant in athletic sports and other public performances in high schools.

As this is written, all America is excitedly seeking potential scientists and mathematicians among young children. Quite commonly, children are stereotyped as academic or non-academic as early as age eleven and twelve. This is common practice in Europe. We may be sure that by typing children at too early an age, we miss and withhold opportunity from many "later bloomers." Numerous highly capable minds do not become intellectuals until the late teens.

Bodily Weaknesses

Some bodily weaknesses tend to be inheritable—the tendency toward heart disease, diabetes, epilepsy, chorea, some kinds of insanity. These inheritable defects must be present in the biological inheritance of both parents in order to affect the offspring. A particular child may not be affected by the specific family defect himself, but may carry it within his genes as a recessive characteristic, and pass it along to his children.

Sex

The primary difference between humans is sex, male or female. One of the interesting arguments of our recent past concerns the significance of maleness and femaleness. Some insist that sex should be taken into account only in reproductive activity, that there are families in which mother should go out to make the living while father keeps house and cares for the children. (This has already happened in some communities in which father cannot get a job and mother finds it easy to get women's work.)

Others insist that every child in the world knows, by the time he is two years old, whether he is to be a man or a woman and what difference this will make to him. Boys and girls need to understand, they maintain, what it means to be a boy or a girl—not only physically but in the culture. The culture sets more of the sex-linked behavioral differences than does nature. These differing points of view are discussed by Pearl Buck [2] and Margaret Mead.[3]

All of us have within us some maleness and some femaleness. The terms introvert and extrovert originally meant predominantly female or predominantly male in personal quality. Some wag recently illustrated the difference by this example: If you ask a woman, "Where did you get that steak?" she will say, "Well, what's wrong with it?" while a man will

---

[2] Pearl Buck, *Of Men and Women* (New York: John Day Company, Inc., 1941).
[3] Margaret Mead, *Sex and Temperament in Three Primitive Societies* (New York: William Morrow and Company, 1935).

say, "At the Super X Market." Some women are quite masculine in their ways; and we don't understand why some "take up" with an unmale, little man. Perhaps we tend in mating to strive for the congenial average of maleness and femaleness in a family. Perhaps nature seeks to strike a balance in mating and thus avoid perpetuating an excessive degree of femininity and masculinity. It is important for the teacher to know that real physical differences explain the differences in behavior between the tomboy and the delicate little girl, between the "he-man" and the "sissy." Some of us believe that high-school athletics give disproportionate acclaim to the early-maturing, excessively masculine boy.

Maintenance Functions

Individuals differ in their store of energy and the rate at which they can release it. Some of us can expend ourselves more completely and restore ourselves more quickly than others. Each of us has an energy budget. When it is gone, we have to take time to build up our supply. It is important to help children and young people recognize their own individual signs that indicate their energy is at a low ebb. It is difficult to tell whether the child whom we call lazy lacks energy or is merely bored. We can gain reliable clues in watching him play. The amount of time required for recuperation from fatigue differs much. Some runners can win a mile race, rest a few minutes, and win a half-mile race. Most of us would have to rest a week after such exertion. The rate at which wounds heal differs. Normal temperatures differ. Do you know your normal temperature? It may vary one or two degree from the general average of 98.6. Do you know your metabolic rate, the rate at which nutrients are converted into energy? You doubtless have noted some very thin people who have unusually hearty appetites, while others of us have to count our calories most diligently lest we become overweight.

Children differ much in the amount of sleep they need. You cannot find in a book the amount of sleep needed by Jim or Nan. You will find the average of the amounts of time mothers report that their children spend in bed. We can judge for ourselves how much sleep we need by seeing how long we sleep when the alarm clock is not set and there is nothing to disturb us. Ordinarily the child who falls asleep at school needs the sleep, although, particularly by the time he has become a college student, he may be finding in sleep refuge from boredom.

Law of

Filial Regression

One law of inheritance, the law of filial regression, explains one of the greater strains of our growing suburban culture. A goodly number of people who leave the smaller towns and rural sections of the country for the city, where they hope to make their marks, are people of unusual or attractive talent. Many of them have brothers and sisters back home who are quite ordinary, but these people, who happened to be born with extra gifts in the arts, or in business, or in science, go to the city to market their special talents. Such a person marries and sets up a family, and expects his children to be as capable, or a little more so, than he. The law of filial regression says that offspring tend toward the average. Stupid parents tend to have children who are a little brighter than they; bright parents tend to have children a little less capable than they. We observe a considerable amount of strain in communities of geniuses and near-geniuses because the children do not measure up to the parents. For example, there are now only two or three major league baseball players who are sons of former major league baseball players. We have little doubt that most major league ballplayers have tried to make ballplayers of their sons. We hasten to warn against making any predictions on the basis of this law.

Physical Quality

Important

Only in

Social Circumstances

No physical quality is important in human behavior apart from the social circumstance of the individual. For example, eye color has very slight relationship to vision. It is possible that dark-eyed people can stand sunlight a little better than light-eyed people but light-eyed people can wear sunglasses. Nonetheless, the appearance of a blue-eyed child in a dark-eyed tribe of people would likely result in a tense social situation. Another example: In former days a midget was thought to be impossibly handicapped. The adult midget today does have difficulty living in a world built for larger people, but he has become highly valuable for certain kinds of work such as riveting in the tails of airplanes. He can get into places the rest of us cannot enter. He would be of little use on a pioneer farm. Abnormally tall boys are now sought by basketball coaches. They used to develop serious inferiority complexes. The popularity of tall and shapely Dagmar greatly reduced anxiety among tall girls. The extent of one's acceptance and friendships in a social situation depends more upon one's own accepting qualities and friendliness than upon one's physique.

Differences to Be Cherished in Human Development

Much of child study, as was noted in Chapter 1, has been devoted to looking for what is wrong with people—for physical and mental defects —rather than to discussing the kind of person with whom we deal. We have tended to subject a child who is different to exceptional treatment. We are rapidly coming to accept the idea that differences in people are to be cherished. Life would be most boring if all people were alike. The term *normal* means *average*. With whatever average quantitative characteristic we deal, half of the population is above and half is below it.

For several decades schools have grouped children according to likenesses. Originally schools separated boys and girls. Some schools still do. Grouping children according to likenesses has made uniqueness a source of difficulty. When our grouping implies that each child should be like the others in his group, to be unique is a problem to a child. An overly tall girl at age ten is often highly self-conscious of her uniqueness. In a group of ten-year-olds she is out of place and a problem to herself and the other girls. In a group of ten- to fourteen-year-olds this early-maturing girl is not conspicuous. A late-maturing boy in a group of boys from twelve to sixteen would not have much of a problem. In a group of fifteen-year-olds he is at a great disadvantage. Problems presented by great variations in the rates of growth are among the ill effects of our narrowly graded school system.

When she was in the sixth grade, Genevieve was the fullback as long as her mother didn't find out about it. Now at age thirty-nine plus, she is the most feminine person of her group. By the time she was in sixth grade, Genevieve had achieved full size and physical maturity. She grew no more. Now she is five feet one, fairly chunky, and a delightful woman. Her noisy, flamboyant behavior which caused her mother much distress when she was eleven, continued into her high-school years. It was her natural way of behaving at sixth grade; the opposition she experienced tended to prolong her extravagant behavior.

Perils of Extraneous Motivation

Let us consider some of the effects on the body of present-day emphasis upon competition in games originally intended as play for enjoyment. We seriously question the value of organized competitive team sports for young children. Social pressure for extreme activity—particularly since we have developed the Little League, Ittsy Bittsy Basketball, and midget auto racing—compels youngsters to keep on playing when they have already exhausted their energy budgets. Nature provides a safety factor which impels us to stop when we have exercised enough. In training distance runners, coaches seldom have them run the entire distance for which they train. The excitement of the race itself will enable the runner to go beyond his safety factor and run the race in full, when he will likely collapse. We require some kind of extraneous motivation—someone chasing us, trying to catch a train, or trying to beat our nearest competitor—in order to exceed our factor of safety in the expenditure of energy.

This principle of the use of the body you can well remember: *one does not violate the well-being of his own body unless highly motivated to do so.* Occasionally one sees the interesting example of such high motivation in a child who is seeking to control his mother by holding his breath. We may have full confidence that if such a child becomes unconscious, breathing will be resumed.

We once saw a fire break out in the main street of a village. As the wind swept the fire down the street, we saw two barbers emerge from their shop, each carrying a barber chair. When the fire was quenched and the danger to their shop had passed, they leaned over to pick up the chairs and couldn't budge them. Stirred by the danger of the fire and the value of the chairs, they were able to rise to the demands of the situation. Almost everyone has done something under emotional stress that has strained the muscles or has given him "cricks" in the back. We must be wary of motivating children to exceed their safety factors in engaging in the great varieties of bodily activity. Ordinarily we can judge these factors in children and youth by watching them in unorganized play. We are coming to recognize the deteriorating effects upon the body of undue pressure to exceed and get ahead as shown in the high incidence of ulcers and heart disease among professional and management people. This is

particularly noticeable among middle-aged men whose jobs demand excessive efforts to excel.

We have been developing the principle that physical qualities do not affect human adjustments apart from the situations in which we find people. Schools must carefully avoid any kind of rejection of a person because of physical uniqueness. We accept the child as a human being. We seek to motivate him along paths indicated by his own physical development and promise. We have attempted to establish the idea that it does matter what kind of body one *is*. However, we must stress the importance of "what kind of person has that body?"

Stephanie is sixty-eight inches tall; her peers are six inches shorter. She is bitter, ill-fated, sure she will not be asked to a dance nor to a wedding of her own. We hope someone can soon help her discern what things are of most worth.

When Henry was twelve years old, polio withered his legs severely. Doctors prescribed years of physical therapy, braces, and special exercises. He decided that he would prefer living on crutches to gambling those years on regaining his legs. He now functions at age forty as a superior professional man. Franklin Delano Roosevelt provides an eloquent illustration of a man who conquered the limitations imposed on his body by illness and went on to achieve greatness in the service of his country.

When his younger brother exceeded his height and weight, Ted was belatedly diagnosed as a midget who would not exceed fifty inches in height. His parents were desolate. Ted, at age eight, seemed to say "So what?" and now is among the happiest, most popular, and achieving boys in his high school. He referees in sports and is realistically contemplating occupations in which normal size is not crucial.

Chuck was born with "rubber bones." He will never be able to stand, nor to sit erectly without braces. When last we saw him, he laughed gaily, read avidly, umpired the fifth-grade ball games from his wheel chair, securely received needed help from other children.

Wisdom of the Body

Contemplation of the wondrous workings of the human body leads us quickly beyond our comprehension. When we take food into our mouths, our mouths "water" to provide sufficient liquid so that the food may be swallowed. Nature seized the opportunity to put into this liquid (saliva) some materials necessary to digestion. Our bodies are built to function best at about 98.6 degrees of temperature. We have a thermostatic control which keeps the body at that temperature in the most frigid climates and in desert heat. When the body needs to be warmer in order to fight germs, the temperature is raised. Callouses form on our hands and feet and any other part of the body exposed to excessive friction so that the skin shall not wear through. When our skin is punctured, the blood coagulates at that point and stems the loss of blood. When we take an unusual amount of exercise and our muscles require more nourishment and more rapid removal of waste, the rate of breathing increases and the heart pumps more blood to the cells needing it. When we have used parts of our body too much and have overexpended their resources, fatigue prevents continued exercise. No one takes thought to secrete saliva, control his temperature, increase the rate of his heart beat. The body is most wise in maintaining its integrity. You will be interested in reading Cannon's classic volume, *The Wisdom of the Body*,[4] which elaborates this theme.

From one point of view the body may be seen as a machine. Certainly it contains many aspects of man-made machines. In the body are levers, lenses, swivels, universal joints, filters, pumps, insulations, radiators, thermostats, and calculators. It is also a complex chemical plant. Practically

---

[4] W. B. Cannon, *The Wisdom of the Body* (New York: W. W. Norton and Company, 1939).

all drugs used to stimulate or depress bodily activity emphasize the effects of chemicals normally found in the body. The body takes in foods in many varied forms, and with water and oxygen converts them into chemicals and energy required by the body. The body manufactures and maintains supplies of acids and alkalies, hormones, and enzymes in its chemical laboratory.

Functioning of Endocrine Glands

To a marked degree, personality is a function of the endocrine or ductless glands, which pour hormones into the blood stream. The glands of internal secretion affect in one way or another the functioning of the body as a whole. The thyroid glands lie beside the trachea in the neck. Their hormones affect metabolic rate, growth, mental alertness, condition of skin and hair. Extreme underactivity of thyroid glands in a young child results in a condition known as *cretinism* in which the individual, while he may grow, maintains the bodily proportions and personal characteristics of an infant. Excessive activity of the thyroid, *hyperthyroidism,* increases the metabolic rate which results in loss of weight, excessive nervousness, and irritability. Abnormal functioning of the thyroid gland can be readily treated. Within the thyroid glands are the parathyroids. They are necessary to life, for the parathyroids regulate the calcium balance in the blood.

Near the kidneys lie the adrenal glands. They are really two-in-one glands. The inner core is called the medula. Surrounding it is the cortex. The hormone released by the medula increases blood pressure, accelerates heart beat, increases the amount of sugar in the blood, increases muscular strength and resistance to fatigue. It makes us ready to fight or flee. The hormone of the adrenal cortex appears to affect the balance of bodily fluids, the tone of various bodily tissues. Extracts of adrenal hormones are now made synthetically. One of them, cortisone, has become well known as an effective aid in controlling arthritis.

The primary reproductive structures of mammals, the male testes and the female ovaries, have functions other than reproduction. The hormones of these sex glands, or gonads, foster the development of feminine qualities in females and masculine qualities in males.

The pituitary glands lie at the base of the skull. Overactivity of the pituitary glands results in excessive development of the skeleton, the condition known as *giantism*. Underactivity results in *dwarfism* and lack of development of the secondary sex characteristics. Normal development of the pituitary seems to be quite essential to the normal activity of the gonads and the thyroids.

Physiologists are not at all agreed upon details of the functioning nor effects of the endocrine system. It is quite clear, however, that it plays an important role in behavior, supplying the organic basis for temperament. The word hormone literally means *excitor*. Our bodies are activated in part by the hormones, but it would appear that the endocrine system works as an organized unit and with the central nervous system to achieve the integrated adjustments and adaptations of the person as a whole. Often personalities are thrown off balance as a result of stimulating independence of particular endocrine functions. The layman dare not prescribe for himself the various extracts now available.

Hearing and Seeing

Through his sense organs, the individual perceives his environment and is able to learn. In school most learning results from seeing and hearing. The mechanism for hearing develops during the later part of prenatal life. After the middle ear has drained, babies respond to definite noises, but seem to lack fine discrimination of sound. Acuity in hearing seems to continue to increase until pubescence. As with all sensations, the quality and intensity of sounds differ from person to person. In terms of sheer sensory stimulation, we are eternally hearing. To most sounds we pay no attention. Children are somewhat responsive to training in tone distinction and other qualities of sound. This training results from specialized attention and interpretation rather than from actual gain in sensitivity.

The teacher needs to know something about ways of identifying children who do not hear normally. Mannerisms such as turning the head, cupping the ear in making an effort to hear can be noted. Many children try to cover up the fact that they do not hear well, although one who has never heard well may not know he has that deficiency. The teacher can use a little game of standing twenty feet from the child who is facing squarely away from him, and in forced whispers call out to the child familiar words of one or two syllables, asking the child to repeat them. Any child showing signs of hearing difficulty should be examined by an expert. Four out of five hard-of-hearing persons are able to hear adequately with hearing aids. Examinations should be given rather frequently during the elementary-school periods, since most of the childhood diseases, such as measles, scarlet fever, and meningitis may lead to damaging ear infections.

Human vision is one of the most intricate, complex functions of the body. The eye, the optic nerve, and the portions of the brain which give meanings to visual sensation develop irregularly and require several years to attain maturity. This development is intricately related to the maturity of the organism as a whole. Vision is so complex and so interrelated to one's total growth pattern that no two children see alike. The teacher who is sensitive to the vision of his pupils watches their coordination. Poor coordination may result from poor teaming of the eyes. The child may have faulty peripheral vision, which he exhibits by tending to run into objects not in the center of his visual field.

It is particularly important to note the extent to which distance affects the child's vision. Does he hold a book or picture at normal distance, far away, or close to his eyes? Does the child appear to work hard when focusing upon a book? Camera fans know the importance of sharp focus to a clear image. The eye accommodates itself to the distance of the object from the eye by altering the thickness of the lenses. This process of accommodation is rather simple in early childhood because the lenses are quite elastic. Young children with misshapen lenses or misshapen eyeballs can in this way accommodate to see clearly. An ordinary visual chart which measures the child's ability to recognize designs or letters will not reveal these defects.

There is good reason to believe that it is a mistake to motivate a child highly to fix his eyes on close objects for a long period of time. The young eye is normally farsighted. To be urged to focus upon objects at less than arm's length for an extended period of time may result later in astigmatism, or nearsightedness. You will note that young children change position frequently when reading. Their wise bodies tell them to change their focal length. Wise teachers do not prescribe the proper posture for reading and writing. One of the ill effects of prolonged televiewing results from the unchanging focal length. Children, and adults too, tend to shift position when viewing in order to vary focal length.

Plight

of Handicapped

In recent times much attention is being directed to the plight of the handicapped child. Handicaps may be placed in three categories: those resulting from incomplete or abnormal development of the nervous system, those resulting from faulty development or damage to the skeleton and muscles, and those resulting from malfunctioning of organs. Each of us is more or less handicapped. There are certain things we cannot do because of the condition of our bodies.

General Disabilities

Educators are beginning to give appropriate attention to disabilities which do not show clearly save through general maladjustment. We can readily spot the child who is blind, or deaf, or maimed. We are more likely to attribute to low intelligence or laziness ailments such as mild malnutrition, substandard metabolic rates, sensory deficiencies, slight brain damage, and the like. For example, we may encounter children who are subject to seizures. A seizure is really loss of control of the body. It may be due to brain damage, or to low blood sugar. Often the child who becomes sleepy or irritable in the afternoon can receive new life from a candy bar.

Dr. Leon Greenspan of the Diagnostic and Evaluation Division of the Queens' Rehabilitation Program[5] reports that among children who are referred to the Division because of poor school work about 50 per cent have either slight brain damage resulting in perceptive or aphasic deficit or emotional problems. Of the brain-damaged children about one-half have slight but clearly evident neural-muscular disabilities. The teacher should be aware of the child who has more than the ordinary trouble putting on his coat or zipping it up, who trips over his own feet. The child who does not listen, who refuses to do his work, who can't sit still may have been born after a difficult labor, may have had an illness in which prolonged high temperature has damaged a portion of the nervous system or he may be simply disinterested.

---

[5] The Queens' Rehabilitation Program is carried on in the Borough of Queens, New York City.

Orthopedic and Muscular Defects

Teachers need to be alert to orthopedic and muscular defects. Because of malfunctioning of damaged structure, some children are slightly crippled and can be helped by a little special training. A slight limp, toes pointing markedly inward or outward or at different angles, uneven wearing of the heels or toes of shoes are indications of conditions that can be corrected with special shoes and exercises. Children crippled by deformities or accident usually require some special help. Most adults tend to give them too much attention. Cripples arouse our pity, which may be an inverted thankfulness that we are not in their condition, and tempt us to overshelter and overcare for them in various ways. We must see them as individuals who need some special help but who are part of the community. These children will grow into citizens and—depending

upon how they are treated as children—will or will not become self-sufficient and relatively independent.

We believe the lame and deformed should be in regular classrooms. They need to grow in the general culture, not a crippled one. Too, the "normal" need them. Too many of us avert our eyes, feel uncomfortable, in the presence of "odd" bodies because we have known no such individuals as persons.[6]

| Food and Sleep | Adequate food and sleep are necessary for growth and the maintenance of bodily efficiency. Many of the children in school today have been reared by parents who are |

overly aware of the importance of nutrition. Some careful students of personal fitness attribute great importance to nutrition. Adelle Davis states:

> Nutrition is a personal matter, as personal as your diary or income-tax report. Your nutrition can determine how you look, act, and feel; whether you are grouchy or cheerful, homely or beautiful, physiologically and even psychologically young or old; whether you think clearly or are confused, enjoy your work or make it a drudgery, increase your earning power or stay in an economic rut. The foods you eat can make the difference between your day ending with freshness which lets you enjoy a delightful evening or with exhaustion which forces you to bed with the chickens.[7]

It seems to us that an undue number of children today have feeding problems. Eating is as natural as is breathing. It takes a lot of learning to reject good foods. In insisting that a child must clean his plate before having dessert, we have given American children the "sweet tooth," and have implied that the term *wholesome* is synonymous with distasteful.

Nutrition

We cite a few commonly accepted facts and principles about nutrition:

> More than sixty nutrients are needed by the body; no one kind of food will supply any great number of them.

***

[6] This is discussed with insight in Lillian Smith's *The Journey* (New York: World Publishing Company, 1954), pp. 12-19.

[7] Adelle Davis, *Let's Eat Right to Keep Fit* (New York: Harcourt, Brace and Company, 1954), p. 3.

Highly refined foods have less nutritional value than unrefined foods.

Energy is produced in the body by the burning of sugar or sugar and fat. The amount of sugar in the blood is known as blood sugar. Breakfast is an important meal for it determines the amount of blood sugar the body will have for the day. To maintain a high level of blood sugar throughout the day, breakfast should combine sugar for energy, protein, and fat which slows down the digestion.

Each meal should combine the three basic nutrients: sugar, fat, and protein —a small amount of sugar and fats, and a larger amount of protein, especially for children.

Low blood sugar results in irritability, lassitude, headaches, nervousness, and fatigue. These symptoms in a child give the teacher a clue to an individual's eating habits, especially his breakfast.

The kinds of soil upon which foods are grown determine their nutritional value. Foods grown on "organic" farms have unusually high nutritional value compared to those grown on poor soil or in chemical tanks with the aid of fertilizers.

The vitamin content of foods is closely related to their freshness. Vegetables and fruits begin to lose their vitamin content as soon as they are gathered, unless they are frozen immediately.

Complete proteins are those containing the eight essential amino acids needed for health. Some sources of complete proteins are wheat germ, milk, cottage cheese, soybeans, meat, and brewers' yeast.

Fat is essential to health. Natural vegetable oils are the richest source of fatty acids. Too little fat may cause overweight.

The most valuable sugar is lactose, which is found only in milk.

All refined, starchy foods serve as sugar when digested and carried into the blood.

Sleep

Indications of inadequate sleep are inattentiveness, lack of concentration, inability to recall names and facts ordinarily known, a heightened degree of irritability, dawdling, and of course sleepiness. The average primary-grade child needs about eleven hours of sleep. If he must get up at seven in order to catch the bus to school, he needs to be asleep by eight o'clock the evening before. In many families, daddy doesn't get home until six or six-thirty. And there are some mighty interesting TV programs on after seven-thirty. We think it likely that soon schools may need to start a bit later in the day in order that the child may spend more of the evening with his family and get more sleep in the morning.

It seems that the normal adult ration of sleep—about eight hours—is insufficient for most adolescents. Of course, individuals differ remarkably in the amount of sleep they need.

New Areas of Knowledge

Knowledge of the body and its functioning is accumulating at a rate so rapid that no one can keep up-to-date in all fields related to it. The scope of this book and the intent of the authors do not permit a thorough review of new insights. However, we do want to mention a few of the new developments to lure you to continue to watch and read about them.

New Drugs: Source of Help or Harm

We can scarcely pick up the Sunday paper without noting some new research on the chemistry of the body and offerings of new drugs, chemicals, and hormones to make us more tranquil, to pep us up, to put us to sleep, to make us fatter or leaner. It is most important that these drugs be used only on the advice of competent physicians. The normal body maintains its own balance. To stimulate or depress the activity of a part of it may throw the system as a whole out of balance. For example, vitamin A is important to health but excessive dosage of vitamin A results in severe headaches. Often these headaches are improperly diagnosed.

Stress Theory

One of the more recent theories, developed by Hans Selye, is known as the stress theory. In his volume, *The Stress of Life*, Selye gathers into a unified theory the work of many specialists, including his own, and describes it in terms that laymen can understand. He defines stress as "essentially the wear and tear in the body." He indicates that changes in the body in both structure and chemical composition which were found twenty-five years ago to result from stress have made it possible to study the effects of stress. He has found that many diseases are caused by stress. He has also studied the body's successful adjustment to stress. This knowledge has contributed immeasurably to our understanding of psychosomatic diseases, those diseases which seem to have strong origins in the emotional realm of life. Selye states:

> Some of the changes (in structure and chemical composition of the body) are merely signs of *damage;* others are manifestations of the body's *adaptive reactions,* its mechanism of defense against stress. The totality of these changes—the *stress-syndrome*—is called the *general adaptation syndrome.* [He uses the letters G.A.S. to indicate this.] It develops in three stages: (1) the alarm reaction, (2) the stage of resistance, (3) the stage of exhaustion.
>
> The *nervous system and the endocrine (or hormonal) system* play particularly important parts in maintaining resistance during stress. They help to keep the structure and functions of the body steady, despite exposure to stress-producing or *stressor* agents, such as nervous tension, wounds, infections, poisons. This steady state is known as homeostasis.[8]

None of us could function without some stress. But when the sources are unrecognized and the stresses are unheeded, when we are keyed up and don't know how to tune down, we can draw our emotional strings so tight that they break. To experience anxiety about the outcome of a purposed endeavor or one's fortunes places undue stress upon the body as an organism.

The school maintains a good many stress-producing features, which seem otherwise unproductive. The importance of tests, making the honor roll, getting on the athletic team or the yearbook committee assume a disproportionate importance in the lives of many children.

Pre-natal Influences

We have gone through a few decades of belief that what happened to the child while still within the womb was quite unimportant to his human development. Montagu has become an eloquent spokesman for the notion that the nine months before the baby's birth are far more important in subsequent development than has been commonly understood.[9] While there is no direct connection between the nervous and blood systems of the mother and the fetus, maternal hormones do reach the fetus, and the common endocrine pool of mother and fetus forms a neuro-

---

[8] Hans Selye, *The Stress of Life* (New York: McGraw-Hill Book Company, Inc., 1956), p. 3.

[9] M. F. Ashley Montagu, *The Direction of Human Development* (New York: Harper and Brothers, 1955).

humoral bond between them. The evidence suggests that unusual emotional stress in the mother prior to birth leaves an imprint upon the neonate—the newborn child—in one way or another.

Research on Brain Functioning

Some of the most fascinating research of our day is that being done by a small group of neurologists, neurophysiologists, and electricians upon the functioning of the brain. The three-pound mass we call the brain distinguishes humans from the other creatures of the animal kingdom. During the past thirty years we have learned enough about the brain to evolve new theories of consciousness and to know what portions of the brain are expendable. Electronic engineers are approaching the skills necessary to make a machine that functions like the human brain. The experts in electronics tell us that if we can tell them what the brain does, they can hitch up a gadget which will do it. It is now rather clear that the highest level of integration, the adjustment of the individual as a whole, takes place deep within the brain, within the reticular system—not in the cortex as was formerly believed. In the cortex, meanings are assigned to stimuli, stored for future reference, coded, and sent to the reticular system, where impulses are issued to the appropriate sensorimotor regions of the cortex to initiate appropriate muscular response.

Some Notes to Teachers

Children should have abundant opportunities to know themselves in as much detail as they can comprehend. Ordinarily, physical examinations are given in a hurry. The results are written down by a nurse or clerk as confidential information for the doctor. Children should share in keeping their own records of physical growth and condition of health. They should know about their shots, their illnesses, and their injuries. Periodic measurements should be recorded with the children.

Ordinarily the child knows his height and weight. He might well know something about his relative strength, how long he can hold his breath, how many dots he can make on a piece of paper in ten seconds, and how his rate compares with other children, how long he can stand blindfolded on one foot, how readily his skin burns in the sun, his normal temperature and how high his temperature goes when he harbors infection, how long it takes him to stop breathing hard after strenuous exercise, the acuity of his hearing and which is his better ear, is he right- or left-handed and to what degree, which of his eyes is dominant, whether he has flat feet or high arches, and so on. None of these characteristics affects his quality as a human being. The school must carefully avoid attaching respectability or privilege or anxiety to superiority or inferiority in any of them. However, it is a bit silly for a child with slow reaction time to yearn to be an outstanding basketball player or a pianist. The highly energetic person will experience marked frustration in being a barber. Among the best bits of advice man has had is "know thyself," and we might add "and like it." The growing child needs to know what is normal and what is possible for *him*.

Suggestions for Further Exploration

▶ With five or six friends, make a number of tests of physical capacity, such as:

How long can you hold your breath after taking several deep breaths?

How many times can you tap a piece of paper with a pencil in ten seconds?

How many details of a picture can you recall after viewing it for ten seconds?

How long can you hold a pencil in the mouth of a coke bottle at arm's length without its touching the bottle?

How long can you stand on one foot with your eyes shut?

What's the lowest and highest musical note you can hum?

Test the distance at which you can read print—for example, on a medium-sized calendar.

If you have enough room, try out the whisper test. At how many feet can you hear and repeat forced whispers of two-syllable words?

After having taken these tests, consider which one of your friends you would choose to team with—if you knew nothing else about them—to go on a mountain hike, to run a sack race, to go duck hunting, to help build a boat, to attend the symphony, to go on a cook-out.

▶ Name the blood relative that you resemble most in appearance. To what extent are you like him temperamentally? Compare your growth patterns; for example, size as a baby, age of walking, age of maturing. Compare your stamina, your reaction time, your body build, general health.

▶ Discover, if you can, these physical characteristics about the young person you are studying:

Does he seem to be an early or late maturer?

Which of his senses seem to be particularly acute?

Is he satisfied or dissatisfied with his body? Is he unduly anxious about any condition of his body? Do you know why?

Do you judge him to be quick or sluggish?

What childhood diseases has he had? Have they left any marked effects upon him?

How does he compare in size and build with others his age?

Does he have any physical condition that sets him apart? If so, how does this condition affect his attitude as a whole?

► Try out some of the tests you have taken with the child you are studying and some of his friends. Note the variations in responses. Reflect upon the importance of these responses in various situations that the youngster finds himself.

► Discuss among your classmates the kind of health information you think it is important for a school to keep about its pupils. Examine some school health records to see what kind of information is usually available. Talk to some teachers to see how this information is used by them.

► A number of films show different aspects of physical growth and development. If possible, view some of the films in the named series:

Ages and Stages Series—National Film Board of Canada
Child Development Series—McGraw-Hill Book Company, Inc.
Health Education Series—McGraw-Hill Book Company, Inc.
Psychology for Living Series—McGraw-Hill Book Company, Inc.

The following three films are ones that stimulate thoughtful discussion:

Heredity and Family Environment (Psychology for Living Series), 9 min., sound, McGraw-Hill Book Company, Inc.

Illustrates the interplay between heredity and environment, limitations set by heredity, capacity to grow and develop one's capacities affected by environment.

Principles of Development (Child Development Series), 17 min., sound, McGraw-Hill Book Company, Inc.

Outlines principles of growth and change from early infancy, establishes the point that all development is the result of maturation and learning, and introduces variables that make each individual different.

The School That Learned to Eat, 22 min., sound, color, Southern Education Film Production Service.

Pictures the approach a school makes in developing nutritional habits of eating by the children in the school and the adults in the community. Excellent depicting of teacher-pupil-adult participation in planning and implementing a project of vital concern to the total community.

Additional Sources You May Find Helpful

W. B. Cannon, *The Wisdom of the Body.* New York: W. W. Norton and Company, Inc., 1939.

Describes the way the body maintains its equilibrium (homeostasis) and meets emergencies. This is the presentation for the layman of the important results of Cannon's researches reported in Bodily Changes in Pain, Hunger, Fear and Rage, *published by D. Appleton Company, 1929.*

Flanders Dunbar, *Mind and Body.* New York: Random House, 1947.

Flanders Dunbar has done a vast amount of research on the relationship between emotional problems and health. This book presents "psychosomatics" in terms the layman can comprehend.

M. F. Ashley Montagu, *The Direction of Human Development.* New York: Harper and Brothers, 1955.

Research from biology, anthropology, and psychology are brought together in this book to show how cooperation and love are necessary for individuals to become social human beings.

Helen B. Pryor, *As the Child Grows.* New York: Silver Burdett and Company, 1943.

This book describes physical development through the period of growth. In it parents and teachers can find guides to understanding inheritance, growth, and maturation as related factors in the developing personality. Particularly valuable is a detailed table of height-weight norms which take into account body types.

Frances B. Strain, *The Normal Sex Interests of Children.* New York: Appleton-Century-Crofts, 1948.

Parents and teachers find this to be one of the most helpful books in guiding the development of children's knowledge and concerns about "Where do babies come from?" Mrs. Strain has published several books on this important and perplexing problem.

4

The Growth and Functioning of Intelligence

Most of the principles discussed in the preceding chapter apply quite as much to chickens, puppies, and monkeys as to man. This chapter deals with man's one superiority over other creatures, his mind. The term *mind* is an abstract term. As we use it, mind refers to various capacities of men to adjust themselves to circumstances by thoughtfully modifying their ways and their circumstances.

For many centuries man has been handicapped in his quest to understand himself by regarding the activities of his body to be separate from those of his mind. We know now that the mind is not an outside something acting upon the body to direct its behavior. The mind is the body in action as surely as is metabolism. Herrick, one of the world's able neurologists says:

> The mind of man, with its capacity for intelligent control of his own cultural development and of the natural resources which are available for his use, is nature's noblest product so far as we know.[1]

Elsewhere Herrick states:

> Mind and body do not exist separately. There may be a body without a mind, but we know nothing about any mind apart from a body. . . . Human nature cannot be understood unless the integrity of this vital process is recognized. . . . The idea that mind is an entity detachable from the bodily organization that generates it and experiences it must be rigorously excluded from all scientific inquiry.[2]

Among all creatures, behavior is interaction between the organism and the field in which it lives. Human behavior, being almost entirely unfixed by nature, is largely determined by conscious intent. We use the term *mind* to include the processes of sizing up circumstances awarely and making aware adjustments to them. We use the term *conscious* synonymously with the term *aware*. The degree of the effectiveness of one's aware or consciously deliberate adjustments measures the degree of his effective intelligence. We use the term *intelligence* to include all of the processes of directing behavior with awareness of purpose and of means for attaining it. When you tell your friends you are going to build a house, they know little of what you actually are going to do. When you see a hornet about to build his house, you know precisely what to expect.

This is not to say that the intelligent person is at any time aware of all his adjustments. The capacity to habituate learned responses makes human life possible. The toddler is extremely aware of his procedure in handling a zipper. The infant exercises much care as he grasps his bottle to put its nipple in his mouth. The young man learning to shave or to smoke exercises similar care in performing these functions. We are able

---

[1] C. Judson Herrick, *The Evolution of Human Nature* (Austin: University of Texas Press, 1956), p. 465.
[2] *Ibid.*, pp. 285-286.

to habituate attitudes and make up our minds that we do not like a person, a kind of food, or a city because we have had a bad experience with a similar condition. The "executive" mind is able to grasp the meaning of a variety of facts and problems and plan action without deliberately weighing each of them.

This chapter is concerned with the development of a human being's ability and disposition to behave intelligently. He is created with a capacity for learning to be intelligent. In a practical sense, intellectual behavior cannot be separated from feeling and personal interest. We have come to use the noun *intelligence* as a collective noun that includes many diverse abilities and dispositions. Abilities are cultivated capacities; all intelligent behavior has to be learned. Learning is a very private, intimate affair. It takes place in a personality. It receives meaning (depth, range, complexity) from the deep feelings that become embedded in our beings in early childhood.

Some Kinds of Mental Behavior

No sharp line distinguishes the mentality of humans from that of other creatures. A few humans behave less intelligently than the average chimpanzee. Animals sense when it is light and when it is dark; they seek shelter from cold winds; they perceive conditions which promise storms. Creatures experience all the sensations that humans experience, but they seldom appear to be aware of their meanings.

Giving Meaning to Sensations

As we give meanings to sensations, we are engaging in mental activity. One does not have to be bright to withdraw his finger from a hot stove; some intelligence is required to become wary of objects which are likely to be hot. A little child reaches for the moon as he would for any other ball. In early childhood perceptions are not in accord with truths. Truths are perceptions, beliefs verified by experience. In fact as we grow, in order to attain truth, we must learn many things which later prove to be untrue. Until the child knows well that the sun comes up and goes down, that the moon and the stars move across the sky, he cannot come to know that the earth rotates. Likely, he must believe that his father knows everything and can do everything in order later to learn that there is a very great deal to learn that neither he nor his father nor his teacher ever completely masters. We must guard against instilling the belief that we have come to final truths. Too many reject evidence, refuse to consider the validity of experience which refutes a "truth" established in their minds.

No one by his own senses could learn that the earth is round or that it spins. Certainly it looks flat and bumpy and unmoving to all of us. Our senses do not tell us that the earth moves about the sun, that it spins at the rate of several hundred miles an hour, that all of us hurtle through space with the earth at about eighteen miles per second. Much of our mental activity utilizes for data the accumulated knowledge and wisdom of the past. By means of language man retains, recalls, transmits, and shares the meanings of his experiences.

Developing Cause and Effect Concepts

The developing of conceptions of cause and effect is a clear indication of mental growth. These concepts develop slowly in the individual and even more slowly among the peoples of the earth. We have known children to be quite mystified to find the wind blowing where there are no trees. According to their experience the wind blows when the trees fan, just as grandmother uses her fan to make a breeze. We once heard a little boy beg his father to make them stop blowing the fire-whistle lest his house should sometime burn. The ancients, with as much raw brain power as we have today, believed that an eclipse of the moon or sun resulted from a celestial dragon trying to devour it. Plato, who must have been among the most intelligent men of all history, believed the sky to be a canopy, the stars peepholes through which beamed the light of the heavens beyond. Aristotle stated that the brain is a huge sweat gland. Too, he held that human slaves were necessary to support free men.

Today most adults believe that a child's learning to read results from systematic teaching by a teacher. Most children learn to read at about the time their teachers engage in systematic teaching; we are not at all sure that one results from the other. By the year 2500, some of our most ardent beliefs will quite likely seem as naive as some ancient explanations seem to us today. Mankind continues to be plagued by a failure to perceive basic causes of poverty and overproduction, by increased amounts of violence among people who have been taught the ways of non-violence, and by wars which nobody wants. Those interested in an eloquent account of man's struggle to become intelligent will want to read Robinson's *The Mind in the Making*.[3]

Distinguished men from varied fields such as General Omar Bradley, Wernher von Braun, and Albert Schweitzer have eloquently expressed our dismay at the disproportionate use of man's brain power to create instruments and methods of destruction in comparison with the use of human intelligence to find ways to live together on this planet peacefully and productively. The point which is essential to note is that every new scientific achievement produces new problems of cause and effect upon which man must use his intelligence if he is to continue to retain his toe-hold upon this planet and extend his progress in civilization. One of today's major problems, to which man's brain power must be applied, is the cause for periodic wars and the probable effects of another world-wide conflict.

Using Symbols

The use of symbols to designate items of experience is basic to mental activity. The extent of comprehension of symbols is a useful indicator of mental competency. When a mark, or a sound, a distinctive touch, or a gesture that has no meaning in itself, *is* meaningful, we are exercising intelligence. Symbolization is not the exclusive property of man. A rat can be taught to go through a black door and to avoid a light one; we have heard of no rat that will hesitate at the sight of the printed word "stop" and proceed upon seeing "go." Doubtless his eyes *see*

[3] James Harvey Robinson, *The Mind in the Making* (New York: Harper and Brothers, 1921).

the symbols as clearly as do ours, but the symbols are too complex for him to interpret.

Mental activity relies upon awareness; it is exercised through grasping meanings, relationships, and understandings. At its highest level, the use of symbols enables man to handle abstractions, to generalize from a specific so that he can apply his knowledge to a wide variety of possibilities, to search out meanings and relationships that are not present but seem to be required to make sense. To use a simple illustration, probably most of you can envision without having the specific experience each time the styles change, the colors and lines and combinations of textures that are becoming to you. You go to shop saying, "I want a mauve cashmere sweater and a charcoal-gray tweed skirt (or pair of trousers)." When symbols are used in abstract thinking by an Einstein, we get a series of symbols, each of which stands for something in his mind (just as the words "mauve sweater" do in yours). These symbols, brought together into hypothetical relationships, result in a theory that changes the direction of the world.

Einstein in developing his theory had to be able to work with many symbols for unknowns that were required to complete the hypothetical possibility he was developing. When tested, his theory proved correct and then he knew that the unknowns for which he had constructed symbols were actualities. Comprehension can result from the slow accumulation of experiences and reflection upon their meanings, or it can take place through a flash of insight that some have called the "aha" reaction. Most of us have read about Archimedes leaping from his bath and dashing down the street nude screaming, "Eureka!" meaning, "I have found it," or as little children would say, "I catch." He had suddenly grasped the principle that a floating body displaces its own weight in the supporting liquid. The youngster's impudent, "So what?" is a high level intellectual demand for meaning.

Imagining—Foresight

The capacity for mental activity enables us to foresee the results of circumstances through imagining what will happen if we do this or that. Only man is capable of "internal experimentation." By means of foresight he can modify his actions, alter his preferences in the light of likely consequences. He is able to choose ways of behaving by weighing and reconciling his preferences. He can hold in his mind many alternatives and project the consequences of each, see relationships among them, and imagine his feelings and total responses to the circumstances resulting from any one of them.

Maintaining Perspective

An important aspect of higher mental processes is the maintenance of perspective, the ability to assign to items of experience and circumstances their appropriate degrees of importance. This ability is the core of humor. The intelligent person does not allow part of his life to become more important than all of it. He remains *whole*some. He seeks "odds" favorable to his gratification and integrity. He does not put all his emotional eggs in one basket with notions such as, "I can't live without you," or "If I don't pass this course, my life is ruined."

Teachers must help children develop an appropriate degree of concern for varied aspects of experience. Herein lies one of the dangers of departmentalized teaching. The teacher of special subjects, if expert, charming, or coercive, is apt to induce an inappropriate degree of importance to his speciality. The maintenance of "statistical perspective" is a significant aspect of adjustment by intelligence. As we step out on the street, we may be maimed by a runaway car. We take the chance. On the other hand, we are "dopes" to walk onto a crowded highway, oblivious to traffic.

Creating

The central function of mental activity we call creation. The creatures have to accept conditions as they find them; man, by taking thought (engaging in reason) can alter himself and his circumstances and make adaptations that are favorable to his integrity and his continued existence. The intelligent individual, or group, determines purposes and pursues them through thinking. *Thinking is the planning of action.* Thought begins and proceeds something like this: What do I want to accomplish? What will happen if I do this or that? What then *shall* I do? With what resources can I work? How shall I proceed? How can I judge the worth of my goals and my endeavors?

Creative urges and creative satisfactions come from within. No one can give another directions for creativeness, nor prescribe for him the ingredients and dosage for a creative experience. A young child may "catch on" that he can make marks in the cereal that he has spilled on the table. This is the beginning of finger-painting. A poet may ponder the meaning of life and express lofty thoughts in sublime form. Both child and poet are engaged in creation. A child is not creating when he traces or even copies a model of Santa Claus for the December window, nor are adults creating when they engage a decorator to beautify the living room while they go on vacation.

One of the writers recalls a school principal who had not been able to accept his "philosophy," but who *had* to enroll in his summer workshop for teachers because she needed the credit. She was sure that she, as principal, should tell teachers how to conduct their classes because she knew more than they; she *knew* that the teachers should tell pupils what to do and how to do for the same reason. To her, planning by participants was "monkey business." In the art laboratory of the workshop she decided to make a flamingo to stand in the garden of her new home. She traced the outline upon plywood and zestfully began to jig-saw along the lines. She came to a curve too sharp for her slight skill. A young man skilled in jig-sawing offered, "Elsie, I'll do that for you." Elsie retorted, "The heck you will! I'll do this if it costs me my arm!" Elsie paused struck by a flash of insight and called to me, "That's what you've been trying to tell me!" After a half-dozen graduate courses she got the point while carrying out an activity quite within the range of sixth-graders. It *does* make a difference whose mind does the planning, whose hands carry out that action.

| Some of the Ways of Intelligence | The intelligent individual is disposed to *look before he leaps.* Through reflection and contemplation he can *foresee* the *outcomes of behavior.* He is able to sense the |

appropriateness of his behavior to the situations in which he finds himself. He does not crack jokes at a funeral, nor express gloomy forebodings at a housewarming. As he grows, he is better able to distinguish between knowledge, belief, faith, and wishes. Men have commonly observed that the more they learn, the more they know they have to learn. The dullard is quite satisfied with what he believes and knows; he makes little distinction between believing and knowing. The intelligent individual differentiates what he has experienced, what he has imagined, what he has heard, and what he has read. He is able to sense absurdity, incongruity, irrelevancy, and error.

The growing child needs to have *ample chance to make mistakes,* to see that some of his plans do not work out, and that he may lack skills and resources that are needed to carry them out. Billy worked all day to make a kite. He rejected daddy's offer to help. When at last the kite rose into the wind, it dove to the ground and was smashed. The next day Billy was more thoughtful, sought some technical counsel, and made a kite that flew to the end of his string.

Adults must guard against offering to a creating child more direction than he desires and requests. They should help when bits of aid promise a gratifying accomplishment on the whole.

We hear of late much rationalization of the traditional practice of "failing" children in school grades and subjects because the child needs the experience of failure. The principle is valid, but common school practice is not in accord with the principle. Failure must be a genuine outcome of lack of foresight, resources, and careful execution of plans. If one forgets to put the baking powder in the biscuits, she fails to make good biscuits. No kind, understanding grownup can make them good, neither will one learn to make good biscuits merely by watching an expert make them. When we address a letter incompletely, it fails to reach its destination. Children do need to fail, but without undue indignity or loss of face. Surely it is as important for Tommy to learn that he lacks the precision of movement necessary to be a draftsman as for Johnny to discover that he has a high degree of precision and does not want to be a draftsman.

One of the clear marks of intellectual acuity is *precision in the use of language.* The more intelligent person speaks of an object or a circumstance as being *wonderful* only if it inspires him with *wonder.* He will not call a fat and ugly woman *nice.* The intelligent individual uses language *nicely.* He can express his understandings and insights in terms comprehensible to those with whom he communicates. He does not behave as if to be intelligent were to be complex or obscure.

The intelligent individual can *defer gratifications* in anticipation of the greater and more dependable amount of gratification that may follow. Students go through a goodly amount of arduous toil and some indignity in order to achieve training and abilities which will enhance the quality of their living in the future. We recall seeing years ago the cartoon strip of *Smitty* who was quite embarrassed for his little brother Herbie who fell for the Boss' trick of offering him a choice of a nickel or a dime. It seemed to Smitty that Herbie always took the nickel because it was bigger. Herbie found it necessary to explain to Smitty that if he should take the dime, the boss wouldn't do it again.

In themselves, *memory* and *knowledge of facts* do not constitute intelligent behavior. They are essential to the exercise of higher degrees of intelligence. Students of education should give serious thought to the fact that many classrooms emphasize little learning other than the memorization of facts, which are meant to be used by the learner only for the purpose of passing tests of "memory for facts." A goodly number of university students with high academic records are little more than speaking bibliographies.

Of course no human activity is possible without memory. Items of experience are recorded somehow (we know not how) in the nervous system. Some persons have much more ability to recall than have others. (They have "sticky brains," and as this is written some of them are making much money on TV quiz shows.) Memory alone is not intelligence. To be remembered, effectively recalled to awareness, an item of experience must have meaning. Most of us cannot repeat a series of more than six or seven unrelated words or numbers. We can repeat exactly a meaningful sentence of many more words. Read this: aco eru dib mun faf bol cac. Now raise your eyes and repeat it! The order of our A B C's makes no sense, yet we learn it when rather young as a necessary convenience in arranging dictionaries, telephone books, and addresses of our friends. For such essential, and otherwise senseless, rote learning we find it useful to use devices such as tuneful jingles. Yet we would feel quite silly in a phone booth singing the A B C song until we reached T. Memory is not trained by memorizing. We best memorize in the terms in which the material is to be used.

Long ago someone observed that *reflection* and *wonder* are the forebears of science and philosophy. Certainly, the disposition to wonder and reflect upon everyday events is an art of effective intelligence. Pavlov's important discovery and description of the conditioned reflex resulted from repeated failures of his attempt to measure the salivary flow of dogs. As he wondered why the dogs' mouths watered before he could adjust his measuring devices, he attained new insights which grew into significant knowledge and understandings through improved control of observations and experiments. A less reflective man than Sir Isaac Newton would have moved to the shade of another tree when falling apples disturbed his repose. We can see someone berating James Watt as a lazy daydreamer as he contemplated the meaning of the rattling lid on the teakettle.

Among the most important factors which distinguish the more intelligent from the less intelligent person is a *realistic sense of adequacy* to meet the problems he faces and to convert his wishes into actualities. Intelligence enables the force of the whole personality to concentrate upon a purpose. A generation ago physiologists and physicists had determined that no man could run a mile in less than four minutes, ten seconds. For many years the world record had stood unthreatened at 4:12. A few years ago the four minute barrier was broken. As this is written sixteen different individuals have been officially credited with running the mile in less than four minutes; by the time you read this, many more will have done so. These men became aware that it could be done; they believed their bodies were adequate to do it.

One displays intelligence in *recognizing his inadequacies.* The authors of this book cannot run a mile in four minutes; they make no attempt to do so. Fortunately, for their mental health, they do not wish to do so. A realistic sense of one's own limitations is an essential feature of intelligent behavior. Abilities wax and wane as one goes through life. Few men beyond age twenty-five have reflexes rapid enough to fly jet planes in combat. As humans grow older, they have less agility, less strength, less dexterity than when they were younger. We recently heard a housemaid comment, "The mind makes dates that the body can't keep."

The social order suffers a considerable amount of inefficiency and obstruction of progress by the ambitions of men who seek to enjoy status and income and position for which they are not qualified in business, in politics, and in the professions. We would recall to you an important principle of biology: the organism will not violate its own integrity unless highly motivated to do so. In terms of the activity itself, one would not care to be an all-Amercan quarterback, president of the United States, the life-of-the-party, unless he regarded himself as actually possessing the abilities to carry out the functions involved. Parents and teachers would vastly diminish the threats to mental health and to social progress by refraining from urging young people to strive to appear to be what they are not, to seek what they have not the capacity to achieve.

Atmospheres

for Mental Growth

The most important feature of an atmosphere favorable to mental growth is the *need* to be intelligent. It is an atmosphere that requires persons to think about what they do. It is a thoughtful atmosphere.

Searching, Questing

The intelligent atmosphere abounds in questions, such as: What shall we do? Do we want this? Must we do it? How shall we proceed? In the intellectual atmosphere real problems require choice, planning, and action. We seek to know, to gain information and comprehension in order to regulate subsequent happenings. Knowledge which functions in intelligence is always held as a guide to action. All distinctively human behavior is social. An intelligent atmosphere involves much interchange of purposes and suggestions and free communication of them. Little effective intelligence can develop where communication is stifled, controlled, one-sided, or flowing in one direction only.

Far too little classroom activity is directed to the consideration of the pupil's own contemporary conditions and current happenings. Knowledge of the past is important only as it illuminates the future. If we are to have an intelligent citizenry, no school child should spend any day without a considerable period of discussion and analysis of what goes on in his group, his school, his neighborhood, his whole community as far and wide as he can comprehend it. Some of the answers his teacher will stimulate him to discover are: How do you know? Are you sure? What more do we need to know? What does it mean? Should *we* do something about it? Seeking to know is an essential ingredient for mental growth. Schools must develop a *liking for* the unknown. We like the way Einstein put the idea: "The most beautiful thing we can experience is the mysterious. It's the source of all art and science."

Exploring Interests

Elsewhere we have stated that the young human lives on the growing edges of his own mind, on the growing edges of his own culture. One of the principal values of the good teacher is to foster and nourish growth as budding abilities and concerns appear. John Dewey defined interest as evidence of dawning capacity. The atmosphere for mental growth includes a high degree of affinity for the interests and concerns of the growers, individually and collectively. Intelligence thrives on successful pursuit of purposes. Success is attainment of purpose; the term does not imply excelling. Little intelligence develops among children who are constantly motivated to perform tasks, attain skills and comprehensions that they cannot yet achieve, or can achieve only with marked difficulty. We believe that more growth in intelligence results from devising facilities and routines for keeping the rabbit alive and relatively odorless than from contemplating the mature insights of Euclid. When we come fully to understand the process of mental development, we shall see that the arts are fundamentals rather than "fads and frills," as all too many citizens now regard them. In the arts one is required to plan, to take stock of resources, and to act in accord with plans and insights that develop during the action.

Associating with the More Experienced

Abundant evidence shows clearly the cultural pull on intelligence. From many kinds of investigations we have seen the importance of the adult in the lives of growing children. Intelligence results in marked degree from thoughtful and aware reaction to the responses of other people. Little children need to talk and to have someone to listen and to respond. A cluster of studies known as the Iowa Studies [4] convincingly validate this principle.

Motivating Oneself

Activities must be carried on for their real reasons as the child perceives them. The youngster washes his hands to become clean or because he is told he must do so, not to pass inspection nor to get a gold star. He reads to find out what someone has written, to learn something he wants to know, to enjoy a zestful tale, not in order to read better, or to be praised, or to escape from the "woodpecker group."

In building the basic structure of mental development, we must eliminate from our activities any implication that the child carries on an ac-

---

[4] These are summarized in George D. Stoddard's *The Meaning of Intelligence* (New York: The Macmillan Company, 1943).

tivity merely for his own instruction. The activity is carried on for its own sake, for the gratification of one's self, or for the amusement or benefit of others. Activities must have some real purpose. We care for plants to watch them grow, to enhance the appearance of the room or the yard. We keep pets because we need to take care of something that is alive, and to watch it live and grow. We spin a top to watch it spin, not to learn the principles of the gyroscope. We read a book to find out something we want to know. We measure with pints and feet and inches and pounds for the gratification of knowing more and more what the world is like and how to describe it—not to build a base for future instruction in science. Learning to gratify one's curiosity is an outcome of intrinsic motivation. We seek to know because we want to find out, not because someone has made an assignment that must be handed in tomorrow morning.

Role of the Teacher

One important way in which the adult fosters the growth of intelligence in children is by helping them distinguish between knowledge, fancy, and wishes. We frequently inquire of them, "How do you know? Can we be sure? Can we find out?" We seek to develop essential respect for authority as they develop discernment for dependable authority.

Today an important function of the teacher is to see that every child has time, place, and the opportunity to observe, experiment, and reflect. The elders must often stifle their mania to teach, to point out lessons, to explain beyond the child's desire for explanations. Rather than encouraging comparison and competition, the teacher must guard against these extraneous motives to excel, or merely to be intellectual.

Someone has observed that we tend to be intellectually sterile from a lack of repose far more than from a lack of effort. Today the well-cared-for child has little repose. He is hurried in the morning to dress properly, to eat a good breakfast, and to be off to school. There his teacher is expected to have plans

for his day's occupation. In a "good" school his play time is managed by the grownups. After school he is likely to have a music lesson, a Scout meeting, or a church meeting. His dinner hour is set; after which he has homework and TV programs to claim his attention. The adolescent's life is even more harried. If the youngster has been a good human, done what was expected of him, he has lived his whole day with no occasion to be in charge of what goes through his own mind, with no time to sit and wonder and reflect. We repeat: The mind is self-generated; it is built from within. Today it is important that the school provide free time for the child to use as he sees fit with a minimum of adult direction and expectation.

Influences Which Retard Mental Development

Intelligence will not develop without opportunity. We do not learn to be verbal, nor to orient ourselves in space, nor to think if we have no opportunity to live among people who do these things. Some children have little stimulation to be intelligent. The adults in their lives do not respond to them. We once knew a couple who talked very little to their two-year-old, waiting for *him* to learn to talk so that they might talk to him. They wondered why he did not talk.

We have referred earlier to the importance of a person's thinking well of himself in the realm of adequacy in mental activities. It is quite common to hear adults insist: "Oh, I am no good at mathematics. I can't even keep my checkbook straight." Relatively little brain power is required for this task, but many—especially those who have been taught arithmetic before they could comprehend it—have a false self-image of inadequacy in mathematics.

A great many grownups are terrified at the prospect of standing up before an audience and giving a simple speech on something they know a good deal about. As they have gone through school, being warned against making mistakes and speaking improperly, having the major attention of the teacher directed to inadequacy rather than to adequacy, the image developed, "I can't do that."

We are particularly concerned today with the conflict between rote learning and the development of intelligence. For many pupils, school experience consists almost entirely of studying to prepare for tests, to learn by repetitious drill the answers to questions they themselves have not asked. We should like to see considerable experimentation done on the influence upon intellect of preparation to take tests. It is our hunch that intelligence does not grow in such circumstances and that learning by drill and rote those responses that involve insight and comprehension interferes with the development of these abilities. Attempting to put an idea into the cortex of the cerebrum so that it can be recited in words before it has permeated the person as a whole contributes to unintellectualism. Certainly, we do not build intelligence in children by drilling and exercising them on tasks that are commonly found in standardized tests. To teach by rote the meaning of symbols before the child has experience with that which the symbol represents is to retard or distort mental growth. To a growing, experienced-based child, *pony* and *horse* are nearly identical words, *horse* and *house* have nothing in common. Symbols have no reality within themselves; they derive their meaning from agreement and from common usage.

We recall an old saying that teaching consists of finding what Jimmy cannot do and making him do it. At present, school practice is often heavily loaded with finding children's weaknesses and attempting to strengthen them. This practice makes it almost certain that the child must respond *dully* to his academic circumstances. He develops images and concepts of himself in terms of dullness in these areas of endeavor. He learns to be dull. He has no time left to do the things in which he has adequacy, because he is kept "practicing" those things in which teacher or mother find him weak or inadequate. Is it any wonder school comes to be a place the youngster "puts up with"?

The teacher who would build intelligence fosters in the child attributes such as, "I can't read so well! But I have good friends who can." "My calculations aren't dependable, I must check them with Josie's. She's a whiz in numbers." Adequacy despite deficiencies is a goal of an intelligent person.

In an earlier chapter we have written of the blight of extraneous motivation. Certainly, the use of mental powers in the pursuit of extraneous goals retards effective intelligence. Students whose primary aim is to make the honor roll, to gain credits and degrees without work, to qualify to make a pile of money are not developing effective intelligence. Striving toward clearly conceived, attainable, and socially useful goals seems to be a fundamental nutrient of mental growth.

The Unintelligent Atmosphere

In many situations we find a condition which is unintelligent as contrasted with lacking in intelligence. The unintelligent atmosphere tends to be devoid of goals. Some writers use the term goal-blindness. We find many classrooms in which the goal of the student is to get the assigned work done and to hand it in. Teachers rather commonly evaluate their pupils in terms of "Did you do your assignment; did you get your work in on time? Is it neat?" The only role which intelligence can play in this situation is in contriving ways to circumvent the teacher.

We have indicated earlier that to teach symbols before experience is to teach unintelligence. One of the writers once taught mathematics. To the satisfaction of his supervisor, his pupils did well on tests. He said to them many times daily, "Don't try to understand this. Just learn how to do it." The learning of a formula without having experience with what the formula represents is an unintelligent approach to problems. To learn that the square of the hypotenuse is the sum of the squares of the two sides of a right triangle has a negative effect upon mathematical comprehension unless one has tested it out to find that it is so. In matters such as these, children *do* need the challenge, interpretation, and extension of meanings by older people.

With the widespread use of tests of mental ability and educational achievement, we have been brought face to face with the problem of the effects upon mental growth of social-class status. It appears that wherever and whenever we investigate this phenomenon we find that the children of the lower (looked-down-upon) portions of the population display, on the average, less mental ability and grow with negative acceleration as they go through our schools. Formerly, psychologists attributed various amounts of native intelligence to various ethnic groups in the population. Today, few responsible students believe that this is true. The works of Davis [5] should be studied carefully for added insight into this problem. It is our opinion that the child's realization of the non-acceptability of his parents and his folks tends to retard his mental development. This is one reason why teachers must carefully avoid implying rejection or an unfavorable attitude toward the parents of their pupils.

---

[5] Allison Davis, *Social-Class Influences upon Learning* (Cambridge: Harvard University Press, 1948, The Inglis Lecture).

Unfavorable comparison restricts the mental development of those compared in the areas in which the comparisons are made. The school would do well to reduce many-fold the occasions for comparing children with each other to the advantage of some and the disadvantage of others.

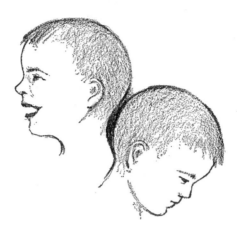

Competition, the effort to excel, should not be promoted in any area in which skill and insight are not firmly established. In most areas of life, competition is quite unintelligent. All civilization has resulted from increased skill in cooperating, not in competing.

Fear of error, dread of being wrong, inhibits the growth of the mind. Some children become so aware of the indignity of making a mistake, of being subjected to unfavorable criticism, that their minds can function in no way other than in seeking escape from a threatening circumstance. Any thoughtful observer can see that an individual or a group bent upon discovering shortcomings, mistakes, or scapegoats accomplishes little in the way of constructive mental behavior.

It must be clear to the reader that we have thus far described mental growth as a function that takes place in an atmosphere of freedom in which the dignity of all humans is respected. Even among psychologists, intelligence is what each chooses to call it. From certain points of view, Adolf Hitler was among the most intelligent men the world has known. From other points of view, he was among the most stupid. Intellectual acuity can serve an infinite variety of purposes. Jesse James was one of the most clever men of his generation. The far-reaching imagination and acute perceptions of Albert Einstein made it possible for mankind to have abundant energy anywhere on the earth—even to destroy himself. We have known a goodly number of pupils whom the teacher thought to be dull who were diabolically clever in annoying him. It is most unwise to attribute to any person lack of capacity to be intelligent without seeing him in a considerable variety of situations. Hogben wisely noted:

> Our parents do not endow us with characters. They endow us with *genes*. . . . Weismann has been amply justified by all subsequent work in challenging the belief that the genes have any sympathetic interest in the way we use the organs we owe to them.[6]

Thus far in this chapter we have considered the ways of intelligence and circumstances favorable to their development. We have assumed that all of these ways are learned. The reader's consideration of the foregoing discussion will reveal to him, we trust, that these ways result not so much from sheer capacity as from disposition, habits, and attitudes.

A central problem of psychology has been to find an explanation for the clearly observable fact that some people behave much more intelligently than others. Thus far explanations are in the realm of conjecture; they are competent guesses. Stoddard has put it tersely in stating: "Boy *A* knows one French word; Boy *B* knows no French word. What neurologist can tell me which is which?"

Theories

of Intelligence

The quest for a simple, unitary explanation for differences in intelligence has led students of psychology down many separate paths. That some people are brighter than others is clear to anyone who has associated with people. For this fact numerous explanations have been offered. We make no attempt here to list or define them in any inclusive way.

Physical equipment and physical condition must surely account for differences in mental behavior. A little child's mind works simply, not merely because he lacks experience but because his body, particularly his nervous system, is simple in organization. A child is born with all the nerve cells he will ever have. Growth and experience cause them to de-

---

[6] Lancelot Hogben, *Nature and Nurture* (London: George Allen and Unwin, Ltd., rev. 1939), p. 11.

velop and establish connections. The amount and quality of experience seems to influence the extent and quality of the developing nervous system. For this reason, and for many others, we cannot neglect the quality of living of a little child.

As individuals differ in quality of eyes, feet, and hearts, so they must differ in the quality of the brain. Some authorities believe differences result from available mental energy. That energy is expended in "mental work" is wellknown. It can be measured by a calorimeter.[7] At present a neurologist cannot distinguish a poor brain from a good brain, unless it has missing or degenerate parts or lesions. More useful to teachers is reflection on some of the explanations of intelligence as a function of human behavior. Stoddard describes intelligence as "a theoretical composite whose elements may be operationally tested." He offers this explanation of intelligence:

> Intelligence is the ability to undertake activities that are characterized by: (1) difficulty, (2) complexity, (3) abstractness, (4) economy, (5) adaptiveness to a goal, (6) social value, (7) the emergence of originals, and to maintain such activities under conditions that demand a concentration of energy and a resistance to emotional forces.[8]

Thorndike set forth three types of intelligence: abstract intelligence, the ability to deal with *ideas and symbols;* mechanical intelligence, the ability to understand *things;* and social intelligence, the ability to understand *persons.* He also defined three dimensions of intelligence—breadth, depth, speed. This conception makes sense. Among little children we can see the carefully thoughtful child who is interested in a wide variety of matters; another who has no time for anything but tools, or music, or pets. We see some who size up social situations readily; others who seem almost devoid of a sense of how other people feel and respond. Speed has been overemphasized as a function of intelligence, yet it is an essential attribute of a city editor or a referee of a basketball game.

Thurstone has devoted many years to studying primary mental abilities among which he can find something in common. Through factor analysis, Thurstone has identified six factors which are functions of intelligence and seem to be related to each other. These factors are verbal

---

[7] This is discussed in C. Judson Herrick's *The Evolution of Human Nature* (Austin: University of Texas Press, 1956), pp. 280-282.

[8] George D. Stoddard, *The Meaning of Intelligence* (New York: The Macmillan Company, 1943), p. 4.

comprehension, word fluency, space, number, memory, and induction.[9] Thurstone states that factor analysis finds application in education and personnel administration in making it possible to recognize in every individual mental and physical qualities which make him unique as an individual.

	Variously productive attempts
Conceptions	to measure intelligence came early
of Mental Testing	in the century. A "flash of insight,"

Conceptions

of Mental Testing

Variously productive attempts to measure intelligence came early in the century. A "flash of insight," which led to modern methods of testing, came to a French physician, Binet, who was requested by his government to find a way to identify at an early age children who should be in special classes for the mentally retarded. He hit upon the idea of finding how much a child has learned out of the many things that all children have the opportunity to learn. To say, "I want a drink," to know one's name, to point to one's nose upon request, to name familiar objects such as a penny or a key, to follow simple directions, to define common but abstract words were among the tasks which were found by Binet to differentiate dull from normal children.

After concluding that ability to perform simple, common tasks did actually distinguish between the retarded and normal children, he hit upon the idea of relating performance to age. This gave us the concept of mental age, which is commonly used as the unit for measuring mental growth. Binet himself never heard of the IQ. This was suggested by Stern, a German psychologist, in 1914 after Binet's death.[10]

Upon learning of Binet's new discovery, American psychologists, social workers, and educators leaped for joy. At last the stupid children in a class could be clearly identified. Americans rushed to France to translate the tests, and brought them back to measure children in the United States. In 1916, L. M. Terman published the Stanford Revision of the Binet Scale, standardized with American children.

Since most of the paupers, criminals, and degenerates who were tested performed poorly upon these tests, low intelligence was deemed to be the cause of all degradation. This trend of thought was somewhat di-

---

[9] L. L. Thurstone, *Multiple Factor Analysis* (Chicago: University of Chicago Press, 1947).

[10] William Stern, *The Psychological Methods of Testing Intelligence,* trans., Guy M. Whipple (Baltimore: Warwick and York, 1914).

verted by a report that the average score of the inmates of a well-known penitentiary was higher than that of the guards. Nonetheless, school masters hastened to identify those young children who had low intelligence and thus no promise. Noting that children seemed to change very little in IQ, educators assumed that the intelligence quotient is fixed and unchanging. Before his death Binet uttered a protest against the "common prejudice against the educability of the intellect."

Quotients can be calculated for all aspects of growth. A boy who is sixty inches tall when the average boy of his age is fifty inches has a height quotient of 1.20. He is twenty per cent taller than the average of his age. We know of no one who records height quotients. The intelligence quotient makes sense to those who believe that intelligence is a unitary factor, that its growth is regular. For these "believers," a child's intelligence quotient can be measured any time during his growth, and his mental age can thereafter be known by multiplying his age by his IQ. This is quite as unreal as to use a height quotient from age eight to calculate a boy's height at age sixteen. The controversy over the unchanging IQ has not yet completely subsided in America. Students who wish to read about it in detail will find the issues discussed in the *Thirty-Ninth Yearbook* of the National Society for the Study of Education.[11]

When America had to raise an army quickly in 1918, the Army requested psychologists to make up an intelligence test that could be given to large groups of people and easily scored. This resulted in the Army Alpha Examination, the first group test of intelligence. Some of our citizens were then shocked to learn that the average fourteen-year-old school child made a slightly higher score on this examination than did the country's young adult males. From this some psychologists concluded that mental growth ceases at age fourteen. Probably it is true that the ability to make the kind of responses called for in most group mental tests does not improve much after age fourteen to sixteen. This seems to be especially true of tests in which time is a factor.

We think it quite unwise to record the results of a mental test in one figure whether it be mental age, intelligence quotient, or percentile ranking. Thus far we have attempted to show that intelligence is an abstract term including a wide variety of functions. To test these functions by

---

[11] National Society for the Study of Education, "Intelligence: Its Nature and Nurture," *Thirty-Ninth Yearbook* (Bloomington, Ill.: Public School Publishing Company, 1940).

small samplings of the individual's behavior and to strike an average of these abilities is to hide evidences of actual potentialities and weaknesses of the individual. To use one word or number to define an individual's mentality is to defy the results of the vast amount of research in factor analysis.

The individual tests most commonly used in America are the Stanford-Binet Test of Intelligence [12] and the Wechsler-Bellevue Intelligence Scale.[13] The Stanford-Binet is regarded to be the most suitable for elementary- and junior-high-school pupils; its results are given in mental ages. The Wechsler-Bellevue yields more meaningful results for adults and near-adults; its results are given in percentiles rather than in ages and quotients.

These individual tests have validity only when administered by trained examiners. A precise testing requires more than an hour of uninterrupted time. It seems to us that some clinics give a disproportionate amount of time to determining a precise measure of a child's mental ability, when precision is not necessary for the problem at hand. One skilled in testing can discern in a few minutes whether a child's mental development is insufficient to meet the demands placed upon him, or if he has abilities that are going unchallenged. Some clinicians use items from the intelligence tests as controlled observations of behavior in order to explore the extent and qualities of mental abilities and the ways they are being used.

A task is useful for measuring growth if it discriminates between ages. For example, very few four-year-olds will respond correctly to the direction, "Give me three pennies" from a handful. A large percentage of five-year-olds can carry out this direction; scarcely any six-year-old fails to do so. Hence, successful performance on this task is a good indication of having reached a maturity level of five years in number concepts, and the ability to follow directions.

Teachers would do well to study some of the standardized individual mental tests to gain perspective on what kinds of tasks can commonly be performed at the successive stages of growth. We cite a few examples for you to study: [14]

---

[12] L. M. Terman and M. A. Merrill, *Measuring Intelligence* (New York: Houghton Mifflin Company, 1937).

[13] D. Wechsler, *The Measurement of Adult Intelligence* (Baltimore: Williams and Wilkins, 1944).

[14] Examples cited are adapted from Lewis M. Terman and M. A. Merrill, *Measuring Intelligence* (New York: Houghton Mifflin Company, 1937).

Age Two

Can point out familiar objects when directed. "Show me the kitty, the ball, the doll, the bed."

Can identify parts of the body. "Show me the doll's hair, eyes, hands, mouth."

Can repeat two digits. "Now say 5–2, 3–9."

Age Four

Can string beads imitatively.

Can use the number concept of two. "Give me two pennies."

Age Six

Can copy a simple string of beads: two round, one rectangular; two round, one rectangular.

Can respond to requests for a number of objects up to ten. "Give me six beads."

Can tell a simple story from a simple picture.

Age Seven

Can respond correctly to, "How many fingers have you on one hand? On both hands?"

Can respond correctly to a request to count sounds, such as: six taps, one second apart, on the desk.

Can use related words to build a sentence, such as: cat, milk, dish.

Age Eight

Can comprehend situations, such as, "Why is a train harder to stop than an automobile?"

Can name the days of the week. Can answer correctly, "What day comes before Thursday, etc."

Can deal with opposite analogies. "Snow is white; coal is ———."

Age eight is the close of the primary school period. Reflect upon the kinds of mental performance commonly expected of children by the time they have completed the third grade. Note particularly that none of the tasks involves the child's reading from the printed page or doing any kind of numerical calculations.

Age Ten

Can remember most of the details of a short selection (six to eight lines) read aloud to him.

Can give adequate meaning to abstract terms such as *pity, surprise.*

Age Twelve

Can copy a slightly complex geometric design from memory.
Can repeat backward five digits spoken to him at the rate of one per second.

Age Fourteen

Can respond correctly to orientation in directions. "Suppose you are going north, turn to your left, then turn to your right. What direction are you going?"
Can respond correctly to problem-solving examples. "Describe how you would measure out exactly three pints of water if you have only a seven-pint can and a four-pint can.
Can define abstract terms such as *courage, charity.*

Age Sixteen

Can handle more complicated problem-solving examples: "If two pencils cost five cents, how many can you buy for fifty cents?"
Can give meaning to proverbs, such as: "A burnt child dreads the fire."

After pondering the complexity and intellectual demands of these tasks, relate them to demands made upon pupils at the various grade levels. For example: does it seem to you that the average person is able to comprehend algebra at age thirteen or fourteen?

We stated earlier that World War I brought us group testing. Since the publishing of the Army Alpha, dozens of tests have been standardized with varying degrees of care, and offered for sale. We shall not name nor evaluate any of them. We should like, however, to make some comments and raise some questions about the use of group intelligence tests in schools. A group mental test is made by presenting many problems to many children, studying their responses to the items to identify those which discriminate between children of various ages, and eliminating those problems which do not discriminate. These items are then subjected to refined statistical procedures to make sure they range in difficulty, and that the differences in degrees of difficulty are similar at all levels. The important thing to hold in mind is that the test items were given to children. In what region was this done? In using the norms of the test the teacher is comparing a group of children, or an individual child, with other real children elsewhere. Children do not do well on tests that are not in their native language. College students who have grown up in one language do not do well on tests given in another language.

Teachers must ponder the fact, however, that the group mental test is likely a valid measure of a child's readiness to do school work as school work is commonly done. If the Latin-American child must read and write in English, the English language mental test does measure his ability to succeed. Hogben has written most wisely on this subject:

> It does not necessarily follow that the intelligence tests give a just measure of all that we commonly mean by the adjective intelligence when we apply it to adults. Probably the intellectual performance of adults depends quite as much on temperamental characteristics ordinarily described by alertness, persistence, curiosity, or a sense of humour as on the type of facility which intelligence tests assess. Hence proposals to limit educational facilities to children who get high scores on such tests are exceedingly dangerous. It is never suggested that the education of the prosperous classes should be limited in the same way. So the political motive is not far to seek.[15]

The norms of a test are always given in precise numbers. Numbers imply great precision and concreteness. Numbers derived from tests are not so precise as inches, pounds, dollars and cents. They are the averages of a given group. Half of the members of the group from which this average was secured were above the norm, and the other half below it. To expect a given child to attain a norm is to expect him to be above the average from which the norm was obtained. Perhaps you recall the cartoon depicting a school principal placating a disturbed mother with the caption, "Try not to worry about it, Mrs. Taylor, we have many seven-year-olds with the mentality of a seven-year-old."

If one is to have his score used in any meaningful way, it is most important to be sure that the child has in fact been tested. Dudley's IQ, as recorded in the office of the junior high school, was 82. This score was the result of one test given to all incoming seventh graders at one time in the cafeteria. Dudley was treated as a dull child and performed dully, in accord with the role assigned him. On the hunch that Dudley had more intelligence than he displayed on this test, one of his teachers administered an individual test three years later. His true IQ was about 150. Upon discussion of this marked discrepancy, Dudley exclaimed, "Aw, that test we took in the cafeteria was baby stuff. Anyhow I broke my pencil." Dudley had not been tested.

---

[15] Lancelot Hogben, *Nature and Nurture* (London: George Allen and Unwin, Ltd., rev. 1939), p. 29.

Rolly was the cleverest T-formation quarterback in his high-school league. His principal was distressed about Rolly's low IQ. On no test could he score better than 85. Rolly's temperament required him to do one thing at a time, and to do it as well as he could. Such orientation does not result in a high score on tests in which limited time is a factor. Such a test was not suitable for Rolly.

Bernice was thought to be an ordinary pupil. She was pleasant, placid, did her lessons in an easy, satisfactory manner. She was not much interested in school work, apparently had not been much interested in the group mental test upon which she had obtained an IQ score of 115. In taking an individual mental test at age nine, she defined the word *treasury* as a "place where a cooperating group keeps its money." This is somewhat superior to the definitions now given in standard dictionaries. Her IQ as measured by this testing was about 200.

We might comment parenthetically that Bernice was done great harm by this testing. The excitement at the clinic, at her home, and at the school over Bernice's being one of the brightest children in all the world gave the child an entirely erroneous conception of the significance of being bright. A child's superior abilities must be employed as assets to the group, never as claims to distinction from it, nor as cause for adulation.

School-wide or even system-wide testing programs can be of value if employed by the teachers in the realm of talent scouting. Many children move along at a congenial pace, carrying out their assignments, avoiding undue exposure to unfavorable comparison as well as to unfriendly envy of their classmates. However, a child's working far below capacity is an important diagnostic sign which leads the responsible teacher to a more thorough study of him.

Rather commonly, children are subjected to blame when they are discerned as working below capacity. Educators are disposed to expect a high degree of relationship between capacity and achievement. We doubt the validity of this expectation. In the realm of intellectual achievement, factors other than sheer capacity, play important roles. One must have enough capacity to carry on an activity whether it be to walk, to stand on one foot in the dark, or to imagine the extent of the universe. But after one has attained the needed capacity, factors such as interest, zeal, and practice are accountable for differences in achievement. This would be a strange world, indeed, if all of us developed all our capacities to their fullest extent. Man has long conjectured, and you might enjoy discussing, the extent to which superior capacity of itself guarantees superior accomplishment. Sir Francis Galton maintained, "Intelligence will out!" Quite an opposite point of view was expressed by Gray in "Elegy in a Country Churchyard."

Today general tests of intelligence which yield a score in one number are used much less than are tests of the particular ability sought. For example, the total score on a test for an accountant is not as crucial as the rareness of his errors. He needs enough intelligence to be an accountant. Thereafter, the quality of accuracy matters more. A watchmaker must have sense enough to understand the mechanism of a watch; he requires delicate precision of movement lacking in most of us. Few creative writers are competent proofreaders.

Translating intelligence test results into IQ's brought classification of individuals according to IQ. Terms such as gifted, feeble-minded, moron came upon us. In clinics these became clinical terms. According to the method used to standardize the tests, the average IQ is 1.00. The term *gifted* has come to designate those with IQ's above 1.30; those below .70 are called *feebleminded*. (Some states have established this definition by law.) In clinics, the term *idiot* applies to those whose IQ's are below .25, and who will grow mentally to be no more capable than the average four-year-old. *Imbeciles* range from .25 to .50, *morons* from .50 to .70. (This is useful information in seeking the appropriate appellation for associates who displease us.)

Gifted children have been studied as likely sources of geniuses and leaders. From time to time the public demands that the gifted be identified early and given special training and opportunity. Immediately upon completing his revision of the Binet Scale, Terman set about to identify a thousand "genius or near-genius" children to be followed through the period of growth. Four interesting volumes have resulted from this identification and follow-up.[16]

---

[16] L. M. Terman, *Mental and Physical Traits of a Thousand Gifted Children,* Genetic Studies of Genius, Vol. I (Stanford: Stanford University Press, 1925). Catherine M. Cox and Others, *The Early Mental Traits of Three Hundred Geniuses,* Genetic Studies of Genius, Vol. II (Stanford: Stanford University Press, 1926). B. S. Burke, D. W. Jensen, L. M. Terman and Others, *The Promise of Youth,* Genetic Studies of Genius, Vol. III (Stanford: Stanford University Press, 1930). L. M. Terman, Melita H. Oden and Others, *The Gifted Child Grows Up, Twenty-five Years' Follow-up of a Superior Group,* Genetic Studies of Genius, Vol. IV (Stanford: Stanford University Press, 1947).

**Learning
to Be Intelligent**

In this chapter we have emphasized the fact that intelligence is a cluster of related abilities which are learned. We recognize that individuals differ in their capacities to learn. Capacities for mental behavior develop into abilities as a result of challenge, opportunity, and nurture. Recently we watched a twelve-year-old struggling to learn to ride a bicycle as a couple of six-year-olds stood by wondering what the trouble was; they had just ridden their bikes two miles across town to call on a friend. The big boy had grown up in a sky-scraper-apartment building in Brooklyn. He had had no opportunity to develop the ability to ride a bike. Being transplanted into a suburban culture at age twelve was putting him at a disadvantage in many respects. The community to which his parents moved is on Long Island Sound, where everyone has a boat. The children grow up in this community knowing about boats and riding their bikes all over town. If a six-year-old inquires how the boat-trailer works, his dad responds, "Look underneath there and see."

When one is helping children learn something, he must have clearly in mind the aim of that learning. We are writing this book for teachers who wish to help children learn to be free men rather than willing subjects. To foster the development of a free man, one uses none of the methods by which dogs are trained to do undogly tricks upon command. Teachers and school administrators must consider deeply the differences between training and education. *Training* implies the use of skill without the learner's thought of purpose. The term *education* comes from a root meaning "to lead out"; it implies helping children become aware of the dignity of persons, and developing their capacities into abilities which may be used for the benefit of others and which will make their own gratifications more secure.

Elmo Roper, a highly competent observer of the social scene, has summed up the function of education as follows:

> The real pulse of our civilization is human lives, lived in freedom and dignity, by men who are conscious of their own stature and deeply respectful of the human potential that all men possess. We will be saved—if we are lucky—by men who are able to use all that is in them—their minds, their senses, and their hearts—as fully developed human beings.
> When schools teach, they teach the whole person. There simply is no

way of compartmentalizing people so that a thing done or taught to them reaches only a preselected part of them.

The primary function of our schools is to teach people how to think, but a submissive person who has learned nothing but to accept what is told him cannot think well. A person who has been educated by forced feeding may be able to display a wondrous amount of knowledge upon request; but it will not have nourished him. Only a free person, who has sufficient confidence in himself to offset the constant battery of pressures from without, can truly think.[17]

Some Principles of Learning

We wish to set forth some principles of learning which teachers may use as guides in planning and evaluating their learning activities.

Learning is a process of reacting to circumstances. The learner learns his own reactions. He truly becomes what he experiences. Feelings and attitudes are the basic determiners in a learning situation. Too, they are the fundamental learnings in experience. Feelings and attitudes cannot be assigned, nor demanded, nor deliberately controlled.

The individual's behavior is directed to bring about conditions favorable to his own interests as he senses them. How-

ever a person behaves, that way makes sense to him. Children need much guidance in learning from their experience to be thoughtful in promoting their own interests and in distinguishing what contributes to their long-range well-being as contrasted with momentary gratification. As teachers give this guidance they must have in mind that people do not prosper by imposing upon others what they are unwilling to accept for themselves.

Children assimilate into characteristic ways of behaving those ways which seem to them essential to the achievement of their own purposes. Human activity is directed to the attainment of purposes. The real outcomes of experience are

[17] Elmo Roper, "Learning Is Total," *The Saturday Review*, May 24, 1958, p. 20.

determined by the purposes of the learner, by his real reasons for his activity. The basic work of the teacher concerns the provision and arrangement of facilities, circumstances, and challenges in terms of the background, level of maturation, interests, and concerns of the learner.

An effective group learning situation permits each participant to perform in terms of his own background, abilities, and concerns, with satisfaction, and with the respect and appreciation of the group.

An effective learning situation provides opportunity for the learners to share responsibility for its arrangement and operation. In it, the children need some things to care for. It must involve genuine planning by the children of activities and occasions for which they have marked enthusiasm. There must be a need for inventing, for contriving, for making out with the materials at hand. The effective learning situation provides free time for reflection and contemplation. It provides opportunity for children to know and interpret conditions in their lives, particularly those about which they can take some action.

| **Meaning of** **Social Intelligence** | We would like to close this chapter with a discussion of the meaning of social intelligence and the consideration of some means for promoting its development. We |

must face the fact that we live in the most schooled generation of man in history; it is also the most destructive, bloodiest generation.

The individual lives now in a highly complex world of machines and organizations too big and too expensive for him to own and manage by himself. Our science and technology offer us limitless amounts and varieties of goods, comforts, and joys without endangering the health and safety of anyone and without the need for enslaving any other man. Progress in civilization has resulted from more and more specialized work and more organization. As men have become more specialized, they have become more productive and more necessary to each other. They have become interdependent. This is the "reason to be" of democracy.

The basic method of democracy is the functioning of group intelligence, the ability and disposition of a social group to come to agreement on common goals and to direct effective action toward attaining those goals. The intelligent group, as does the intelligent individual, determines purposes and pursues them through *thinking*.

Methods commonly used in school assume intelligence to be individualistic and largely non-cooperative, despite the fact that modern life presents problems too complex for the individual to solve, and demands specialized skills and knowledges too varied to be carried in one small head. Group enterprise taps and mobilizes the skill and wisdom of individuals. Numerous studies show that the individual lacks the capacity to think clearly by himself, to set aside his vested interest in being right. He requires the checks and balances of other individuals. To know truths and to act in accord with the best wisdom available, man normally seeks conference and counsel and opportunity for discussion. The teacher who would lead a group toward ever more intelligent behavior seeks to help the group attain a high degree of consensus in setting goals, in realistic appraisal of resources and opportunities for reaching them, in wise planning of procedures and in appropriate designation and acceptance of responsibilities for implementing plans. The teacher makes sure that all concerned parties are heard, that marked enthusiasms and marked dissents are justly weighed, that the mild desires of a majority shall not outweigh the strong concerns of a few. A genuinely democratic group seldom votes; voting tends to emphasize disagreements.

In circumstances where the leader exercises the authority of status, as do most adults in schools, the group cannot become intelligent unless it clearly understands and accepts as reasonable the imposed limits of its freedom of choice and action. Too often, discussions in classrooms and staff meetings are merely exercises in guessing what the leader has in mind or will accept. Once freedom of choice has been offered the leader may not exercise veto power.

A significant function of the teacher is the discovery, release, and marshaling of competencies within the group. He holds fast to the principle, however, that individual competencies and tools are to be prized as assets for the group, and are not claims to distinction or privilege. Because Josephine can spell exceptionally well, she shall read proof on the magazine, not receive a pat on the head nor a certificate of merit for being the best speller.

If we are to have a cooperative world, we must have people disposed to cooperate. We regard as intelligent the individual who is sensitive to the quality of living of other people. The cultivation of this sensitivity is a major function of education of social intelligence. The teacher must feel and behave with genuine concern for the inner good feelings of every pupil.

The socially intelligent individual is motivated by an active feeling of personal responsibility for the well-being of mankind. He claims nothing for himself that he does not work to achieve for other people. As the child develops in a school social group, he must experience ever-widening opportunities to be genuinely valuable to others in his immediate environment.

The socially intelligent individual is disposed to act in accord with his foresight of human outcomes. He cultivates skill and resources for predicting social outcomes of behavior. The individual subverts his own interests to the wishes of the majority in situations which require common action. He maintains, however, active resistance to the encroachment of the leader and of other members of the group upon matters peculiarly personal and private. Perhaps the entire group must go to one place—to the museum, the post office, or on the pregraduation trip to Washington or Chicago or San Francisco. Everyone must abide by the group decision if he is to participate. However, the group may not demand that each boy part his hair in the middle or wear white trousers when he takes a tour through the museum.

Socially intelligent people respect genuine authority; they are skeptical of the authority of status. They learn discernment in judging the worth of the opinions and proposals for action of other persons. They grow in respect for relevant data and testimony. They respect the leadership of competency as they recognize its worth in the attainment of goals.

To build these qualities in people, those in positions of leadership must make them function in the operation of the group. The activities of the group must require group enterprises. The group must be more than a number of individuals pursuing their individual purposes in congeniality and proximity. These activities are carried on in accordance with the principle that democracy is a group of persons voluntarily working together to enhance the quality of living of each one of them.

Some common educational practices seem to interfere with the development of social intelligence. Most destructive among them is the promotion of individual or in-group determination to gain advantage, to have its own way. We have known teachers to comment to a parent, "Your Susie is the best reader, or the best cooperator in the room." The motivation of individuals to excellence rather than to being of genuine worth to the group is directly contrary to the achievement of genuinely intelligent group enterprise. We must move rapidly from concern for "Who shall have his way?" to the proposition, "What way will bring the greatest satisfaction to the most of us?" Commonly, teachers imply the expectation that certain individuals among their pupils will have the "right" answer, the best suggestion. Often these "right" children are beamed upon by the teacher to the pain of their associates. This practice has given us the term *egg-head.* Our politicians are most wary of any suggestion that they are scholarly. Some years ago a prominent political leader said proudly of his candidate at the national convention, "He represents no thinking group."

In evaluating the individual's contribution to group endeavor, we must express appreciation of the *contribution, not* of the *contributor.* Discriminating praise of the individual seems to act as a strong, habit-forming drug. Group appreciation of contributions and achievements seems to be a prime motivator toward human gratification.

In our time man's greatest developmental task, that edge of rapid growth of civilization, is the achievement of world-wide cooperative living. Modern technology leaves no neutral ground between peace and war. Teachers and pupils must grow rapidly in the knowledge of how other men live, of the circumstances that make life good, of the world's resources for richness of life. School must carry on ways of living together which promote personal responsibility for the condition of mankind everywhere. It must carry on group enterprises directed to continued improvement of the quality of living. *Mankind must learn to live by intelligence!*

Suggestions for Further Exploration

▶ Note some of the things the individual you are studying or some other young human does or says that indicate his level of mental maturity. Discuss these with your classmates to see how much agreement exists among you.

▶ Try to recall all the situations during the past week in which you have "given up" on something you started. Can you analyze why you did not complete what you started? Was it due to lack of capacity, waning of interest, temperament, or a combination of all these?

► Construct an opinionnaire of twenty-five items ranging from statements of fact to ones of belief and ask a group of your acquaintances to respond in terms of a five-point scale. For example:

	Absolutely True	Probably True	Don't Know	Probably False	Absolutely False
1. A man will at some time land on the moon and return to earth.					
2. The distance between San Francisco and New York City is about 3000 miles.					

Discuss the responses you receive noting differences in opinion and in individual intensity of belief about matters we cannot be sure of.

► Note during the next week instances of behavior which you would call "stupid." Ask yourself these questions:

Did the individual know he was behaving stupidly? If not, why didn't he?

If he did, how did he respond: try to laugh it off, cover it up, bluff his way through it, blame someone else, or. . . .

What caused the stupid behavior, as you see it, in each instance?

► Note during the next week instances that make you say or think, "My, wasn't that smart!" In each case try to analyze the ways of behavior that were displayed.

► With some of your classmates list individuals who seem to have a genuine sense of humor. Do these people have other intellectual characteristics in common? Can they laugh at their own mistakes and incongruities?

► Observe a group of children. Note those that during the discussion hold out, refuse to go along with group decisions. See if you can relate this quality to other qualities in personality. Do you judge these children to be particularly bright, average, or below the average, or do they seem to include all three categories of description?

► Observe a group of young people making a decision. See how many people in the group contribute to the discussion as the subject is being considered. Observe how differences of opinion are handled by the group and by the leader. Do any people change their positions during the discussion? How is the decision made: by vote, by consensus, by strong-arm methods, by one person? How much commitment to the decision by the group as a whole do you surmise there is? Try to test it out. How well do individuals understand their own responsibilities in relation to the decision? Discuss this experience with your classmates in terms of its meaning relative to social intelligence.

Additional Sources You May Find Helpful

John Dewey, *Interest and Effort in Education*. New York: Houghton Mifflin Company, 1913.

This early little book is among Dewey's clearest statements that interests reveal the growing edges of the mind and that the effort which educates and builds the mind must come from the inner drive to grow and to know.

William Heard Kilpatrick, *Philosophy of Education*. New York: The Macmillan Company, 1951.

The mature reflections of a pioneer student of educative methods. This book was written after fifty years of distinguished teaching by one of America's master teachers.

George Mead, *Mind, Self and Society*. Chicago: University of Chicago Press, 1934.

Students of society commonly agree that this book is among the most important contributions to our understanding the human mind as a social product.

Jean Piaget, *The Origins of Intelligence in Children*. New York: International Universities Press, 1952.

Jean Piaget's original research on young children is recorded in this book. He emphasizes the importance of the perceptual activity in the development of intelligence. He believes that mental faculties develop by being used. The last chapter summarizes theories of intelligence—very useful. This is difficult reading but we recommend it most highly.

James Harvey Robinson, *The Mind in the Making*. New York: Harper and Brothers, 1921.

Many leaders of modern thought regard this book to be among the most important influences upon their conceptions of society and of man. It traces man's long struggle toward realizing his human potentialities. Dr. Robinson's insights, gained from lifelong study of human history, are expressed simply and profoundly.

5

The Cultural Origins of the Individual

Of all creatures humans are born least capable at birth. A human infant can do nothing but metabolize. He is born with no ready-made *human* behavior, rather he must learn all his human qualities as nature matures his special capacities to learn them. He learns to behave like a human being through associating with other humans by the process of acculturation. A child requires several years of care merely to stay alive. To remain human, all of us require the care and concern of other people throughout our lives.

**Human Behavior
Is Learned**

Nature has been most wise in providing that humans are born with no fixed ways of behaving and in requiring a long period for humans to grow to adulthood. Because they require the care of other people and constant association with them, the very young learn to be like those who care for them. We use the term *care for* to mean providing for the child's basic needs.

Have you not been astounded to observe how easily a little child comprehends his mother who is rattling to him in a language incomprehensible to you? He comprehends fully though he has had no instruction such as you had in that language in school. Young children in Madrid use Spanish quite well. Even the slow learners learn French in France. Yet some of America's brightest youth have difficulty learning Spanish, French, and German. We learn our language, religion, manners, values, politics, prejudices, preferences, and aversions from the people with whom we grow. A human being is the product of his own special culture (sometimes we call this a subculture). He is the product not merely of his nationality, his community, his church, his family but of his own responses to his family, his neighbors, his own world of people. By growing with people, a child learns to be like those with whom he grows. We believe Walt Whitman caught the import of this thought in the following lines:

> There was a child went forth every day,
> And the first object he look'd upon, that object he became,
> And that object became part of him for the day or a certain part of the day,
> Or for many years or stretching cycles of years.[1]

The child's need for prolonged care is essential to his development and to his life as a human. One of the fundamental aspects of human life, not shared by the lower animals, is that we learn to care for those for whom we care. Long have teachers said of some of their pupils, "Only a mother could love *that* child." Now we know that a mother, in meeting that child's deep needs for food, cuddling, and comfort, learns to love the child. And the baby learns to love her. Fathers who wish to be loved

---

[1] Walt Whitman, "There Was a Child Went Forth," *Leaves of Grass* (New York: Aventine Press, Inc., 1931), p. 372.

must care for the baby, too, and share in the feeding, cuddling, diapering, bathing, lullabying. A most interesting study of the relationships of fathers to their children who were born during the father's absence from home during World War II has been made by Stolz.[2]

Children learn to love, respect, and value those persons who care for them. Nature has sought to make it mandatory that a mother feed her infant child in frequent periods of warm cuddling. (Much interesting work has been done in the last few years on the effects of children losing their mothers. The film "Maternal Deprivation in Young Children"[3] eloquently portrays these effects.) Thus father-love is much less a theme of poetry and song than is mother-love. All too often we have known mothers to neglect their fundamental role or leave the basic care of the child to someone else, then to be quite hurt to realize that the child preferred the other person.

Common Attributes of People in All Cultures

Let us examine the likenesses of people in all cultures. We believe that baby Moses, baby Cleopatra, baby Napoleon, baby Socrates, baby Gandhi, baby Florence Nightingale, baby Columbus, baby Hitler, baby Eisenhower were very much alike. How they became so different is one of the basic problems we discuss in this chapter. Each was born by a woman; each was born helpless at a low level of creature functioning; each was born with a need to accept food, with the necessity to rely upon older people to whom he must make his wants known; each was born male or female and learned early what this meant to him in the particular culture in which he grew. All cut their teeth within a narrow range of months, assumed erect posture, walked independently about the same period of development. Whether they approached walking by cruising around a playpen or by holding on to saplings, viewed their mothers as threats or havens, knew no father or peered eagerly from the window to see him come home every day, played baseball or threw mudballs into the Euphrates depended upon the time, place, and human ways of their

[2] Lois Meek Stolz and Collaborators, *Father Relations of War-Born Children* (Stanford: Stanford University Press, 1954).

[3] *Maternal Deprivation in Young Children*, 30 min., sound, New York University Film Library.

culture. Each had an urge to grow, to relate to other people, to be some-body within his own intimate group, because of whom he was and what he could do.

Each Individual's Culture Unique to Him

The babies mentioned above became remarkably different persons because of the uniqueness of their bodies, the cultures in which they grew, their own responses to the events of their daily lives, and the demands and opportunities of life as they experienced it. Very often teachers, neighbors, and parents are perplexed by the extreme differences in children from the same home. They assume that each child in a family has the same culture. Let's take a look. In a two-child family, one may have no sister, but a brother; the other child has no brother, but a sister. One is the older, the other the younger. Perhaps the older was not yet wanted by his parents, but he taught his parents to love babies; the younger was most welcome. Or, perhaps, the second child came earlier than wanted and felt his intrusion. Often expectations for girls are quite different from those for boys. Perhaps Lydia matches the pictures her parents have of what their child should be; Jimmy looks like cousin Mortimer. A child's culture consists of the behavior of the people with whom he grows, and the way he feels about that behavior. Interpersonal behavior tends to be specific in terms of the attitudes of the persons involved. Merely knowing the general aspects of a culture, be it the family, the neighborhood, or the nation, will not enable us to know the private world of an individual within that culture, apart from knowing him. Germany produced Hitler and Einstein during the same time span.

Dominant Themes of American Culture

The cultural expectations of the people around him critically affect the way in which a child develops. Convincing evidence indicates that some very young children experience the trauma of being a disappointment to their parents. Mom and Dad wanted a girl and got a boy. Brown-eyed parents got a blue-eyed baby. Father expected to sire an all-American football player and found his son temperamentally opposed to violence. Our present culture has many themes that exert strong molding forces upon the young. Let's consider some of these dominant themes.

The Success Theme

America has long prided itself upon its social mobility. The "rags to riches" theme, with which our literature abounds, has permeated the culture. We recommend Marquand [4] as one of the outstanding current writers on this theme. Many of us grew up on the Horatio Alger stories. Even today, "great businessmen and potent industrialists interrupt their affairs to gather" [5] each year in New York City for the presentation of the Horatio Alger Award, which is given to a few men who have risen from humble origins to success. The success theme is emphasized in expressions like "the American dream," and "a self-made man." Advertising in fashions, in automobiles, in practically every phase of living accents the importance of material success. We recently heard a woman who is allergic to mink wryly remark that her husband's success in his work depended upon his driving a big car and his wife's wearing mink. What girl on the Lower East Side of New York does not dream of wearing a mink coat as she cruises along in a Cadillac?

Boys especially are expected to be striving, energetic, "eager beavers" in our culture. They are expected to "get ahead." We are much less concerned with girls becoming successful in professions and in business. Of course, boys feel this pressure, and some of them feel inadequate to measure up to these expectations. From any point of view from which problems of maladjustment are considered, about five times as many boys as girls appear. Delinquents, slow readers, behavior problems, and emotionally disturbed young people are for the most part boys. Nothing in the basic nature of the sexes explains this. The difference, it appears, is in the expectations of the culture. The cultural expectation to be successful, to "get ahead," is much more demanding for males than for females. This is particularly true for the middle-class male child. [6]

---

[4] John P. Marquand. See *Point of No Return* (New York: Bantam Books, 1952), and many others.

[5] R. Richard Wohl, "The 'Rags to Riches Story': An Episode of Secular Idealism," *Class, Status and Power*, eds., Reinhard Bendix and Seymour Martin Lipset (Glencoe, Ill.: The Free Press, 1953), pp. 388-395.

[6] Arnold W. Green, "The Middle-Class Male Child and Neurosis," *Mental Health and Mental Disorder*, ed., Arnold M. Rose (New York: W. W. Norton and Company, Inc., 1955), pp. 341-357.

There are few situations today in which the youthful male has the freedom to climb down the social ladder, as well as up, and maintain his self-respect. According to Dorothy Canfield Fisher,[7] Vermont is one of the rare places which still gives people this freedom. She cites a school principal who found himself pale, tired, and nervous at the end of each school year, but vital and composed as he worked at carpentry during the summer. He resigned and became a carpenter and continued living in the same community. In many places, accepting work with his hands after having been a professional would have caused this man and his family so much anxiety that the decision could not have been made. A square peg would have remained in a round hole.

One way in which the success theme is reflected in child-rearing practices is our undue concern about earliness. While mothers today usually are counseled to go slow in toilet-training, weaning, and introducing new routines, many still feel considerable anxiety about these matters. Comparisons are made with neighbors' children, and mother is likely to feel her child is a bit inferior if he does not respond as early as Joey or Phyllis to these cultural impositions. The demands made of an American human being between birth and six years greatly exceed those made by most other cultures. The middle-class American culture is said by many anthropologists to be the most restrictive culture in child-rearing practices. Murphy states that one seldom hears a baby cry in India: "Infants are nursed for two years or longer and in fact often wean themselves. . . . There is little systematic toilet training; few children are forced; they seldom receive bewildering punishments for something their bodies needed to do." [8] This easiness is characteristic of a great many cultures, especially those we sometimes consider underdeveloped. The effects of child-rearing practices are still subject to considerable difference of opinion among competent authorities.[9]

So many parents and doting aunts deem it a mark of distinction for a child to cut his teeth earlier than his cousins, or to read before other chil-

---

[7] Dorothy Canfield Fisher, *Vermont Tradition* (Boston: Little, Brown and Company, 1953), pp. 317-338.
[8] Lois Barclay Murphy, "Roots of Tolerance and Tension in Indian Child Development," in *In the Minds of Men* by Gardner Murphy (New York: Basic Books, Inc., 1953), p. 49.
[9] Robert R. Sears and Associates, *Patterns of Child Rearing* (Evanston, Ill.: Row, Peterson and Company, 1957).

dren of his age! There is no reason to believe that a child who cuts his teeth earlier will have better teeth. Nor is it logical to believe that a child who reads earlier than another shall ultimately be a superior reader. Teachers and parents should consider that the word *precocious* literally means "too soon done."

Some teachers take great pride in having their pupils perform in ways that express their precocity. We seriously question the practice of exhibiting and applauding children in performances that are not in keeping with their age. Adults praise and applaud eight-year-olds who sing "hot mamma" songs, play the Virgin Mary in the Christmas pageant, dance the polka on TV with grown men, not because they perform so well, but because they are so young, so cute! Adults must be most wary of using children for their own entertainment. We take a dim view of the morality of persons in the entertainment industry who make personal fortunes by using little children to amuse and entertain adults.

We are probably paying a heavy price for using our high-school youngsters to entertain the public by highly publicized and emotionalized sports, the principal motivation for which has become defeating rather than the enjoyment of the zest of playing. This motivation is an inevitable concomitant of "Keeping a little bit ahead of the Joneses." Public display and contrived contentiousness have become so prominent in our adolescent culture that we frequently hear it declared that they are functions of human nature. If this were true, we would find adolescents the world over responding in a similar manner. We don't!

When being a success becomes so important to the individual that his self-respect is damaged if he does not keep up with all the others in all ways, his mental health becomes precarious. Much of the school's culture reflects adult attitudes that place success above all else.

Conformity

Conformity has become such an overriding theme of our culture that many powerful voices are now raised against it.[10, 11] Fromm analyzes the alienating effects of conformity with insight and clarity:

---

[10] David Riesman, et al., *The Lonely Crowd* (New York: Doubleday Anchor Books, 1953).

[11] Wm. H. Whyte, Jr., *The Organization Man* (New York: Doubleday Anchor Books, 1956).

The mechanism through which the anonymous authority operates is *conformity.* I ought to do what everybody does, hence, I must conform, not be different, not "stick out"; I must be ready and willing to change according to the changes in the pattern; I must not ask whether I am right or wrong, but whether I am adjusted, whether I am not "peculiar," not different. The only thing which is permanent in me is just this readiness for change. Nobody has power over me, except the herd of which I am apart, yet to which I am subjected.[12]

The anonymous authority which supports conformity is referred to as *it* or *they. They believe, they said, it isn't done that way here* are phrases repeated thoughtlessly. The school culture, with its inordinate emphasis upon regimentation and standardization, reinforces this strand of the larger culture. Report cards are sent home periodically with comments from well-intentioned teachers: "Gertrude is not adjusting as well as she *should.* She seems content to work by herself." In too many classrooms pupils are treated as automatons—working from the same workbook, reading from the same readers, taught from manuals prepared in one central office for teachers all over the country, and given the same time to produce the designated assignment which is the same for all.

One small detail of conformity is in compulsively honoring the clock. We are painfully "time aware." Do we have so much more of importance to do than does the Oriental, or than peoples of many other cultures who use time as they want to rather than being used by time? "I haven't time," "When I get time," "I must go now—I have an appointment at 4:00 and another at 4:30," are refrains that all of us sing.

Impersonality

As our country has become more and more urban, we have embraced structures in our organized living that allow a minimum of interpersonal relations and these are frequently on a superficial level. Families may live side by side in an apartment building and have no more communication than an occasional pleasantry about the weather. The structures that characterize modern American cities are designed to keep communication from flowing. The problem of impersonality is accentuated by the high degree of mobility in our culture. Industry, education, and communica-

---

[12] Erich Fromm, *The Sane Society* (New York: Rinehart and Company, Inc., 1955), pp. 153-154.

tion tend to get more and more centralized. The problem is well stated by Mumford:

> The very extension of the range of community in our time, through national and worldwide organizations, only increases the need for building up, as never before, the intimate cells, the basic tissue, of social life: the family and the home, the neighborhood and the city, the work-group and the factory. Our present civilization lacks the capacity for self-direction because it has committed itself to mass organizations and has built its structures from the top down, on the principle of dictatorships and absolutisms, rather than from the bottom up: it is efficient in giving orders and compelling obedience and providing one-way communication: but it is in the main still inept in everything that involves reciprocity, mutual aid, two-way communication, give-and-take.[13]

Education, too, is an impersonal affair for thousands of pupils. Today over half of the country's children go to urban schools. These tend to be large, factory-like structures controlled from a central office with the aid of an intercommunication system. The principal's eyes may be in a teacher's room without the teacher's being aware of it. Privacy and a sense of intimacy with one's pupils is difficult to achieve under such conditions. In large schools individual children do not come to be known as people by the school staff. The youngster is fortunate if his homeroom teacher knows him as a person. Many secondary-school pupils go through school without becoming known to a single individual on the school staff.

The impersonality of the school encourages practices that emanate from a lack of trust. Individual conferences are hit-and-miss affairs. Some schools forbid a male teacher to be alone in a classroom with an adolescent girl. Recently, one large city school system issued an edict a few weeks before the close of school forbidding any teacher to inform pupils or their parents if the pupil had to repeat a grade. The intent was to avoid conferring with parents. These examples give some indication of the extreme antisocial conditions that sometimes come about when people do not have an opportunity to know one another well enough to develop trust in and mutual respect for each other.

Pupils in large schools have little opportunity to develop their unique capacities. In a school of 2000, only a few can have the opportunity to sing in the glee club, to play in the band, to work on the newspaper, to be a

---

[13] Lewis Mumford, *The Conduct of Life* (New York: Harcourt, Brace and Company, 1951), p. 276.

member of the student council, to belong to the debating team, or....
And who can get to know the principal well in a school that size?

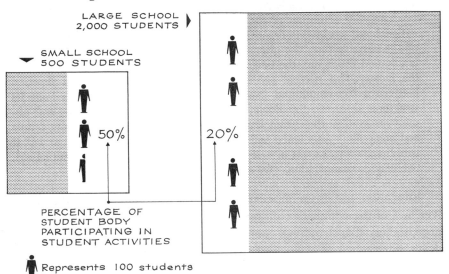

Students in a large school have fewer opportunities for participating in extra-curricular activities than students in a small school.

Ambivalence about Women's Roles

Our culture is unsure of women's roles. Women today are freer than they have ever been save in a few matriarchal societies. Yet they are discriminated against in many realms. Ask any female professor and she can brief you about woman's position in the academic world, or observe for yourself the ratio between women teachers and women principals. Not only are they at a disadvantage in the economic world, but their homes have become less satisfying to them. Modern gadgets have made housework so simple and undemanding as to be non-satisfying. Rare is the woman today who does her own baking, her own sewing, or her own preserving of foods. The centralization of business has taken the husband and father away from home from early morning to late evening. No longer does the wife look forward to her husband's dashing in for lunch with a bit of gossip and a word of praise for the tastiness of the noon meal.

Today most young women plan to work until they get married. Many undertake a kind of work that can be left during the child-bearing years and resumed later. This is one reason for many young women entering the teaching profession, and accounts in part for the large drop-outs. The kind of adjustment required in keeping a home and working outside the home has its attendant pressures. A husband's dignity may be hurt because his wife works outside the home. Family relationships disintegrate as husband and wife express conflicting views about the wife's working and tenaciously maintain them. A first-generation American, whose original culture disapproves women working outside the home, faces a special problem. When a wife secures money of her own, she is no longer willing to accept the second-class citizenship her former culture imposed upon her. The situation may become impossible if a wife earns more than her husband. Mothers who have been reared in the "genteel" tradition may press a daughter to go to school "to be finished" rather than to equip herself for a vocation. If a daughter expresses her interest in a vocation that is looked upon as a man's job, the pressure becomes more intense.

The girl child is acculturated to being docile, sweet, gracious. She may find herself uncomfortable and inadequate in a highly competitive situation. The same kind of discord that occurs between wife and husband takes place between girl children and those families coming from cultures that have more rigid attitudes toward women. Girls are expected to excel in aesthetic pursuits, to abhor mathematics and science, and our schools succeed in perpetuating these cultural imprints.

These dominant themes of our culture—the importance of success, the need to conform, the impersonality of living, and ambivalence about women's roles—are reflected in school culture. These themes encourage certain qualities of personality: the urge to be "better than" at the expense of others, overconcern for what others think, lack of knowledge of self, herd-mindedness, and a sense of aloneness. Rollo May eloquently expresses our feeling toward aloneness: "The fear of being alone derives much of its terror from our anxiety lest we *lose our awareness of ourselves.*" [14]

Cultural Roadblocks to Full Development

Some aspects of each particular culture exercise restraining influences on human development. Just as the excessive teasing in Bali develops a placidity that finds expression in the beautifully controlled Balinese dance, so do the dominant

---

[14] Rollo May, *Man's Search for Himself* (New York: W. W. Norton and Company, Inc., 1953), p. 32.

themes of our culture tend to produce people who have certain values, who accept without question the ways of their culture. One major difference between the Bali culture and ours is that ours is a diverse culture. Groups of people have different values, different ways, and have an opportunity to maintain their differences. The diversity of our culture is not an unmixed blessing, however, for it produces problems for many individuals.

We may find ourselves in situations in which our ways are not accepted or in which we do not understand what is expected of us. Then confusion, distortion, displacement, or submission may occur. In this section we examine some of the situations in which cultural roadblocks to full development occur frequently enough to present serious problems to the culture as a whole as well as to the individuals involved. We might add parenthetically that no culture can afford to sanction conditions that hamper the full development of individuals within it.

Rejection of the Individual

The human spirit has little toleration for rejection. Studies made with newborn infants indicate that a newborn baby seems to sense whether or not he is welcome to his mother. Rejection may result in illness, apathy, anxiety, or hostility. Cultures that treat children as welcome and wanted human beings rear quite different personalities from those which subject the children to frustration and denial. We recommend the many studies by Mead [15] as documentation of this basic tenet.

Among the most important tasks of education is identifying and eliminating from school procedures their many rejective practices. Ability grouping, honors societies, special privileges for special merit, marking, reports to parents—each must be examined to see how implicit and explicit rejection harms the individual.

Rejection of One's Group

Another important cultural difference, felt by individuals, is the degree of acceptance one's group has within the culture. Numerous subcultures make up what is known as the American culture. In New York City, for instance, many nationality groups have subcultures of their own. Individuals of a given subculture tend to cluster together and thus keep alive their own distinctiveness. While it is commonly recognized that the child

---

[15] Margaret Mead and Martha Wolfenstein, *Childhood in Contemporary Cultures* (Chicago: The University of Chicago Press, 1955).

must be accepted by the persons with whom he is intimately associated, scant attention is given to the equally basic need that his family, his immediate culture, be accepted by the larger culture in which they live. This is the basic evil of the segregation of minority groups.

As efforts are being made to integrate the schools of America, several testing projects have been carried on to measure the academic achievement of Negro and white pupils in a given community. The authors have had the opportunity to examine many of these results. At the first-grade level, the Negro children come up to norms as well as the white children. They continue to hold their own until the later part of the third or fourth grade, at which time they drop sharply and continue to lose ground from then on. This is the age when children begin to grasp the fact that they are rejected and their folks are rejected because of skin color. This same phenomenon occurs in both Northern and Southern school systems.

We once heard a missionary, returned from the Belgian Congo, say that he had more success in teaching written and spoken English to the children of primitive people than he had teaching it to children of Latin-Americans in a junior high school in southwestern United States. He attributed the difference to the fact that the African natives had no sense of their parents' being rejected, while the Latin-American natives lived constantly in an atmosphere of rejection by the dominating, whiter community. Test results in our schools attest the lower functioning of the children of day-laborers and servants in communities everywhere. This has been rationalized as a function of biological inheritance; it is much more likely a function of a feeling of rejection and of cultural deprivation.

Rejection of One's Class

Probably the most damaging cultural rejection is that of certain social classes. This phenomenon is eloquently described in the works of Allison

119

Davis.[16] Having used slaves so long for arduous toil and finding it neces·
sary to excuse the practice to God and to conscience by declaring the slave
to be an inferior being, man continues to look down upon persons engaged in hard, unpleasant work, however valuable their labor may be. In
building a new country, America has needed the best talents of all its
people and thus has avoided rigid class consciousness for all but highly
identifiable laborers—its Negroes. We have a long way to go, however, in
building bridges of solid respect and acceptance between the various
social classes. The public school could be a dynamic institution in this
process. Nearly all studies show the reverse to be the case—the public
schools tend to support and solidify the existing class structure of the
community.[17]

The large majority of school teachers tend to come from the middle
class. Most school-board members usually come from the more conserva-

---

[16] Allison Davis, *Social-Class Influences Upon Learning* (Cambridge: Harvard
University Press, 1948, The Inglis Lecture).

[17] A. Hollingshead, *Elmtown's Youth* (New York: John Wiley and Sons, 1949).

tive elements of this social class. The school develops a subculture that represents those who make its policies and who are employed by the school. In most schools this subculture is non-representative of the total community. Yet this culture is superimposed upon all the pupils who are predominantly (taking the country as a whole) lower class. The imposition of this new culture creates many anxieties and discontinuities among children who have only partially assimilated the values of their *own* culture and who are unfamiliar with the values of the new one.

In growing up in the lower class, a child learns particular ways of satisfying his needs that are different from the ways of middle-class children. Fighting is acceptable behavior, indeed it is required; grabbing food from the table and eating on the run is habitual; language is graphic and direct; emotions are freely expressed. When the child comes to school, he discovers these behaviors are all frowned upon, indeed prohibited. He recognizes that he is being pressed to reject, give up, these ways, but in so doing he feels he is rejecting his family. Taba capsulizes the problem facing the schools:

> . . . Can schools institutionalize cultural variations in procedures of curriculum making, of learning and teaching so as to allow all students to use their previous learnings, to reduce anxieties for those who undergo a sharp cultural transition from home to school, and to enhance learning opportunities for all? [18]

The schools' cultural bias in favor of middle-class pupils is demonstrated by the use of rewards and punishments. Pupils from the lower-class receive a disproportionate amount of punishment and are rewarded much less frequently than pupils from the middle class.[19] Lower-class pupils' dropping out of school causes much less concern than does the middle or upper-class pupils' leaving before graduation.[20] The question of morals gets entwined with the behavior exhibited by lower-class children. In trying to "correct" the child, the teacher often unintentionally teaches him that his language, his fighting, his expressions of anger are bad.

---

[18] Hilda Taba, "Educational Implications in the Concepts of Culture and Personality," *Educational Leadership,* December 1957, p. 185.

[19] Louis E. Raths and Stephen Abrahamson, *Student Status and Social Class* (Bronxville, New York: Modern Education Service, 1951, pamphlet).

[20] James S. Davie, "Social Class Factors and School Attendance," *The Harvard Educational Review,* Summer 1953. Vol. 23, No. 3, p. 179.

Comparisons

Recently we heard a person of considerable consequence insist that the need to look
down upon some other humans seems to be a
part of human nature. We can find no evidence
of this in nature, apart from creature puppy-
like physical rivalry. The tendency to judge by
comparison, however, is now a powerful force
in Western culture.

Our children are plagued by the persistence of Plato's notion that God maintains
everything in perfection in Heaven. There is
the perfect person, the perfect lamp, the perfect television set, the perfect space-ship. If we
accept this theory, we may logically assume
that two individuals who are unlike differ in
degree of perfection and thus in worthiness.
Our language with young people is replete
with "Which did you like best?" "You are the
finest boy a mother ever had." "Why can't you
write as well as Josephine?" Our tests evaluate children by comparing their output with
that of other children. Often prizes are offered
to the "best citizen," thwarting our struggle to
make good citizens of all our children. The
reader can probably call to mind many situations in which children are invited to gain
satisfaction from looking down upon and belittling other people. Once this source of gratification is learned, it follows that all too many
people gain satisfaction from belittling. This
is displayed in envy. We like the way Frank
Lloyd Wright says it:

> . . . Odious comparisons dog the footsteps of
> all creation wherever the poetic principle is
> involved because the inferior mind learns only
> by comparisons; comparisons, usually equiv-

ocal, made by selfish interests each of the other. But the superior mind learns by analyses: the study of Nature.[21]

Envy is a potent motive, but it has to be taught. Advertising proclaims "You can be 'belle of the ball,' 'stag of the herd,' the envy of the many," if only you will buy and use *this* toothpaste, *that* shaving lotion, *our set* of books. Being envied is surely among the most shaky and soluble foundations for healthy happiness.

Teacher's Role in Cultural Differences

We have been emphasizing the importance of the teacher's understanding of and respect for the individual's cultural background. Teachers tend to come from a rather particular culture. A goodly number of their pupils come from another culture. Teachers are very much concerned about the use of "bad language," and the cultivation of proper language usage. To a considerable portion of our people, these are problems of scant importance. When a child says, "We ain't got nothin'," we understand him quite well, but insist to him that his language is incorrect. We urge that teachers be exceedingly wary about discrediting children's folks by insisting to their pupils that their language and their ways are unacceptable. Recently, we heard a teacher say to a group of children, most of whom were from Puerto Rico, "Do you want to be immigrants all your lives? Do you want to be like your mothers and fathers?" We have a hunch that the surest way for this teacher or any other to effect changes in her pupils is to make them *like* her so well that they wish to be *like* her.

The teacher must strive to see a pupil as a whole, not merely as a learner of lessons. He comes to the teacher as a product of *all* that he has previously experienced. Has he known grownups as friendly, helpful people, or as demanding, unjust people? Each individual has his own particular conception of teachers which he has derived from his special culture. Some cultures demand that the teacher be revered. In many subcultures that we have experienced, the culture says the teacher must be set apart, left alone. Some youngsters have learned that fun and can be gained only by defying or deceiving grownups. A few

---

[21] Frank Lloyd Wright, *A Testament* (New York: Horizon Press, 1

one of our students reported shortly before Christmas that she heard that ominous silence which mothers of three-year-olds dread. She called to her little boy, "Johnny, what are you doing?" He replied, "I'm not doing anything. How can I do anything with you and Jesus and Santa Claus watching me all the time?" This young mother vowed to change her ways with the child. It is likely that considerable time and contrivance were required for his teacher to gain Johnny's confidence and become a positive addition to his culture.

Developing Rich School Culture

An important purpose of the school today is to make sure that every child spends a good part of his time in a culture suitable for children. In this school culture much time should be spent in continuously evaluating the dominant values, ways, and skills of the larger culture. Accepting this role, the school seeks to make the grounds, buildings, and classrooms suitable places for young people and manageable by them. We deem it particularly important that pupils are able to play a significant part in arranging and maintaining their physical environment. The school furniture should be such that a variety of child needs can be satisfied by its use. For many pupils, the "physical culture" of a school consists of the backs of other children and whatever face the teacher presents. Pupils should be able to turn the lights off and on, to do something about arranging ventilation and heat, to clean up their own messes.

In their room should be the important cultural tools and gadgets: materials for writing and duplicating, basic art materials, maps and globes comprehensible to them. As older people, we rather lament the disappearance of the clock which needed to be wound and set. If we would grow scientists and mathematicians, children and young people must have in their everyday surroundings magnets, batteries, magnifying glasses, binoculars, an abundant variety of useful "junk," meaningful books, and appropriate magazines and bulletins. If we would grow people who love music, the day by day living space of the pupils must include simple instruments upon which they can make melodies and rhythms, and appropriate records for a phonograph which they can run themselves.

Relating School Culture to Larger Culture

It seems to us that the school often promotes an excessive degree of cultural isolation from modern life. Children and youth go through school with people of their own age. Even within schoolrooms, pupils often are divided into groups of similar ability, knowledge, and skill. The individual's assimilation of his culture results from interactions with persons different from himself. We need to examine practices of special classes for children of like handicaps. Should blind children live in a sightless culture, or borrow the eyes of others? Does a child who reads haltingly need to be with some others who read well?

We have been saying at some length that every immature human being needs grownups in his life. The adult response to a child challenges and shapes his growth. Modern life has decreased the opportunity of young people to know grownups in non-status roles. In a simple rural culture, young people know the storekeeper, the blacksmith, the janitor, the doctor—each as a person. We have a notion that it is important for the school to involve more adults without professional status in the lives of pupils.

It used to be easier to relate the school culture to the larger culture, for there was more stability in the larger culture. Today we cannot assure the young learner that he will have the kind of culture that he grew up in or that he is in now. This makes the task of the school difficult. The Balinese culture can produce a group of people who test high on a "test devised for schizophrenics in the West," without being concerned about the problem of schizophrenia. Balinese culture can tolerate a large amount of schizophrenia because the whole culture is so unified and stable that it has found useful ways to take care of the schizophrenic personalities that are produced by the culture.[22] Our culture is fragmented; it is highly ambivalent about many values; it is rapidly changing and is likely to change more rapidly during the next twenty years. Teachers must spend considerable time thinking intelligently about the problems created by the culture.

Eliminating Roadblocks to Development

Some aspects of culture seem to hinder, divert, even stop the full development of young people. We referred earlier to the extreme effects of disturbing the young child's affectional pattern. The loss of the mother is the most eloquent example of such disturbance. Often a child comes to

---

[22] Kenneth Soddy, ed., *Mental Health and Infant Development* (New York: Basic Books, Inc., 1956), pp. 174-179.

school, having known only love and acceptance, and suddenly encounters marked efforts to change him, to restrict him, to set him apart. With some children, marked shock results from moving from the zestful acceptance of kindergarten to the prescribed lessons of first grade. This is not to suggest that the ways of the kindergarten be changed. A New Zealand teacher remarked sadly, "You Americans seem to believe that the creative things—games, puzzles, easels, paints, clay, and the like—are needed only until a child is six."

It is rather common today in the lives of pre-school children that mother plays the role of sole interferer with childish ways. Father works away from home. Neighbors seldom correct or restrain child behavior unless it is most extravagant. The fact that mother is the chief disciplinarian may present a rather severe emotional problem to the child. A good deal of discussion and professional concern must be directed toward broadening the concern that neighbors have for children of the neighborhood. We doubt if a family alone can rear children in the most promising circumstances for growth. We need a return to neighborhood concern for the well-being of children.

A powerful restraint upon wholesome development is the undermining of a child's self-respect. Every human must think well of himself. Concepts that are built by the words "naughty," "good," "bad" have no place in the mind, conscious or subconscious, of the teacher. Too often adults describe as "good" the child who is not *childlike,* and as "naughty" the child who is being quite normal, but in a place or circumstance not meant for children.[23] In a subsequent chapter we shall discuss in detail ways in which the teacher can learn more about the cultural background of children. Simple, factual data of the kind usually found in school records is important. The number of children at home, the kind of work the father does, whether or not the mother is employed outside the home, who the other adults who live in the home are, the intactness of the family—these may be important, but none has any meaning in itself. For example, we commonly believe that children from broken homes are at a serious disadvantage, but we cannot know the effect of this circumstance upon a child unless we know the child.

We learn much about the effects of the circumstances of living on children and youth if we provide them with sufficient freedom so that

[23] Karen Horney, "The Tyranny of the Should," *Neurosis and Human Growth* (New York: W. W. Norton and Company, Inc., 1950), pp. 64-85.

they are able to reveal themselves to us. Among young children, we learn much by listening to their conversations; by watching them play, noting the roles they assume when playing house or school or church; by noting them in their creative moments, as they paint, write, dance, and work with clay. Older pupils reveal themselves, too, if they are free to express themselves without anticipation of correction or judging. Teachers can learn very little from pupils' work that is turned in merely for a mark.

It is most important to know parents as people, rather than merely as mothers and fathers of certain specific pupils. Schools are rapidly learning to hold informal get-togethers at which teachers can get to know parents, rather than merely confer with them about the behavior of their children.

In earlier times when the school and the teacher had specific lessons to teach, when the pupil gained and prospered at school solely in terms of the degree to which he learned these lessons, it was relatively unimportant that the teacher sense and appreciate each child's own peculiar culture. Today, when education is compulsory and we have become aware of the complexity of growing people, and have matured morally so that we want to make life good for every child, the teacher cannot teach effectively without an understanding and appreciation and acceptance of the child as he is. The teacher must expect every child to function upon the growing edges of his own life, in those areas of concern that are then alive for him. Really, the child can function in no other way. The teacher seeks to provide challenges, opportunities, and some necessities for a child's positive action and reaction in his group.

Among all creatures, the basic reactions are acceptance and rejection, attraction and repulsion. Every creature tries to maintain his own integrity, to defend himself from attack. When the child responds negatively to a situation, be it a great storm or a great poem, the experience is negative in his cultural development. Today's teacher seeks to provide circumstances and situations which call forth positive growth in effective, happy living. The child *learns his experience.* Experience derives its quality from feeling. Only the teacher who senses a child's feelings about a situation knows what the child is learning.

Suggestions for Further Exploration

► Take a walk home with the person whom you have chosen to study. Listen carefully to his talk and see if you can discern his culture as he sees it. Try to get invited into his home so you can learn something of the family culture.

Jot down your observations and add to them as you learn more about this individual. Exchange your observations with one of your classmates. Discuss your findings together.

▶ If you are working with a group of young people, try to find out the roadblocks imposed by their culture to their full development.

▶ Follow one youngster through a day of school and jot down all the comparisons that you hear, either from adults or other youngsters. Ask yourself what you think about the use of these comparisons.

▶ Do the same thing, only this time listen for rejections. Try to catch some subtle ones. See, if you can, if there are rejections of any one group. Try to analyze why.

▶ Do you know well a member of a group that is often rejected by your community? If not, try to begin getting acquainted with someone in whom you are interested from this group. As your acquaintance develops, try to discern the ways in which his culture has affected his attitudes toward himself and his family.

▶ Many excellent films are available depicting various aspects and influences of culture. We especially recommend the following:

A Balinese Family (Character Formation in Different Cultures Series), 17 min., sound, New York University Film Library.
    Shows the child-rearing practices in a Balinese family.

Bathing Babies in Three Cultures (Character Formation in Different Cultures Series), 9 min., sound, New York University Film Library.
    Shows mother-child relations at bathing time in New Guinea, Bali, and modern America.

Family Life of the Navaho Indians, 31 min., silent, New York University Film Library.
    This film shows the way in which the Navaho culture is inculcated upon the Indian child, even though the Navahos exist as a part of the American culture.

Forgotten Village, 67 min., sound, Brandon Films.
    This film, set in a remote Mexican village, is of unusually fine technical quality. John Steinbeck co-directed and Burgess Meredith narrates the film, which is concerned with the conflicts that arise in cultures in transition.

Additional Sources You May Find Helpful

Ruth Benedict, *Patterns of Culture*. New York: Mentor Books, 1948.
    A classic written by an anthropologist of note. Especially good discussion of the ways culture affects human development and the need to appraise current cultural influences.

Allison Davis, *Social-Class Influences Upon Learning*. Cambridge: Harvard University Press, 1948, Inglis Lecture.

This is a terse, simple description of the fundamental cultural differences between middle- and lower-class families. Dr. Davis maintains that the school's curriculum and value system are not appropriate for children of the lower-class.

Kenneth Eells and others, *Intelligence and Cultural Differences*. Chicago: University of Chicago Press, 1951.

A report of a comprehensive study that the University of Chicago under the leadership of Dr. Allison Davis has been sponsoring for a number of years on the relationship between intelligence and cultural differences. Some thought-provoking material on the bias of intelligence tests.

Erich Fromm, *The Sane Society*. New York: Rinehart and Company, 1955.

This book is an evaluation by a highly competent and human psychiatrist of the subtle effects of conflicting values within the culture. His presentation of the concept of "anonymous authority" and its restraining effect upon human freedom is especially valuable to those seeking to understand contemporary human behavior.

Margaret Mead, *Coming of Age in Samoa*. New York: Mentor Books, 1949.
————, *Growing up in New Guinea*. New York: Mentor Books, 1953.
————, *Sex and Temperament in Three Primitive Societies*. New York: Mentor Books, 1950.

These three paperbacks contain much of the research Margaret Mead, eminent anthropologist, has contributed to our fund of knowledge about man. From the study of these cultures, the student of human behavior is able to understand more fully those attributes that are common to all men and the complex ways in which culture shapes our personalities.

Lewis Mumford, *The Culture of Cities*. New York: Harcourt, Brace and Company, 1938.

This book recounts the development of cities as commercial enterprises which gave scant thought to the quality of living of the people who dwell in them. Mumford eloquently and sensitively describes the psychological effects of the city upon the individual.

James S. Plant, *Personality and the Cultural Pattern*. New York: The Commonwealth Fund, 1937.

Dr. Plant was one of the wisest individuals of our generation working directly with children who were having trouble adapting to the cultural demands made of them. His wisdom and comprehensive experience is reflected in this book.

6

The Meaning of Human Personality

A father stands at the window of the hospital nursery gazing at all the babies born in the hospital during the past few days. Which baby is his? What distinguishes it from all the others? What kind of seven-year-old will he become? What kind of adult? Will he be a physical education teacher, a violinist, a businessman, or. . . . . . ? What will be the joys and sorrows encountered as the child grows in this particular family? These are some of the questions that father vaguely feels as he catches his first glimpse of his first-born. When he knows which baby is his, he realizes that in this small speck of humanity is the raw stuff from which personality comes.

We have to look to the mother and father, and back at least another generation to the grandparents, to get any understanding of the forces that need to be "reckoned with" as we try to understand what produces an individual's personality. Montagu [1] describes the infant at birth as a "culturally undifferentiated animal." The process of becoming differentiated as a unique human being begins as the *social* process begins during birth. We say *during birth* rather than *at birth* because many psychologists believe that the birth process itself has lasting effects upon the infant. A long, difficult birth process may produce a trauma, it is claimed, that shapes the individual's perceptions of his world.

While disagreement exists on the validity of the idea of birth trauma, we do know that, regardless of the child's physical organism, he is shaped and molded by the culture in which he lives. He begins to develop a personality as soon as he is born. A precise definition of personality at this point would be somewhat meaningless. Let us just say that, when we talk about personality, we mean that which differentiates this human being from all others. One's personality consists of the ways in which he functions with other people. Personality is an "umbrella" word which we use to include interactions, doings, characteristic ways of behaving, manner, speech, likes, dislikes, temperament, and the manner in which all these items are put together to produce a *self*. Personality is what makes you, you. It is what you do with yourself rather than merely what happens to you. When we talk about personality, we must come to a clear understanding of the term *self*. "Who am I?" is the unanswered question that pursues all of us throughout life.

Development	Each of us is continuously developing a self. The self is learned
of Concept of Self [2]	from others. While the qualities of one's self are shaped extensively in infancy and early childhood, most

individuals retain enough plasticity so that the self continues to be shaped,

---

[1] M. F. Ashley Montagu, *The Direction of Human Development* (New York: Harper and Brothers, 1955).

[2] This chapter contains some difficult concepts. It requires careful reading and supplementing from additional sources.

and to some degree, changed throughout life. Chances are that the shaping and changing are in the direction of and in harmony with the patterns set down during the first few years of life. Let us then examine the influences on the newborn infant as he begins his life work of developing a self, of becoming a personality.

Influence of the Body

The child's body sets certain limitations for self-development. He is a boy or she is a girl. Genetic factors establish different thresholds for responding. One child may respond more quickly and intently to motor stimuli while another's sensory responses may be more acute. These differences are noted almost from birth. Some babies are far more active than others. Some sparkle, others glow. Some sleep almost constantly, while others tend to be wakeful. Some seem much more irritable than others. In Shirley's longitudinal study of twenty-five infants,[3] she observed that these infants had distinguishable personalities from birth and that the personality remained consistent up to three years after birth. These same children were studied at sixteen years of age by Neilon [4] and were found to have maintained a high degree of consistency in their personalities.

At the moment of conception, patterns and limitations of physical development are determined. What the individual is to do with his body within the confines of its limitations is determined by the vast variety of cultural influences he experiences and by his physical and psychic vitality. He comes to accept the fact that he is a short person, or a poorly coordinated person, or one inclined toward irritability, or a curly-haired person, or a person with a dark skin. How he feels about these characteristics and what he does about them are the significant factors in the development of the personality. These feelings and doings about our unique characteristics develop from our associations; they come from the *people* with whom we interact.

---

[3] M. M. Shirley, *The First Two Years: A Study of Twenty-Five Babies, Vol. III, Personality Manifestations.* Institute of Child Welfare Monograph Series, No. 8 (Minneapolis: University of Minnesota Press, 1933), pp. 72-73, 576-577.

[4] P. Neilon, "A Personality Follow-Up of Shirley's Twenty-Five Babies" (master's thesis, University of Minnesota, 1946).

Influence of One's Family

Let us return now to the father gazing at his newborn child. What do he and mother see when they look at their child? This is perhaps the most important question we can ask as we trace the development of human personality. The child builds his images of himself from the pictures of those with whom he grows. As he seeks food, warmth, and relief, he is learning the feel of love; and he learns to love those who care for him. Or he may learn the feel of neglect, of harshness, and feel the lack of love. He becomes then a lack-love baby. The Rene Spitz [5] and other films [6] vividly portray the effects of lack of love upon infants.

For nearly every infant the feel of the world into which he has been thrust comes from his parents. The kinds of feelings that parents have about themselves and about each other are communicated to an infant. So we say that some school-age children reflect growing in a secure world. This means that as these children grow, they feel that they are loved and wanted, that they have a place. They are secure. Lois Murphy reports: "... in instances in which mothers expressed happiness and joy in having a baby, and reported that the baby was more fun than they had imagined possible, the preschool child was free and open in his emotional responses, able to express his problems in one way or another and to handle his tensions." [7]

The parents' feelings toward the baby make up his emotional climate. Their true feelings may be masked by a veneer of social acceptability. We remember a model who resented the intrusion of a baby upon her professional career. She used the verbal language of love and acceptance in caring for her child, but the more powerful feeling-language quickly and irrevocably communicated to the child her conflict, rejection, and resentment of him. He grew into a confused child because his emotional environment was ambivalent.

Parents are often unaware of their deeper feelings. Many authorities believe these feelings are communicated to the baby and have effects upon

---

[5] Rene A. Spitz, *Grief* and *Genesis of Emotions* (Film Studies of the Psychoanalytic Research Project on Problems in Infancy Series). Each is a 30 min., silent film, distributed by New York University Film Library.

[6] Jenny Aubry and Genevieve Appell, *Maternal Deprivation in Young Children*, 30 min., sound, distributed by New York University Film Library.

[7] Lois Barclay Murphy and Associates, *Personality in Young Children* (New York: Basic Books, Inc., 1956), pp. xv-xvi.

his personality. The parent's overt self may be solicitous and over-protective; his covert self may be poorly-organized, frightened, and immature.

Thus far we have talked about the baby's body and about the parents' feelings toward themselves, toward the baby, and toward each other as the determining factors in the growth of the baby's personality.

Influence of Child-Rearing Practices

The feelings that the parents have about their child make a difference in the way they handle him. Debates about parental discipline of children have been long and heated but seldom have they changed any opinions or unearthed conclusive evidence. Most scientific studies support the thesis that children reared in more permissive homes are healthier personalities than those from homes which practice strict discipline.

A recent study by Watson [8] analyzed a rigorously selected sample of children from "child-centered, permissive homes" with a comparable sample of children from strict homes on nine dimensions of personality:

Overt Behavior

Independence—Dependence
Socialization—Ego-centrism
Persistence—Easy discouragement
Self-control—Disintegration
Energy—Passivity
Creativity—Stereotyping

Inner Feelings

Friendliness—Hostility
Security—Anxiety
Happiness—Sadness

The children from permissive homes were significantly more healthy on four of these nine dimensions (independence, socialization, friendliness, and creativity). On three of the dimensions (self-control, security, and happiness), no differences were discerned between the two groups of children. On the dimension of energy, the psychological testing revealed no differences, but teachers rated those from strict homes as being more

---

[8] Goodwin Watson, "Some Personality Differences in Children Related to Strict or Permissive Parental Discipline," *The Journal of Psychology*, 44, 1957, pp. 227-249. This study was made in 1956 in Westchester County, New York. The sample included 78 children.

energetic. On persistence, teachers rated no differences but psychological testing revealed that the children from strict homes fell into one of two extreme categories—unusually persistent or easily discouraged. Children from permissive homes maintained a better quality of intellectual activity in the face of frustration.

Chess is now in the midst of a longitudinal study of eighty-five children to determine if reaction patterns observed in very young babies remain stable throughout childhood and adolescence and if individual reaction patterns are intrinsic or experientially determined. She states: "Our consistent finding has been that the response of the child to the parental approach in various areas and at different ages has been determined, not only by the attitude and behavior of the parent, but also by its own specific reaction pattern." [9] In her discussion of the study, she indicates her hunch is that reaction patterns are but slightly related to child-rearing practices. Her study has not extended long enough to draw definite conclusions from it. This is another study, it seems to us, that illustrates the difficulty in attributing behavior to a single cause. It is our belief that the way one *uses* his individual reaction patterns is markedly affected by child-rearing practices.

Personality as Intentional Dispositions

Allport extends our thinking about the structuring of personality by proposing the concept that "the most comprehensive units in personality are broad intentional dispositions, future-pointed. These characteristics are unique for each person, and tend to attract, guide, inhibit the more elementary units to accord with the major intentions themselves." [10] He defines intentional characteristics as "the individual's primary mode of addressing himself to the future. As such they select stimuli, guide inhibitions and choices and have much to do with the process of becoming." [11] This quality of "future-pointing" leads one to the concept that the personality is always *becoming*. The self is never finished.

[9] Stella Chess and Alexander Thomas, "Characteristics of the Individual Child's Behavioral Responses to the Environment" (mimeographed statement, 1958).

[10] Gordon W. Allport, *Becoming* (New Haven: Yale University Press, 1955). p. 92.

[11] *Ibid.*, p. 89.

"Personality is not what one has, but rather the projected outcome of his growth." [12] As a growing, becoming structure, one's self has *power* because it is unfinished. It is moving, pushing, forming, and reforming. The intentional dispositions of personality act as a compass to set the directions in which the self is continuously shaping itself; they help to keep the individual on his own course.

Self-Realization a Basic Motive

Many psychologists agree that the basic motive in life is the maintenance of one's self. This is called self-realization by some, self-actualization by others, self-consistency by still others. The human organism will not violate its own integrity. The dominating purpose of all life seems to be the fulfillment of one's self. Why does Hillary's [13] self find it necessary to engage in dangerous exploration while Salk's [14] self seeks the quiet intensity of the laboratory? This book will not answer that question, but it is one worthy of your contemplation.

Others' Perceptions of Us a Factor

Man is the only creature who can talk to himself or who can have an attitude toward himself. This attitude is a composite of his interpersonal relationships. As a baby grows, he sees himself as the center of his universe. All within his grasp is his. He reaches out and grabs a toy, "Mine! Mine!" Mother speaks to him as she snatches away a sharp instrument, "Bad boy! Aren't you ashamed of yourself?" and the baby's perceptions of what others see in him are in the process of forming. Let's see how this works.

A child who has had polio, for example, and who has learned by the subtle nudges of his culture that he can't do things other children can do, finds it difficult to accept himself as an equal participant in life. He may hesitate to take part in the many gang activities of growing boys, to let himself get interested in girls, to engage in sports, to drive a car. In contrast to this Marcia, who has no nerves in the bottom of her feet, is learning to ice skate. When her aunt inquired how she was getting along, she

[12] *Ibid.*, p. 90.
[13] Sir Edmund Hillary, English mountain climber, who was the first man to scale the highest peak of The Himalaya, Mt. Everest.
[14] Jonas Salk, scientist who developed vaccine for poliomyelitis.

replied, "When I have someone on either side of me, I can skate as well as anybody."

Jim grew up in a home in which things were more important than people. As a toddler, he was often punished for intruding upon the place that was granted to things in his parents' value scheme. He had his hands slapped for breaking a bit of costly chinaware; he was always dressed in "good" clothes and scolded if he got them soiled or torn. He was told repeatedly not to get dirty, not to touch, to be a good boy, to make his mother proud of him. So he would not "mess up" the house he was kept in a playpen until he was three. You fill in the rest of the details. The pictures that Jim was developing of himself during this time were unconsciously, and at times consciously: "I'm a nuisance; I don't count. I'm a bad boy; I get in the way. Clothes, rugs, toys, and pictures are more important than what I want to do." Once a person has firmly established and organized into a structure these perceptions of himself, they serve as a screen to block out later perceptions that experience brings to him.

Our concepts of our "selves" are frequently vague, and we seldom know their sources. We never see our "real" self. We know how others see us only through clues they give us, the ways they behave toward us, and the ways they accept us. At best we get a partsome and distorted picture.

Development of One's Perceptions of Others

As a child matures and learns, he perceives that he is apart from the rest of his world, that those "others" out there have pictures of him which are communicated to him through feelings. He also learns that his feelings have an effect upon the "others." If he cries, mother runs. In this process, associations are established which give the child's world a uniquely peculiar flavor that is all his own. No two of us see the world

137

outside ourselves in the same way. This aloneness of the individual is a major theme of literature both today and in the past. Man's journey through life is always to some degree a lonely journey, and it is always a search for fuller realization of social relationships. If one is blocked in realizing himself, distortions and maladjustments occur. Adler says:

> It is always the want of social feeling, whatever be the name one gives it —living in fellowship, co-operation, humanity, or even the ideal-ego—which causes an insufficient preparation for all the problems of life. In the presence of a problem this imperfect preparation gives rise to the thousandfold forms that express physical and mental inferiority and insecurity.[15]

The Phenomenal Self

A further step in the formation and interpretation of perceptions is identifying with the perceptions of others and incorporating them within one's own self. To illustrate, a belittling remark about an individual's family becomes an insult to him. His family is a part of him and is, therefore, a part of his self-concept. Syngg and Combs call this the "phenomenal self" and describe it as including "all those parts of the phenomenal field which the individual experiences as part or characteristic of himself." [16] The phenomenal self includes—in addition to all the *vital* perceptions that the individual identifies as himself, the self-concept—*all* the perceptions the individual holds about himself regardless of their importance or clarity to him. We may see ourselves as responding to the cause of the underdog. This is a part of the phenomenal self. We may see ourselves as finicky about our food. This also is a part of the phenomenal self. Each one of us has a host of perceptions about himself that, when organized into a gestalt (a whole), become his phenomenal self.

The phenomenal self develops through the process of growing up with other human beings who influence our behavior. The phenomenal self is particularly powerful in those areas of behavior that have significance for the individual. The phenomenal self is relatively stable. It has an inner consistency which reflects the values of one's private world. It changes and develops as the individual grows, but the changes tend to be in directions harmonious with the organization and structure of the

---

[15] Alfred Adler, *Social Interest: A Challenge to Mankind* (New York: G. P. Putnam's Sons, 1938), p. 110.

[16] Donald Snygg and A. W. Combs, *Individual Behavior* (New York: Harper and Brothers, 1949), p. 58.

self. Unless an abrupt and powerful happening intervenes, changes in the self are generally the emergence of latent or nascent qualities. While it sometimes appears to adults that some adolescents create different selves as they grow into maturity, chances are that the process is one of releasing the latent qualities which have been hidden or unnoticed prior to adolescence. Changes caused by nascent qualities are ones that could be predicted if we understood enough about psychosomatic functioning.

Cultural Components

Many of our perceptions are culturally oriented. We shall give just a few examples. The Japanese culture places great value on cleanliness and precision. Their pictures of self are reflected in the art, drama, and dance of Japan as well as in the self-concepts of the Japanese people. After studying forty-seven cultures, Whiting and Child found that no culture studied was less permissive with children than that of the American middle-class family.[17] What effect this lack of permissiveness has upon inner hostility and anxiety is a matter for serious study. The importance of time and success are two themes of the American culture that affect our self-concepts. These and other dominant themes in our culture are discussed in Chapter 5.

The manner in which cultural pressures harmonize or conflict with the inner growth pattern of individuals is an aspect of personality development that needs further study. Many cultures give a child until puberty to establish self-concepts without much curtailment of freedom.[18] By placing so much emphasis upon time and upon earliness the American culture may be damaging the personality by arresting the inner growth pattern.

In growing, human beings seem to go through cycles of rapid growth, followed by periods of leveling off when learnings tend to become organized and consolidated. If the culture places unusual stress upon the individual at the time his growth is consuming most of his energy, we get out-of-focus behavior. The pre-adolescent period is an example of this disharmony. At the very time when the individual must meet a host of growth problems, our culture frequently says to him, "We shall place you in a big school where no one really knows you, and ask you to decide

---

[17] J. W. M. Whiting and I. L. Child, *Child Training and Personality* (New Haven: Yale University Press, 1953).

[18] Kenneth Soddy, ed., *Mental Health and Infant Development*, Vol. I (New York: Basic Books, Inc., 1956).

now whether you want to be a mechanic or a scientist for the rest of your life."

Perceptions

Create

One's Environment

Folk wisdom states, "You get out of life what you bring to it." We see the deeper meaning of this as we study the ways self-perception changes the environment. An outgoing, friendly person attracts friends, and so lives in a more friendly environment than one who rejects people. Each person's environment is what *he* perceives it to be. His perceptions of his environment tend to make it, in fact, the way he thinks it is. A world federalist's view of a large item for foreign aid in the national budget is quite different from an isolationist's view. A teacher who perceives that children should be seen and not heard lives in a different classroom world from the teacher next door who encourages active discussion. The first teacher's feelings about talking are quite likely to create a high level of hostility within his classroom.

Perceptions Affect Roles

Up to this point we have been discussing perceptions in a generalized way. Now we want to relate our perceptions to the roles we assume throughout life. An overworked truism is that man is a role-playing animal. An individual becomes more aware of this if he becomes conscious of the conversations he has with himself when he is trying to come to a decision. Let's suppose your term paper is due today and you do not have it completed. You probably have many imaginary conversations between yourself and your professor explaining the predicament you are in. As you engage in these conversations, you assign yourself and your professor a variety of roles. You try these out until you finally decide what to do and what to say. Of all the roles you might assign yourself, however, you select only a few from which to choose. Why? The other roles are ones you do not perceive yourself taking because they are not compatible with the pictures you have of yourself, with the pictures you think others have of you, or with the statuses and feelings involved in the situation. The first two alternatives have been discussed. Let's examine the way status and feelings function in the roles we play.

If you feel the professor has genuine affection for you and some understanding of your problem, you may take a role of the professor's friend. You simply tell him your need for more time; you assume that the professor will see your plight and cooperate. If you have feelings about your own inadequacy in the course and have developed some pictures in your head of the professor's aloofness and strictness, you may take a role of a special interest pleader. You devise a "trumped-up" excuse and expect the professor to accept the excuse as valid. Remember, this is the same professor we are discussing. Each student in the class has assigned a slightly different role to the professor—not so much because of his experiences with *this* professor, but because of his own perceptions of himself in relation to *all* professors. Professors spell status and authority to the student who has formed perceptions about these concepts from all the relationships he has had with adults. The student's perceptions will not be changed overnight by finding one adult who doesn't fit the composite picture in his mind.

To carry our illustration a step farther, let's suppose the student has assigned the professor the role of an authoritarian tyrant. Because the student feels this way, he acts as if the professor were a tyrant. This behavior makes it much easier for the professor to assume an authoritarian air and actually to some degree play the role that the student has assigned to him. Recently a student remarked to his professor, "You are defensive with me." The professor had just listened to a long tirade from the student about "succeeding in spite of you (the professor)". The professor realized that at the time he *was* defensive with this student. He had accepted the role the student had assigned to him. How dramatically we see the "bad boys" in a school living up to the roles the school has given them, or the "giggly adolescent girls," or the "teacher's pets"!

Let us summarize. Our conceptions of status and authority are central to the pictures we have of our roles. As teachers of children and youth, we must form healthy concepts of status and authority in our own minds so that we may help those we teach develop them, too.

The manner in which we carry out roles is ascribed by the culture. Many popular sayings and routine actions reflect this. "The play must go on," says to the actor that he must not allow his personal life to step upon the stage. "The customer is always right," says to the saleslady that she must not argue if used merchandise is returned. The doctor leaves his telephone number wherever he goes. "The woman always has the last word," or "A woman has the right to change her mind," indicate the ways in which sex roles have been defined by culture.

A generation ago much was written about the extrovert and the introvert. Extroversion was associated with maleness and was defined as a general tendency toward outgoingness; introversion was associated with femaleness and was considered a turning in. Today we realize that this classification of personality types is too simple to be of much value. All of us are part introvert and part extrovert; some situations elicit responses predominantly of one type, other situations result in responses of another type. The most introverted female may turn into an extrovert if her own self is threatened. Recently in New York City much amusement resulted from a group of mothers thwarting a city planner's designs to turn a playground into a parking lot by placing their baby buggies in front of the bull-dozer and standing guard until the bull-dozer was taken away.

Sometimes today we speak of the free personality as being on one end of a continuum as contrasted with the inhibited personality on the other; or we note that the aggressive personality is at the opposite end from the withdrawn or submissive personality. These labels are generalized descriptions only. They really do not help us know an individual in a functional way. The farther we go toward the extremes, the more variations we find in the specific category under consideration. There are more apparent differences, for example, among withdrawn individuals than among the same number of personalities that might be labeled well-adjusted.

Scott is a withdrawn boy. He can be found aimlessly doodling or just sitting most of the time. He is confused in his feelings about his parents. His mother hovers over him intermittently and then seems to forget he's around for long periods. He seldom sees his father and when the father does appear for a short time, Scott is confused by the feelings he senses in his home. Nothing in school interests him. He spends a lot of time daydreaming. He can be found just wandering around by himself almost any afternoon after school.

Sam also would be labeled "withdrawn" by most observers. He seems unconcerned with those around him. He is usually unchosen when the class is asked to select individuals with whom they would like to work. He reads a great deal, has a consuming interest in machines. His parents are quiet people. He feels secure in his world. His parents love him and respect his individuality. He understands what things are important to him and he is able to secure enough of these ingredients to give him a feeling of worth and a sense of direction. Are these two boys alike? Obviously not.

Life-Style a Useful Concept

Personality is too dynamic to be classified into types that have much meaning. A more useful concept is that each of us has a *life-style* which is unique to him. One's life-style develops much of its uniqueness from the things he is vitally concerned about. Allport believes that one of the capacities most urgent in the human is *individuation*, which he defines as "the formation of an individual style of life that is self-aware, self-critical, and self-enhancing." [19] In the process of becoming, each of us is constantly pushing toward his own individual self-realization. In the early years the life-style of the individual begins to take shape as the person endeavors to establish a firm sense of security. To the degree that he succeeds in gaining security, the human being is free to grow. If he becomes blocked in this process, to the degree that he is insecure, his growth is impeded. His sense of being at home in his world, of trusting those around him is of utmost importance in his development. You can identify quickly some familiar life-styles of our real and fictional heritage. Uriah Heap has become a symbol for the fawning person, Quisling for the treacherous one, Pollyanna for the unwavering optimist, Buffalo Bill for the adventurer, Will Rogers for one who is wise and possesses easy, bubbling humor.

Is the life-style learned or is it native? It is both. Each of us accepts certain parts of his culture as vital concerns to the self, because he has

[19] Gordon Allport, *Becoming* (New Haven: Yale University Press, 1955), p. 28.

lived in this culture and not another. But we are selective. The selective process is related to "what we have to *select with*" as well as "what there is to *select from*." A child peculiarly sensitive to sound may take things related to sound from his culture and incorporate them into his self as vital concerns that another neglects. His life-style may be pointing toward a life's work in electronics as applied to high frequencies utilized in modern communication. All that we have discussed in this chapter in terms of our self-perceptions, the ways others see us, the feelings generated by our perceptions and those of others, the kind of folks we have, the kind of bodies we have, the effects of the culture, and our perceptions of roles are interrelated in the forming of our life-style. While each of us has many facets to his personality and functions in varying ways depending upon his perceptions of a situation, each is unique. This uniqueness is what gives to each his personality.

Significant Personality Deviations

We have discussed the uniqueness of personality. Indeed, an individual's personality is his own, and a dynamic democracy values uniqueness of the individual. This value is expressed in the social context by finding useful functions for the individual's uniqueness. Society tends to establish norms and in so doing sanctions certain behaviors and condemns some others. Societies vary tremendously in what is accepted and valued as normal behavior. The simpering modesty of the Victorian Age is not valued today and individuals adopting such conduct might be ridiculed. The degree of withdrawal required of a Buddhist monk is considered abnormal in our culture. The interplay between men and women accepted in American culture is taboo in many others. Many countries openly accept a double standard between men and women while our culture pretends a single standard and has built this pretense into its legal structure. Each culture, then, establishes its own norms which change from period to period, but which tend to *change slowly* and to have inner consistency. Those considered abnormal deviate so markedly that they present a hazard to the continuance of the culture and require individual treatment.

Causes for Personality Deviation

Something within the individual which places him out of communication with his culture results in personality deviation. The *mental defective* may be so unable to communicate as to find it impossible to carry out his life functions with safety. In such cases, institutional care has to be provided. The *emotional defective* may live in a fantasy world that has little resemblance to reality. He is in communication with *his* world but it is a world that is unknown to others. He, too, must be cared for institutionally.

Other deviations are less extreme. Our society does not sanction the prostitute, but we seldom institutionalize her. Any serious violation of a group norm, such as robbery, assault, or drunkenness, is punishable by laws established to encourage people to accept the norms of the group. Some interesting struggles have taken place as vigorously motivated individuals have sought to change group norms. The fight of the suffragettes to bring the vote to women was one such struggle. Today we are watching the norms of one section of the United States changing as integrated schools become an accepted pattern. This process is creating personality adjustments and maladjustments on the part of millions of people. As a result of a legal mandate to integrate public schools, some individuals are making tremendous growth toward the life-style that they have been pointing toward up to this time; others are finding their growth impeded by lack of intentional dispositions in this direction. The healthy personality is one that can meet new situations as they arise and work with them creatively, so that warping and stunting of the capacity to grow is avoided. Sudden changes, too much uprooting (especially during the early years), and traumatic experiences may produce deviations so marked as to be labeled abnormal by society.

| **How to Study Personality** | No one method or approach is adequate in studying personality. Since personality has cultural, social, physiological, psychological, and genetic components, the dynamics of all these influences must be explored as one tries to gain insight |

into the motivations of another human being. This we call a multidimensional approach. In this approach we are not concerned with trying to measure the relative strength of each of these components. Rather our goal is to examine how all of these interdependencies are related to create the uniqueness which is identifiable as a human being, different from all others. In applying the multi-dimensional approach to the study of personality, we shall now enumerate and briefly describe a number of processes that are discussed more fully in later chapters.

Self-Understanding a Key Dimension

The teacher who hopes to understand those he teaches must have an awareness of himself—his own wishes, fears, blind spots, and expectations. He must have some sense of how others perceive him. He must be developing continuously his own self-awareness and self-realization. This concept is developed more fully in Chapter 16.

Understanding Individual's Life-Space

A teacher who has some self-awareness and a feeling of its importance in his teaching is in a position to acquire some tools for studying the personalities of those he teaches. The first tool is that of gaining as complete a picture as possible of the young human's life-space as seen through his eyes. By life-space we mean the following: (1) the actual physical dimensions of the pupil's daily life; (2) the constellation of forces that are significant in his life; (3) the feelings he has about himself and those whom he includes in his life-space.

PHYSICAL DIMENSIONS OF LIFE-SPACE. Each individual has a daily life-space composed of thousands of details. The over-all effects of his life-space upon the individual require study. One way for the teacher to assess these effects is actually to travel the life-space of the pupil, asking himself as he does so, "What are the probable feelings that this pupil has as he travels over this area?" Variations in life-space are tremendous. Manuel may live in a rural area. He walks to school along a country lane, breathing fresh, clean air; seeing a profusion of blossoms; receiving the friendly greetings of numerous adults and children. Marjorie passes a number of saloons on her way to school. She sees carousers staggering home along streets lined with foul-smelling garbage cans. She fears the greetings of those she meets, especially if she is becoming an attractive young woman. Jack walks along a block in which *Keep Off the Grass* signs are posted in each lawn. Along the way he picks up his buddies who, like him, have been carefully trained where to walk and in what company. Judy, age ten and the only girl in a block, walks to school alone. She watches from a distance the group of boys accumulating on the way to school. And so it goes! Try traversing the life-space of some of the boys and girls you know, and see what is added to your understanding of them.

CONSTELLATION OF LIFE FORCES. Knowing the physical dimensions of a pupil's life means little unless we also know something about the significance of these forces. We usually assume that his own family is important to the pupil. At certain periods of development the neighbor next door may be as dynamic a force. Some of the forces that yield relevant data to the teacher are: family patterns and structures, relatives, play groups, social-class status, race, religion, school pressures, and expectations.

The *family,* of course, constitutes the most likely potent force in the individual's life. Some of the phases of family life that teachers find it helpful to understand are these:

Does the family have two parents living in the home? Is the relationship between mother and father a reasonably healthy one?

What is the birth order of this child? Is he the oldest, youngest, middle child, one of many, an only child? How does this matter to him?

What is the sex distribution of children?

Are there other adults living in the family?

What is the space arrangement for the family?

Does the child seem to be reared on a short-leash, a freer leash, in an indifferent climate?

What activities, if any, does the family participate in as a group? Does the family have fun together? How?

How does the family respond to routines?

Are there any unusual features not common to families in general, such as: chronic illness of a member, handicapped sibling, well-known member famous for either socially approved or disapproved reasons?

Relatives often are a powerful force in the life-space of children and youth. Many of us recall the influence of a grandparent, aunt or uncle, or cousin. Certain nationality groups have family ties that extend to the relatives in such a strong affectional way that the relatives are considered almost a part of the family group. TV comic, Sam Levenson, whose "Cousin's Club" meets regularly once a month, although it numbers forty or fifty people, is an illustration of this kind of feeling. Children from Jewish, Italian, or Puerto Rican families are likely to have unusually strong affectional bonds with their relatives. Lack of relatives may be a force in the individual's life also. A young human who has never known a grandparent, or who has few, if any, close relatives, has a life-space quite different from one who has ready access to a number of cooky jars after school or the emphatic ear of an understanding, but not-so-closely-involved aunt or uncle.

The *play groups* in which an individual grows up are forces in his life-space that require serious and careful study as one tries to understand another. Some points to consider are:

Does the child or youth have play groups in his neighborhood? Are there other "kids" who live in his block or within walking distance? Is he accepted by the play groups of his neighborhood? If so, what roles does he play in these groups? If not, can you assess why he is not accepted?

What are the play groups like? Are the others about his own age, or are they varied in age? Are the groups predominantly of his sex or the opposite sex, or mixed? Has he had lifelong membership in the play groups; or did he come in after their mores were well-established?

How varied are the play groups? Do they include members of different races, religions, social-class status groups, differing social, political, and economic attitudes?

Social-class status factors as they relate to the family's position in the neighborhood and the children's positions in their peer groups are dynamic forces in one's life-space. A boy or girl whose parents are perceived by most of the children as being of lower social-class status than the majority often comes to see himself as inferior, less well-accepted, and in turn less accepting. On the other hand, the youngster whose parents own half the town may be perceived as a snob, a sissy, or an "aloner."

Since the majority of teachers are from the middle social class, we tend to assume that all our pupils have our values, our manners, and customs. When we encounter pupils of a lower social-class status for the first time, our tendency is to reject them. We do not understand their values. We do not approve of their language. We are sometimes shocked, sometimes incensed, by the kind of language and behavior the children bring to school with them. The language used by these children is not meant to offend the teacher, nor is it perceived by the children as unacceptable language. It is just what they have heard all their lives. A great deal of acculturation is necessary to change one's language. Even with most careful tutoring, moments of stress will elicit a return to one's familiar way of speaking. You recall George Bernard Shaw's famous play, *Pygmalion*, converted by Lerner and Loewe to the Broadway hit, *My Fair Lady*, which has some very amusing examples of language reversion.

The teacher, too, considers that a child from a home with fewer advantages in the way of learning tools (books, magazines, music, pictures, games, toys) is likely to take more time in acquiring some of the academic skills expected at any given age.

Race and religion are factors that operate in a way similar to social-class status. They are significant only if they encourage the individual to develop feelings about himself and his folks that are blocks to his own mental health. The teacher who is searching for explanations notes if race or religion may be factors that are causing the individual concern.

School pressures and expectations often turn out to be blocks to the full development of a human being. Many youngsters get along superbly everywhere but in school. The child's personality must be studied as a whole, not just the special part of it that he reveals during school hours.

FEELINGS ABOUT ONESELF. All that we have said about life-space is meaningless unless we know how the individual himself perceives his own life-space and how he feels about what he sees. The physical dimensions of the life-space of two chronic invalids in a hospital ward may be quite similar. One, however, is an eternal griper while the other perceives the daily events in a humorous way.

As we study the life-space of an individual, our major focus is, "How does _____ see this? Is this a source of annoyance, a source of pleasure, or does he perceive it at all? How intense and enduring are his feelings about this? Manuel, who walks to school in an idyllic setting, may be so angry or resentful that he sees neither birds nor flowers, and does not feel the tang of spring in the air; whereas Marjorie may see the garbage-can world she walks among as an exciting adventure. One child living in such an environment wrote of the beauty of the iridescent colors made by a few drops of oil on a dirty puddle of water! The teacher who perceives this quality of feeling in his pupils has the means for understanding them. With this understanding, the details of the physical dimensions and the cluster of forces in each life serve as fascinating bits of the personality mosaic.

Understanding of Individual's Life Crises

Another phase of a child's life that often illuminates his personality is the crises that he has met. Each life has many hazards. Knowing how these hazards are met and what kinds of *traces* they have left in the individual is important for a teacher. In the physical realm, we examine illnesses. When did the illnesses occur? How severe were they? Did they require hospitalization? Did they leave impairments? How were the illnesses related to other strong experiences in the child's life? In the emotional realm, we examine parent-child ties, sibling relationships, and adult-child ties. Has the child suddenly been deprived of a parent by a death or divorce in the family? Does the child feel he has a place all his own in the family? Does he feel any unfavorable comparison between himself and a sibling? Does the child feel closer to one parent than another? Has he been uprooted from his home and his playmates frequently? Has any traumatic experience such as fire, violence, or accident left its mark upon him?

Play a Source of Understanding

Each of us expresses his real self most completely when he is in situations that he structures. These are *play* situations and, as we are using the word, play is applicable to all ages. Chapter 15 discusses play and its contribution as a tool in understanding children and youth. An understanding of the meaning of play and the creative processes is a rich source for knowing human beings—young and old.

Signs of a Healthy Personality

Let's see if we can summarize our thinking by drawing some guide lines for a healthy personality. You recall the discussion of vitamins of personality in Chapter 2. As each individual expresses his unique personality, he is felt in more or less positive, constructive ways. The teacher's primary role is to help each pupil to realize most fully himself, that which has significance for him. As we work with our pupils toward self-realization, we accept certain criteria as the marks of mature, socially useful individuals. What are the criteria?

A healthy personality is one that is coming to terms with authority. Developing constructive feelings about authority is a lifelong task for most of us. We are healthy if we recognize our own particular problems in relation to authority and if we are working to resolve them. A healthy attitude toward authority is capsulized in the folk saying: "Great men never feel great; small men never feel small."

A person having a healthy personality is able to accept himself, to admit his shortcomings and his strengths. Sometimes we call this security. We are growing toward greater maturity as we grow toward greater and greater security. This implies the ability to carry on honest self-criticism. Only by changing our pictures of ourselves can we grow.

We visualize a healthy personality as growing in certain social directions along a continuum. Certainly a personality that is not growing is no longer healthy, regardless of how far growth extended before it ceased. We see the process as follows:

Dependence _____	Independence
Inadequacy _____	Adequacy
Insecurity _____	Security
Ego-centeredness _____	Altruism
Competitiveness _____	Cooperativeness

Summary

This chapter has presented some of the personality theories that have wide acceptance today. Hall and Lindzey [20] state that most personality theories conceive of man as a purposive creature who functions as a total organism (known as holism); that the self-concept has a prominent role in most theories; that the psychological environment (or how man sees his environment) is held to be significant in most theories; and that there is a growing tendency to give explicit attention to group membership determinants. You will recognize these as aspects we have discussed.

---

[20] Calvin S. Hall and Gardner Lindzey, *Theories of Personality* (New York: John Wiley and Sons, Inc., 1957).

We have not presented a history of personality theory nor tried to identify the many existing schools of thought. Some theories have been omitted because they are not consistent with the general orientation of this book. They tend to be less well-supported by psychologists, which is not to say that they are useless theories. Time may prove them to be more fruitful ways to view mankind than the prevailing concepts which we have discussed. Other aspects of personality have been barely mentioned. We say little about unconscious motivation, for example. Since the functioning of unconscious motivation is assumed throughout the book, we felt that a better way to use the space was to discuss the areas included. Some excellent sources, which have been published during the past few years, are listed at the end of this chapter. Your study of some of the original sources as well as the compilations of materials about personality theory will help you fill in the gaps in this presentation.

Suggestions for Further Exploration

▶ Think back about what kind of baby you were by recalling discussions your family has had of your childhood. Do you see certain continuities in your personality?

▶ Study the behavior of your college classroom group. See if you can identify some roles that students have assigned the professor and each other. Can you discern what roles are assigned to you or perceived by your classmates as ones that you assume?

▶ Try to discover the various roles the boy or girl whom you are studying assigns to the adults in his life: his parents, you, his teachers, his club leader, the policeman, the minister, his relatives.

▶ Write a paragraph describing the personality of the youngster you are studying. Include what you think his self-concept is, his phenomenal self, his perceptions of others. Discuss your thoughts with some of your classmates.

▶ Try to make a thorough investigation of the life-space and life crises of the youngster you are studying. What do these portend for the becoming personality?

▶ Many excellent films have been produced to help in the study of personality. If possible, view some of the following, which are only a few of those available:

Angry Boy, 33 min., sound, Mental Health Film Board.
   This film shows the help available through a guidance clinic for a boy whose hidden hostility is expressed through stealing.

Feelings of Hostility (Mental Mechanisms Series), 27 min., sound, National Film Board of Canada.

The story of Clare is traced from childhood to young adulthood. Her determination to succeed through her intellectual capacity is traced to the hurts experienced as a child which made giving and receiving love difficult.

Feelings of Rejection (Mental Mechanisms Series), 23 min., sound, National Film Board of Canada.

The story of a young woman who has learned to be dependent upon her parents. Briefly shows therapy methods that are used in helping her face her problem.

Shyness, 23 min., sound, National Film Board of Canada.

Excellent for showing great differences among shy people. Tells story of three shy children.

This Is Robert (Studies of Normal Personality Development Series), 80 min., sound. Distributed by New York University Film Library.

A longitudinal study of a child from two to seven. An aggressive, difficult child learns how to handle his problems more effectively with wise guidance at home and school. Excellent to show development in personality characteristics over a period of years.

Additional Sources You May Find Helpful

Gordon W. Allport, *Becoming*. New Haven: Yale University Press, 1955.

An important summation of the thinking of a wise man who has studied personality most extensively. This is a thin book which many people find they want in their personal libraries so they may go to it again and again. A lucid and meaningful treatment of life-style.

Henry P. David and Helmut von Bracken, eds., *Perspectives in Personality Theory*. New York: Basic Books, Inc., 1957.

This book which includes papers from nine different countries grew out of a symposium held in Montreal by the Fourteenth International Congress of Psychology. The thinking of the European and American psychologists about personality theory is well presented.

Calvin S. Hall and Gardner Lindzey, *Theories of Personality*. New York: John Wiley and Sons, Inc., 1957.

This book is unique in that it is the first source book that makes a survey of existing theories of personality. The first and last chapters help to unify the book. The first chapter gives the reader the attributes to look for in personality theory and the last chapter summarizes the degree of agreement about these attributes.

Arthur T. Jersild, *Child Psychology*, 4th ed. Englewood Cliffs, N. J.: Prentice-Hall, Inc., 1954.

In the foreword Dr. Jersild says, "I have taken a full leap in emphasizing the concept of the self as an essential consideration in the study of all features and phases of developmental psychology." His book is helpful in explaining the development of the self.

Kurt Lewin, *A Dynamic Theory of Personality*. New York: McGraw-Hill Book Company, Inc., 1936.

A difficult book but one that the serious student should make his own. Lewin was among the first to develop the concept of the meaning of life-space and the dynamic forces that affect our behavior.

A. H. Maslow, *Motivation and Personality*. New York: Harper and Brothers, 1954.

In this book Maslow synthesizes holistic and dynamic principles in coming to an understanding of motivation. Excellent discussion of self-actualizing people in Chapters 12 and 13.

Arnold M. Rose, ed., *Mental Health and Mental Disorder*. New York: W. W. Norton and Company, Inc., 1955.

This is an important book in the field of mental health. We especially recommend to you Section V, "The Social Psychology of Personality Organization and Disorganization." In this section you will find an excellent discussion of some of the important components of personality.

7

The Meaning of Character

We once knew a placid, undemanding, uncomplaining infant. Relatives and neighbors said, "Isn't he a good boy? He is so little trouble." A year later this child was recognized to be physically and mentally defective. At a funeral not long ago we heard someone comment upon the departed somewhat as follows: "She was such a *good* woman. She never did anything wrong." A period might have been put after *anything*. As long as anyone could remember,

this woman had rocked in her chair—indoors in the winter, on the porch in the summer—doing nothing to benefit any person, merely living on the rental from the land left her by a husband who had died in rather early middle age.

Goodness

an Active Process

For many centuries the goodness or, as some would put it, the *character* of a person has been judged by what he did not do. The inference of this chapter is that goodness must be judged by what people *do* do. Goodness is an active process. We intend to make no clear distinction between personality and character. (Someone has wisely observed that the quickest way to stop an intellectual discussion is to call for a strict definition of terms.) Perhaps it is enough to say that personality is what one really is, while character evaluates a person's behavior in terms of what his society expects of him. We shall use the term character to mean characteristic behaviors which affect other people. An individual's basic character consists of those features of his personality which now and henceforth affect the well-being of other people. Character is judged by the extent to which other people can count upon a person's behaving in given ways.

In popular and practical terms when one inquires about another's character, he is asking: "How good is this person?" A standard dictionary defines the term *good* as "satisfactory for its purpose." A good cow is one that gives nutritious milk in expected quantities. A good automobile is one that enables us to travel safely and rapidly without breakdown. A good vacation is one that comes up to our expectations. Thus, a good man is one in whom the expectations of what we wish a man to be are realized. When we speak of a *good* human, we must specify "good for what?"

To some teachers a good pupil is one who causes no confusion, follows directions precisely, raises no questions outside the scope of the lesson, and remembers what he was told and what he was assigned to learn. To other teachers a good pupil is one with an active curiosity, a resistance to being imposed upon, a determination to be helpful, and an abundance of self-respect. Librarians are unhappy with children who sing in their presence, music teachers are equally unhappy about children who do not sing.

Surely all of us agree that a social group—be it family, classroom, neighborhood, or nation—needs to expect certain kinds of behavior in its individuals and to be intolerant of other kinds of behavior. No one can behave just as he pleases, just as his creature impulses momentarily impel him to act. In present-day society, no one would live long behaving upon momentary impulse. An individual's safety, as well as the convenience and comfort of others in his environment, requires some imposed modifications in his behavior. We do not expect him to learn *by experience* not to run into a street carrying heavy traffic, nor to engage in exploratory manipulations of the automatic washing machine. Neither do we expect him to learn to stay out of the street by being tied to a post, nor to avoid the washing machine by threats of dire punishment. We build his character by helping him understand and foresee the consequences of his behavior. In the long run, we expect him to judge the goodness of his acts by contemplating what type of behavior promises the greatest good for the greatest number of people for the longest period of time.

The Goal of Character Education

Many of the readers of this volume have been reared in the doctrine of original sin, the notion that man was conceived in sin and born in iniquity, and that he becomes good by learning to shun all creature impulses. Many thoughtful people have come to a more significant interpretation of the meaning of original sin. An infant is born completely selfish; he cannot perceive, nor do we expect him to be concerned about, the well-being of other people. No one regards him to be sinful, but were he to remain that way as he grows stronger and more competent, he would become intolerably wicked. As the infant grows in perception and understanding, he can sense and foresee the effects of his behavior upon other people and upon his relationships with them; he modifies his behavior in terms of those effects. Certainly modern society cannot survive unless most people develop a high degree of concern and active responsibility for the well-being of other people everywhere, always. This is the goal of character education.

According to the Scriptures, upon which many of us were reared, one of man's early questions was, "Am I my brother's keeper?" Certainly in modern times we have become our brother's keeper, whether we know him or not. There are few people so situated that their behavior does not affect the well-being of numerous other people. Thus, we are increasingly concerned that every person be "satisfactory for his purpose." Imagine the confusion in the Empire State Building should the elevator operators pause to have another cup of coffee rather than report for duty at eight o'clock! Some years ago in the rush hour in Washington, D. C., a streetcar motorman decided that he had had enough. He set the brakes on his car on Pennsylvania Avenue and walked off across the Mall. In a few minutes the city's traffic was snarled. A school system can tolerate very few school teachers who are prone to say, "How good the bed feels. I will stay in it today and not go to school." Now and then we observe a person using his car on the highway as a thrill-toy, or as an instrument of aggression. The states have found it necessary to make laws stating that, regardless of how he feels, a person cannot drive his car above a prudent speed nor make improper turns to enjoy the scurrying of pedestrians. Those who issue drivers' licenses are beginning to see that the character of the driver is quite as important as his eyesight and mechanical dexterity.

Goodness and Conformity

To most of the people of the world, the goodness of an individual is measured by the extent to which he conforms to the ways and beliefs of the people with whom he lives. In some sections of our country marked suspicion is directed toward the person who speaks of his evening meal as "dinner." We once knew a farm community which judged its preacher to be incompetent and dismissed him because he did not know how to harness a horse—he had been reared in London. In some communities a woman who adds color to her cheeks and lips is thought to have loose morals, while in others a woman who does not do so is judged to take no pride in her femininity.

Goodness relates to circumstances of time and place. The pioneer mother might in clear conscience say to her child, "Go out and see if you can find some nuts and greens for our dinner." Imagine the plight of a child seeking to obey such admonitions from his mother in a modern city. Thoreau, whom most of us regard to be an exemplary man, today would be heavily fined for trespassing. Daniel Boone would be in jail for hunting out-of-season. In his acceptance speech after receiving the Nobel prize for literature in 1950, Bertrand Russell related that the two Estonian children he adopted during the war could not be taught to refrain from

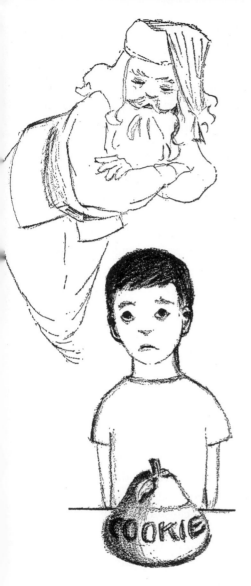

stealing potatoes from the neighbors, despite their abundance in the Russell cellar. The children had spent their early years foraging for food wherever it might be found. Good behavior is behavior appropriate to circumstances.

Anyone who has lived with an infant knows that he has, at birth, the capacity and the tendency to resist the imposition of outside force. In his splendid book, *The Envelope*,[1] Plant has defined the functioning of personality as that point of compromise between the urges of the individual and the demands of his culture. The individual with exceptional character and mental health is the one who has achieved congenial compromise between the demands of society for his conformity and his own personal impulses.

We doubt very much the wisdom of parents and teachers who say to children that some outside, unperceivable power or pair of eyes is watching to judge the goodness of what they do, whether it be the recording angel or Santa Claus. This seems to us to be taking unfair advantage of the less mature. This is a cowardly shifting of responsibility to contrived and inaccessible powers. More important, when the child grows up enough to comprehend the fictitiousness of these characters, his reasons for being good vanish. Character is based upon a sensible security in dependably productive ways of behaving: habits, routines, manners, customs, institutional codes, moral codes, laws.

---

[1] James S. Plant, *The Envelope* (New York: Commonwealth Fund, 1950).

All of us find much security in our habits. William James referred to habit formation as "man's most precious conservative agent." Our habits, our routines, our ways of behaving, require little planning and little thought, and save time, attention, and energy for creation and for adjustment. We find it quite difficult to relate to people who have no predictable ways of behaving, who follow no set schedule for meals, who go to bed and awaken at varying times each day, who appear punctually one time, hours late another. Each of us puts on the right shoe before the left one, or vice versa, and few of us know which. If we had to think and plan each time we tie our tie or wiggle into a girdle, we would have very little time for more important matters.

Teachers commonly agree that those activities in which all pupils must take part every day should be rather sharply routinized. It seems that the human organism develops habits quite apart from cultural demands. One who has been accustomed to having his dinner at six o'clock may develop ulcers if the time is changed suddenly to seven. Some travelers who, let us say, live in New York and fly to California in a few hours find themselves awakening at four o'clock in the morning, which is seven o'clock back in New York.

It is unwise to reduce to habit behavior about which one should be thoughtful. Too, it is unwise never to allow an exception to occur. One who can never stay up late or delay his dinner is a "stick" indeed. We want behavior to be sensible, appropriate to circumstances, rather than sheer habit. We seriously question the wisdom of reducing a human's behavior to a concept of orthodoxy in which one says, "Because I was born a Democrat, or a vegetarian, or a female, I must behave in this given way because 'we' have always behaved that way." Man does not live well when he views life through a rear-view mirror. Man is gifted with intelligence which enables him to take stock of situations, employ foresight, note new circumstances, and decide how to behave in terms of the situations in which he finds himself.

A goodly number of us were reared in an atmosphere in which goodness was seen as being very gloomy. It was almost an attitude of penitence. Some of us were reared in a culture which demanded that we work very hard all week and insisted that we could not work nor play on Sunday. This made sense in a pioneer culture in which there was always more work to be done than a man could do. I recall one preacher who insisted that it was immoral to laugh on Sunday. In my childish innocence, with perhaps a bit of skepticism, I asked this clergyman if the idiot boy who lived down the block and laughed all the time, on Monday and Friday as well as on Sunday, would go to hell for his transgression. He replied that the ways of the Lord were indeed most mysterious, but in terms of His law this boy must be punished for his transgressions. We have learned enough of the laws of nature to know that man probably invented the Sabbath as a time of recuperation from arduous labor. Too, we have learned that lack of occupation is not rest. In fact, modern psychology assures us that we rest only when we play.[2]

Motive

Is the Raw Material

of Character

In the long run, character is determined by one's basic motivations. Man shares with all creatures the one basic motivation: protecting his own integrity. An amoeba recoils from threats, is attracted by promise of nourishment and comfort. All animals are peculiarly equipped for warding off threat and responding favorably to promise of gratification. In man we see the basic motivation of maintaining, realizing, and extending his capacity for gratifying experiences and for avoiding threatening circumstances. Man's peculiar equipment is his brain.

Many centuries ago a wise teacher observed, "As a man thinketh in his heart, so is he." More recently Freud explained to us that the wish is the father of the thought. In the field of economics and social intercourse, Thorstein Veblen showed us that we all tend to think and to make decisions in terms of our own interests. In less dramatic terms we can say that motives are the stuff of character. If we want to know a child or any other human, we must try to discern what he is trying to accomplish— "What makes Sammy run?" Is the meticulously polite gentleman whom we encounter in our travels trying to entice us into a game of poker, using his marked cards, or does he genuinely care how we get along? Is the seven-year-old in our second grade so very "good" because he is afraid of us, because he has carefully imposed habits, or because he is sick? Is the tax collector who goes to great trouble to return to us the three cents we overpaid extremely careful in managing his affairs, or is he trying to build up a reputation for being honest in matters of small consequence to divert our attention from his phony accounts?

Man's motives and thus his character grow and change, as do all the

---

[2] J. Huizinga, *Homo Ludens* (Boston: The Beacon Press, 1955).

other aspects of his being. With his vast capacity for imagining and contriving, man builds for himself the most likely circumstances for maintaining himself. The infant seeks little beyond being comfortable and growing. He comes into the world with neither concern for nor perception of other people nor of human qualities. His character develops with the increased complexity of his nervous system and with his experiences. We do not deem it odd to hear a child of three wailing loudly because he cannot have what he wants when he wants it; nor do sensible people feel compelled to provide it for him. We do feel impelled to call the police or a psychiatrist upon hearing a full-grown man or woman screaming loudly on Main Street because someone has denied him momentary gratification. The philosopher, Thomas Hobbes, observed, "A wicked man is but a child grown strong."

We believe that the most important teaching done by parents and teachers consists of the motives they offer boys and girls for doing what they do. Children and youth must become quite confused in learning that in some circumstances they must be very considerate of how other people feel, and in others they must ignore others' feelings and try to defeat them. For example, Jerry must offer his friend first choice of the goodies at a party, but he must try to outscore him on a test at school.

Scrambled Motives Scramble Character

Little children are taught at home and at school that they must implicitly obey those whose status they recognize. They get in serious trouble ofttimes by obeying an older child who is not concerned with their good. The reader can reflect upon nations which have been admired for the ready obedience of their children and who have been repeatedly victimized by unthinking following of evil leaders. Obedience in itself is no virtue. To be able to decide wisely whom to obey is a high-level human quality.

Some children are taught that excellence is a high-level human gratification, that they must strive to be better than most people. This striving can be reduced to absurdity if a person or a group of persons is declared to be better than another without any facts to back up the declaration. This is clearly the foundation of racism, which justifies persons of one color insisting upon their superiority to persons of another color without any consideration of what either is able to do. To some, persons with one kind of schooling are deemed superior to persons with another kind of education, regardless of what they know or are able to accomplish.

It has long been a major temptation of elders in a society to subject younger members to their domination. In fact, a large part of society regards goodness as being the extent to which the young accept the rules and regulations of their elders. This is probably the result of mankind's long history of living in slavery. To those who owned and controlled other people, a good person was one who accepted domination; a bad person was one who resisted that domination. The degree of badness was measured by the effectiveness of the resistance. In the early part of this century one of the major wickednesses of a child was impudence, speaking to a grownup as the grownup spoke to him. Few sins transcended that of a child's treating an adult as the adult treated the child. A child who, being subjected to a beating, struck back was the most nefarious of sinners. This attitude still prevails extensively in child-rearing and in school keeping. This tale has been commonly retold of late, but for those who haven't heard it, it is priceless and meaningful. A father while belaboring his son with a strong strap said to him, "You know, son, I'm doing this only because I love you." The son replied, "I can hardly wait to get big enough to return your affection."

It seems to us rather obvious that mankind could have made no progress ever by complete acceptance of the domination of the elders. Character consists of what one is trying to do. If a person is simply trying to remain safe, to be free from threats or possible reprisals, he cannot grow. To us, the current popular yearning of many grownups to impose excessive regimentation and indignity upon children and youth is one of the most severe immoralities of our time. The assumption by some parents and teachers of the right to subject youngsters to indignity seems dangerous and wicked. A friend of ours tells of encountering a woman in a park recently beating a small child. The friend inquired of this adult, "Whose child is that?" The reply was, "He is mine. You don't think I would be treating anyone else's kid like this, do you?"

Throughout recorded history, man's most pressing moral problem has been the extent of the right of some men to own and control other men. Man's improvement in goodness has followed the path of giving up his right to own and to control, and of extending to all other persons the rights and living conditions which he desires for himself.

Jesus of Nazareth was quite a radical in His time when He insisted that man was not good merely because he refrained from doing evil things. Concepts such as "Love thy neighbor as thyself . . . Do unto others as you would have them do unto you. . . By their fruits ye shall know them," were new and more mature moral principles. America's Declaration of Independence and the Bill of Rights, which colonial citizens insisted be added to their Constitution, define high principles of human dignity and limitations of the rights of some people to infringe upon the rights of others. Emanuel Kant gave us his imperial dictum, "So act that thy acts might be universal law." We like the statement of Mumford, "Whatever nourishes the personality, humanizes it, refines it, deepens it, intensifies its aptitude and broadens its field of action is good: whatever limits it or thwarts it, whatever sends it back into tribal patterns and limits its capacity for human co-operation and communion must be counted as bad." [3]

On the occasion of the eightieth birthday of William Heard Kilpatrick in 1951, Eduard Lindeman made these comments on the good man:

> The good man is the man who doesn't expect a perfect society or a perfect individual. Perfectionism seems an impediment to the good life. Perfectionism is not the final goal but the ever-enduring process of perfecting. This is the good life.
>
> The good man avoids extremes; he avoids either-or's. He avoids false antitheses.
>
> The good man does not resort to blame-fixing, persecution, yet realizes that he is involved in the problems of mankind.
>
> The good man doesn't ever expect to be released from conflict. Wherever there is life, there is conflict. This calls upon man to formulate a new concept of belief in something.
>
> The good man knows how to work in and through groups, but steadfastly refuses to become collectivized.
>
> The good man insists upon his right to dissent.
>
> The good man knows how to use the perspective of humor. He sees himself as comical. This humor comes out of experience, throws a kernel of truth on our affairs that can't be got at any other way. Humor rests upon a solid belief. You can't use it unless you have faith in your fellowmen.
>
> The good man doesn't permit himself to be used by others as a means to external ends nor will he use others.
>
> The good man feels no compulsion to assume superiority to other people or to exercise inferiority.
>
> The good man insists in being and in acting as if the whole human enter-

---

[3] Lewis Mumford, *The Condition of Man* (New York: Harcourt, Brace and Company, 1944), p. 415.

prise is an experiment. The outcome is an experiment and continuing but it is a continuing adventure—exciting, an adventure in which the road is always better than the end. You can always have more fun if you enjoy the process.

New Conditions

Demand

New Characters

Now that we humans have become so numerous and have become concentrated in the more favorable climates of the Earth, the behavior of any individual is a matter of concern to other inhabitants. Little children who like to make mud pies, splash in the water, and leap from here to there constitute a considerable hazard in the modern city apartment, even in the suburban ranch house. The teen-ager, who in former years satisfied his quest for excitement and expressed his willingness to take risks as he broke and raced wild horses, is a serious menace today as he seeks the same gratifications in a hot-rod on a busy thoroughfare. His attempt to find the extent of his courage by jumping from high cliffs or by challenging a newcomer to a fight now becomes a public menace as he plays modern "cops and robbers" in the crowded city.

Character and Morals

Morality refers to the observance of principles of conduct which have come down in a social group through many generations. Most of the world accepts the Ten Commandments (or their counterpart in other religions) as a valid statement of restraints upon the individual which have held for thousands of years and which few individuals will openly violate today. A moral code is made up of highly emotionalized standards; deviations from the code engender emotional responses in other people.

After a long period of exile, the term *conscience* has been reinstated as an important concept in the formation and stability of character. We have many interpretations of conscience. As little children, we were taught that conscience was an inborn, still, small voice of supernatural authority telling us right from wrong. More skeptical persons have viewed conscience as our negative conditioning and our memory of things we feared to do as little children. It seems quite likely that some of the motive force of conscience stems from the distress we feel at departing from habits of response, just as some of us feel some distress at finding ourselves in a dark room in which the furniture has been rearranged. We urge you to read Fromm's book *The Sane Society*,[4] in which he describes his concept of anonymous authority. For most of us, anonymous authority is the authority of fixed ways of believing and behaving which gives all newness in ideas, beliefs, and ways of behaving something of an immoral flavor, since these new ways threaten the ways familiar to us. We view conscience as those inner controls upon ourselves which oblige us to consider our own behavior in this light: "If everyone behaved as I behave, what would the world be like?"

As little children, we learn early that the ways of our families are the right ways. Persons who differ from those ways, as viewed through our morally immature eyes, are wrong; else we must be wrong. Since our self-respect can scarcely entertain the notion that we are wrong, it follows that the others are wrong. We would urge that young people be taught that, in making most of life's decisions and choices, more than one right way can be found. When life was simple and changed very little from one generation to the next, man was able to establish fixed and dependable ways of behaving which were satisfactory for living. Today, with the extremely rapid change in our mode of living and in the circumstances for human enjoyment, conscience alone—save as it impels us to consider the well-being of all persons affected by our behavior—is an insufficient guide to conduct. In a simple culture, people worked during the light of day and rested when their part of the world became dark. A man seen on the street after midnight was surely up to no good. Now he may have just gotten off the swing-shift at the factory and be spending his after-work time in much the same way as those of us whose work is finished at four or five o'clock in the afternoon. In the farm country, anybody who slept in the daytime, unless he was sick or very young or very old, was not a good person. Today many of us find it necessary or more congenial to work in the artificial light of the night and do our sleeping in the daytime.

Those of us who develop good character in the young must see conscience as a growing, emerging, learned quality of the personality. Let us examine some of the moral concepts that do need to change with time and circumstances. Conscience supported solely by ancient codes of conduct permits much current evil in our world. Few persons on earth

---

[4] Erich Fromm, *The Sane Society* (New York: Rinehart and Company, Inc., 1955).

would excuse a man for pouring poison in the baby's bath, yet how many of us consider it a moral problem for certain companies to pour tremendous amounts of poison into streams used by many people or to pollute great quantities of air that all people breathe? Few of the world's citizens regard as murderers the *manufacturers* of devices intended only to kill human beings. Since young men, who believe the moral admonition that it is wrong to kill another human, experience marked conflict in wartime, a part of preparing people for war is to persuade them that the potential enemy really is inhuman—more like beast than man. We like Sandburg's comments on this subject:

> The little girl saw her first troop parade and asked,
>   "What are those?"
> "Soldiers."
> "What are soldiers?"
> "They are for war. They fight and each tries to kill
>   as many of the other side as he can."
> The girl held still and studied.
> "Do you know . . . I know something?"
> "Yes, what is it you know?"
> "Sometime they'll give a war and nobody will come." [5]

When one man lays plans and slays another man he is subjected to most extreme legal reprisal. When a motorist allows his car to become mechanically defective and loses control of it on a busy street killing several people, he may be excused because he did not intend to kill them.

We express extreme moral indignation upon seeing a youth snatch twenty-five cents from a smaller boy. We note scant indignation being directed to the buyers and sellers of homes when they loudly proclaim that a racial minority is moving into the neighborhood and that owners should sell while the prices are still good. Thus the members of the first group are deprived of their homes and the members of the next group are deprived of the full value of their purchases.

We teach our young that they must not bear false witness, yet any day we hear it proclaimed by the press, radio, and television that each of many cigarettes is much healthier than any other, that each of dozens of hand-lotions is more likely than any other to make us look like we do not work with our hands. The reader might ponder the extent to which the bearing of false witness is becoming an important profession—impor-

---

[5] Carl Sandburg, *The People, Yes* (New York: Harcourt, Brace and Company, 1936), p. 43.

tant enough that we even award degrees to our youth for becoming proficient in it. We cite *The Hidden Persuaders* [6] as an excellent source discussing this phase of modern living. Some schools tell every pupil that he could be valedictorian if he would try, knowing full well that only one can be.

It is interesting to comment upon the role of growing up in terms of approved morality. It is most difficult to teach a little child to bear false witness, to lie. One of the oldest of our moralities is our respect for authority, respect for status, be that authority the parson, the president, the mayor, the policeman, the teacher, the parent. Many grownups never become free from the fear of displeasing their parents. We note with dismay that some of our students who are teachers accept from their principals the indignity of public ridicule and fault-finding which they would accept from no other person on earth. When they were little children, they learned to be afraid of the principal and they have never outgrown their fear. By some this might be called conscience.

Allport observes that "If we encounter in a personality fear of divine punishment as the sole sanction for right doing, we can be sure we are dealing with a childish conscience, with a case of arrested development." [7] He continues to point up that conscience grows in three important respects: external sanctions give way to internal; experiences of prohibition and fear give way to experiences of preferences and self-respect; specific habits of obedience give way to self-guidance, to a broad schemata of values that confer direction upon conduct.

We have been urging that a brittle and fixed conscience is inadequate to twentieth-century living, that inner controls guided by intelligence must serve as dependable guides. Let us consider some other present-day problems. On the busy street the double-parker saves himself a few steps by inconveniencing hundreds of people, who must drive past him in single file. The pedestrian who walks into the street against the red light inconveniences numerous motorists and seldom saves himself any time. The motorist who beats the red light endangers the well-being of a goodly number of pedestrians. Traffic laws cannot be based upon long-time morality, nor upon the impulse of conscience. They result from careful study to provide the safest, freest-flowing movement of people—motorists

---

[6] Vance Packard, *The Hidden Persuaders* (New York: David McKay Company, 1957. New York: Pocket Books, Inc., 1958).

[7] Gordon W. Allport, *Becoming* (New Haven: Yale University Press, 1955), p. 73.

and pedestrians. Only by competent observance of these regulations can people experience convenience from them. Rarely is their violation regarded to be immoral.

In days past, a good man saved a considerable part of his income. That income was largely goods and real property, a part of which he could lay aside for times of meager production. As this is written, we are being urged to dig into our savings, not to leave our money in the banks; instead to support a more liberal program of social security which will relieve the individual of fear of want and starvation should he lose his job or become unable to work.

Few of us would deliberately throw a handful of soot in a child's face. Yet many Americans hold stock in corporations whose factories belch smoke needlessly into the air for all to breathe. In a farm culture, a man was his own boss and he could work as he felt. He could choose to go fishing or paint the barn or dig post-holes with his own feelings being of valid importance. Modern business, industrial, and social organization put great stock in punctuality, in one's being where he is needed at the time he is expected to be there. For our time the notion that conscience is the inner voice of the herd will not suffice.

Conscience must impel us to be thoughtful, to respect facts, to employ mankind's highest level of ability: the capacity for altruism—the sensing and caring about how other people feel. Altruism is prompted by true concern for others, which can be summed up in the admonition, "As you do to the least of these, you do unto me." In 1958 we passed through what some commentators called a mild recession. It was said to be minor because only six or seven million people were out of work. A mature conscience would not consider this minor for those seven million people. We have been trying to locate Bill Maulden's wartime cartoon in which he showed a dozen or two slain men lying about a bomb crater—the subtitle: "It was only a minor engagement!"

Developing Goodness in the Young

Let us now consider some ways and conditions for building goodness in the young. We wish to view character not as conformity but as a creative, developing, generous growth, from the complete selfishness of the crib to a sense of world-wide responsibility for the well-being of all people. In the life of every child there must be a sense of moral orderliness—in his family, in his neighborhood, in his whole world as he perceives it. To this orderliness a reasonable degree of conformity is practicable and desirable. The subsoil of good character is a system of habits necessary for living smoothly and congenially with a minimum of friction and wasted motion so that more important, more humane activities can be pursued.

To some of the elders moral education has meant teaching a system of "thou shalt's" and "thou shalt not's," based upon supernatural sanction, with promise of punishment to violators. It is interesting to consider whether the precepts enunciated by the world's great religious leaders have been pronounced because they seemed to be true—that they were not made true by the prophets' utterances of them.

All social groups behave in terms of a system of values to which they adhere. We need to teach the young that *we believe when we cannot know,* that belief is certainty without knowledge, that as knowledge accumulates, beliefs are modified. Men of high moral principles once believed that malaria was the result of bad air. One of the lessons of history is that man has tended to become quite upset about threats to his belief. As the King says in *The King and I,* we are quick to fight about those things that we don't know are so. Man has seldom been annoyed by another's rejection of a fact. Some of us might well note that we can judge the sureness of our own knowledge of a subject by how emotional we become in discussing it. We can't get in much of a fight about the time of day; we often have noisy discussions about what time a sixteen-year-old should get home at night. Most of the people in the world are still flexing their muscles and amplifying their voices for the beliefs we express in our Declaration of Independence and our Constitution. Much blood has been spilled in the efforts of some men to impose their beliefs upon other men.

When American schools were first started, adults held a great faith in the value of precepts in moral education. All early readers and storybooks for little children carried moral lessons. It is quite unlikely that reciting precepts, such as "Honesty is the best policy," has much to do with the disposition to be honest. Opportunities for finding satisfaction in honesty are far more productive. Arousing in a child the impulse to do a good thing without giving him immediate opportunity to do it relaxes rather than strengthens his character.

Slogans have been heavily relied upon as guides to conduct. One organization for boys has as its slogan, "Do a good deed daily," which is misinterpreted by some to mean that once you have done your good deed you can do as you please the remainder of the day. Today we start our fights and our football games by singing "The Star Spangled Banner." Most legislatures have imposed upon teachers and students the obligation of pledging allegiance to the flag whenever they meet together. We have scant reason to believe that blind repetition of slogans improves love of country. Too often we hear persons proclaim loudly "I love America," when they love few Americans; when they ruthlessly deface the countryside with ugly mining operations, and scores of acres of identical houses; when they toss garbage on America's streets, and belong to organizations that are undermining American ideals. We are sometimes wearied by grownups who insist "I love children," but can't stand the childish behavior of any one of them. We are inclined in such circumstances to agree with Shakespeare and say, "Methinks thou protesteth too much!" We do

not deplore the use and repetition of some slogans. We once knew a three-year-old who stopped hitting other children when his mother repeated to him several times daily, "Hands are to love with, not to hit with." And a few years later, his father bought him boxing gloves for Christmas! A goodly number of teachers have reported hearing some youngsters say to others, "I can't hit you now because this is Brotherhood Week. I'll get you next week."

We would like the adult community to give up, as rapidly as the inertia of habit will permit, calling childish behavior *naughty* or *bad* or *good*. Instead of proclaiming "You are a bad boy," we would better inquire, "What were you thinking about when you did that? Did you think how Josie would feel when you hit her?" Certainly we are actively undermining character when we tell boys and girls that their normal childish behavior is bad. We refrain from running through the halls not because running is naughty, but because the building is poorly constructed, there are too many children in the hall at a given time, Mrs. Jones' migraine headache can't take running, or the principal has pictures in his head that we must respect.

The young human does not learn character by thoughtlessly accepting the domination of his elders. A basic condition for character development is the opportunity to make thoughtful choices in planning enterprises, and to live by these choices. Goodness results from foresight, from the clarity of the preview of the probable effects of certain behavior, and from a feeling of personal responsibility for these effects. In general, those aspects of behavior which we call character are learned to a marked degree in accord with the principles guiding all learning. Thus growth and maturity in the insights made possible by growing intelligence affects one's ability to be dependably good. We recall knowing a feeble-minded girl who was so devoted to her teacher that she stole her pocketbook whenever she got a chance. She was then carefully taught that she must not steal Miss Rino's pocketbook, and she did not steal it thereafter. However, she would steal her handkerchief or steal someone else's pocketbook. This girl did not have the mental power to generalize from her specific teachings.

Certainly the culture itself, the family, the neighborhood, and associates at school are the most important factors in character building. It is important that the moral tone of these groups be harmonious. A home or school confused in its beliefs, at cross-purposes in its values, will undermine the child's character development. A teacher who urges all pupils to be polite and considerate while subjecting them to the indignity of public correction undermines character. All of us can remember instances in which a grownup in extreme rudeness demanded that a child be courteous. No character was taught by that procedure.

As the individual makes choices, he must live by them if his behavior is to result in positive learning. Little Tommy was so moved by his visit to a poor section of the city and by an appeal that old clothes be sent to a settlement house which he visited that he packed up all his garments, excepting those he wore, and sent them off to the poor. His mother was so delighted with this premature outburst of generosity that she immediately replaced all his garments with shiny new ones and threw in a pair of cowboy boots as a bonus. She thus robbed him of the learnings that come from having to live by one's own choices.

Some of us are worried by the current expectation of immediate rewards for good behavior. "What is in it for me?" may be taught by a school that gives marks, maintains honor rolls, exercises the credit system, gives special privileges for special endeavor. A well-known columnist giving personal advice received this inquiry: "Don't you think if a person gets all A's and B's on her report card she should get something for it? Especially if her parents have an above-average income?"

Throughout creation the elders have sought to control the morals of the younger and other subjects by acts of reprisal for "bad" behavior and promises of pleasure for goodness. In all cultures hell is pictured as the most uncomfortable place imaginable while heaven is a composite of all cherished pleasures. Doubtless character is built by the reward-punishment, pleasure-pain principle. Goodness will be adopted as a way of life if it brings gratification. Goodness or morality is a long-range, widespread view of human satisfaction. To be effective the rewards must be the logical outcomes of behavior and must never be confused with bribes, or promised rewards. Bribes undermine character. It appears that the basic rewards, apart from creature comforts, are: appreciation of associates, acceptance, and the granting of additional responsibilities in a group. The only effective punishment is a genuine sense of failure to attain one's inner goals.

We wonder at the strength and persistence of the notion that the infliction of bodily pain upon a child is necessary for his proper character development. So many grownups express the belief that the adult not only has the right but the obligation to inflict injury upon a misbehaving child. The practice of inflicting bodily pain was developed by kings to control their subjects and by slave-owners to control their slaves. In terms of moral principle it is no more right for a large person to control a small person by physical violence than for a large nation to control a smaller one. You might ponder the extent to which we call a child good as he exhibits the qualities slave-owners sought to develop in their subjects. Today our cities are calling "bad" many young humans who are doing nothing more than engaging in childish behavior in inappropriate circumstances.

The facilities for learning to be good are quite as important as the facilities for learning to be a typist or a football player. Boys and girls will keep off the grass and cherish its beauty if they have other adequate open space in which to play. Youngsters will be relatively inactive and quiet in the living room if they may go elsewhere to express their exuberance. A wise historian has observed that civilization has been a process of giving up low-level freedoms in order to secure them at a higher level. Restriction is good for the young only if it makes sense to them by making their lives more free and more gratifying. Wise teachers do not restrict children merely to accustom them to restrictions. Without seeming soft in our attitudes, we should like to insist that it should be reasonably easy and immediately sensible to be good.

This chapter has been offered neither as a deep scientific explanation of character nor as a set of directions and principles for building character. It is intended principally to stimulate you to be thoughtful about the moral and character problems of our time and to take your full share in promoting good living for those about you as well as for all young human beings everywhere.

Suggestions for Further Exploration

► If you are studying a person age ten or over, talk with him to get the answers to the following questions. After your talk, study the responses you get to see if the deductions and inferences of this chapter seem valid to you.

What things do boys and girls your age do that adults think are wrong?
What things do boys and girls your age do that adults think are right?
What do *you* think makes a *good* person? (You'll probably have to probe a bit. Search for answers that pertain to in-school and out-of-school activities.)
What do adults do that boys and girls your age think are wrong?

► Jot down all the ways you are dependent upon others and all the ways others are dependent upon you. Does this help to make vivid some of the problems of being "your brother's keeper"?

► What are some of the non-conformities your community, your school, your social group frowns upon? What do these attitudes mean in character development?

► Spend a couple of hours in a public school noting all the appeals to altruism and all the appeals to selfishness that are made by the teachers and other adults. Discuss your findings with some of your classmates.

► List some important problems of modern life that demand the functioning of conscience. How have moral concepts changed since the Roman Empire? The beginning of our nation? The turn of the century? (You might want to discuss this with your parents.) What do you predict will be the functioning moral concepts of 2060 that are different from present-day ones?

Additional Sources You May Find Helpful

Brock Chisholm, *Can People Learn to Learn?* New York: Harper and Brothers, 1958.

A dynamic statement by the former director of the World Health Organization on world problems and the moral issues they present to man. Excellent chapter on education in the modern world.

Erich Fromm, *Man for Himself*. New York: Rinehart and Company, Inc., 1947.

A perceptive statement on the theme that every individual is the nucleus of his own universe and yet man cannot exercise human qualities without being concerned about how others are faring.

Lewis Mumford, *Faith for Living*. New York: Harcourt, Brace and Company, 1940.

An essay on the values that are enduring in our culture.

T. V. Smith and Eduard Lindeman, *The Democratic Way of Life*. New York: Mentor Books, 1951.

A classic discussion of the values of democracy, presented as ideals by Smith and empirically by Lindeman. The discussion by Lindeman is most helpful to those who wonder about the functioning of the classical ideals of democracy in a modern technological culture.

William Graham Sumner, *Folkways*. Boston: Ginn and Company, 1906.

Written by a minister at Cambridge who became acquainted with people from differing cultures of the world. By visiting with these people he perceived that morals are relative and a function of the circumstances in which people live.

The creeds of the great religions of the world and statements of philosophers who represent varying cultures are rich sources to explore as you consider the meaning of character. A very few are listed below.

The Bible—encompasses the Hebraic-Christian belief.

Bhagavad Gita—a great Hindu epic encompassing the prevailing Brahmanic belief.

Laotzu's *The Way of Life*—a Chinese philosopher of 600 B.C. whose words were recorded by those who came after him.

Kahlil Gibran's *The Prophet*—a Syrian-American philosopher's attempt to state the great truths of life as he saw them.

The Koran—the scriptures of the Mohammedans.

Growth from Conception to Young Adulthood

This section presents detailed information that you as a beginning student need in order to understand the boys and girls with whom you are working or plan to work. Since growth is a continuous process, teachers need to understand, as much as can be ascertained, what happens to the individual from conception to the time that he leaves high school. Ideally, our story would extend through the entire span of life, but since we have limited space and you have limited time, we shall be satisfied with discussing what have

177

come to be known as the "growing years." We hope that your inquisitiveness will lead you to investigate other ages and stages.

You may wonder at the amount of space devoted to the pre-school years. Today a teacher deals with one small segment of the lifespan of a growing child. No phase of any process can be seen clearly nor its special functions appreciated without seeing and experiencing it as a whole. Many teachers and parents display near mania for rushing the child out of whatever phase he is in.

We believe that child life would be much richer and teaching more effective if all teachers-in-training, whether for first grade or twelfth-grade physics, were to spend much time with pre-school children. At this age change is so rapid as to be readily perceptible. One can see wonder, curiosity, experimentation, and gratification arising from new insights and skills. The changing and ever-vital roles of the elders (teachers) are clear. Behavior cannot be demanded; learning (lessons) cannot be assigned. We hasten to add that no wisdom results from flitting here and there to observe the cute, characteristic behavior of little children. It takes time to watch and perceive the process of growth. Did not American education make a grievous mistake when it moved the older children away from the little ones? Too many parents have grown up knowing few younger children until they hold their own.

We have been confronted with a dilemma in writing this section; namely, how to discuss growth in an organized, integrated fashion without appearing to endorse the concept that growth can be divided into discrete, normative stages that apply uniformly to all children. At one time we planned to discuss the *mental* development of the individual from birth through adolescence; then the *physical,* the *social,* and the *emotional.* This division of the human being into four separate entities denied our basic philosophy. We discarded that scheme. What we have decided to do is *consider the individual whole* but for the sake of clarity to discuss important aspects of six developmental phases of life, holding in mind that human beings do not pop from one stage to another as a cocoon pops into a butterfly.

The six phases are arbitrary and represent nothing more than convenient pauses for observation and interpretation. We begin with the pre-memory age; this is followed by the pre-school years. From this point on we use the school divisions as convenient pegs upon which to hang our discussion: early elementary childhood (ages five to eight); the middle years of childhood (ages nine to eleven); early adolescence (ages twelve to fourteen); adolescent-young adult (ages fifteen to eighteen). Our primary focus is to discover the tasks the individual himself is really working at as he matures. These are called the developmental tasks [1] of growing up and contrast with what society demands of the individual. The concept of developmental tasks is used because it seems less misunderstood than that of the "needs" of individuals since it combines both the *personal* and *social* achievements necessary for continued development in living in one's culture. As we discuss these developmental tasks, we probe into the why's of behavior as they emerge in relation to the tasks at hand and as they have significance for future growth.

We use *growth* to mean the progressive development of the individual in all the ways in which he is capable of maturing. The process of growth in a sequential, patterned manner is characteristic of all life. This process when applied to the physiological being is called *maturation*. All life has within its structure the urge to grow. Observe the simple plant life, lichen, split the rocks as it absorbs enough food to grow. Plant a bean seed in a pot of soil and watch the tiny germ split the hard, tough bean as it springs to life. Take note of a newborn colt and return in a few hours to see its wobbly legs already strong enough to support its cavorting. All life has within it the determinants to grow as the species to which it belongs grows; an acorn yields an oak and a pine scale a pine tree. Each of these has progressed step-by-step through sequential patterns. Not

---

[1] Robert S. Havighurst, *Human Development and Education* (New York: Longmans, Green and Company, 1953).

all the specimens of a species grow at identical rates nor to identical extents. Some specimens grow much faster and more wholesomely than others. Even among seeds that have been carefully selected for superiority or among animal life wherein eugenics has been applied to produce uniformity, variations in rate and form of growth result. This leads us to the answer to one of our first *why's*. Today we accept the fact that all life is intricately and inexorably linked with environment. Growth and survival depend upon some satisfactory adjustment to environment.

You need to know some of the principles that govern growth. One of these is the principle of *differentiation.* By this we mean that growth proceeds from the simple to the complex, from the general to the specific. You will note that in the beginning of prenatal life the first cells are all the same kind. As growth continues, various cells are differentiated to form specialized tissues and organs; some become skin, others nerves, others bone, some fat. The general becomes specific. Differentiation occurs also in the acquisition of learning skills. The infant first learns to press both feet against the ground, then he differentiates his muscular and neural coordination so that he learns to press first one foot and then the other. Later he learns to make continuous movements with both feet and still later continuous movements but in opposing directions. In the psychological realm most of us as adults still see things generalized at first. We look into a nursery thinking, "Why, all those babies look alike." Then nurse holds up the baby *we* came to see. Immediately we differentiate. This baby *is* different. We have gone in our perceptions from the general to the specific.

A second principle of growth that is a corollary of differentiation is that of *integration.* As new skills are acquired, new learnings taken in, as the body grows and changes, the individual is called upon to integrate these "newnesses" into his old self. This requires a process of disorganization so that a higher organization may emerge. All life is a process of differentiation and integration. During periods of growth in which differentiation is the dominant process, the individual is more restless; he is more demanding of his environment for he is reaching out to take in all kinds of experiences. We say that he is hard to handle at these times. Such periods are followed by periods of integration in which the human being is assimilating that which has been taken in. He is learning how it fits with all the rest of him. He is trying it out in various situations. He is learning to be comfortable with it, to make it part of himself. These periods of growth are pleasant, smooth. The individual is less demanding and we adults are pleased. As you read this section, you will note that as the infant grows to adulthood there is an ebb and flow between differentiation and integration. During the first fifteen months, for example, he learns to walk and to work his voice box. He learns, too, how his family feels about his explorations as he begins to toddle. Then follow a few months of integration when he is a delight to himself and to us before some other developmental tasks demand his differentiating again.

Reorganization into higher, more inclusive patterns is another principle of growth. A child learns first to walk by utilizing opposing movement. As the body becomes organized to achieve more intricate balance, a tricycle may be mastered. This is followed by a bicycle which requires even higher, more inclusive patterns of balance and of opposing movement. As growth occurs, the individual is capable of mastering more complex patterns of thought requiring a reorganization of ideas and data. The baby's use of his arms is more highly integrated as he matures so that he can reorganize his movements to use his thumb in opposition to his fingers. These are illustrations of more inclusive organization through differentiation.

We have discussed previously the principle of *unevenness of growth*. Not all parts of an organism grow uniformly. Many early adolescent girls are uncomfortable about their big feet. They are victims of uneven growth patterns. The unevenness of growth during adolescence makes boys seem unnecessarily clumsy as they stumble over furniture, drop china, and the like. Nor does growth proceed at a uniform, steady rate. Growth occurs in spurts, but there is some degree of predictability as to when growth spurts are likely to occur. The infant's first year is one of tremendous growth. This is followed by a few months of relative stability before he goes on to other growth patterns. One important fact to remember is that growth peaks heighten the individual's susceptibility to damage. Growth spurts place an emotional strain upon the youngster, for he is having to make many adjustments very rapidly. This leaves him confused. During such peaks, outside pressures and restrictions should be held to a minimum if the individual is to attain his full potential of uniqueness. This is the reason for our great concern about the unduly restrictive quality of the school during the early adolescent years.

By their *interests*—self-generated activities—children *reveal* their *growing edges*. This principle of growth is frequently ignored in our schools. When a child first stands alone and recognizes his achievement, he does it again and again. Mothers are "worn to a frazzle" keeping up with the child who has just learned to walk. The toddler who has gained the independence to be outdoors by himself can't spare time for meals or naps. Nature seems to provide the *urge to practice dawning capacities. This is drill.* Drill which is imposed before capacity has dawned retards development. The child must have needed space and freedom to develop new capacities. The meaning of new behaviors must be recognized. For example, when the child grows enough to climb out of his crib, we do not spank him back into it, nor put a lid on top of it. We provide him a bed without sides and put pillows on the floor.

Another principle of growth that one needs to understand in working with growing boys and girls is that social, emotional, and mental development tend to be closely related to inner physical growth. Physical growth often gives us the cues that something is happening in the less observable areas of life. This is particularly true in the early years. It is important to discern *individual* patterns and rates of maturation of those we teach if we are to understand their perceptions of their own developmental tasks at any given point of maturation. Aldrich stated:

> In the early years of childhood, physical and mental functions are so merged in the plan of growth that they cannot be considered separately. In fact, at this age mental growth is measured by physical accomplishment. Since this is so, there can be no mental hygiene as sharply distinguished from physical hygiene. Considerable physical *care* is good mental hygiene in infancy. To give a baby all the warmth, comfort, and cuddling that he seems to need; to meet his wishes in the matter of satisfying and appropriate food; to adjust our habit-training to his individual rhythm; and to see that he has an opportunity to exercise each new accomplishment as it emerges; these are the beginnings of a forward-looking program in mental hygiene.[2]

[2] C. Anderson Aldrich and Mary M. Aldrich, *Babies Are Human Beings* (New York: The Macmillan Company, 1954), pp. viii-ix.

8

The Pre-memory Age

Stop to consider—what is the first memory you have? Are you sure you actually remember this experience or have you heard the story told so often that it *seems as if* you remember it? Do you recall wondering as a child why you couldn't remember when you were a baby? Do you sometimes look at an infant now and wonder what is going on behind those bright eyes as eager hands reach out toward you? This is one of the mysteries of life. How does memory begin and

why? We have entitled this chapter the pre-memory age because we wish to discuss growth from conception to about two-and-a-half years of age. Sometime around this age impressions survive in vague memories. Since we cannot remember this span of our own lives, our major source of data is what we can learn from observing the growth process in others. Since the first nine months of life occur inside the mother's womb, this segment is subject to limited observation. Much then has to be *inferred* about life during this period.

Prenatal Life

Today each of us consists of about twenty-six billion cells, most of which are continuously being re- newed as the old ones wear out. These twenty-six billion cells are organized into the most complicated living structure known on this planet—involving continuous chemical reactions of infinite variety, and voluntary and involuntary functions that utilize the higher laws of physics. Because so little about prenatal life is known, the student needs to consider this discussion as suggestive rather than conclusive. We present a simplified description of growth before birth, as it seems to occur, and indicate some of the significances of this process to the student of human behavior.

Conception

Life begins with conception. It really begins for each of us as a particular sperm (male germ cell) and a particular ovum (female germ cell) begin their process of maturation. All cells of the human body with the exception of germ cells have twenty-four pairs (forty-eight) of chro- mosomes, which are rod-like structures present in the nucleus of each cell.[1] Before germ cells can unite, a process known as reduction-division takes place. This means that each germ cell splits into two cells, each of which carries one-half of the forty-eight chromosomes. Not until this occurs can fertilization take place. Within each chromosome, it is believed, are the genes which are the trait-carrying bits of life. Since no one person can have

---

[1] For a more detailed discussion of this phenomenon, consult Theodosius Dobz- hansky, *Evolution, Genetics, and Man* (New York: John Wiley and Sons, Inc., 1955), pp. 44-71. It is now believed that each cell has forty-*six* chromosomes. (The precise number seems of little importance to the classroom teacher.)

transmitted to him through the genes more than half of the total number of traits available within the chromosomes, the chances for individuality increase to infinite degree. At the time of fertilization, reduction-division has taken place; the ovum and the sperm are ready to unite to form a new life.

The chromosomes within the sperm are of two types, the X-chromosome and the Y-chromosome. In the reduction-division of chromosomes, some sperm cells carry twenty-four X-chromosomes, and some carry twenty-three X-chromosomes and one Y-chromosome. All of the chromosomes in the ovum are X-chromosomes. If the ovum joins with an X-chromosome sperm the sex of the individual is female; if with a Y-chromosome sperm the sex is male. Thus far, no way to control this process has been found.

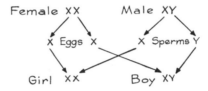

Sex is determined at time of conception. If male contributes X-chromosome, new individual will be female. If male contributes Y-chromosome, new individual will be male. Adapted by permission from Elements of Genetics, 3rd ed., *by E. C. Colin. Copyright 1956, McGraw-Hill Book Co., Inc.*

The sperm is microscopically small and is vigorous. Sperm cells are plentiful and very much alive. They have the capacity to swim and are provided with whiplike tails. The male has a continuous supply of sperm cells so he is almost always capable of impregnating the receptive ovum. In contrast, the female normally produces only one mature ovum each lunar month. It lives about a day. Since the sperm can live for several days in the woman's body, fertilization may be the result of sexual intercourse within a period of three or four days each month. The ovum is smaller than a flyspeck, but is visible to the naked eye. It is lethargic.

Prenatal Growth

When the sperm and ovum unite, they immediately begin to divide and multiply, adhering to each other. This accumulating organism is called the *zygote* and is designated by this name during the first two weeks. After that we call the organism an *embryo* until the beginning of the third lunar month (eight weeks); from then on the organism is known as a *fetus* until birth when it becomes a *neonate* (newborn) very briefly for a period of about two weeks. These names, you understand, are just convenient labels agreed upon by biologists. They do not designate discrete periods of growth. The zygote spends its brief life of two weeks becoming embedded in the uterus of the mother and preparing its home within the womb.

During the process of implantation, as it is called, three special structures are formed to provide nourishment for and to protect the newly-begun life. These are the *placenta,* the *umbilical cord,* and the *sac.*

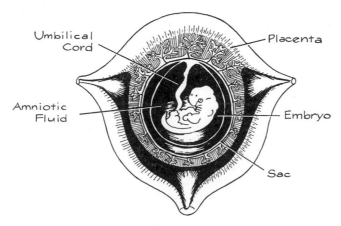

Human embryo in the uterus. Adapted by permission, Encyclopaedia Britannica, *1953 edition, Vol. 19, p. 169.*

At the point where the zygote puts out feelers which push through the blood vessels in the uterine wall, the placenta develops. The feelers branch and intertwine until they finally form a fairly solid mass. This is the placenta. The baby-to-be floats in a sac, filled with amniotic fluid, that is connected to the placenta by the umbilical cord. The umbilical cord, attached to the zygote, has blood vessels but no nerves. The maternal blood flows into the placenta carrying oxygen, hormones, viruses, water, and nutrients. Some of these substances are sucked from the placenta into the umbilical cord and carried to the embryo. The wastes of the embryo are carried back to the placenta and filtered back into the mother's blood. In other words the umbilical cord carries food from the placenta to the embryo and waste from the embryo back to the placenta. The placenta serves as a screen through which whatever reaches the life within the sac must be filtered. While the umbilical cord connects the mother and the embryo, no direct connection exists between the maternal and embryonic blood streams.

During the life of the embryo, which you remember is six weeks (from two weeks to eight weeks of age), most of the structural organization of a human being occurs. The embryo, measuring about an inch, is suspended in its two-inch sac. Within that inch-long body are the beginnings of bones, muscles, nerves, sensory organs, internal organs, arms and legs. The

Embryonic development of human organism. Adapted by permission from Textbook of Healthful Living, *5th ed., by Harold S. Diehl. Copyright, 1955, McGraw-Hill Book Co., Inc.*

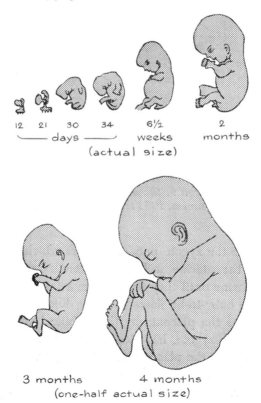

| 12 | 21 | 30 | 34 | 6½ | 2 |

└──── days ────┘   weeks   months

(actual size)

3 months   4 months

(one-half actual size)

heart, which begins as a simple tube, has begun to beat; the spinal cord is laid down in full; blood flows through microscopic arteries, and muscles are capable of twitching. The face has taken on human characteristics. We note that the embryo grows from the head down and from the central axis of the body toward the extremities. As an illustration of this, the head of the beginning fetus is one-half of its total length; at birth, the head is one-fourth of its length; in the adult, the head is only about one-tenth of the total height. The baby first performs intentional acts with the muscles of the face, later the throat, and still later with arms and legs. Coghill describes the significance of this principle as it relates to learning throughout life:

> The principle may be stated thus: The behavior pattern from the beginning expands throughout the growing normal animal as a perfectly integrated unit, whereas partial patterns arise within the total pattern and, by a process of individuation, acquire secondarily varying degrees of independence. According to this principle, such an entity as a "simple reflex" never occurs in the life of the individual; complexity of behavior is not derived by progressive integration of more and more originally discrete units; the conception of chain reflexes as usually presented is not in accord with the actual working of the nervous system. On the other hand, within the total, ever-expanding integrated organism as a whole, partial patterns emerge more or less and tend toward independence and dominance, but, under normal conditions, always remain under the supremacy of the individual as a whole. An inappropriate degree of independence or dominance of a partial pattern constitutes abnormality or perversion of behavior.[2]

Beginning with the third lunar month we call the life within the womb a fetus. From then until the seventh lunar month (twenty-eight weeks), this bit of life becomes what we recognize as human. By the third lunar month his sex organs are well enough formed to distinguish his sex. His nails begin to emerge; his teeth begin to take shape deep within his small gums; nerve cells appear and begin to form connections. His beginning kidneys are even capable of secreting a small amount of urine. The fourth month is distinguished for the beginning of many movement patterns which are life-long. Arms and legs move; hands open and close; the head rotates; the mouth opens; the tongue and lips move. By this time the fetus is about six inches long and weighs about four ounces. In the fifth lunar month, the mother probably first begins to feel the movements

---

[2] G. E. Coghill, "The Early Development of Behavior in Amblystoma and in Man," *Archives of Neurology and Psychiatry*, 1929, Vol. 21, p. 989.

of the baby. In former days, it was believed that this was when the baby came alive; this period was then known as "the quickening." By now the fetus has twelve billion nerve cells, all this human will ever have. The cerebral cortex has become differentiated into several layers. By the end of the sixth lunar month all of the essential anatomy and physiological processes have been established. The skin is red and wrinkled. The glands are coming into action. The digestive system begins to work. From this point on growth is largely an increase in size, complexity, and organization.

The baby has a 10 per cent chance to survive if he is born during the seventh lunar month and a 50 per cent chance during the eighth lunar month. This gives some indication of the importance of the quality of growth after the baby's anatomical structure is complete. From the seventh lunar month to birth, the fetus grows in length from about fifteen to twenty inches and from about two and a half pounds to about seven pounds. During the last two lunar months he fills out rapidly, his skin fades from red to pink, and he begins to shed his prenatal body hair. He may start sucking his thumb—thus exercising a function much needed at birth.

This brief description can do little more than introduce you to the wonder of life and entice you to explore more deeply this period of growth. Note the suggestions at the end of the chapter. As you read about prenatal life, notice the many applications of the principles of growth. Perhaps you are asking *why* it is important to include a discussion of prenatal life in your study. In addition to knowing how life starts so that you may understand the continuity of all behavior, the thoughtful student discovers his knowledge of this period of life explains many behaviors for which no other causes are found.

Prenatal Inheritance

Each of us, as we have seen, inherits a set of genes which are uniquely our own. No other person has a set like ours. These genes set patterns and limits to what we can do, for in them are carried our traits. We also inherit our environment. What we become is the result of the dynamic interaction between our genes and our environment. The environment for each of us also is unique. It is never the same for two individuals. The closest we come to identical heredity is the prenatal environment for identical twins (the result of one ovum), as distinct from fraternal twins which are the result of the simultaneous fertilization of two ova. Fraternal twins are no more related than other siblings. If you are interested in a more detailed study of twins, read Newman.[3] In most cases, limits set by the genes constitute ceilings so high that they do not thwart development. Furthermore, genes may be changed by environment. We are witnessing the threat of this today as the percentage of radiation in the atmosphere is being markedly increased. Much can be done to insure an optimum environment for prenatal existence.

Effects of Prenatal Environment Upon Growth

Nutrition of the mother is an important factor. Studies by Sontag,[4] Sanders,[5] Warkany,[6] and Murphy[7] show that maternal nutrition in the early stages of fetal growth does affect the infant. Mothers who have inadequate nutrition during pregnancy usually give birth to infants who have white striae in their tarsal bones at the end of the first postnatal month. Physical abnormalities seem to be related to maternal nutritional factors, especially a deficiency in vitamins B, C, and D, and in calcium and phosphorous. One of the most significant studies on the effects of nutrition was carried on at Harvard between 1930 and 1941. This study of 216 mothers and their infants showed that "every stillborn, every infant dying during the first few days after birth, with one exception . . . all prematures,

---

[3] H. H. Newman and Associates, *Twins: A Study of Heredity and Environment* (Chicago: University of Chicago Press, 1937).

[4] L. W. Sontag and L. M. Harris, "Evidence of Disturbed Prenatal and Neonatal Growth in Bones of Infants Aged One Month," *American Journal Disturbed Children*, 1938, 56:1248-1255.

[5] B. S. Sanders, *Environment and Growth* (Baltimore: Warwick and York, 1934).

[6] J. Warkany, "Etiology of Congenital Malformations," in *Advances in Pediatrics* (New York: Interscience, 1947), p. 1.

[7] D. P. Murphy, "The Outcome of 625 Pregnancies in Women Subjected to Pelvic Radium Roentgen Irradiation," *American Journal Obstetrical Gynecology*, 1929, 13:179-187.

192

and all functionally immature infants were born to mothers who had had inadequate diets during pregnancy."[8]

While the blood stream of the mother is separate from that of the fetus, the placenta does permit small molecules to penetrate to the fetus. Thus a chemical reaction in a mother caused by an emotional upset or over-fatigue or smoking or drugs is reflected in the fetus. A definite neurohumoral connection exists between the mother and the fetus. In other words, secretions from the endocrine glands pass through the placenta. Infants whose mothers are hyperactive or who have been severely disturbed during pregnancy exhibit irritability and hyperactivity more frequently than infants of calmer mothers. Such infants are frequently feeding problems and subject to gastro-intestinal disturbances. The use of quinine during pregnancy has produced congenital deafness in many cases. All of these are factors of the environment which usually can be controlled—at least to some degree. Teachers need to be aware that the physical and emotional well-being of the mother during pregnancy can make a difference in the development of the child.

Any child who is having trouble in school and who has had a difficult birth should be examined for possible damaging effects. Some brain damage is so slight as to go unnoticed. Knowing that birth was difficult may lead to the kind of skilled examinations that make possible accurate diagnoses. Seeking remedies is wasted effort unless we know the causes for behavior.

Birth

Birth is an incident in development. The normal range of gestation for the human is from 240 to 300 days. Great progress has been made in the last decade in saving premature babies. In America 70 per cent of all babies are born in hospitals. Today many specialists believe that drugs administered during childbirth are harmful to the baby. As more knowledge points to the possibility for psychological as well as physiological injury during birth, childbirth practices are being studied carefully. With the need that arises in large institutions to manage schedules and routines, many thoughtful people feel that the family, and especially the infant, have lost much of the emotional pleasure of birth through following

[8] B. S. Burke, V. A. Beal, S. B. Kirkwood, and H. C. Stuart, "Nutritional Studies During Pregnancy," *American Journal of Obstetrical Gynecology,* 1943, 46:38-52.

hospital procedures. Sometimes the mother is so heavily drugged that she feels as if she is being prepared for an operation rather than a birth. She hardly knows when her baby arrives and sees little of it during her stay in the hospital. Father is allowed only a glimpse through the nursery window. Other children, if there are any, are not allowed even that. The atmosphere is sterile and the baby is treated as an inventory item—carefully handled and provided for—but lacking love.

If we take seriously the theories coming from the field of mental health, these first few days are important in determining how the baby feels about his very different world. Many authorities claim that these early days tend to set the infant's responses; therefore they counsel a more intimate arrangement than that described. The rooming-in plan of some hospitals is one solution. The baby is left with the mother and the father may join the family group for short intervals each day. The mother learns the feel of her baby from the very beginning and the baby has warmth and arms to support him. Many maternity sections of hospitals in so-called "underdeveloped" countries are equipped with a cradle that swings from the foot of mother's bed. As the baby whimpers or cries, the mother reaches out with her foot and rocks him. Sounds like a good arrangement for the first few weeks at home! The trend today is to help both mother and father know what is taking place throughout pregnancy and to include father in the birth process itself to as great an extent as good judgment permits. Much more care is exercised in the use of implements and drugs, and mothers are taught ways to help in the actual delivery of the baby.

The Baby

"Even newly born babies became active, hard-working members of society instead of static bundles wrapped in flannel," said Dr. Aldrich, noted pediatrician, in 1938. What can this "active, hard-working member of society" do at birth? He has been described by many romanticists as "trailing clouds of glory," as being an "angel from Heaven." A few realists describe the newborn infant as an alimentary canal with a noise-maker at one end and the power of elimination at the other. The neonate, as he is called for a couple of weeks, begins immediately to make adjustments to a new environment consisting of solids, instead of the fluid existence he was accustomed to during the nine months within the womb. He immediately begins to function as an individual separate from his mother. In short he begins a change-over from fetal to postnatal functioning; these are his immediate developmental tasks.

When he is born, he can be held in a large hand. He is wet, wrinkled, and scrawny. He probably looks more like an old man than our mental picture of a baby. He can sleep and wake and cry and suck and wave his arms and legs around. He responds to stimuli. He grasps. He has a number of reflexes which help to sustain life during these early days. He can breathe and increase the amount of oxygen he takes into his system through yawning. He clears his nose with a sneeze, his throat with a cough. He secures nourishment by crying, rooting, sucking, and swallowing. He is able to defend himself through crying, withdrawing from painful stimuli, and becoming startled. The startle reflex, or Moro reflex, is called forth by two stimuli: a sudden, loud noise and an abrupt loss of equilibrium.

In fetal life circulation was through the umbilical cord. A few minutes after his first cry his internal circulation patterns begin to take hold. He soon begins to breathe with his own lungs and in a few hours to take in food through his mouth and to eliminate waste. All of these internal processes have been synchronized with infinite precision. An excellent illustration is the functioning of the respiratory and circulatory processes. At birth the baby's lungs are incompletely expanded and do not begin to fully function for ten days or so. He comes equipped at birth, however, with a million or two extra red blood cells. These extra cells are on hand to supply the blood with the necessary oxygen that the lungs are incapable of supplying. As the lungs expand, these extra blood cells gradually decrease until the normal supply is reached. This occurs at the time the lungs are fully expanded.

Even at birth babies behave in individualized fashions. Some are cuddly and curl up when held. Others are tense and still. Others are sprawly and seem loosely put together. Some spend most of their time sleeping and seldom cry. Others are restless and whimpery. Some cry for food every two or three hours. Others are content to be fed less often. Some react with great vigor while others only mildly notice the same stimuli.

The first few months of baby's life is a story of superb nerve and muscle coordination progressing in a synchronized manner so that nerve tracts and muscles are developed as they are needed. Thus baby becomes a person. During the *first year*, the body increases in size, adding about twelve inches in height and fifteen pounds in weight and improves in function. The baby acquires six temporary teeth and grows hair. He learns to recognize his mother, to sleep through the night, to eat solid food, to begin communicating, to get around on his own. He begins a life-long process of differentiation and reorganization. He develops his sensory facilities. In this process he learns some basic attitudes of trust or distrust and experiences emotions which are beginning to become differentiated from pleasant or unpleasant into anger, fear, joy, apprehension, excitement, and curiosity. He is learning to perceive his world and at the same time learning how this world feels to him. He spends the next three months (roughly from twelve to fifteen months) consolidating the learnings of his first year. Then follows another spurt of growth which is concentrated mostly on language development and learning an awareness of self which Erikson calls autonomy.[9]

Baby's growth requires all phases of his being. We shall trace the progress of his most urgent developmental tasks and indicate what baby requires from his environment in order to grow wholesomely. At this age we know that if baby's physical behavior is satisfactory, his mental and sensory growth are healthy. He cannot perform physically in a purposeful way until the central nervous connections are well-established and capable of dictating types of responses. Growth takes place in an ordered manner. When the muscles are ready, the nerves arrive.

The baby's acts are influenced by his emotions which are aroused by the satisfaction or blocking of his drives and also furnish additional drive to practice and make perfect. Each baby's growth proceeds along the same sequence of acts, but wide variations exist in the rates of growth. The student must expect to find a wide margin of individual differences whenever ages are given. One reason for becoming familiar with growth at this age is to learn how markedly individuals do vary within normal ranges in their rates. The progress of an individual from baby to "yearling" is so dramatic that no one can miss the principles of growth that are so often obscured at later stages.

---

[9] E. H. Erikson, *Childhood and Society* (New York: W. W. Norton and Company, Inc., 1951).

Sensory Development [10]

The baby's sensory equipment is not completely developed at birth. He learns to use his equipment more purposefully as his ability to receive impulses through his sense organs increases. The brain learns to function more effectively by interpreting the impulses sent to it more fully and building connections between the senses. As this occurs, the infant's power to respond selectively increases. As the baby gradually experiences and matures, he comes into full control of his sensory powers. Hearing and taste are more completely developed than sight, at birth. We know little about smell except that the baby can recognize the odor of milk, can detect the strength of odors, and can discriminate between odors.

Taste and smell are so closely related that it is difficult to isolate one from the other. Babies seem to prefer sweet tastes from the start and are able to differentiate between tastes. Most babies do not like sour tastes. Considerable evidence indicates that most babies have a built-in control that leads them to select the food their bodies need and to regulate the amount and intervals of food. We recommend Clara Davis' [11] experiment as a fascinating study for you to explore. Most pediatricians today teach young mothers to recognize the cues baby gives about his preferences in eating. If an issue is not made of eating during the early weeks and months, eating problems seldom emerge except as temporary manifestations of new growth tasks.

The baby's retina is only partially developed at birth. Probably objects are only dimly and vaguely perceived and appear colorless. It takes about four months for the retina to become fully developed. About ten weeks after birth the nerves connecting the eye and brain are completely formed; but baby cannot focus his eyes for several months because the nerves and muscles controlling focus are not yet coordinated. The cross-eyed appearance of young babies is not a matter for concern until after the time for the focus mechanism to begin to function. Baby uses whatever vision he has and in so doing makes possible the development of ever

---

[10] The authors are indebted for much of this material to C. Anderson Aldrich and Mary M. Aldrich. Their little book *Babies Are Human Beings* is a classic that parents and teachers universally enjoy and find of value.

[11] Clara M. Davis, "Results of the Self-Selection of Diets by Young Children," *Canadian Medical Association Journal*, 1939, 41:257-261.

more accurate interpretations of his world. By the end of a month or five weeks he will follow a moving light with his eyes, and by the end of the second month he recognizes objects and attaches meanings of pleasure to some, such as his bottle, and displeasure to others. By the end of four months eyes and hands have become synchronized for purposeful behavior. His eyes are now complete, but they will be far-sighted during his early childhood—probably until he is eight or nine. As the eye itself has been developing, the brain has been building nerve connections between various parts of the brain and between the brain and the sense organs. As these connections mature, memories and sensations are stored up and the brain improves its interpretations of the messages it receives and sends. The selective process has begun to work. Likes and dislikes are functioning. The baby is becoming a discriminating human. For a detailed study of baby's development, we refer you to Gesell's *Infant and Child in the Culture Today*.[12]

In contrast to the relatively slow development of seeing, the baby's hearing apparatus is complete at birth and the nerve tracts are all laid down. As soon as the amniotic fluid is drained out of the neonate's middle ear, he hears. Hearing is closely related to his fear of loud sounds, so the baby associates emotion with hearing much earlier than with seeing. He is six, seven, or eight months old before he develops enough selectivity to be afraid of a strange or horrible sight. Often a crying baby will stop to listen to a whisper in his ear. He early learns to associate a soft voice with loving hands, and a harsh voice with abrupt, jerky movements. He responds to music early and by nine months is able to move to music. Hearing is the child's avenue to speech; it enables him to attain his full stature as a human being through language.

The neonate seems able to feel comfort and discomfort immediately. He responds with his whole body to pin pricks or pressures. An empty stomach makes him cry. Food is comforting to him, a pleasurable sensation. Since eating is probably his most important function at this time, his mother's cuddling is most necessary to him while he eats. Freud calls this the "oral" stage of development because life's satisfactions are found largely through the mouth. As mother cuddles, fondles, and holds him during his feeding time, he learns to trust his world, to feel good about

---

[12] A. Gesell and F. L. Ilg, *Infant and Child in the Culture Today* (New York: Harper and Brothers, 1943).

his existence, to associate comfort and care with adults. His emotional and social outreaches are being formed. Small babies seem able to sense the mother's real feelings though she may not be aware of them herself. If she resents the baby, she seems to communicate it to him. Lacking maternal love from some adult (it need not be the blood mother), the baby fails to develop the confidence and trust his nervous and muscular system needs in order to develop wholesomely.

The second bodily process, elimination, also has elements of comfort and discomfort in it. The process of relieving the body of the distension felt when the bowels need to move is basically a pleasurable feeling. As long as the baby is confined to the crib, most mothers accept the fact that his elimination functions on an involuntary basis. We are now in the waning portion of an era of early toilet training that has yielded few positive results for anyone except the manufacturers of laxatives. The child's feeling of pleasure in elimination cannot take place if he is asked to eliminate when he doesn't want to. Keeping this gratification intact is the best insurance for adequate functioning of the digestive tract. By carefully studying the child's elimination habits and putting him on the pot at the time when he automatically moves his bowels, mother can accomplish this. His brain soon learns to associate elimination with the pot and with his own satisfaction afterwards. Permanent training results and baby's feelings have been kept healthy. Whatever happens, the child must not be shamed for soiling his pants. Sexual and elimination processes can too easily become confused in a child's mind at this age if shame is used in trying to train him.

The Smile

Baby's first unnecessary act is to smile. This occurs at about four weeks of age. We might add parenthetically that baby first sheds tears soon after his first smile—during the second month. Blind babies smile. Premature babies smile about four weeks after they should have been born—an indication of the developmental nature of the smile. In a few days baby is smiling upon invitation from mother. This is the beginning of conscious communication. In a few more weeks baby is laughing and his laughter is intermingled with his first speech sounds, which are ready to function by this time since the central nervous system has made connections with the vocal cords.

Development of Speech

The baby's first cries are involuntary acts, but he soon learns to use cries to secure what he wants. Many people hear a baby's cry as an expression of great anguish, but a sensitive mother can tell whether the baby's cry is one of hunger, or weariness, or merely practice for his vocal cords. She understands that the cry is baby's first language.

Baby's first language is expression of raw feeling. The expression of feeling is immediate and clear. Delight, pain, anger, and fear are made known without restraint. From observing babies we can see the need for knowing a person in order to discern what he means by his language. Experts cannot tell by hearing a baby's cry whether he is mad, sad, or glad; mother knows. Curbing display of the emotion does not diminish the feeling. Young children are likely to interpret the admonition "stop crying" to mean "stop feeling that way." Numerous adults are ill because they learned as children that it is wrong to feel strongly. Consider if you know less useful advice than "stop worrying; don't be afraid." In accepting this advice, we worry about worrying and are afraid to be afraid. As children grow, they learn more specific, more productive, more acceptable languages of emotion.

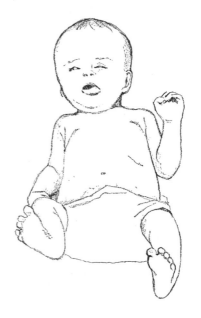

When baby is in his third month, he spends most of his waking hours practicing the few sounds he is able to produce—sounds which may have been made accidentally at first. Even a deaf baby begins to make these first babbling baby sounds. Usually his vocal cords are in good condition, but lacking the ability to hear, he has no chance to develop his perceptions of sound. He soon becomes mute as well as deaf. To learn to push air over the vocal cords, to use tongue, lips, palate, and mouth to secure the desired results is a complicated task for baby. Soon he has developed to the point of imitating the voices of others. As mother leans over the crib, baby utters, "da da." Mother responds with, "da da." The sound of his voice and of his mother's furnish further stimuli. A circular reflex is established for more sound producing. It is well to state here that the Broca area of the brain, the portion controlling the manipulation of sound and speech, is the most highly specialized area in motor development.

The development of speech is one of baby's most important social functions. When he begins to babble, he takes a giant stride toward becoming a real member of the family. Parents find it intriguing for baby to echo back their "da da's" and "ma ma's" in similar tones and inflections. It is doubtful if baby associates his sounds with mother and father, but he doesn't need to, for the parents are quite ready to make the association! When daddy returns from work, baby's accomplishments are proudly displayed and brothers and sisters join the family group around the crib cooing and gooing—much to baby's delight *and their own.* Baby has found a way to give the family enjoyment and zest and to receive much adoring attention. He is learning to become a communicating human.

His progress in speech, from this early experimentation at the age of three or four months until he is around two and a half, is one of the phenomenal learning feats in his entire development. During this time baby learns to associate objects with their names, to speak many words, to obey simple commands and some prohibitions, to put words together to form short sentences, and to begin to express relationships through words. Briefly, the development in speech progresses in the following sequence: [13] Sometime between nine and ten months he is able to imitate sounds and words of others. This newly acquired function is practiced in an atmosphere of much socialization in which those around him help him associate a word with an object. Frequently the first word he uses that is associated with an object is *mama.* Most babies begin to use words that they associate with objects sometime between fifteen and eighteen months. Before the baby uses his associations in speech, he shows that he comprehends the associations by obeying simple commands and prohibitions.

As with adults, the words baby understands far exceed the vocabulary he is able to use. The first words he uses are generally nouns. They constitute over half of the speech of the two-year-old. A specific term is frequently generalized to stand for all like objects. Thus "daddy" may be the postman, the milkman, the bus driver, the delivery boy, and other

---

[13] Dorothea McCarthy, "Language Development in Children," in *Manual of Child Psychology,* ed., L. Carmichael (New York: John Wiley and Sons, Inc., 1954), pp. 492-630.

men. "Bow-bow" may be all dogs. Soon baby learns to put words together. He may say, "Me go . . . I do it . . . Me up . . . No, me want it . . . No nap . . . Milk all gone." These short sentences gradually become longer and expressive of more relationships. The connecting words may not be in the child's vocabulary but he expresses cause and effect, purpose, and reason. When overturning his cup of milk, he says, "Milk spilled. No more milk." When being wrapped up to go outside, he inquires, "Going to play in park?" If he hears another child crying in the park, he asks, "What for she cry?"

Children this age love repetition and strong rhythmic movement. They repeat nonsense syllables over and over and in so doing gain control of their new-found vocal powers. They beseech you to read them a story and the story they ask for is one with repetitive rhymes or phrases. They enjoy having you set your movements with them to a rhythmic, repetitive pattern such as, "Up we go." Babies respond to music at a very early age and learn to love it if adults are wise enough to make it a part of their culture without emphasizing "good taste" too early.

The development of speech illustrates the principle of differentiation in growth. At first all sounds seem to baby to be undifferentiated, but as nerve connections and muscles develop, baby learns to differentiate between pitches, inflections, sources of sound, varieties of feelings that sounds produce in the mouth and throat. Finally the young learner differentiates between a wide, wide variety of sounds and meanings. Few of us ever completely master the process of differentiation in language. Indeed, the language sets up some formidable barriers with its frequency of homonyms and its breadth of origins. How puzzling it must be to a runabout to learn that a "choo-choo" is a train and then to hear us say, "We must *train* that dog to heel!" He goes to Sunday School and learns that good *souls* go to Heaven and then hears his dad remark that his shoes need new *soles*. He learns from his story book that a king *reigns* and then it *rains!* Yet by the time baby becomes a runabout of two and a half he usually has a vocabulary of around five hundred words which he uses with considerable accuracy.

The sequence of steps we have discussed in language development may be telescoped by some children to such a degree that they cannot be sorted out. Some children seem to blossom into short sentences from the babbling stage. Some cling to their babbling much longer than others. As in all learning, the quality of satisfaction experienced, the emotional overtones felt by the baby during the time this developmental task is on

the timetable for accomplishment affect the quality and rate of the learning. We have seen in earlier chapters how babies who lack love do not
learn to talk. We have wondered how much the mother's talking to her
baby influences his speech development. Recently we have observed
closely two mothers with their infants. One of the mothers is quiet, reserved, and reticent. She just doesn't talk much to anyone. Her children
developed speech much more slowly than did those of the other mother
who is a gay, talkative individual.

What can adults do to help baby along with this task of becoming
a communicating human? We can provide him with an environment of
trust and confidence. We can respond to him, answering in his terms, as he
makes his first funny noises, by laughing, smiling, and noise-making with
him. By such behavior we stimulate baby to continue his practice; we
assure him that the world is not harsh, cold, forbidding.

Use of Hands, Arms, and Head

Baby is born with a reflex grasp, but he cannot voluntarily "let go of"
an object for another six months. During the first few weeks baby has
to make a change-over from involuntary grasping to voluntary grasping.
It takes over a year for this function to develop fully. Here we have an
example of another principle of growth—the reorganization into higher,
more inclusive patterns. As baby matures, he is able to reorganize his
grasping mechanism so that it serves a higher purpose.

Baby discovers his hands about the fourth month and begins to play
with them. He spreads his fingers, watching the process. He sticks everything he holds into his mouth. He needs objects to handle. No toymaker
has improved upon three or four spools loosely strung together. Baby
needs some objects that do something in response to him: sway, rattle,
roll. Floating toys in the bath move with his splashes. Dangled baubles
sway. His eye muscles are exercised. Baby attempts to get both hands to
come together and great is the day when he succeeds, for again a
maturation has been reached. At about the sixth month, he learns to
transfer objects from one hand to the other. He also discovers his feet
and begins to grasp them. He pulls them up to his face for inspection.
Inevitably the day comes when he succeeds in getting his big toe (which
may be any part of his foot) into his mouth. He probably has learned
to roll over by now and is able to push himself up by his hands when on

his stomach. And then during the seventh month, as baby is sitting up to be fed, he begins the delightful game of dropping objects from his feeding tray and banging objects together. Again baby's socialization needs are being met as he and mother or older brother or sister play at dropping and retrieving. Incidentally he is gaining much needed skill in "letting go of" objects.

When baby is about eight months old, he uses his hands for crawling. He tries to feed himself, and by the ninth month he begins to manipulate objects between his thumb and fingers. He enjoys "pat-a-caking" and playing simple games that involve manipulative skills such as passing a toy back and forth. He develops consider-able skill in finding and picking up objects and becomes increasingly able to handle smaller objects with more precision. An ex-cellent film that illustrates the synchroniza-tion of baby's grasping power and eye de-velopment is *Life Begins*.[14]

By the time he is two years old, our young learner is able to feed himself quite well, to manipulate many sizes and shapes of objects. He loves boxes and bottles and spends many hours filling and emptying them with anything available. He learns to put small objects inside larger ones and begins to get some notions about matching shapes. He is able to manage block building if he is lucky enough to have large blocks as part of his environment. If not, boxes or pans serve as adequate substitutes. He is curious about the feel of things. Before he learns to feed himself with a spoon, he practices feeding himself with his hands. He is learning to control the hand-to-mouth coordination movement with precision. He is also learning about the textures of foods. He is making a whale of a mess of himself and mother's floor, but this doesn't distress *him*. If mother can tolerate this hand-feeding stage, she will probably find spoon-feeding presents no trouble when the time arrives for it. He enjoys all kinds of textures—the squoosh of mud, the graininess of sand, the oiliness of crayons, the resistance of hard surfaces.

---

[14] *Life Begins*, 60 min., sound. Distributed by New York University Film Library.

Baby's use of his hands and arms can only develop as he learns to control his head. You probably recall how a newborn infant's head jerks and wobbles when he is held upright. All of us have heard the admonition, "Put your hand behind the baby's head!" When our ancestors walked on all fours, the muscles at the back of the neck needed to be stronger than those in front. Our bodies seem to carry many useless vestiges of our evolutionary past. This is one of them. Baby can lift his head when on his stomach but it takes three or four months before nerve and muscle tissue support these movements when baby is held upright. As soon as he learns to hold his head steady, he begins to notice what is going on around him. So at about three months, baby begins to work intensively on the control of his arms and hands. This is another illustration of how growth proceeds from the head downward.

Locomotion

Baby's locomotion at birth is limited to some very restrictive reflexes, such as the Moro (startle) reflex, and his ability to wave his arms and legs around. He really can't go anywhere. He can't even turn over. We have seen how he learns to control his head and how simultaneously he gains control of his hands and arms and learns how to move himself through the use of his hands. During the fifth month his ankles begin to straighten and about this time he learns how to roll over completely. He can pivot on his protruding belly and can get from place to place by rolling. He pushes himself up when on his stomach; then mother has to watch out, for baby is about ready to make his first independent lunge. He will not develop these capacities in a soft crib. He needs a clean floor.

For several weeks baby has been practicing holding his head and chest high while supporting himself on his forearms. His next development is to raise his body and support himself by the palms of his extended hands. Soon he learns it is possible to lift both his chest and pelvis off the surface at the same time. This gives him freedom of movement, and he uses it from then on. Baby makes his first lunge sometime between the fourth and sixth month. The distance from a lunge to a crawl is almost imperceptible. If you doubt the creativity of young humans, observe a number of babies crawling. You'll find almost as many distinctive crawls as babies. Some learn to crawl backwards before going forward. Some use a sideward movement. Nearly all have some distinctive quality.

The neural and muscular development needed for crawling is similar to that needed for sitting. At birth baby will fall face forward if you set him up. In the third and fourth months he begins to push forward his neck and shoulders while lying on his back and then to hold up his head and shoulders while lying on his stomach. When he learns to push himself backward as he sits, he is about ready to master sitting alone. This usually occurs by the eighth month. Just about as soon as he can sit alone he is pulling himself to his feet.

In harmony with the principle of growth extending downward (the cephalocaudal law), the last major task the baby accomplishes in gaining control of his body is to learn to walk. The sequential steps are given below:

> The newborn baby, when supported, will sometimes make a few reflex steps without attempting to keep his back rigid or to hold up his head.
> At four months or so, after he has learned to control his head, he adopts the toe stance with his feet close together. The stepping movements are almost lost but he learns to bounce up and down at this time.
> He pulls himself from a sitting position to standing with support.
> With his back upright and his arms outstretched for balance, he places his feet far apart to widen his base as he stands alone.
> He gains the courage to step out with the same wide spacing of his legs and a very uncertain gait. Finally, when he is sure of his balance, he puts one foot before the other and acquires accurate control over equilibrium.
> It is interesting that the alternate arm movements which are a definite part of walking appear at a later date.[15]

The Runabout

Babies usually graduate into runabouts or toddlers some place between fifteen and eighteen months. A few learn to walk at about a year. Walking proceeds from standing alone, hanging on to tables or chairs to get ahead, then taking a step alone, then walking longer

---

[15] C. Anderson Aldrich and Mary M. Aldrich, *Babies Are Human Beings* (New York: The Macmillan Company, 1954), p. 46.

distances holding on to daddy's finger and then gaining enough confidence to go it all alone. The time the baby walks depends somewhat on the courage and confidence he has acquired as he has grown to this point. He walks more securely in hard-soled shoes since his toes still tend to curl. At the time the baby walks, as Aldrich so clearly states, baby's world changes. He is able to make himself a nuisance and he does. The house has to be baby-proofed. Dangerous gadgets must be kept out of reach; valuables moved to higher shelves—for baby learns to climb soon after he learns to walk. Mother begins to fear the long silence which she anticipates will be followed by a crash. Baby learns the words, "No, No! Don't touch!" and frequently, "You bad child!" This is commonly known as the "No! No!" stage of development.

For the student of human development, there is an important insight to be gained from this bit of growth. Walking is one of man's most distinctively human characteristics. We want our babies to learn to walk— many of us try to rush them into walking by the artificial stimulation of walkers. (The walker may be a household necessity for the busy mother of an active one-year-old, but it does delay walking for a few weeks since the motive to get about is satisfied.) Yet when the change in behavior occurs that accompanies walking, we are unable to cope with it. We, through our own inadequacies, develop negativism, feelings of shame and doubt and confusion when we punish or restrict the child who is following through on his own developmental growth pattern. The expectation of change and the readiness to accept it is basic to constructive child care. Parents and other adults who are responsible for this age must consider carefully the kind of preventive planning that makes punishment *unnecessary* for behavior that is *necessary* for the growth of an individual at any age. When we discuss early adolescence, we shall note the same tendency of adults to punish the adolescent for that which he must do to become an adult—namely, to gain his independence. When a child walks, he has taken his first major step toward the goal of ultimately being a self-directive human. He must gain gratification from walking. Let's be sure we do not handicap him in his quest for autonomy at this age.

From the time the child begins to walk he grows in his desire to do things for himself. He insists upon trying to dress himself. He feeds himself. He spends most of his time touring around his environment by one medium of transportation or another. If he sits on daddy's lap, he squirms, and insists upon playing "trot-a-horse." He loves to go piggy-back. He

likes anything that moves, from doll carriages, to tractors, to cars, to fire
engines. If he is sitting on a chair, he is probably banging both heels
against it. He has his own peculiar way of getting himself seated on a
chair. He usually carries something by using both hands. He is the busiest
little person you ever saw. Perhaps this is the reason Aldrich calls him
a "hard-working citizen."

Most of his responses are whole-bodied responses. He walks over
people and objects that are in his way with no awareness of having done
so. If he sees an object in his path, he is likely to be diverted by it for a
few seconds and then moves on to some other exploration. He is becoming
aware of other children; and when he encounters them in the park or at
play, he is likely to poke them as if to try to find out what they are like.
Often he will go up and throw his arms around another child his own
size with so much gusto as to unbalance the receiver of this doubtful bit
of affection. He likes picture books, songs, rhymes, and rhythmic games.
Sometimes you find him just standing near another child watching him
at play. Frequently he plays alone. He seldom plays with another child
for long intervals.

**Differentiation
of Perception**
As the baby grows during these
first two and a half years, he is beginning to develop a self. At first,
we believe, he perceives the world
as indistinguishable from himself.
He exists in a non-differentiated world. He knows wetness, light, dark,
hunger, feeding, noise; but he does not connect any of these qualities
with a source or as something apart from himself. Piaget says:

> During the earliest stages the child perceives things like a solipsist who
> is unaware of himself as subject and is familiar only with his own actions.
> But step by step with the coordination of his intellectual instruments he
> discovers himself in placing himself as an active object among the other
> active objects in a universe external to himself.[16]

In this chapter we have traced the beginnings of the coordination of these
"intellectual instruments."

The experiences of the baby create meanings which gradually permit

---

[16] Jean Piaget, *The Construction of Reality in the Child* (New York: Basic Books,
Inc., 1954, p. 352. We suggest you read the entire chapter entitled "The Elaboration
of the Universe," pp. 350-386.

him to see himself as a separate entity and to recognize objects outside himself as being separate from him. During this pre-memory age he looks upon objects as means to satisfactions or dissatisfactions. A great many adults do, too. The developmental task that only begins during these years and is of consuming interest in the pre-school years is that of locating and understanding "I, me, mine." This is one of the most puzzling and difficult tasks that awaits our young human. The roots of how he feels about himself, what he sees when he finally comes to understand, "I, me, mine" are put down during this period of life. They are subject to change, of course, but their first growth unmistakably affects the development of the self. The baby and the toddler begin work on other developmental tasks, too. They begin to get a feeling of "rightness" and "wrongness," and they may learn to distinguish maleness and femaleness.

Summary

In this chapter we have tried to tell the story of the beginnings of life. Since our discussion is necessarily limited, you have to go beyond these few pages to supplement your knowledge of this stage of life. We hope that you will find the suggestions and resources at the end of the chapter of value. They have served us well through the years.

We have tried to demonstrate how all growth is integrated, and how no one segment—such as the mental, with which the teacher is most directly concerned—is understandable apart from the total growth pattern. We have tried to pull out of the early years of growth some principles that must function if we are to guide wisely. We would like to summarize these principles:

The basic motive force of all creatures is the quest for gratification (pleasure), and the avoidance of unpleasantness (pain). The child as a whole moves toward comfort and warmth, recoils from unpleasant and painful circumstances.

Every human being has an inborn resistance to the imposition of outside force. In all growth we see a thrust toward independence, self-sufficiency. A healthily growing human is in charge of his own life as much as his capacity and resources permit. Teaching is a process of utilizing individual developmental growth patterns, wisely timed and "teased out," through recognizing budding interests which are the evidences of dawning capacities.

The growing human learns self-control gradually. To urge perform-ance before the child has capacity for it is to delay and distort growth. Example: Urging baby to use a spoon and keep his hands out of his food before needed neuro-muscular controls have developed is to delay spoon-feeding.

The process of living is ever-changing. To resist change, even to lament it, is to invite trouble. Example: Baby climbs out of the pen in which he has played peacefully for months. From that point on the play-pen is better used as a refuge for father to read his evening paper.

Change is gradual not precipitous. Baby changes from breast to bottle by less frequent breast feedings, more frequent bottles. The early bottles are taken while cuddling warmly against mother's breast. Sudden change startles the psyche as surely as a loud noise disrupts composure.

Integration, wholeness of personality, takes place through specializa-tion. Use of the hands improves as thumb and fingers can act independ-ently. But it's always the child who picks up the toy, not his thumb and his fingers.

Every human differs from all others. One knows little about one baby through intimate knowledge of another. Little Billy seems to relish the warm humidity of his wet diapers; Bobby screams with outrage until his are removed. Nellie gurgles with glee in a piggy-back ride; Lottie de-mands to be put down at once.

Suggestions for Further Exploration

▶ Visit a museum or university, if at all possible, and study preserved fetuses at various stages of development.

▶ Visit a nursery in a hospital and observe the neonates you find there, noting the varieties of behaviors you find.

▶ Spend a few hours around a baby beginning to learn to talk or to walk. Watch for a couple of weeks to see if you note any progression in skill. Watch him "drill." Count the number of times he repeats one action.

▶ Spend a few hours with a two-year-old and note how his behavior differs from that of a one-year-old. For a few minutes imitate every move he makes.

▶ Select any phase of baby's development that particularly interests you, such as hearing, seeing, speaking, and make a detailed study of it from conception to two and a half.

► By referring back to this chapter, make a timetable by months of baby's accomplishments so you have a summary of what to expect of baby at any age. Allow for overlaps in places where there may be varying rates of growth.

► Develop a profile (the life story) of the individual you are studying to cover the first two years of his life. Fill in as many of the details of development as you can find out from him, his folks, or from records. Hypothesize what the details are that you cannot verify. Include in your profile such information as:

A description of the circumstances of his birth

A description of the individual at birth: weight, length, any details that indicate uniqueness

A description of the beginnings of talking, crawling, walking

► Develop a list of examples emerging from your own life that illustrate the principles summarized at the end of this chapter.

► Much understanding comes from viewing some of the many excellent films depicting the early years. We list a few of the well-known ones.

Baby Meets His Parents (No. 1 in the Series on Personality Development), 11 min., sound, Encyclopaedia Britannica Films.

Depicts the ways in which the treatment baby receives shapes his personality.

Expressive Movements (*Affectomotor Patterns*) *in Infancy,* 42 min., silent. Distributed by New York University Film Library.

Depicts the relationships between expressive patterns of crying, smiling, and the like with patterns of manipulation, locomotion, and interpersonal relations. Emphasizes individual variations which seem to be inborn.

Life Begins, 60 min., sound, Encyclopaedia Britannica Films.

This film is a classic showing Dr. Gesell's work at the Yale University Clinic of Child Development. The film was made at the Clinic and provides a record of the development of infants from birth to eighteen months.

Life with Baby, 18 min., sound, March of Time.

Another of the Gesell films growing out of candid-camera sequences photographed at the Yale Clinic.

The Smile of the Baby (Film Studies of the Psychoanalytic Research Project on Problems in Infancy Series), 30 min., sound, New York University Film Library.

Shows the varied responses of infants between two and six months to human beings and indicates some of the reasons for the differences in these responses.

Additional Sources You May Find Helpful

C. Anderson Aldrich and Mary M. Aldrich, *Babies Are Human Beings*. New York: The Macmillan Company, 1954.

Dr. Aldrich, mentor of Dr. Benjamin Spock—author of widely used child care books—and his wife wrote this book primarily for parents. We find it valuable in helping us understand how nature has provided the baby with a developmental pattern for growth that must be honored if we are not to thwart growth. Excellent chapters on eating, elimination, and sleeping.

Charlotte Buhler, *The First Year of Life*. New York: John Day and Company, 1930.

Dr. Buhler is a thorough and comprehensive student of early infancy. This book is a classic among her writings.

L. Carmichael, ed., *Manual of Child Psychology*, 2nd ed. New York: John Wiley and Sons, Inc., 1954.

A comprehensive compendium of researches in the area of child growth. Excellent for detailed analysis and documentation.

E. H. Erikson, *Childhood and Society*. New York: W. W. Norton and Company, Inc., 1951.

A significant presentation from a psychoanalytical orientation of the development of the child's critical alternatives as he grows. His attitudes of trust or distrust developed as an infant affect his perceptions of the world throughout life.

Arnold Gesell and Catherine S. Amatruda, *The Embryology of Behavior*. New York: Harper and Brothers, 1945.

Arnold Gesell and Frances L. Ilg, *Child Development*. New York: Harper and Brothers, 1949.

Dr. Gesell has made most comprehensive studies of behavior of infants and children and developed norms for behavior from birth through twelve years. A student of child development needs to know Dr. Gesell's work at the Yale University Clinic of Child Development.

M. S. Gilbert, *Biography of the Unborn*. Baltimore: Williams and Wilkins, 1938.

An analytical study of prenatal development. A classic in the area of prenatal biographies.

Wilbur E. Martin and Celia Burns Stendler, *Readings in Child Development*. New York: Harcourt, Brace and Company, 1954.

Excellent first-hand source material on physical growth.

Willard Olson, *Child Development*. Boston: D. C. Heath and Company, 1949.

The writings of a careful scholar who has followed a group of children from birth into adulthood (longitudinal study). A careful reading of this book helps one respect the wide range of individual differences possible within normal behavior.

Jean Piaget, *The Construction of Reality in the Child*. New York: Basic Books, Inc., 1954.

A fundamental book but very difficult to read. A detailed description of how a child develops his concepts of his world.

L. Joseph Stone and Joseph Church, *Childhood and Adolescence*. New York: Random House, 1957.

Particularly valuable for this age as it draws on research done at Sarah Lawrence and Vassar College in the Department of Child Study.

Kenneth Soddy, ed., *Mental Health and Infant Development*, Vols. I, II. New York: Basic Books, Inc., 1956.

Excellent recording of proceedings of the Seminar on Mental Health and Infant Development held in England in 1952, sponsored by the World Health Organization. The Seminar was attended by child development specialists, anthropologists, and others. Especially useful in acquainting the reader with child-rearing practices in many parts of the world. See discussion of "Child Development Patterns in the United States," pp. 87-100.

9

The Pre-school Years

We left our toddler at two and a half an active person, a "hard-working citizen" bent upon establishing his identity as an individual. He has acquired much skill in locomotion and is well on his way in language development. He is by all odds the most active member of his family group. But in spite of all this activity, rare is the individual who remembers these days. Burr [1] found that only thirty-nine

---

[1] A. R. Burr, *The Autobiography* (Boston: Houghton Mifflin and Company, 1909).

autobiographies out of the three hundred he studied made any reference to the first three years. The quality of these early memories reveals the way in which perception develops. Plank quotes Kendon's description of his early memories as illustrative of the nebulous form of memories.

> Memories of very early days are strangely detached. Though we may be at any moment the sum of all our experiences, many experiences which must have been important in their influences upon our later lives have been quite forgotten and what suddenly flashes into mind is something bright but trivial, with no place in the story of our lives to account for its survival. These memories are neither striking nor significant, they are like little detached pieces of jigsaw puzzle.[2]

As the child grows, his perceptions become more distinct, so that memories do become a part of nearly all five-year-olds.

Our culture has regarded this period of life (from two and a half to five years of age) as relatively unimportant in personality development since the child is too young to understand or to remember. A great deal of experience is built into the infant's rapidly growing nervous system earlier than it can reach the awareness or conscious level of recognition and retention. The principal thesis of this chapter is that the quality and appropriateness of experience in the pre-school years markedly affects the whole course of development. The central nervous system enables the individual to make adaptive adjustments to his environment; environmental action stimulates development of the nervous system.[3] To deprive the toddler of rich and zestful experience is to stunt his growth as surely as a malnourished sapling grows into a scrawny tree. This chapter describes the process of growth during these highly impressionable years. We call them the pre-school years simply because most children this age do not attend school. We shall say a word about the need for nursery schools in our culture as we conclude this chapter.

The pre-school child is more open than he will ever be again. He is inclined to be more direct, spontaneous, and free in his responses than

---

[2] Emma N. Plank, "Memories of Early Childhood in Autobiographies," in *The Psychoanalytic Study of the Child,* Vol. VIII (New York: International Universities Press, Inc., 1953), p. 383.

[3] For a full description of this idea consult: R. W. Gerard, "Higher Levels of Integration," in *Biological Symposia,* Vol. VIII, ed., Robert Redfield (Lancaster, Penn.: The Jaques Cattell Press, 1942), pp. 68-74.

later in life. He cannot be taught to lie. Perhaps this is the meaning of, "Except ye be as little children ye shall not enter the Kingdom of Heaven." His world is expanding to include a great variety of objects, new experiences, and additional people. His development is multidirectional since this is an age when learning is rapid and results more from his kinds of experiencing and less from the developmental patterns laid down by nature in the muscles and nervous system.

The developmental tasks of the pre-school child are to gain more skill and control over his body, especially the function of elimination; to further differentiate between sexes; to develop his language ability; to sharpen and expand his perceptions of reality, and to begin to distinguish between reality and fantasy; to continue establishing his identity and importance as a person; to continue developing concepts of right and wrong; and to become a social individual related through emotional ties to those around him. Need we say that the child's sense of success or failure in achieving these tasks consists of the feelings and perceptions he has about his world. These tasks demand the energy of the whole person interacting with whatever environment is his. They can be accomplished successfully only as the individual's body matures and as he feels encouraged by his own social world as he perceives it.

The pre-school child is very much an individual. Since he has not had time to learn all the "normal ways" of his culture, we find a wide, wide range of behaviors. Some are much more babyish than others. Some already have become "aloners;" others are quite aware of and curious about other children. Some show marked creativeness; some are willing to follow routines without rebellion. Some are easy to handle, and seem to want to please adults, while others seem determined to have their own way. Some are punishing; others seek punishment. Some are restricted in movement and inhibited in responses. Some are timid; others aggressive. Some have many other children with whom to play. Others are *only* children in a household of doting adults. Some have mothers who are tender and loving and have much time to spend with them. Others have mothers who provide them grudgingly with the minimum essentials of life. Keep in mind as we discuss the pre-school child that you will find many variations of the central theme presented. Your study of this age group will mean more if you are able to observe some pre-school children in a variety of situations.

Control

of the Body

The rate of physical growth slows down during this age. It will not reach the rate of the infant's growth until puberty. A child's height increases only about nine inches from two to five years. His rate of gain in weight decreases gradually until he is gaining only about five pounds a year when he reaches kindergarten. His proportions change during this period. He ceases to be the cherubic figure made famous by Renaissance painters and begins to take on adult proportions. At five his head is about the size it will be when he is grown. His legs, at five, are about 44 per cent of his height. When he was two, his legs were 34 per cent of him.

Motor Development

The child improves in the functioning of his motor skills as his body takes on more adult proportions and he has time for more practice. In fact most five-year-olds are highly graceful individuals. He masters the problem of asymmetry which has kept him carrying objects in two hands. As he grows into asymmetrical functioning, he learns to swing his arms in alternating movements with his feet as he walks, and learns to ride a tricycle with alternate foot movements.

We recently observed a little girl learning to ride a tricycle and were somewhat amused at the keen understanding of her slightly older sister and dismayed at her mother's lack of understanding. Mother and the four-year-old and Jane, two and a half, were coming down the street. Jane was on the tricycle but obviously was having difficulty making the thing go. The older sister had run ahead a few feet. Mother was admonishing Jane, "Push down on the pedal, Jane. Push!" The older child, sensing the difficulty, ran back to the family group saying, "You know what, mom, I think we better let Jane practice for a few more years or days." (Thus the four-year-old showed her concept of time.) Then standing behind Jane she patted her on the back. Mother paid no attention to this bit of advice but motioned the older sister aside with another instruction, "Push, Jane, push!" Jane pushed once and stopped. More admonitions from mother yielded no results. Finally mother, exasperated, grabbed Jane abruptly from the tricycle and motioned for the older child to get on. Jane wailed and went into a brief temper tantrum. Her mother scolded her and gave her a slap.

As the older sister wisely remarked, given a little more practice Jane will master the tricycle. Nagging before she is ready to learn will not increase her learning speed.

The pre-school child is able to scale ladders, climb jungle gyms, jump, and run with some precision of movement. He may learn to skip at this time. He still gains his major satisfactions from moving. His coordination improves. This is the age of the big muscle development which has become in many nursery schools a major emphasis that has tended to block more complete experiencing. Murphy, on the basis of years of study of this age, sounds a wise word of caution about limiting experiencing to any one emphasis:

> ... Thus in the nineteen-thirties awareness of the fact that two-year-olds have so recently developed the capacity of locomotion led to an over-emphasis by nursery school educators on large-muscle activities and their role. This often left out of account the wide differences in need for or interest in these large-muscle activities.[4]

Control of Elimination

Gaining complete voluntary control of elimination is a developmental task that most children accomplish during the pre-school years. At two and a half, 40 per cent still have daytime toilet "accidents." The manner in which toilet training is given is of lifelong importance, as we stated in the previous chapter. The lower-class culture is usually more relaxed in its attitude toward early toilet training than is the middle-class culture, although this varies with geographical regions.[5] In addition to interrupting the natural developmental process of gaining control of the sphincters, attitudes of shame and uncleanliness that are often inculcated at this

---

[4] Lois B. Murphy and Associates, *Personality in Young Children* (New York: Basic Books, Inc., 1956), p. 189.

[5] Allison Davis, *Social-Class Influences upon Learning* (Cambridge: Harvard University Press, 1948), pp. 12-22.

time are of lasting harm. It is as natural for a child to be interested in his feces as it is for him to notice any other object around him. It is also as natural for him to be interested in his genitals as it was for him to be interested in his feet when he discovered them. No mother would think of slapping her baby for sticking his big toe in his mouth, or saying "Dirty, Dirty! For shame!" It makes as much sense to the toddler to respond with disgust and shock when he matures to the point of noticing his feces and being interested in his genitals.

The tasks with which we can help the pre-school child are: learning to make the associations that are necessary to gain voluntary control of both bowel and bladder elimination, and keeping healthy, unashamed attitudes toward all his body. As a footnote we might add that under severe emotional strain or fatigue, children will lose control of their bladders for many years after they begin school. We hope the era is almost over when children are shamed and held up to public ridicule for such behavior. Yet we wonder as we read this account by a teacher written in 1958:

> I was brought up sharp by seeing Patricia ready to go home as soon as everyone else. Usually she is the last to leave. "Oh, look! Here's something on the floor," said a little girl standing by Patricia's desk. I detained Patricia and *confronted her with the telltale evidence*. At first she was embarrassed and denied having had an accident. Finally she admitted that she had not been able to make it out of the room in time. I had a little talk with Patricia and she realized more speed on her part would have prevented the accident.

This teacher didn't realize how her own feelings of shame were revealed in the words, "confronted her with the telltale evidence." She may have been projecting her own middle-class values, learned as a child, onto Patricia whose family and neighbors did not respect the same values.

Differentiation in Perceptions About Sex

The pre-school child usually notices the anatomical differences between boys and girls, especially if he lives in an environment that provides any freedom. You doubtless are familiar with the cartoon of the little boy and girl this age peering down the insides of their panties and saying, "There *is* a difference!" This captures the attitude of the pre-

schooler toward sex differences. Lillian Smith in *The Journey*[6] deals
most perceptively with the discovery of girlness and boyness by some
children this age and their budding interest in getting the animal kingdom
classified as male or female. Sometimes little girls and boys, too, want
to stand up "like daddy" to urinate. These perceptions are about the
extent to which a child differentiates between the significance of being
boy or girl, until he is between four and five. In dramatic play the boy
takes the mother's role as readily as the father's—probably most boys
prefer to be the "mother" since it is a more dominant role in their perceptions.

The child, especially the middle-class child, frequently learns during
this stage of life that adults have many anxieties about sex and often he
becomes confused about sex functioning and elimination. Someplace
along the age continuum he receives sexual gratification from manipulation of the sex organs. Freud calls this the phallic stage to designate the
area of gratification shifting from the anal to the genital region. One does
not need to be Freudian or accept all of his theories to recognize that
human beings do have a progression in the sources of their gratifications.
Considerable evidence post-dating Freud is consistent with the basic
hypothesis upon which he based his developmental pattern of sexual development. Freud believed that the child falls in love with the parent of
the opposite sex; but, recognizing the futility of displacing the more
powerful rival, starts to identify with him.[7] Thus the boy begins to
identify with his father about five and through identifying begins to
learn the masculine role. Conversely, the five-year-old girl identifies with
her mother and learns how to be a "little lady." An illustration of this
identification process furnished by a teacher reads:

> When his father came out Kenny (age five) smiled broadly and relaxed;
> he took his hand for a few seconds but dropped it as they started to move
> toward the elevator. As they came near me, Kenny said, "Here's my Daddy.
> I am going to get my hair cut; Daddy is going to get his cut, too. George
> cuts my hair and then he cuts my Dad's." Just then the elevator arrived and
> I heard the father tell Kenny to wait while I got on. As soon as we were
> in the elevator, Kenny told the operator that "me and my Dad are going to
> get a haircut. Does George cut your hair, Joe?"
> At this point Kenny looked at his father and saw that he had removed

---

[6] Lillian Smith, *The Journey* (New York: World Publishing Company, 1954), pp.
112-117.

[7] Of course, this is a very simplified explanation of the process of identification.

his hat; very self-consciously Kenny took off his own cap. The father had his hat in one hand, his other was resting on the elevator railing. Kenny took up this same pose even though it put quite a strain on his arm. When the elevator reached the ground floor, Kenny, with an eye on his father, waited for the other passengers to leave the car and then followed his father out. We said good-by. I noticed that Kenny smiled up at his father, lengthened his stride in an effort to match his father's, and the two men were off.

Let's return a moment to a consideration of masturbation. Much harm is done by making an issue of masturbation and threatening the child with dire consequences that are untrue, and that may frighten him so much as to block natural sexual development. While scientific attitudes have shifted greatly since the beginning of the century, parents are frequently quite anxious about this phase of sexual development.[8] Chisholm, former director of the World Health Organization, has an excellent discussion of the effects of our attitudes toward masturbation. We recommend his discussion to you. He describes mother's probable reaction upon discovering her child masturbating, which he calls "a perfectly normal and healthy exploration of his total environment." Mother disapproves and shows horror and disgust. She may slap the child's hand and reinforce her words by, "Stop that, dirty, dirty, if you do that Mother won't love you any more." Chisholm continues:

> . . . A taboo, guarded by fear of loss of love, is set up, which has the effect of rendering his body permanently dirty and disgusting, and of crippling one of his most important physiological and his most important biological functions. . . .
>
> It becomes necessary for the frightened child to stop his normal experiments whenever anyone else might see him . . . but the mother is suspicious. . . . The next time she takes further steps to enforce the taboo by means of threats to tell the father, threats that such behavior will lead to insanity, or still worse, threats of the displeasure and vengeance of an all-powerful and all-seeing God, who watches the child all the time and can even see him in the dark and under the bedclothes. . . .
>
> The social consequences of learning to repress while young are all destructive, but the mother feels that she has done her duty.[9]

---

[8] To get a picture of the shift in attitude toward masturbation from the beginning of the century until now, we recommend that you read: G. Stanley Hall, *Adolescence,* Vol. I (New York: D. Appleton and Company, 1904), pp. 432-453.

[9] Brock Chisholm, *Can People Learn to Learn?* (New York: Harper and Brothers, 1958), pp. 98-99.

Masturbation, like any other growth process, should be treated casually. The growing child has a better chance of accepting a more mature developmental pattern if parents' fears and punishments have not established masturbation as the ultimate form of sexual fulfillment.

At this age children may ask questions about life, especially if another baby is on the way. Such questions should be answered simply, giving the child the information he has asked for without trying to give him a full course in sex education and genetics. One little boy, who had been so exposed, remarked, "You know, they say I'm the way I am because of my blue *jeans.*"

Language Development and Perception

When we left our toddler at two and a half, he had about five hundred words at his command. He has around two thousand words in his vocabulary when he first goes to school at the age of five. This increase has not come about without sharp attention and much drill on the part of our small learner. Try listening to a three- or four-year-old. He enjoys rolling sounds around in his mouth and throat. Over and over he will repeat nonsense rhymes, rhythmic syllables, and chants. As you read aloud, he will join you in reciting the text. We like the *New Yorker's* account of a five-year-old's concept of a speech, developed from much listening, no doubt:

> In Central Park the other afternoon, a five-year-old advised a contemporary that his father was going to make a speech at his club. "What's a speech?" he was asked. "I'll make a speech," said the five-year-old, and went on, "Doors are dangerous. You mustn't throw toys. You mustn't pinch necks, because it makes you cough. God isn't an animal and mountains don't die. When you play with a hoop, be careful or you'll get a splinter in your finger. You mustn't throw your car in the river, because it will get rusty and you may need to ride in it." The contemporary looked properly edified.[10]

In his language he still sees objects as action symbols to satisfy his needs and interests. A delightful illustration of this is the recording of four- and five-year-olds in *A Hole Is to Dig:*

A face is so you can make faces.
Dogs are to kiss people.

---

[10] *The New Yorker,* June 21, 1958, p. 24.

Hands are to hold.
A hole is to dig.[11]

His growth in language shows development in his perceptions. He begins to put himself in another's place—the first dawnings of a sense of the "other." As he plays mother, for instance, his conversation may go like this child's did:

> Oh, dear, I just never get enough sleep. I have so much to do. I just wish I could be left alone to sleep as long as I want to. . . . Mother must hurry and get the dinner ready so Daddy can eat on time because he'll be tired when he gets home and I don't want to upset him.

As a toddler, he had begun to associate objects and names. During these two and a half years he takes several additional steps in conceptual development. He begins to learn to distinguish between objects that are somewhat alike but have different characteristics. For example, he can tell a horse from a cow or a pig from a dog. He can tell that a truck is different from a car or a trailer. His next step is to be able to designate characteristic functions as going with certain objects. For example, trains go "choo-choo," cars go "putt-putt," babies cry. As he makes these distinctions, he first perceives only differences. His ability to abstract likenesses and develop categories from them develops about the time he enters kindergarten.

We must note that all of these steps in language development are contingent upon the child's development in perception. From a vaguely felt indiscriminate mass, sharper and sharper definitions emerge. These definitions concern time, space, and people. The toddler has little notion of time except as a signal for him to perform his daily functions. By the time he has reached five, he begins to sense a future but his time framework is still wobbly. One four-year-old illustrated this concept when he said, "I saw you on Sunday. I think it was Sunday." Chanting the days of the week, he continued, "Yes, Sunday, because Friday is before Saturday, and Saturday is before Sunday." His reaching back into the past is in terms of himself. He is curious to hear about himself as a baby. He still has a distance to go before he can tell time; and, of course, he does not necessarily understand time if he can tell it. This explanation of how a

---

[11] Ruth Krauss and Maurice Sendak, *A Hole Is to Dig* (New York: Harper and Brothers, 1952).

child's perceptions develop is only one of many that might be given. Smillie raises this question: Do we not read much of our adult need for "expectation, prediction, and comparison" into the child's responses and thus judge him less mature because his responses are "basically (of) the world of the immediate?" He tells of Michael who, in a testing situation, saw no reason to categorize a dress, for "A dress is a dress." [12]

Space concepts at this age are limited to the immediate environment of the child. He has some perception of down, up, around, beneath, inside, on top of, beside; but he is a rare four-year-old if he has much concept of distance and space. He still finds it possible to believe that the people seen on the television screen are real people and are shut up "inside the box." Circumstances of living have psychological effects upon children's concepts of space. Children who feel insecure are inclined to depict this feeling by drawing tight, small figures. Children living in close, crowded city dwellings probably have a different perception of space than those who live in the wide open spaces. The authors have observed such children for several years and have found that they tend to feel themselves small and less significant compared to children who live with more space around them. For an interesting discussion of the psychological implications of space as revealed in children's drawings we recommend that you read Lowenfeld. He summarizes a most insightful discussion of the meaning of space as follows: "Not only does the significance, which is assigned to the self, change with regard to the importance it has in relation to environment, but the spaces also change with regard to the emotional significance they have to us." [13]

While the pre-school child may be able to count to ten, he seldom understands number concepts beyond two or three. The counting is mere recitation of rote symbols. If you ask him to make groups, he forms groups of two or sometimes of three.

Distinction Between Reality and Fantasy

As the child's perceptual world becomes more definite, his ability to distinguish between reality and fantasy becomes more accurate. Two

---

[12] David Smillie, "Reality, Possibility, and Children," *ETC.—A Review of General Semantics*, Vol. XV, No. 3, Spring 1958, pp. 163-168.

[13] Viktor Lowenfeld, *Creative and Mental Growth* (New York: The Macmillan Company, 1947), pp. 171-176.

characteristics of this age that teachers and parents must understand are the "big lie" and the "imaginary playmate." You probably have heard the story of the four-year-old who refused to do as his mother requested because a big black bear in the front yard stood in the way. When he was sent to his room to pray to God for forgiveness and was later queried about the results of his praying, he replied, "God said he would be scared of that big black bear, too." One cannot consider these figments to be lies. The child still perceives his wishes to be realities. He is, therefore, omnipotent through his imagination. Since we become wing-clipped mortals all too soon, let us not take away this power from the pre-school child! Kenny felt "mighty powerful" as he told his comrades that his father was getting him a knife with a radio attached to it. When others expressed some doubt because they had never seen such a contrivance, Kenny calmly remarked that it wasn't made yet, that his father was inventing it. He then put an end to all further questions by announcing that the radio was magic because no one could see it but himself.

You might find it interesting to ask your class how many of them had imaginary playmates as children and what functions these playmates served as you remember them. A beautifully poignant story of one such make-believe playmate is told in *The Dollmaker*.[14] Little Cassie Marie entertained herself in a Detroit munition workers' housing development by playing and talking to Callie Lou who was smaller than she and who needed all kinds of care. Cassie Marie was the baby of a large family of Southern mountaineers who were transplanted to Detroit during the war. As one reads this story, the need Cassie Marie had for Callie Lou becomes quite evident. Not all imaginary playmates are so urgently needed as was Callie Lou, but they frequently serve as a friend, a conscience, a scapegoat, or a retreat. If accepted as a part of the child's life, imaginary companions usually disappear when the child is six or seven. Sometimes they live until the child is as old as ten.

Dreams are real to the pre-school child. He has not yet learned to distinguish between what he dreams and what is real in a more substantive way. Sometimes you find a three-year-old trying to pick something off a page of a book. He believes the pictures are real.

---

14 Harriette Arnow, *The Dollmaker* (New York: The Macmillan Company, 1954), pp. 229-336. A most sensitively written story illustrating how uprooting causes disintegration in one family.

**Establishing
Identity**

The pre-school child makes great strides in untangling his life-long search of "Who am I?" He still sees the world revolving around himself, but his world is becoming more sharply defined and he is becoming more aware of the other people in it. He is beginning to be aware of a family structure although he has scant notion of the meaning of relationships in a family. He is likely to ask his nursery-school teacher if that man (the teacher's husband) is her daddy. He enters this age as a negativistic human being, but he usually grows out of this attitude as he gains greater control of his internal functioning. His self-awareness is largely made up of what he can do, how he feels, and what he perceives the responses of others are toward him.

**Developing
Conscience**

The pre-school child begins to develop a conscience at about the same time that he begins identifying with his parents. The quality of his conscience is largely dependent upon his parents. The ways in which they use love and punishment as the child's initiative carries him into ever-widening spheres of behavior determine his basic attitudes toward himself. If he is unduly restrained and confused, he is likely to develop into either a submissive, withdrawn person whose ego is so weak that he cannot think for himself or an aggressive, angry person. You may recall the discussion of personality functioning in Chapter 2, pages 32-35.

Parents must, of course, set limits, but limits within which there is ample room for moving about and exercising choice. These should be consistent and clearly defined. *Limitations should be limited in number.* The number of taboos should be kept to a minimum. If the child knows he must keep the living room floor picked up, he should have a place where he can play without this taboo. The first beginnings of a sense of right and wrong are established by the child's having a chance to be responsible for his own acts thus learning the *consequences* of behavior. In this way self-control is developed. If he tears the arm off his doll, he has to be satisfied with an armless doll. Chisholm states:

> While still quite young he should be able to overcome some of the immediacy of the demands of his infancy and to forgo minor satisfactions

226

THE PRE-SCHOOL YEARS

today for better ones tomorrow. . . . Even at the expense of a little passing pain every child needs to learn that his own behavior produces inevitable consequences.[15]

In setting limits parents should try to avoid making absolute issues of behavior. Diverting the child's attention to something else is a better way to handle problems that arise. When punishment is given, it should follow immediately the behavior that necessitated it, and should be administered without feelings of reprisal or holding a grudge. The middle-class child who is told that his father will take care of him when he gets home may see little relationship between his father's punishment and his behavior. On the other hand, the youngster who gets a quick slap on his bottom followed by a hug soon afterward may be developing a greater understanding of consequences.

Social Development

The child's social development, interwoven as it is with all other phases of his being, is observed most clearly in his dramatic play. You recall, that as a toddler, his play was of short, familiar, disjointed themes. By the time he becomes five he is engaging in elaborate dramatic play involving complicated themes and fanciful explorations. In addition to dramatic play, he engages in play for the sensory pleasure he gains from it: such as swinging, hammering, sampling textures and tastes. He begins by using one color as he paints, adds another one as he matures a bit, and then progresses to an intermingling of many colors, allowing his fancy to carry him where it will as he plays with the dripping paints. You will find a more extended discussion of the meaning of play in Chapter 15, pages 428-434.

While the toddler is primarily a solitary player, the pre-school child develops to the point where parallel play gives way to spasmodic group play. The progression by a nursery-school child is illustrated by the following excerpt:

This semester Hanya (age four) has become a group member. Sheila, Roseann, Stella, and Lourdes are her particular friends. These girls enjoy playing house and their friendship grew from this interest. Hanya has

15 Brock Chisholm, *Can People Learn to Learn?* (New York: Harper and Brothers, 1958), pp. 105, 108.

recently felt free to join almost any group of children at play. I have noticed greater willingness to share materials in the last two weeks. Her conversations are longer—in the play-house group they are continuous throughout the play-time. Last semester there was very little verbal inter-play. Last fall Hanya would wander into a group and leave if no one accepted her. She almost always sat quietly painting or cutting or working with clay or dough for long periods, every morning. She refused to do rhythms or any activity in which the total group was engaged in a vigorous way. This semester she enjoys the days when records are put on, and she interprets the music without being aware of anyone else around her.

The child's dramatic play abounds in domestic scenes. As he plays these out, he is not concerned with appropriateness of role as it relates to sex or age. He recognizes status and since the child perceives mother's role as being of higher status than father's, this is the role most often played. Or perhaps it is the role played so frequently because it is the role most familiar to the child. As his social circle widens, he plays out scenes involving the fireman, policeman, postman, grocery-man, doctor, or any other person who has come to have meaning in his life. Children this age accept activity roles to play out. If daddy goes to the office, his role has little lure for the pre-schooler, in comparison with the truck driver. They love to "dress up" and show considerable growth in placing themselves in another's place as well as dress. Mother's shoes are in constant jeopardy.

As the socialization process takes place, children become imitative of each other. One person may start a chant and have it picked up by the entire group. As we note from the above illustration, children have to learn to talk to each other. Before they advance to this stage, they talk to themselves or at each other in a disconnected fashion. By the time group play has become a part of the child's life, he has developed some capacity for empathy. At two, a child may break into tears when another child cries, but it is believed that the child does not differentiate himself from the crying child. Later he consoles a hurt child. One of the interesting aspects of observing children is to note those who show strong empathy for others. Are they the individuals in the group who seem to have unusually strong feelings?

The pre-schooler is quite aggressive at times. Leadership patterns begin to emerge during the later part of the pre-school age. Often an individual who has an unusually strong identification with an adult assumes a leadership role. However, he cannot be a leader unless others are willing to follow him. He may have skills that others seek to emulate. At this age he may be the individual who has considerable imagination, curiosity, and initiative. Or he may just be bigger and therefore more forceful or more mature.

During play, quarrels are frequent, intense, short-lived, and usually insignificant. At two and a half, most quarrels are silent tugs-of-war over the possession of a toy. After three, quarrels are more likely to involve boys than girls (perhaps differentiation in sex behavior is beginning to take hold) and are the result of physical attacks or disputes over who is going to play with what and who will be in charge.[16] These quarrels consist of physical combat and loud cries until about age five when verbal denunciation begins to supplant the physical struggles.

The child gains an increasing mastery over the materials he uses in play. He stays with his materials longer and they come to have more specific meanings for him. Block building is a favorite pastime for the pre-school child. At first his structures are poorly organized and sprawling, but as he reaches five his ability to build tall structures that don't topple is really something marvelous to behold. Often these structures are used as play areas for days at a time. Parents should be helped to see the importance of large blocks or some substitute as a part of the play equipment of the pre-schooler. A five-year-old's imagination seems more limited than that of a three-year-old for the older child insists that playthings have some semblance to reality. He does use his imagination in contriving to develop this reality from what is at hand. Therefore, he can roll up a blanket and make a doll out of it, but he won't use a plate or a pan as the three-year-old might do.

A few generalizations may be made about the way in which play at this age reveals social and emotional development. Children seem concerned about keeping themselves whole, about losing parts of their bodies.

---

16 H. C. Dawe, "An Analysis of Two Hundred Quarrels of Preschool Children," *Child Development*, 1934, 5, pp. 139-157.

Their talk is likely to contain many references to cutting off arms and legs. They sound quite blood-thirsty, but they are showing their anxieties about maintaining their identity. They are often concerned about death or about losing their place in the family. The yarns adults tell children in our culture about death don't relieve their anxiety any and often make it more difficult for individuals—even as adults—to accept death as one of the processes of living. In their play, children generally make adults appear as individuals who can do as they please and who can control children. Teachers are generally played as ogres, or at least as distinctly unfriendly to children, whether a child has ever had a teacher or not. We wonder if these pre-school children are sensitive enough to have picked up some of the feelings our adult culture frequently exhibits toward teachers.

Children this age are beginning to perceive some of the differences observable among people. Their responses to the differences they behold depends largely on the responses of the adults they trust. Lillian Smith in her beautiful book *The Journey* tells of how she saw Carl, the village idiot, as a child. Her perceptions were distorted for:

> I was used to a world where questions were not answered and usually not asked. The lights had not been turned on in childhood when I was young and sometimes it was a very dark place as we children groped our way, each finding his own path through the mysteries, laughing and crying in the wrong places, trembling at harmless things and sometimes accepting the brutal with ease.[17]

How very important it is for adults to be able to deal with children's questions simply, truthfully (as we know truth), and directly! The questions that these pre-school children raise concern the real fundamentals: birth, death, the body, evil, differences in race, religion, dress, and speech. As teachers and parents we must be ready for these questions, as was the nursery-school teacher who described a white child's reaction to her:

> Christine asked me to pick her up. Then she rubbed my face and kissed my cheek. She gave me a long, long look. Finally, she said, "Teacher, you are black like Debra, aren't you?" I said, "Yes, Christine, but the color of my skin makes no difference in the way I feel about you *or* Debra. I love you and I love Debra."

---

[17] Lillian Smith, *The Journey* (New York. World Publishing Company, 1954), p. 17.

**Physical,
Mental, Emotional,
and Social Growth**

During this two and a half years, we have watched our "cute" toddler grow in so many ways. His body has become taller, thinner, more like an adult's. He has learned to control it through added coordi-nation and muscle and neural development. He has started to build the foundations for much of the mental growth that is to take place during the next three or four years. He has much sharper and more accurate understandings of reality; he is beginning to recognize number concepts; to have a sense of past and future time; to appreciate more space to move about in and to learn some of the restrictions such enjoyment brings. His emotional growth has progressed until now he can reach out to another in a genuine act of "feeling with," and he is becoming more and more a social creature. Never will he have more basic personal dignity than now. He requires respect for himself as a person.

This is the age when adults are tempted to exploit children by showing off their cute (early) behaviors. When we place children in the limelight to behave in ways that are not childlike, we laugh and beam, not because the child's performance is good but because he is so young and earnest. We laugh *with* a child, never *at* him. Training a child to sing, dance, recite, "play a piece," that is not in keeping with his own inner impulses is to thwart and pervert wholesome development. Adults do much harm by expressing admiration of behavior which is normal and appropriate for later stages of development. Training a child to do tricks, as one trains a dog, inhibits his human development.

The Child

—A Family Product

At this period of life the child assumes the human ways of his folks. If they express zest for life in laughter and "happy talk," the child does so. If they seek to control others by violence so does their tot. Recently we saw a three-year-old in a supermarket hit a customer who was in his way. As the mother smote the child a heavy blow, she screamed, "Haven't I told you to stop hitting people?" The child takes into the world the language patterns of his folks. Polite words, dirty words, patterns of sentence structure are acquired from the family and playmates. We believe that a fertile source of "problem children" may be teachers who are overconcerned about "bad language," and thus tend to reject the child and his folks. *The little child cannot fail to assume that his family's ways are right ways.*

During this period some children display envy of adults who show interest in other children. It is necessary to a child that he maintain control of the adults important in his life. At age two and a half, Rosie was savagely biting other children in the nursery school. Her mother was humiliated, her teacher was mystified. Rosie's life seemed good in every respect. Thoughtful observation and reflection revealed to the teacher that she frequently admired little girls with neat hair-do's and pretty ribbons. Rosie's hair was too short and fine to curl or hold a ribbon so she was biting children so adorned. After a small ribbon was ingeniously attached to her hair, Rosie stopped the biting.

Appropriate

Atmospheres

for Growing

Pre-Schoolers

The pre-schooler requires abundant care, sound mothering. He needs to dwell in circumstances that permit much freedom in relative safety. Too, he needs the security of a ready haven from threats of danger, somebody to make the minor repairs of inevitable hurts and scratches, someone to reassure him when he is hurt or frightened. In this stage, play is the child's business. He has not yet been perverted into distinguishing between work and play. His purposes go beyond staying alive, and comfortable, and learning to be a biped. Now his purposes are to learn to use his body to find out what his world is like, to develop and practice the important functions of the culture in which he grows. For his important work, the young human has to have space, materials, and tools as surely as does the builder of houses or sputniks.

These youngsters need to play in soil and water. They need large objects they can handle—boxes, barrels. A little child needs a big ball, not a little one. Hoops, wheels, and barrels that turn and roll are essential. The pre-schooler must run, climb, and jump, swing, hang, and let go. Nature requires him to be active with his whole body. The motive for his activity must come from within himself. He needs dolls, simple dishes, rags, old clothes with which to play house, school, and church. Play is the oldest and most meaningful of the projective techniques.

Toys

What is a good toy? In an earlier chapter we defined *good* as suitable for its purpose. Today toy-making and selling constitute a major industry. A plaything is any suitable tool for a child. It has a variety of uses. A ball can be looked at, rolled, bounced, kicked, tossed, caught, batted. A carpet sweeper is a pull-toy, a scooter, a sweeper. A tricycle is a push-toy, a set of wheels to spin, a means of transportation. A box can be a boat, a table, a fort, a storage bin, a house. A good toy requires the child to do something in order to use it. It must respond to his behavior.[18] Toy manufacturers are caught in a dilemma of providing appropriate playthings for children and attracting purchase by those who have the money to buy them, the grownups. Their problem is confounded by the fact that most toys are purchased as showy gifts for Christmas and birthdays rather than as appropriate tools for children.

Modern homes provide scant space for children's necessary activities. The *parents* of a normal child are likely to become *problems to him*, often to the extent that they *call the child a problem*. Mother takes a dim view of her upholstered chairs being used for bouncing; she is not likely to welcome the making of mud-pies in her house. The neighbors on the floor below express marked distaste for children racing and jumping. The keepers of the fine lawns and flower-beds are the natural enemies of small children, to say nothing of the millions of children who are reared in

---

[18] Ethel Kawin, *The Wise Choice of Toys* (Chicago: University of Chicago Press, 1938). This book discusses fully the role of toys in the life of the child.

crowded, city dwellings where there is not even a lawn with a *Keep Off* sign for miles.

One of the most profound social changes of our time is the family's loss of land and space. Few modern housing developments have taken into account children's need for useful areas of earth. We believe it imperative that neighborhoods make sure that every child is within ready reach of some space in which he can freely be a child and where mother is not afraid to take her eyes off him. The "tot-lots" that some cities have begun to develop are a step in this direction. The small children of this country need thousands more of them. Moral uplift of the adult community seems necessary, also. Too many grownups value their roses and manicured lawns more highly than their neighbor's children. In the modern city parents alone, on their own, cannot provide adequate, appropriate atmospheres for the growing of pre-schoolers. This concern must become, in the opinion of the authors, as urgent as that our older children have effective schooling. A society cannot leave to chance the quality of living of its young children and expect to grow fine humans by later providing schools, clinics, jails, and mental hospitals.

Schools

for Pre-Schoolers

The recent growth of the nursery school is an expression of increasing concern for the well-being of young children. Thus far, nursery schools and play schools are provided principally for the offspring of the wealthy and the very poor. They are maintained at public expense in a few cities for the children of mothers who must be employed outside the home. Increasingly, churches are offering their facilities for weekday use of children who are too young to be admitted to public school. One of the most hopeful developments is that of the cooperative nursery school in which parents pool their resources and time to provide good living for their children. We hope that in the long run all neighbors will participate in this cooperative endeavor.

The good nursery school is a place built and maintained for little children in which they can live as little children need to live. There is a minimum of teaching "lessons," an absence of training young humans to do cute tricks for exhibition.

The adult community has been slow to accept the validity of the nursery school. "A child belongs with its mother" is loudly proclaimed from bench and pulpit. The good nursery school enhances, does not substitute for, family life. Indeed, in this crowded and dangerous world which requires mother's constant watchfulness over her child as she does her housekeeping, her marketing, and seeks some measure of gratification for herself, the mother has become the sole and constant interferer with the normal, essential impulses of childhood. This may be the basis for "momism." Careful studies show clearly that relationships between parents and children are markedly improved by the child's having a place to be free, safe, and secure during part of the day. Too, children who have attended nursery school show more continued zest, variety of interests, fewer personality problems, and an accelerated rate of mental growth. Nursery schools must guard against the danger of limiting the child's relationships to those of his own age only. The wise nursery-school staff involves parents and older siblings in activities. We believe with Dr. Aldrich that: "The greatest educator of all time will be the person who shows us the way to conduct children through the preschool years so that this baby eagerness to learn is maintained." [19]

Suggestions for Further Exploration

▶ Visit a nursery school and make the following observations:
Contrast the social development of the three's and the near-five's. Document with incidents and discuss.
List the materials and equipment this school has that are not available in most homes.
Talk with some of the nursery-school teachers. What do they think is important in nursery-school education; what do they find most satisfying in teaching this age, what least satisfying?

▶ Talk with the parents of a few nursery-school children to see what they think their children are getting from attendance at nursery school.

▶ See if you can reconstruct your earliest memory. Think about why you happened to remember this particular incident.

▶ Go to a park or some place where mothers of pre-schoolers gather. Listen to their talk to see if you can discern the concerns they have about their three- to five-year-olds.

---

[19] C. Anderson Aldrich and Mary M. Aldrich, *Babies Are Human Beings* (New York: The Macmillan Company, 1954), p. 43.

▶ Spend an hour with a three- to five-year-old. What have you learned from the experience?

▶ Continue the profile you began on the individual you are studying. Find out what he remembers about his life before five.

▶ Films depicting this age which we recommend you view, if possible, are:

Frustrating Fours and Fascinating Fives (Ages and Stages Series), 22 min., sound, National Film Board of Canada.
> Studies of these ages at home and school. Suggestions for the guidance needed by the fours and fives.

Long Time to Grow: Part I, *Two- and Three-Year-Olds in Nursery School;* Part II, *Four- and Five-Year-Olds in School* (Studies of Normal Personality Development Series). Each part is 37 min., sound, New York University Film Library.
> Excellent; show the characteristics of children from two to five, the kind of schooling that is helpful to their growth, and the kind of help they need from adults.

Terrible Twos and the Trusting Threes (Ages and Stages Series), 22 min., sound, National Film Board of Canada.
> Shows these two ages playing on the playground of a nursery school. Excellent opportunity to see the social development of two- and three-year-olds.

When Should Grownups Help? (Studies of Normal Personality Development Series), 14 min., sound, New York University Film Library.
> Pre-school children are shown in various situations; in some, they require the help of grownups. Designed for discussion purposes—the outcomes of four episodes are left to the audience to discuss. Excellent teaching device.

When Should Grownups Stop Fights? (Studies of Normal Personality Development Series), 15 min., sound, New York University Film Library.
> This film is similar in structure to the previous film; four episodes are shown and the audience is expected to discuss them after watching some introductory sequences which set the stage for the discussion.

Additional Sources You May Find Helpful

> Susan Isaacs, *Intellectual Development in Young Children.* London: Routledge and Kegan, 1930.
> ———, *Social Development in Young Children.* London: Routledge and Kegan, 1933.
> > *These two books are classics in the field of nursery education.*
>
> Harriet M. Johnson, *School Begins at Two.* New York: New Republic, Inc., 1936.
> > *An appealing description of the values of nursery school education.*

Catherine Landreth, *The Psychology of Early Childhood*. New York: Alfred A. Knopf, 1958.

A comprehensive treatment of the first six years. Excellent summary of pertinent studies documenting the findings. Able use of illustrations. Dr. Landreth has had many years directing nursery schools so her work comes out of her own experience as well as being documented by the research in the field.

Lois Murphy and Associates, *Personality in Young Children*, Vols. I, II. New York: Basic Books, Inc., 1956.

These two volumes are a report of the research carried on at Sarah Lawrence and Vassar Colleges in nursery schools over a period of several years. Excellent treatment of the meaning of play in childhood. Volume II is a case history of Colin, one of the children studied. Most helpful to those who wish to understand the nursery school age.

Play School Association, Inc., 41 West 57th Street, New York, N. Y.

This association has many inexpensive materials describing the philosophy and methods of early childhood. We would recommend that you write for a list of their publications.

George Stoddard, *The Meaning of Intelligence*. New York: The Macmillan Company, 1943, pp. 382-392.

These few pages give some rather significant effects of nursery-school experiences in the Iowa Studies that were carried on in the thirties.

10

Early Elementary Childhood

Up to age five or six today's children are much like little Mohammed, little Marie Antoinette, little Simon Bolivar, little Abraham Lincoln. Their purposes and basic ways of achieving them seem eternal and universal, but at five or six each culture begins to cause differentiations among its children. In America, the six-year-old must become a reader; he must dress properly and assume responsibility for frequent changing of the dirt on his face and hands.

> The first day of school—'that most important, most beautiful morning'—as a teacher herself described it, looking back on her own childhood.
>
> From the door of home to the door of school—what momentous steps! They are taken, to be sure, in a mixture of 'giant' and 'baby' strides, and not without a looking backward to the well-known walls of home. But they mark a real transition.[1]

A part of this experience is the ache in the parent's heart to see his little boy or girl growing up. Ewald expresses this feeling so beautifully: "And I take him to school and see how he storms up the steps without so much as turning his head to look back at me."[2]

At five, the age with which we start this chapter, the child is still primarily a member of his family. By about eight, he has become irrevocably a member of larger groups composed of his peers: his class at school, his neighborhood gang, the children at the community center, the Cub Scouts, his religious group. He has jumped out of his mommy's lap. This chapter traces the development of the child during the years of his first steps into his expanding world—the time when he is too big to be a baby and too little to be the free-roaming soul he dreams of becoming, the years from five to eight. He requires extremely elastic but strong apron strings.

The developmental tasks upon which our young human is working are ones he continues throughout his elementary school life. Havighurst describes these as "three great outward pushes. There is the thrust of the child out of the home and into the peer group; the physical thrust into the world of games and work requiring neuromuscular skills; and the mental thrust into the world of adult concepts, logic, symbolism, and communication."[3] While these are the human's pre-eminent concerns during the childhood years, they are in reality a continuation of his former growth patterns that take on new shapes and dimensions as he matures into more complex functioning. You need to read this chapter and the following one as the first and second parts of the continuing development of the child up to the years of puberty.

---

[1] Lucy Sprague Mitchell, ed., *Know Your Children in School* (New York: The Macmillan Company, 1954), p. 17.

[2] Carl Ewald, "My Little Boy," in *The Scribner Treasury* (New York: Charles Scribner's Sons, 1953), p. 312.

[3] Robert J. Havighurst, *Developmental Tasks and Education* (New York: Longmans, Green and Co., 1948), p. 15.

The

Physical Thrust

By the time our young human has become five, his growth has slowed down to a steady rate. He has ahead of him a period of five, six, or seven years of continuing, slow growth before he begins to "shoot up" into manhood or womanhood. During these years he grows about twenty inches and likely doubles his weight. As he grows, he loses the last vestiges of his baby looks. By five he is able to feed himself, to lace (and tie) his shoes, to accomplish much of his dressing. He can do all of his dressing according to his own standards. If he is a boy, he gradually begins to assume a look of muscular strength during the next few years. His person becomes less and less tidy-looking and his possessions are definitely marked as belonging to "The Court of Boyville." [4] A girl becomes scraggly-looking at play, but she still finds many opportunities to appear as a dainty little girl fond of ruffles and lace, pretty hats, and grown-up looking purses. A pair of new patent leather slippers still brings a sparkle to her eyes in spite of her usual helter-skelter appearance. At five, handedness is usually well-established and the child begins to use his hands in many small movements requiring dexterity.

By six the baby teeth begin to come out. Then follows the "toothless gap era" about which some authors wax poetic, doubtless reading into the age their own long-outgrown yearnings for adventuresome living. The six-year-old is likely to go to extremes in behavior. He laughs and cries easily. He is loving one moment, aggressively hostile the next. He seeks independence and becomes apprehensive when he gets it. He is quick, active, and in a hurry to get on with things. He is susceptible to quick, violent outbursts and much contentiousness. He seems to be assertively growing into a new level of independence. [5] This shifting from a stable individual to an ambivalent one is frequently upsetting to parents who do not know that this is part of the developmental pattern of "sixness." One mother says, "Sharon now rebels against me; she used to be so easy to handle. What could be making her act this way?" She is acting this way

---

[4] William Allen White, *The Court of Boyville* (New York: McClure, Phillips and Company, 1906).

[5] Arnold Gesell and Frances L. Ilg, *The Child from Five to Ten* (New York: Harper and Brothers, 1946), pp. 88-130. Contains an excellent behavior profile of the six-year-old.

so she can learn to be a mature, grown-up person. This step is as necessary as progressing from crawling to walking. This is an age of exploration that ranges farther and farther afield as the child's motor powers and independence increase.

By six the girl is about twelve months more mature than the boy. This maturation differential between boys and girls increases up to puberty. By then the girl is usually two or three years more mature than the boy at the same age. At eight, permanent teeth begin to appear, starting at the front and working backward. The process of the permanent teeth erupting continues until age eleven or twelve. The oversized permanent front teeth give the eight-year-old a toothy look that can hardly be described as attractive.

Learning Physical Skills

We left our pre-schooler with a mastery of alternating movement. He was able to ride a tricycle skillfully. This is one of the last fundamental maturations needed before a child can have complete control of his body. At four or five the child puts this newly-gained skill into use by swinging his arms as he walks in alternating rhythm to the steps. Many five-year-olds can ride a two-wheeler if one is at hand and space is available to operate it. The currently used auxiliary wheels, meant to keep the two-wheeler upright, retards learning to use a two-wheeler. With the mastery of alternating movement, comes grace and sureness. From five to eight the child is busy trying out a variety of physical skills and perfecting others. He takes great delight in putting his body through unbelievable contortions, thus drilling himself in his newly-dawned capacities. He much prefers to walk on top of ledges than on the sidewalk. He fancies himself a future trapeze artist.

This is the age when the child's indispensable toy is a ball. He has played with balls before; now he begins to aim, to make a ball do what he wants it to do, in contrast to his aimless throwing of a year or two before. With balls of various sizes, textures, and shapes comes the use of the bat, so that the ball may have more uses. "One-ole-cat" and "two-ole-cat" and other ball games seem to sprout like mushrooms wherever small boys congregate. It is interesting to note cultural differences in the kinds of toys children of similar ages have in various countries and to relate the toys to children's developmental needs. In Mexico, for instance, nearly every child has a balero—is a toy requiring much the same muscular coordination and precision as throwing a ball.

It is especially noticeable that youngsters at this age find their most urgent impulses to learn in the activities of slightly older children. The six-year-old, seeing his eight-year-old elders daring to drop from a tree limb six feet above the ground, gains marked satisfaction from dropping to the ground two feet below his dangling feet. He feels no inferiority of comparison. This is one of our more urgent principles to be considered by the organizers of schools, most of whom have accepted the idea that a group of school children should be as nearly alike as can be arranged.

All kinds of kicking skills become a part of the child's repertoire of games. Kicking rocks down the road or street, "kick the can," simple forms of soccer, kick-ball are all a part of the child's play between five and eight. Generally speaking, the older the child the more highly organized the game becomes. Piaget's [6] study of the ways in which playing marbles changes with the age of the players is a classic bit of documentation of this principle. Piaget found four stages of rules. The first or *motor* stage consists of handling the marbles and formulating "more or less ritualized schemas, but since play is still purely individual, one can only talk of *motor* rules and not of truly collective rules." The second stage begins whenever the "child receives from outside the example of codified rules." This usually occurs sometime between ages two and five. The child looks upon rules at this age as "sacred and untouchable, emanating from adults and lasting forever." This stage is designated as *egocentric*, for the child continues to play by himself or with others, but with no thought of trying to win. Sometime between seven and eight, the beginnings of group play

---

[6] Jean Piaget, *The Moral Judgment of the Child* (Glencoe, Ill.: The Free Press, 1948), pp. 1-103.

emerge. This is known as the *cooperative* stage. Since each person wishes to win, mutual rules are agreed upon temporarily, but they may be changed by general consent. Not all are agreed upon the rules. Later the rules are *codified* or fixed. All are aware of them and certain of their details. This occurs between eleven and twelve. The only way of changing rules at this final stage is by enlisting general opinion. As the child internalizes the rules, he becomes more free in applying them as his group and he himself consider best.

Running, jumping, swimming, climbing, hanging in precarious positions, skating, diving, and playing ball are all means by which the five-to eight-year-old gains finer muscular control and strength. Much is made of daring to try dangerous physical feats. As the child grows during this period, greater sex differences in play occur. How much the parting of the ways between boys and girls is culturally induced is not known. Nearly every culture has discrete behavior for boys and girls.[7] That these patterns are so varied leads one to question the inherent qualities of them. Boys, as mentioned earlier, become more muscular and have more strength than most girls. Today's child-rearing practices give more freedom to girls than formerly. With this freedom has come greater participation by girls in what used to be considered boys' games. On a playground today in a modern primary school, the girls take as active and as vigorous a part in the ball games, and the running and jumping games as do the boys. By seven, girls often begin playing games that are not attractive to boys, such as jacks, hopscotch, and jump rope.

Making one's way with the peer group begins to depend on skill at the approved games of the group. The importance of skill continues to increase throughout the early elementary and middle years. This is particularly true for boys. Many boys become misfits because their environment, illness, or impairment has left them meagerly equipped to play games with their peers. This has been the theme for many stories and plays, some of which we mention at the end of this chapter.

Most children learn the skills needed for games without help from the school. If a child cannot throw a ball, or is not adequately skilled in certain games, a wise teacher tries to contrive ways for the child to gain these skills. These are the years to tackle this problem. If the child finds he cannot make his way with his peer group, he often rejects the idea of

---

[7] Margaret Mead, *Male and Female* (New York: William Morrow and Company, 1949), pp. 3-21.

trying. A vicious circle is established. The child can't. He says he doesn't want to. Lacking the courage to try, he creeps ever more steadily into the shell separating him from his own peer culture. Often disproportionate interest in reading reveals this anxiety. Many delinquent boys are unskilled in games.[8] They begin to channel their need for attention and achievement into less acceptable patterns of behavior. This makes them even less acceptable. We are not implying that all unskilled children become delinquents. This is only one manifestation of maladjustment that frequently occurs if the peer culture is rejected and rejecting. By the time the child is nine or ten, it is a little late to undo the emotional and social malformation that may have occurred during this age.

The early elementary child discovers that he can make his body perform lots of tricks that are uproariously funny to his peers—slightly less so to adults. He wiggles his ears, crosses his eyes, makes his tummy shimmy, stares without blinking, and practices making identical movements in opposite directions with his hands. He persists in performing these feats for any audience that gives him a slight nod of approval, and he is distressingly generous with encores.

Developing Wholesome Attitudes Toward Body

As the child grows physically, he is refining and acquiring attitudes toward his body. As a toddler, he became aware of himself as a boy or a girl and he mastered his problems of bodily control. The ages from five to twelve are often called the *latency period,* for the body's sexual functions are more or less at rest until the onset of puberty. If the child has not come to think of the body as dirty or evil, he will enjoy his body during this period; he derives great pleasure from physical prowess.

During these primary years the child assumes more responsibility for his own health habits. Meals and sleeping hours are established by adults, but ingenious youngsters often find ways to alter the rigidity of these routines. "Please, mom, let me stay up just this once for 'Captain Video'!" Most children are by this age bathing themselves, with an occasional supervisory inspection and are responsible for brushing their teeth and caring for their elimination without monitoring. Middle-class families work most diligently to establish habits of cleanliness, regularity, and

---

[8] Howard A. Lane, "The Social and Educational Backgrounds of Young Delinquent Boys" (unpublished doctoral dissertation, Northwestern University, 1934).

proper eating habits.[9] We dare say that most parents feel frustrated in these efforts. We counsel patience and time as the two most important ingredients of success. This theme is humorously presented in "The First Dress Suit." [10] Perhaps you recall the hours you spent before a mirror in the bathroom behind a locked door as you preened yourself for your first date.

The American culture seems to have succeeded in making the eating habits of children a problem in the midst of plenty. We must again point out that this is peculiarly a middle-class problem. School teachers and parents alike have accepted elaborate devices for *encouraging* healthy, growing organisms to eat. Some insist that a child must taste everything on his plate, thus denying individual differences in a highly individual matter. Others insist on a clean plate and hold out dessert as a bribe for finishing a meal, thus accentuating the desirability of desserts which we withhold from him because they are not as good for him as meat and vegetables. If food habits are sensibly and individually established in the pre-school years, the child will eat well and nourish himself adequately —unless he learns that eating is an area in which adults panic and therefore is an ideal area of controlling mothers. Lower-class parents are much more relaxed in their attitudes toward habit formation. We know some mighty fine adults from lower-class homes who seem to have as healthy body habits as any other people we know. This makes us wonder!

The Social Thrust

As the five-year-old goes to school, he looks back toward home and he hesitates. This glorious day for which he has waited so long carries also its measure of heartbreak. As described in *Heaven in My Hand*, the indecision is not for long. The little boy says to his mother, "There is water in mine eyes, but it is not Crying Water . . . I shall have no need of thee tomorrow." [11] At five he retains much babiness, but dawning manliness can be seen in his eyes. He is willing to be cuddled; he wants mom or dad to tuck him in and kiss him goodnight; he often comes

---

[9] John R. Seeley, R. Alexander Sim, and E. W. Loosley, *Crestwood Heights* (New York: Basic Books, Inc., 1956), pp. 52-69.

[10] R. Medcraft, "The First Dress Suit," in *One Act Plays for Stage and Study,* Fifth Series, by Samuel French (New York: French and Company, 1929).

[11] Alice Lee Humphreys, *Heaven in My Hand* (Richmond: John Knox Press, 1950), pp. 46-47.

running back to dad if he encounters a strange dog on a walk; he also runs ahead to explore all by himself. He likes to help mom as she does her household chores.

As he grows into "sixness", we probably find him on the outskirts of the gang, tagging along, listening, absorbing, making out that he is participating and oftentimes he really is. He has come to accept the older boys and girls as his models and tends to imitate their walks, their speech, their mannerisms.[12] He is much less interested in being a cooperating, helpful member of the family for a few months, but he regains this desire again around seven. By the time he is eight, his transition to a peer culture is almost complete. He no longer looks back and waves as he hurries out to play and he is reluctant, so reluctant, to be called in. As he makes this transition, he may run away from home a number of times. Perhaps you recall the cartoon depicting the defiant-looking youngster of six, hobo stick slung over his shoulder, saying as he slams the door behind him, "And you won't see me again until dinner time!"

Accepting Peer Culture

We have noted how the development of skills is an important criterion in gaining group acceptance. This seems to be universal with all classes in our culture. At five, the child is just beginning to try out all manner of new experiences. He explores his world to the hilt. If he has been to

---

[12] A charming and sensitive depicting of this phase of growth is found in the film, *Little Boy Lost*, screen play written by George Seaton (Paramount Films, 1953).

nursery school, he is probably more developed in social interchange than if kindergarten represents his first experience over the threshold of his family. At nursery school he has likely gained confidence and poise in being away from home. Likewise his parents may have learned some of the processes of letting their baby grow up. They may have learned some constructive ways of cooperating with the school in helping the child to become an accepted member of his peer group. Whatever the child's first organized, continuous experience away from school, it is quite as important at this time for the parents to understand their roles as it is for the child to go from the home. Kindergarten or nursery school or first grade may be a negative or positive experience depending partially upon the parents' perceptions of healthy growth.

You recall that the pre-schooler was just beginning to play *with* other children. This facility expands rapidly during the primary age. By the time the child is six, he has learned to play with a number of children for a considerable length of time. He also enjoys playing circle games and other simply organized group games. The following sensitive description of a six-year-old's play captures many of the characteristics of this age:

> I noticed that his attention was wandering to a small child near by, who was playing with a truck at the base of a tree. He said to me, "Can I go play with him?" I gave him permission. He went at once, and just stood near the child, watching the boy with the truck, not quite ready to join in. After a few minutes he too squatted down, poked at the earth with a stick, and said to the other boy, "I'm making a road for my truck." The other boy at once started to help him, and from then on it was a joint project. Larry said, "This is a bulldozer—it's going to move this big tree."
>
> For the next little while, the road building continued, Larry contributing most of the conversation regarding how bulldozers worked, how big they are, who drives them, the size of the stones they move, and how they tear up trees. Both children made imitative noises when the machinery was supposed to be in operation. Larry's facts were amazingly accurate, and it was obvious he was drawing upon personal observation, not just hearsay. He referred to having seen a road built through the mountains where he had lived before, and his father's taking him to see a bulldozer.
>
> After about fifteen minutes the other child was called away by his mother, and Larry immediately left his play, brought his truck over, and said to me, "When is Mummy coming back?" When I said it would be in a few minutes, he took his truck and went to stand inside the gate to wait for her. When she arrived, he eagerly took her hand and brought her over to me, describing with pleasure his play with the other child. He held onto her hand for some time afterwards.

At five and six boys and girls play together and play similar games. Dolls, dramatic play centering around home activities, transportation (trains, boats, planes, cars), spacemen, and cowboys—or the current prototype of cowboys—are the major themes of play. Gradually as the mores of the peer culture take hold, the gulf between boys and girls widens. Frequently they continue to play together in neighborhood groups, but the girls play games the boys want to play and are accepted in the boy play in a begrudging way, at the verbal level at least. By nine the child has absorbed the rituals and forms of his own group or gang, as he calls it, and he gains his major satisfactions from the acceptance of his buddies. Like many other social forms, the formation of gangs seems to come at an earlier age than formerly, especially in those communities in which parents tend to pressure their children to grow up quickly. The authors have found the emergence of gangs even in kindergarten. These gangs have all the characteristics of gangs of seven-year-olds. Memberships shift quite rapidly; rituals for becoming a member are well-established; the group's avowed purpose is to be together and thereby to exclude others; an air of secrecy and bold endeavor pervades the organization.

Play of the early elementary child begins to become highly ritualistic. The sing-song rhymes that we remember as adults set standards of behavior that must be observed with fidelity. As you walk along the street, watch an eight-year-old avoid stepping on any of the cracks in the sidewalk chanting: "Step on a crack, you break your mother's back." Or see how he avoids walking under a ladder repeating: "Walk under a ladder, you'll be the sadder." Observe him hold his breath as he crosses a bridge or stamp his palm with his thumb and make a wish when he sees a white horse. Listen to the ritual of pins and needles when two playmates utter the same words, or note the lengths to which two girls will go to avoid passing on opposite sides of any barrier such as a post, a tree, or a gate. They remind each other by calling out "bread and butter" when they do have to go on opposite sides. These rituals vary from one part of the country to another, but all groups have them. They continue to function through childhood and sometimes carry over into adolescence. Relics of these rituals remain with some of us as adults.

A part of the play that comes sometime between five and eight and continues through childhood is the use of a secret language.[13] This may

---

[13] C. Brownstone, "Why Children's Secret Languages?" *Parents' Magazine*, 1940, 15:30-31, 38, 40.

be a form of pig Latin, Double Dutch, or some other adaptation that is designed to exclude the adults who happen to be around. This develops, we might add, into more complicated patterns with the adolescent who is continuously creating new vocabulary to express his own culture, and to conceal himself from adults. One of the difficult tasks of adults is to keep abreast of the latest "jive" talk. Using a word that made its debut last year but has recently been replaced marks one definitely as "old fogy." No doubt we have just been so marked by some of you as you read this paragraph.

If you live in a neighborhood where there are many children between five and eight, listen some summer evening as the children are called in or as they go out after dinner for the last few minutes of play. The street rings with their sing-song patter—sweet sound of childhood. "Oh, Roger, come on out, Rogerrrrrrrr! Billy has a girlllllllllllll! Billy has a girlllllll! I know something you don't know. I know something you don't know!"

During this period in the child's social development, attitudes emerge toward people that are likely to remain with him for life. He learns to be generally inclusive in his choices of friends or to be exclusive. If he becomes exclusive, he rarely knows that he is. His environment may be so contrived, however, that his group of friends include only those who are quite similar in background, race, or religion. The film, *The High Wall* depicts this very well.[14] How many children hear repeatedly as they grow up, "*We* don't play with that kind." He learns to feel with other people, and he often develops a friendship with one person who becomes his pal. Some psychologists believe this "pal" relationship is the basis for the first feelings of tender love that later are rechanneled into heterosexual forms. A beginning of the feeling of tenderness emerges. Teachers must be wary of breaking up these tender attachments.

Learning Sex Roles

During early childhood, the youngster's sex role becomes definitely established. At five the boy child would still just as soon play a mother's role as a father's; by nine the boy child wouldn't be "caught dead"—in his language—playing the mother's role. During these years, he learns quite

---

[14] *The High Wall*, 32 min., sound, distributed by New York University Film Library.

definitely that our culture expects boys to be strong, protective, stoic. Tears are the stuff of sissies. "Cry-baby" becomes a label of derision, and so American men weep inwardly and develop ulcers. In many communities if he is a lower-class boy, he is expected to fight, to be outwardly aggressive. If a middle-class boy, he must fight in self-defense but not pick a fight. He is not supposed to show tenderness or weakness. The girl learns that she is expected not to be as boisterous or active or strong as her brother. "Whistling girls and crowing hens come to no good ends," is a folk saying that our culture has absorbed. Daintiness and sweetness are prized virtues in females. A girl may cry, not swear. She is expected to stay closer to home, to be more interested in activities of the home and to help mother with household affairs.

Our culture imposes quite a burden upon the boy child since he tends to grow up rather exclusively in a female society, often lacking satisfactory male models. *Crestwood Heights* [15] is a story of one community illustrating this circumstance. This is particularly true in suburban living, when the men of the community leave on the seven-thirty train for work (or hop in their cars) and do not return until six or seven in the evening. Many of these communities are known as "bedroom communities." Today few children have the opportunity to form any clear idea of what their fathers do when they go to work in the morning.

During the primary years, the child is consistently interested in babies. He is not able to understand how babies come to be, and he doesn't much care for a biological explanation. He seeks information about babies and his play involves having babies and caring for babies.

The Mental Thrust [16] In early childhood the young learner has to discover the shapes, feels, tastes, smells, sights, and sounds of his world. He is a curious human and the world is full of mysteries that must be unraveled. He has a million questions to be answered and every answer poses another batch of questions. What is it? What makes it go? How does it work? Where is it going? Why is it hard, soft, green, red? Just as the mouth was baby's

---

[15] John R. Seeley, R. Alexander Sim, and E. W. Loosley, *Crestwood Heights* (New York: Basic Books, Inc., 1956).

[16] Willard Olson, *Child Development* (New York: D. C. Heath and Company, 1949).

major avenue for finding out about the world, at five the eyes, ears, hands, and legs are the major media for discovery. The five-year-old needs to have many opportunities to try out all his sensory equipment in a vast variety of situations. He should be surrounded with all kinds of materials so that his life experiences are rich and varied. The kindergarten room and play space includes toys that challenge his mechanical and structural senses such as large blocks; puzzles, requiring the fitting together of various sizes and shapes; dolls of many different sizes, textures, and capabilities (it is important to have dolls that are flexible, that can be cuddled); as many pieces of machinery as the ingenuity of the teacher can contrive, such as simple motors (they need not work). Facilities for climbing and swing-

ing should be available for the development of muscles that are awaiting exercise and stretching. Experiences with clay, paints, games, story books, pictures, simple musical instruments, plants, and animals—all are necessary if our five-year-old is to develop as wholesomely as his capabilities allow. Indeed, these materials should be available to the child throughout the primary grades, for these are the stuff out of which learning is fashioned. One other ingredient is necessary—a wise and loving teacher who can do some of the things that primary children want to have done and who can so guide the boys and girls in their discoveries that they have many opportunities for planning together, for sharing, for accepting responsibilities both for their own behavior and for the well-being of the group, for caring for property, for discussing, for becoming aware of their own and others' needs.

Learning the Three R's

During the primary grades most children learn to read, to write, and to do simple calculations. The muscles and nerves of the hand and arm have developed enough by six that most children are ready to learn to write. The eyes have matured by age six or seven so they are ready to focus for more extended periods on the relatively small print found in most books. Many children's eyes do not become adapted for fine, close work until eight, however. These children should not be pushed to spend any more time than the wisdom of their own bodies dictates in focusing upon the printed page.

The five- or six-year-old child brings to the task of writing the same concentration and dedication of purpose that he brought to walking at an earlier age—if he is the one who initiates the writing. He works with his whole body as he seeks to gain control of his neuromuscular powers. Sometimes this proves a frustrating task for our young learner. His desires often outdistance his skill, but he perseveres nonetheless. Gerry was such a child:

> As he spoke, Gerry came to his mother with a sheet of paper and a pencil and asked her to print his name for him to copy. He squatted on the floor beside his mother, took on a look of intense concentration and started to print underneath the letters. It was evident that this was not an easy task, his whole body was involved. His facial muscles moved continually, he frowned, his tongue kept coming out between his lips. He clutched the pencil in his right hand while his left hand anchored the paper firmly to the floor and was placed so that he could make erasing movements with his thumb. His whole body moved and there was constant shifting of his feet.
>
> After a short time it was evident that he was having considerable difficulty. He had covered several pages and was by no means satisfied with the results. Finally he leapt up, picked up the paper and rushed to his mother with it, teeth clenched, face red, and body rigid. Almost in tears he said, "I can't make this one," at the same time he scored the paper with his pencil until it tore. Crumbling up the paper in both hands he rushed out of the room, breaking into tears just as he disappeared.

Children today are usually taught manuscript writing in school, since it corresponds to the letter formation found in printing. They seek to write their own names, many of them at age five. They wish to dictate stories to the teacher and finally to write stories on their own "writing power." In school, the child is helped in letter and number formation, in spacing, in establishing relationships of letters, words, and sentences. Teachers would be wise to re-examine the steps by which a child learns to feed himself with a spoon as he guides a child in learning to write. Few indeed are the six-year-olds who have failed to learn how to feed themselves. Neither will many fail to learn how to write if we go along *with* the developmental process of hand and arm coordination rather than attempting to impose uniformity of growth and performance. By the time the child is eight or nine he writes. We smile a bit ironically as we consider the tremendous effort elementary teachers put into securing uniform writing that meets certain preconceived standards and then examine the writing of our graduate students, most of whom learned to write according to these standards.

Among the many values peculiar to communicating by writing is that one can communicate with another without facing his immediate response. Teachers must guard against correcting a child's writing if they expect to learn about a child through his writing. Bobby's parents learned much about him through an earnest bit of genuine writing. Bobby, age eight, had been visiting his neighbors frequently. They almost always gave him things, many of them made in Japan. One day the woman neighbor gave a candle to a little girl who was there, also, but gave nothing to Bobby. He came home and wrote the following letter to the woman's husband, Mr. Gooch. This he was about to deliver (it had an Easter stamp on it) when his mother discovered it and restrained him. The letter was written in ink and had on the outside of the envelope, "To Mr. and Mrs. Gooch." Bobby had a three-month-old sister. He had been the only child and these neighbors had been quite understanding of him. The letter read as follows:

Dear Mr. Gooch   I

want you to look at this carfly because I will be Gone, if
you want me to stay you had better acte quick? take a scarf
and ty it around the tree out in the lot beside your house.
I will see it and then you have me back again. but this
mens that you are going to give me a fair pick betawn the things
that you are going to give outher people.
                                    yours truly
                                    if you do this?

Bob.   ps thinks for what you have done enehow

Children growing up today live in a reading culture. We dare say that if the school gave no formal instruction in reading, most children would learn to read. Most children come to school already "reading" in a variety of situations. The five-year-old brings the mail to mother saying, "We got a letter from grandmother today." He has in his way read the envelope though he may recognize no word on it. He goes to his record collection and picks out "Peter the Wolf" to play. He has read the label on the record—in his way. The child who is surrounded by attractive books, which he may handle in his own way, learns to read sometime between ages five and eight. A few learn at four; a very few may not learn until nine. As with eating, the child soon "catches on," especially children of upward-striving middle-class parents, that he can use reading as a weapon to control his mother. Her anxiety about early reading is contagious. As he catches on, he unconsciously realizes that this matter of such great concern to her puts him in a favorable position for managing the adults in his life. He becomes anxious and he cannot read.

Each child should be given many chances to find out that reading is just an aspect of the process of communicating by writing. As he dictates his experiences to you and has a chance to read them back with you, he learns this fundamental fact. Reading is a personal matter and should be personalized by the school as it is taught. Individual differences affect the time at which the child begins to read, the facility with which he reads, and what he chooses to read. We teachers must take into account these differences and see to it that our primary rooms contain a wide variety of attractive books of a wide range of difficulty about many, many childhood interests. The teacher's task in helping the child with this developmental task is to challenge him to *think* as he reads, and to provide an atmosphere of confidence and trust that will encourage him to explore by reading the material found in books. Our culture needs people who have the ability to think critically, to evaluate what is read. This attitude toward the written word is begun in the primary years at the time the child is learning to read.

We see a parallel in our culture between the adult's anxieties about eating and reading. Both of these are processes in which the child is eager to participate and to learn the necessary skills. The middle-class insistence upon earliness and for proper, approved ways of doing things has created emotional blocks that have resulted in making both eating and reading problems for many children in spite of their natural need to succeed in both, perhaps we should say *because* of their great desire to succeed.[17]

The child who cannot yet write must have opportunities to dictate messages to someone who can read and respond to them. If he cannot yet read, he needs others in his life to read to him, as do the authors of these lines when they misplace their spectacles. The activities of the primary grades must be so managed that every child can participate fully in complete dignity and self-respect regardless of the degree of his skill in writing and reading. Reading is important, it must never be crucial to a child. We urge your deep and thoughtful study of the ultimate effects of separating a classroom of children into superior, medium, and incompetent readers. A child who cannot read well needs a pal who can, and will seek one just as surely as the undersized lad will seek a friend who is a good fighter.

The following outline shows the kinds of language experiences that are desirable for a school to provide, and the ages at which these experiences are appropriate. Note the wide overlap of ages at which any experience is considered an appropriate part of the curriculum.[18]

Language

* *Experience given emphasis*
o *Experience occurs*

ORAL EXPERIENCES	K	1	2	3	4	5	6	7	8
Simple requests	*	*							
Answering questions	*	*							
Conversation in small informal groups	*	*	*						
More formalized conversation in larger group	*	*							
Sharing time (show and tell) with class group	*	*	*	*					
Relaying messages	o	o	o	o					
Telling a story	o	o	o	o	o	o	o	o	o
Planning and discussing class activities	o	*	*	*	*	*	*	*	*
Reciting rhymes and poems	o	o	o	o	o	o	o	o	o

[17] For a more detailed discussion of this point of view consult C. Bühler, *The Child and His Family*, trans. by H. Beaumont (New York: Harper and Brothers, 1939).

[18] *Design for Human Growth* (Wilmette, Ill.: Wilmette Public School District No. 39, 1958).

	K	1	2	3	4	5	6	7	8
Dramatic play-recreating, impersonating or imitating a character or part	✻	✻	✻	o	o				
Dictating a story, letter, experience, a poem or song	o	o	o	o					
Creating or making up a story	o	o	o	o	o	✻	✻	✻	✻
Telling about an incident or personal experience	✻	✻	✻	✻	✻	✻	✻	✻	✻
Making an announcement		o	o	o	o	✻	✻	✻	✻
Reading to group		o	o	o	✻	✻	✻	✻	✻
Taking part in a discussion	o	o	✻	✻	✻	✻	✻	✻	✻
Making simple introductions of people		o	o	o	o	✻	✻	✻	✻
Taking part in telephone conversation		o	o	✻	✻	✻	✻	✻	✻
Giving directions for a game or other activity	o	o	o	o	o	o	o	o	o
Telling jokes or riddles		o	o	o	o	o			
Giving simple book reports			o	o	o	o			
Speech improvement activities		o	o	o	o	o	o	o	o
Giving simple report—such as Student Council report		✻	✻	✻	✻	✻	✻	✻	✻
Choric speaking			o	o	o	✻	✻	✻	✻
Giving social studies reports					✻	✻	✻	✻	✻
Giving book review or report (evaluating material)					✻	✻	✻	✻	✻
Dramatizations	o	o	o	o	o	✻	✻	✻	✻
Participating in and conducting class meetings					✻	✻	✻	✻	✻
Reporting to class group as a representative		o	o	o	✻	✻	✻	✻	✻
Current events reports					✻	✻	✻	✻	✻
More formal introduction of people such as for assembly programs						✻	✻	✻	✻

LISTENING EXPERIENCES

	K	1	2	3	4	5	6	7	8
Listening to stories or poetry	✻	✻	✻	✻	✻	✻	✻	✻	✻
Listening to conversation in small groups	o	✻	✻	✻	✻	✻	✻	✻	✻
Listening to experiences of members of group	✻	✻	✻	✻	✻	✻	✻	✻	✻
Listening to group instruction or direction	✻	✻	✻	✻	✻	✻	✻	✻	✻
Listening to radio or TV programs	o	✻	✻	✻	✻	✻	✻	✻	✻
Listening to music records	✻	✻	✻	✻	✻	✻	✻	✻	✻
Listening to story recordings	o	✻	✻	✻					

LISTENING EXPERIENCES (cont.)	K	1	2	3	4	5	6	7	8
Listening to film commentator or other audio-aids	o	*	*	*	*	*	*	*	*
Listening for phonetic training—(Discriminating between various sounds)	o	*	*	*					
Listening to group discussions	o	o	*	*	*	*	*	*	*
Listening to reports		o	o	*	*	*	*	*	*
Listening in audience situation—assemblies, etc.	o	o	o	o	*	*	*	*	*
Listening in class meetings					*	*	*	*	*
Listening to individual instruction or direction	*	*	*	*	*	*	*	*	*

WRITTEN EXPERIENCES

	K	1	2	3	4	5	6	7	8
Dictating ideas to be written by teacher—simple stories, letters, news or description of picture	o	*							
Writing a caption for a picture—labels, signs	o	o	o						
Writing a note		o	*	*	*	o	o	o	o
Writing an invitation		o	o	*	*	o	o	o	o
Writing simple story		o	*	*	*	*	*		
Writing poem		o	o	o	*	*	*		
Writing a group experience		o	*	*					
Writing simple letter (a permission note)			*	*	*	o	o	o	o
Writing friendly letter (a thank you note)			*	*	*	o	o	o	o
Writing about an experience		o	*	*	*	*	*	*	*
Writing a play			o	o	o	o	o	o	o
Writing a song			o	o	o	o	o	o	o
Writing on greeting cards		o	o	o					
Writing in booklets, class newspapers, etc.			*	*	*	*	*	*	*
Writing simple report				*	*	*	*		
Writing an outline						*	*	*	*
Writing a social studies report—using research material						*	*	*	*
Writing a business letter—asking for material, etc.						*	*	*	*
Writing for school paper						*	*	*	*
Writing a book review					*	*	*	*	*
Taking notes (for room meeting, etc.)					o	*	*	*	*
Formulating answers to thought questions					*	*	*	*	*
Creative writing—stories, poems		o	o	o	*	*	*	*	*

256

ORAL ABILITIES	K	1	2	3	4	5	6	7	8
To express idea so that it is understood	*	*	*	*	*	*	*	*	*
To carry on conversation with individuals	*	*	*	*	*	o	o	o	o
To talk to class group	*	*	*	*	*	*	*	*	*
To tell a story, recite a poem	*	*	*	*	*	o	o	o	o
To contribute to a discussion	o	o	o	o	*	*	*	*	*
To contribute to a planning session		o	*	*	*	*	*	*	*
To contribute to an evaluation discussion			o	o	o	*	*	*	*
To give an oral report				o	o	*	*	*	*
To discuss a problem and give views			o	*	*	*	*	*	*
To use telephone		o	o	o	*	*	*	*	*
To pronounce words properly—using dictionary when necessary					*	*	*	*	*
To interpret or portray a character in play	o	o	o	o	o	o	o	o	o
To organize ideas for a story, report, discussion					*	*	*	*	*
To speak from notes							*	*	*
To give information clearly and accurately					*	*	*	*	*
To give details when needed					*	*	*	*	*
To speak with poise (physical and emotional composure)					*	*	*	*	*
To use simple parliamentary procedure					*	*	*	*	*
To ask clear questions	o	o	o	o	*	*	*	*	*
To use correct grammatical forms in conversation, reports, etc.	o	o	o	o	*	*	*	*	*
To speak clearly and with pleasing voice					*	*	*	*	*
To speak concisely					*	*	*	*	*
To participate in panel type discussions								*	*
To discriminate in choice of words								*	o

LISTENING ABILITIES

	K	1	2	3	4	5	6	7	8
To listen courteously to individuals—conversations	*	*	*	*	*	*	*	*	*
To listen courteously in group situations—discussions	*	*	*	*	*	*	*	*	*
To listen for directions or instructions	*	*	*	*	*	*	*	*	*
To listen for explanations, understandings	o	*	*	*	*	*	*	*	*
To listen for information, details, etc.	o	*	*	*	*	*	*	*	*

257

LISTENING ABILITIES *(cont.)*

	K	1	2	3	4	5	6	7	8
To listen for cues or implied meanings							*	*	*
To listen to music, radio, poetry	*	*	*	*	*	*	*	*	*
To listen to a discussion	o	o	*	*	*	*	*	*	*

WRITING ABILITIES AND SKILLS

	K	1	2	3	4	5	6	7	8
To dictate a short sentence	*								
To dictate an idea, a story, a caption	*	o	o						
To write a story		o	o	o	*	*	*		
To write a poem		o	o	o	*	*	*		
To create story, poem, play, program					*	*	*	*	*
To write simple letters (permission to take trip, etc.)		o	*	*	*	o	o		
To write friendly letter—an invitation, a thank you note			*	*	*	o	o	o	o
To write business letter			o	o	*	*	*	*	*
To write simple report				o	*	*	*	*	
To write complete sentences	*	*	*	*	*	*	*	*	*
To write ideas in paragraph form						*	*	*	*
To understand letter structure—friendly, business					o	*	*	*	*
To proof read						*	*	*	*
To write simple outline						*	*		
To write report—book, special interest, social studies with good organization of ideas					o	*	*	*	*
To write minutes of meeting—room, Student Council						*	*	*	*
To write articles for bulletin, newspaper, room, school						*	*	*	*
To write with variety of expressive words							*	*	*
To keep bibliography, book lists							*	*	*
To present written material in correct form—heading, centering, indenting, spacing, paragraphing							*	*	*

Growth in language ability takes a giant step during these years; the primary child begins to catch hold of the idea of symbolization. As he reads, he learns that these few marks "stand for" something. He begins to differentiate between the reality and the symbol although this, like many other tasks, is lifelong in its accomplishment. He begins to be able to develop categories and to recognize likenesses as well as differences between the various items within a category. He begins to think in abstract terms although he acquires little skill in handling abstractions during the primary years. His interest in cause and effect is high. He becomes curious about natural phenomena, speculating on the cause and origin of the wind, what happens when it lightnings, why we can hear a jet plane but cannot see it, and what causes the streak it leaves in the sky. All of these are subjects for conversation. He seeks to add to his storehouse of knowledge and in so doing gradually develops organization and integration of his knowledge. He is beginning to feel the need to master the knowledge that he recognizes is all around him.

The primary child's language reflects rather accurately the quality of language spoken in the home. Many children from lower-class homes meet their first rejection by the school when the teacher informs them that "nice people don't talk like that." Yet all the adults they know do talk that way. The teacher is often shocked by some of the vocabulary that lower-class children use. He interprets the use of certain words as deliberate attempts by the children to offend or to shock the teacher. Shame and humiliation result. The child is confused for he does not know in what ways he has offended. Teachers need to know the mores of both lower and middle-class living if they are to relate with wisdom and understanding to their children.[19]

A few children have speech difficulties. These occur more frequently among boys than girls. Usually such difficulties have an emotional base and may need to be diagnosed by the best available medical and psychological services. Stuttering is a speech difficulty that still defies solution. For years it was believed that one common cause of stuttering was changing a left-handed child to right-handedness. Present knowledge makes this seem quite unlikely. As far as is known, stuttering seems to have an emotional base. Sometimes young children stutter for a short while and then outgrow it. Some instances of stuttering are due to a traumatic experience

---

[19] M. M. Hughes, "Learning New Ways of Behaving," *Childhood Education*, 1945, 22:125-131.

that the child has had. One such instance was Michael, age five, whose mother was about to give birth to her second child. One day Michael started to stutter. His speech before this time had been quite normal. His mother was at a loss to explain the sudden turn in her child's development and after several days of his continuous stuttering took him to a clinic for diagnosis.

The physician probed to see if anything had happened to explain Michael's behavior. The mother knew of nothing. She was advised that probably the stuttering would disappear as suddenly as it had appeared. She began to listen carefully to Michael and to spend more time with him. One day she had to reprimand him rather sharply. Michael burst into tears and cried out, "Donald said you would throw me in the garbage!" This was her clue. She discovered that Michael's playmate, Donald, who had been taken away from his home because of his mother's death when her second child was born, had been filling Michael full of the horrible notions of what would happen to him when he got a little brother. Donald's favorite way of disposing of Michael was to have his mother throw him in the garbage can and put the lid down so tight that he couldn't get out. It was after a visit from Donald that Michael had begun to stutter. Soon after Michael's outburst, his mother noticed that Michael was no longer stuttering. Mother in the meantime had been reassuring Michael that no such fate awaited him.

More and more is becoming known about aphasia. Many children who have slight brain damage have speech problems due to aphasia. Frequently, this is accompanied by reading and writing defects due to perceptual difficulties. Teachers are in many instances the first casefinders of these problems because, since they are objective, they are able to see deviations that parents do not recognize. Some children have formed incorrect speech habits because they live with people who speak indistinctly. It is important to know whether a child's speech difficulties are caused by structural deficiences, brain damage, emotional disturbances, or poor habits, or some combination of these factors.

Primary children learn to tell time, to count, to add and to take away. They begin to get a concept of space and distance beyond their own experiencing. They are interested in sizes and shapes. The concepts of spatial relationships become quite realistic. The people in the drawings of an eight-year-old tend to be smaller than the houses, for instance. Comparisons are made as a part of daily living so that concepts of more and less, longer and shorter, larger and smaller, now and then, today, yesterday and tomorrow, gradually become more complex in their structure. A child visits another's house and comments, "We have two bedrooms in our house, one for me and one for Daddy and Mummy. You just have one— for you." He goes to school and counts the number of children absent each morning. He begins to keep track of how many days it will be before we go on our trip to the pet shop. He counts out the cookies for each child at a party or the crackers at milk time.

Arithmetic is the shorthand of quantitative thinking, an especially compact language. No sensible person would seek to teach the shorthand of an *unknown* language. Until a child knows the meaning of three and six, more and less, add and take away, divide (share) and multiply, it is quite useless and stupefying to instruct him in the intricacies of arithmetical formalities. First-grade children who have had experience with money—feeding the rabbit two carrots, seeing if we have enough eggs for breakfast—can come up with the right answer to: "Have we enough money to buy what we have listed? How many carrots will we need to feed the rabbit for a week? If daddy and Uncle Fred eat two eggs and the rest of us eat one, how many eggs will we need?" Few youngsters of five can comprehend the conventional way of writing arithmetic down.

Comprehension of arithmetical processes seems slightly related to general development and maturity. In these primary years degrees of comprehension and skill in dealing with numbers should receive no more attention nor occasion no more gratification in teachers and parents than the size of the child's feet. The classroom, however, should abound in gadgets and concerns requiring the consideration of quantity: pennies, dimes, nickels, dollars, feet, inches, pints, cups, pounds, quarter wedges, half wedges. These must be real quantities, not mere symbols.

Achieving Independence

The primary child continues to work on his lifelong task of becoming an independent person. By the time he is seven or eight he is usually entrusted with finding his own way to school. This may, of course, come earlier if the school is nearby. He begins to make choices of friends. In middle-class families, this is likely to be quite subtly managed by the parents, so the child may not be as autonomous as he seems. In lower-class, urban families, friends tend to be limited to those who live on the same block. As the child grows older, he begins to realize that *adults may be criticized,* that the wisdom of adult authority may be questioned. This is a big *step toward autonomy.* As he gains more status among his own peer group, he becomes more independent of adults.

A wise parent does a bit of judicious contriving to help the child gain independence. Note how skillfully the mother in the following incident nudged her fledgling from the nest:

> Nick and his mother greeted me at the door of their apartment. We sat down for a few minutes; the mother announced that she and Nick had been planning to go to the sixth floor to deliver a Red Cross receipt. She turned to Nick and suggested that he might go without her. Nick said, "But that's where they have the big dog and he jumped on me before. Do I have to go?" The mother answered, "But, Nick, that is how he makes you feel welcome. He forgets that you are a little boy." Nick pressed close to his mother and said, "Do I have to go by myself? I don't want to go. That dog scared me; he knocked me over; maybe this time he will bite me." Mother reassured him by saying that Patsy was just showing him how glad she was to see him. She said, "Remember to call her Patsy, stand firm, and say, 'Down' firmly. Then she will know you are her friend."
>
> Nick with his feet firmly apart said, "I'll say it like this, 'Down, Patsy.'" His mother told him that sounded fine. Nick said, "OK, I'll go. I won't let that old dog knock me down this time." As his mother reached for the envelope for him, he asked, "What floor do I go to? How will I know which door? Maybe she won't be there. Do I tell Joe (the elevator operator) to wait for me?" The mother explained that he was to ask for the sixth floor, and the number was on the envelope, "6N, like your name, Nick." She showed the envelope to him, and told him that the door was right near the elevator, and that when he had delivered the envelope, he should ring the elevator bell and Joe would come for him. She also told him that if no one answered the bell he was to bring the envelope back. This explanation seemed to satisfy Nick and he prepared to leave. His mother told him that she was going to make tea and he could have cake when he got back. He smiled broadly and left.
>
> After about ten minutes there was a peremptory ringing of the doorbell and Nick could hardly get in fast enough to tell us about his trip. "Mummy, Patsy jumped up and she licked my face and I didn't even wiggle and do you know what—Patsy's going to have puppies real soon. Her mother said that I can go and see them. She'll tell me when they are borned. She has to go to the hospital to have them borned." He was so

excited that he could not speak fast enough to tell us of his experiences. He said, "Patsy let me feel her tummy where the puppies are. How many puppies will she have?" His mother said, "You weren't afraid of Patsy this time, were you?" With a shrug of his shoulders he answered, "Nope, I like her." Then he asked for his cake and sat down and concentrated on eating it.

Contrast this mother's treatment with the one described in the following incident. This child is a year older chronologically, much less mature emotionally:

As Rhonda was talking, she dropped into the habit of nervously interlacing her fingers, looking up at her mother every other minute with attitudes that suggested fear and need for approval. If Rhonda mispronounced a word, her mother immediately corrected her. Rhonda then always said, "Excuse me," and looked at her mother hesitantly as if to say, "May I go on?"

By the end of the primary years, the child is usually free to choose what he is going to wear on most occasions, what TV or radio programs he wants to listen to (within reasonable limits), where he is going to play—outdoors, indoors, in his room, or elsewhere. Children of seven or eight need to feel that they are responsible, that they can be entrusted to help with some of the household tasks. This is particularly important if the older children are given a great many jobs to do and thus included in a more adult way in the family. We recall Nathaniel whose mother did not allow him to go to the corner store on errands because he always lost the change, or broke the bottles, and his older brother was far more dependable.

For several weeks Nathaniel had been visiting the neighbor who lived down the hall as soon as he got home from school. The neighbor sent him on errands and had found him quite trustworthy. One afternoon Nathaniel's mother happened to be visiting the neighbor as she was instructing Nathaniel about what to get at the store. Much to his mother's surprise, the neighbor gave Nathaniel a five dollar bill to pay for his purchases. His mother protested, but the neighbor said Nathaniel had managed situations like this before and always got home with the correct change as well as the groceries in good condition. Nathaniel was seeking from the neighbor the responsibility that he needed but was denied in his own home because the older boy was available.

| **Developing** | The child began the process of |
| **Conscience** | developing a conscience as a pre- |

schooler through his identification
with his parents. This process continues and becomes more differen-
tiated during the primary years. He begins to recognize rules that govern
behavior; once he recognizes them, he insists upon their rigid application until he learns later that rules are not ends in themselves. A child's
insistence on adhering to the letter of the law is illustrated by this incident:

> His mother said audibly, "Tommy is angry with me today, and I really
> don't blame him in a way, aren't you, Tommy?" He looked up momentarily
> but made no reply. His mother went on to explain, carefully directing her
> remarks to both of us, "He promised to take his Babar book to his teacher
> for Friday, when Mrs. Sloan asked to borrow it for David, who is sick in
> the hospital. We both forgot about Friday and lent it. We can't get it back
> in time for him to take it to school. Tommy is quite upset about it." At
> this point Tommy lifted his head and almost shrieked with anger, "But I
> promised and you shouldn't forget." He gave the ground a vicious stamp.

This is the age of "It's not fair!" for he expects all things to work out
according to the rules. He still interprets the rules as primarily established
for his benefit. When they work against him, "It's not fair!" The child
begins to develop means for avoiding his sense of guilt when he does not
live up to the rules. The processes of rationalization and self-justification
begin to operate. The teacher has excellent opportunities to help the
child understand what he does when he rationalizes by helping him become aware of the "others" who are concerned. The teacher's use of rewards and punishments is more apt to make sense to the child if he begins
to understand the processes by which his conscience is developing.

The flowering of the awareness of the feelings of others begins to
take place during the primary years. This is one of the satisfying experiences of teaching this age. Observations from teachers read:

> I was interested to see Trudy's response as one of the children bumped
> into a corner of the cupboard. The child burst out crying. Trudy immedi-
> ately left her blocks, went over to her, put her arms around her and com-
> forted her. She began rubbing the hurt side and probably would have
> succeeded in rubbing the hurt away had not Miss R. interrupted to ques-
> tion the hurt child. Trudy stepped back a little, but stood quietly with a
> look of deep sympathy on her face, as if to say, "I'm so sorry you got hurt.
> I'll help if I can."

I've recently noticed he is more tolerant of others. At the start he would not accept the behavior of the most immature in the group. But just this week he most thoughtfully helped Jim with his jacket and zipped it for him.

More and more she gives love and care to others; for example, she'll comfort, pat and kiss children who are crying or hurt. Sometimes she'll run and hug me. Often she comes at me from behind or the side so I'm grabbed unexpectedly and can't see who it is. One time I decided to turn the hug into a piggy-back ride. Evan was thrilled and delighted.

School for Primary Children

What kind of school is needed for the five- to eight-year-olds? This is the question that you must put to yourself as you plan to teach. The school of today is largely the result of circumstances of living that no longer prevail. In the past, long summer vacations were necessary so that the children would be available to help during the growing and harvesting seasons. Classes were organized into chronological age groups because this represented a convenient way of making assignments and officiating at recitations when the curriculum was limited to "the three R's." Today we no longer have an agrarian culture.

As we write this, several million children are about to be turned out on the streets of New York City, Chicago, Los Angeles, St. Louis, and dozens of other large cities for two summer months, most of them with no plans as to how they shall spend their time. A majority of their homes are too small and uncomfortable and crowded to be used for any constructive purposes for children. Many of the social agencies that provide recreational facilities for children and youth during the school year close or curtail their city services at approximately the same time as school is adjourned for the summer. Today it makes no sense to limit school to nine or ten months and to allow expensive school plants to remain idle while children roam the city streets in search of some constructive and interesting ways to "fill up" the summer days. Parents who can afford it spend more money for a few weeks of summer camping than for a full year of schooling.

Enough children are born in New York City, or any other large city, so that groups of children could be organized into classes whose birthdays occur in the same week or on the same day, if we had any assurance that such an arrangement would create a better learning environment. We have little more reason to believe that grouping children who are born the same year is the most productive way of organizing elementary schools.

Today we know enough about how learning takes place and about how children develop to warrant some sharp revisions in present practices so that experimentation may lead us to more wholesome grouping of children for their schooling. We hear much criticism of our schools, but those who criticize—for the most part—would have us "return to the good old days." The schools then in reality were not so good even for their day and are unrelated to present problems and present knowledge.

In the next few paragraphs, we are going to present some of our ideas for an ideal school organization. Some of these ideas you may agree with, and some you may not see at all. We are trying to whet your appetite to think of some creative schemes for trying out. As you read these paragraphs, ask yourself if they seem to take into account the developmental tasks that the primary child must work on, whether he wishes it or not, because they are the tasks that are an inevitable part of his growth sequence. What would you like to add to the primary school in which *you* plan to teach? [20]

We believe the primary school should be a small (no more than 350 pupils), neighborhood school so that teachers, parents, children and other adults may come to know each other well and share their common concerns for *all* the children of the neighborhood.

We believe that all the teachers might well feel responsible for all the children in the school at times when the children are not actually in *a* classroom.

We believe that a teacher should be able to live, work, and play with

---

[20] Howard Lane, "Moratorium on Grade Grouping," *Educational Leadership,* March 1947, Vol. 4, No. 6, pp. 385-395.

a group of children for at least two years. Nine or ten months is too short a span of time for a teacher to come to know children and their parents significantly. A child, then, might have only two teachers during his primary years or he might have only one. We would like to remove the grade designations and simply enroll a child in the primary school the day he becomes five with the understanding that he shall remain there until he is eight or nine, depending upon his developmental needs.

We believe that children might be grouped into classes of twenty-five that would encompass an age span of three or four years. Thus, Miss X might have a class composed of 5 five-year-olds, 10 six-year-olds, 5 seven-year-olds, and 5 eight-year-olds. As groups are formed, criteria are used for developing a somewhat balanced group in terms of temperament, intelligence, rates of maturation, friendships, interests, size, and needs. In thus grouping children, we would make it impossible to standardize and routinize the curriculum, and the emphasis would come to be one of learning from each other's differences.

We believe that each classroom should be equipped with a variety of modern gadgets for modern living. We are thinking of primer-type typewriters; record players and duplicating machines manageable by children; motors; science paraphernalia, including microscopes and batteries; simple musical instruments; arts and crafts materials; dolls, and housekeeping equipment.

We believe that each classroom should include some growing plants and animals, a variety of building materials and a work bench with simple tools, many, many books, beautiful pictures, color, and space to move about in. We would keep the environment simple but rich in creative possibilities, all of it manageable by children.

Given these circumstances, we believe the teacher would be in a position to do something creative about the curriculum. The program should be a continuous discovery in which the children are finding answers to their questions, are having doors to new worlds opened, and are having chances to evaluate and integrate that which is discovered. The children themselves must be involved in their own learning processes. Their purposes must be worked upon. Their eagerness for *knowing* must be utilized. Much of the child's time would be spent managing his own living environment, just as it is spent outside school hours and in adult life. The tasks of keeping the building clean and attractive, paper picked up, the plants and animals cared for, the news shared, the trips planned, the talents discovered and shared, the milk ordered, the lunches accounted for—all would be handled so that learning would emerge from them. As these functions are performed, the child discovers the need to drill or practice so that he may hold up his end of the responsibility. This does not occur by itself. The teacher is skillfully guiding, asking questions, making material available, giving personalized attention first to one and then to another.

This type of learning occurs in a few schools of our land. You can help make it possible in many more if you believe in it.

Suggestions for Further Exploration

▶ Write a description of the primary school in which you would like to teach. Describe the competencies and personalities of the teachers, the kind of community, the kind of building and equipment, the pupils. Where do you see yourself in this school?

▶ Identify three primary-school children of the same age and make a maturity profile of the three in terms of the following developmental tasks: developing conscience, achieving independence, language development, skill development. See if you have any hunches about your findings.

▶ Visit a speech therapist if you can and become acquainted with the work he does with primary-school children.

▶ Visit a children's library and become acquainted with some of the recent books developed for children. Be sure to see the Cadmus Books and the Newberry Award winners.

▶ Talk with the individual you are studying, if he is in primary school or older, to find out what he remembers about his primary years. See if he remembers any of his teachers. If so, what does he remember about them? Try to find out when he learned to read and if he remembers it. Ask yourself why you think he remembers what he does. Continue your profile of him and focus on the developmental tasks discussed in this chapter as they relate to your study.

▶ The following films will be helpful to you in understanding the early elementary child:

From Sociable Six to Noisy Nine (Ages and Stages Series), 22 min., sound, National Film Board of Canada.
>   This film depicts many of the characteristics discussed in the chapter: the secret-club, beginnings of play with own sex, and differences between the social behavior of boys and girls.

Learning Is Searching (Studies of Normal Personality Development Series), 30 min., sound, New York University Film Library.
>   The process of a third grade in searching for the information they seek,

their trials in solving their problems and their methods of sharing their information is skillfully shown in this film.

Passion for Life, 80 min., sound, Brandon Films.

A film that every schoolteacher should have the opportunity to see. Sponsored by the Film Board of the United Nations, it has won many awards. The story is set in a small village in France and shows the struggles that a wise schoolteacher has as he tries to change some of the patterns of education in this village. The film is based on a true story. French soundtrack with English subtitles.

Books for Children

Utilizing Theme of Not-Belonging As It Relates to Lack of Skill.[21]

Adam Allen, *New Broome Experiment*. Philadelphia: J. B. Lippincott Company, 1944.
Shows how one city boy becomes the scapegoat for the rudeness of other city boys and how, by developing an appreciation of rural skills, a city boy makes his place with farm boys.

Leona Bruckner, *Triumph of Love*. New York: Simon and Schuster, Inc., 1953.
A family decides to keep in their home a child who is born without arms.

Dorothy G. Butters, *The Calico Year*. Philadelphia: Macrae Smith, 1953.
An older sister helps to give Tina the feeling of security she needs.

Dorothy Canfield, *The Deepening Stream*. New York: The Modern Library, 1930.
The development of a young girl from an introspective girlhood to a happy and satisfying marriage.

Marion Garthwaits, *Shaken Days*. New York: Julian Messner, Inc., 1952.
The "odd child" in a family of four learns to make friends in a new school.

Emma Jacobs, *A Chance to Belong*. New York: Henry Holt and Company, 1953.
A son helps his Czech-refugee father understand his need for recreation and friendship outside the home.

---

[21] These books and their annotations have been adapted from Margaret M. Heaton's *Reading Ladders for Human Relations* (Washington, D. C.: American Council on Education, 1954). We are substituting this type of listing in place of books relating to this age level for your study. See the preceding and the following chapters for references that will help you understand this age more fully.

Marie L. Killilea, *Karen*. Englewood Cliffs, N. J.: Prentice-Hall Inc., 1952.
Family cooperation, faith, and courage help a child with cerebral palsy adjust to her handicap.

Frances Fullerton Neilson, *Giant Mountain*. New York: E. P. Dutton and Company, Inc., 1946.
Ronnie's unsocial French-Canadian father does not realize that he is keeping his son from entering into village activities.

William Saroyan, *The Human Comedy*. New York: Harcourt, Brace and Company, 1943.
The story stresses loyalty to a small group and shows how its influences may be felt in the community.

Jesse Stuart, *The Beatinest Boy*. New York: McGraw-Hill Book Company, Inc., 1953.
An orphaned little boy chooses a grandmother, learns skills, and gains appreciation of mountain living.

11

The
Middle Years
of
Childhood

He wandered out into the yard, even to the sidewalk, even, at length, to the corner, where he could see them coming from three ways at once. . . . Nearly all of them walked in two's and three's, and members of these groups often called to others of the groups. You could see how well they all knew each other; any number of people, a whole world.[1]

In these few sentences Agee gets to the heart of the differences between the five's and the nine's.

[1] James Agee, *A Death in the Family* (New York: McDowell, Obolensky, Inc., 1957), pp. 213-214.

The five is standing at the corner longing to be a part of the activity of those bigger ones, seeing their friendships as something to cherish but not understanding what it is about them that is so fascinating. He continues: "Why was it that . . . there was some kind of a strange, tight force in the air all around them that made them all seem very much together and that made him feel very much alone and very eager to be liked by them, together with them?" [2]

This sense of togetherness just for the sake of being with one's pals is the most dominant characteristic of the nine-to-twelve-year-olds. We are using the *middle years* as a term to describe this age since it seems to us less confusing than the term pre-adolescence. You will find that both terms are used. The gang emerges as the social structure most powerful in the lives of this age. The gang exists not only to include but also to exclude. The developmental thrusts described in the preceding chapter continue to function, but with different meanings and they are expressed in different kinds of behavior.

The Physical Thrust

This is the age when physical skills are more important than they will probably ever be again. During these years, most children who do not learn how to play, with a fair degree of skill, the accepted games of the culture usually do not learn at a later date. If by nine, the child does not seem to be gaining the skills he needs for acceptance by his peers, the teacher tries to discern how the child feels about his lack of skill. A few will not be concerned. Their life-styles have already taken on different patterns. Most of the youngsters, however, will care. The teacher works with these to help them develop skills, for the lack of skill is a hazard to their acceptance in the peer group. This acceptance is so desperately needed that it is sought in devious ways. If it cannot be attained through skill at games, the child may try more unacceptable ways, such as buying his place in the group by providing special treats or equipment for the gang. Usually the gang accepts such proffers with casualness and continues to reject the giver.

---

[2] *Ibid.,* p. 218.

Sex Information Needed

During the years between nine and twelve the boy, in his intensified search for manhood, likes to feel that he has acquired forbidden information. Smutty stories are told and retold, usually with scant knowledge of their meaning, but with an awareness that their meaning is something that "gets" adults. Elimination and sex information are frequently confused and are of equal importance to the teller. Girls have as much interest in sex as do boys, but they do less talking about it.

Some sexual experimentation occurs, perhaps at the suggestion of an older boy or girl. A homosexual experience with an adult is not an infrequent occurrence at this age. The middle years display marked interest in all matters that grownups indicate they are too young to consider. More complete sex information needs to be given during the middle years. It may come from any adult or older youth who is close to the child, and from whom the child seeks information. The parent may be so close that the youngster feels more comfortable getting his information from some adult whom he trusts outside the family. This may be a teacher, a club leader, an uncle or aunt, or an older brother or sister.

The type of sex information the middle-year boy or girl seeks and needs includes the biological facts involved in growth and reproduction and the psychological understandings attending mating. The latter is transmitted to a child implicitly by one's own attitude toward sex experiences and toward the opposite sex, and by one's own feelings about love,

273

274

home, family, and children. The feelings of the one giving sex information to the youngster are so important and integral a part of the process of attitude formation about sex that wise adults consider carefully how and when to give sex information.

Generally we err by waiting too long, for youngsters exchange considerable information at earlier years than we adults are inclined to believe. If a youngster's first sex information comes from someone who gives vulgar, smutty, incorrect, or inadequate facts and interpretations, the parents' task of helping the child form wholesome attitudes becomes infinitely more difficult. If youngsters feel that the adults in their lives—their parents, teachers, club leaders—accept them as they are, they provide the cues of when they are ready and how much sex information they want and can understand. Because the range of maturing varies so markedly, no precisely appropriate time can be recommended. Some time between nine and eleven, however, boys and girls want to know the "facts of life"; they may be disadvantaged if they have not been so instructed.

Sudden Growth a Problem

During the middle years a girl, starting to grow into adulthood, may shoot up overnight to find herself head and shoulders taller than her classmates, with developing breasts and newly felt emotions that cannot be shared with those who do not show signs of maturing. This frequently happens to a few girls in the sixth grade, occasionally in the fifth grade. A girl may develop feelings of inferiority unless a wise adult is handy to help her understand the processes of growth that she is experiencing and to reassure her that her present oversize may in the long run be advantageous to her—that she is now more of an adult than her classmates and, therefore, will be treated in more adult ways. Very occasionally a boy has a spurt of growth during the middle years. His concern is not with his added size but with his new feelings.

Girls who are having trouble growing up frequently turn in upon themselves and become quite withdrawn. They may spend many hours in their rooms alone—reading, daydreaming, preening themselves before the mirror. Much of their practice of adult roles is carried on surreptitiously. They dare not risk the glare of publicity or the chance of making a mistake. Physical manifestations of insecurity come out in nail-biting, fidgeting, withdrawing from the group. They fall in love with stars of TV and screen whom they can adore in complete safety and absence of responsibility.

Growth during later childhood is more steady than at any other period of a person's life. Health is usually good with a minimum of diseases. Health habits continue to be the source of considerable conflict between parents and children during the middle years. While children have gained enough control of themselves and enough skill to carry out the desired routines of hand-washing, teeth-brushing, bathing, and dressing neatly, these represent areas of little importance to the middle-aged youngster. They also present available avenues for proclaiming independence from adult control. The boy's shirt tail is more likely to be out than in, his desk a mess, his pockets full of "trash," his papers crumpled and dirty. We recall the incident of a lad who was admonished quite severely by his teacher for emptying his pockets upon his new desk in the new school building. She chided him, "Ralph, you aren't going to scatter all that junk around our pretty room!" He replied, "Mrs. Jones, I don't call *your* stuff junk."

Among the most pressing problems of all periods of life is maintaining an even pace of growing in various aspects of development. The middle-aged child is a full-fledged person with enough sheer strength and brains to maintain himself, to be independent in a simple culture. Yet he is a child, quite dependent upon his elders for food, shelter, and comfort. He is very slightly cognizant of the validity of cultural demands upon him. Private property, the inviolability of the neighbor's lawn, the essential deceit of manners, dressing in terms of conventionality, rather than for comfort, are concepts beyond his comprehension and concern. What heed shall he give commas, capital letters, tenses and spelling in his writing as long as the recipient knows what he means by what he writes. At this period it is most important that the elders respect the ways and values of children if they seek to gain acceptance of their own values.

Adult admonitions are more likely to be ignored than directly challenged. The youngster can overlook the unreasonableness of his parents' and teachers' requests unless he is nagged too continuously. Then frequent blowups may occur which are out of proportion in intensity to the significance of the item that has brought about the outburst. The youngster is protesting not against the particular incident but against being treated like a "baby."

Nine has a tremendous appetite. He heads straight for the refrigerator after school, and this appetite continues for a number of years. Girls frequently become finicky eaters during pubescence, not the boys. The stories of the growing boy's appetite are legion. Any mother can document such stories.

The Social Thrust By nine most children have made the transition from being home-bound humans to being members of groups of their own age-mates. Often these groups have tremendous sway over the behavior of the boy or girl. At the same time that this is happening, boys are developing a social structure separate from girls. Since there are some marked differences, we shall discuss the social development of boys and girls separately; then we shall describe some of the social developments common to both sexes.

Social Development of Boys

Boys take on the semblance of hating girls, of disdaining any activities that might remotely smack of femininity. They associate femininity with love, romance, sentiment, tenderness, softness, tears, and other forms of "weakness." It is a bit difficult for a fellow to maintain this attitude when he has smashed his finger or lost his dignity. Their toughness is expressed not only through their talk but in the books they choose to read, the movies they attend, the television programs they watch, the games they play, the names they give themselves. Any "he-man" of nine would rather be known as Tinker, Stinko, Fatso, Toothpick, Mealy, Piggy, or Freckles than as Tom, Dick, or Hans. Boys assume an attitude of superiority by virtue of strength, dare-devilish schemes, greater range upon which to run. (Some males seem not to grow beyond this period of their development.)

Near the end of the latency period, they show signs of reaching toward adolescent roles. The boy's first recognition of the existence of girls as something different from himself is likely to be teasing. This is probably as definite a phase of the development of love-making as is discernable in the maturing process. He may stick his foot out in the aisle as a girl passes his desk, or give her a poke as he goes by, or untie her hair ribbons or the sash of her dress, or stick out his tongue at her, or chant a teasing rhyme such as, "Sally had a party. No one came but a big fat smarty!" He is expressing the radiant hope and joy of all young things, but "In Boyville it is a shameful thing to flaunt the secret of the heart." [3]

The gang life of the middle-year boy is a mixture of medieval ritual and frontier escapades. Names of gangs vary from *The Pirates, The Knights, The Dick Tracy Club, The Alley Rats, The Toreadors,* to *The Dirty Dozen.* Eight- to nine-year-old gangs have little organized purpose other than to serve as hide-outs from adults where fellows may meet their pals to exchange yarns of escapades and to plan ever more daring, more dangerous adventures.

Most of the activities have a "cops-and-robbers" flavor. Their imaginary exploits far outdistance the actual doings of the club. Another function of the club or gang seems to be to have a place to "just sit." It is important, however, to sit with one's buddies. The eight's and nine's are often found just sitting around, usually so the legs and feet can dangle while the hands are free to finger contents of pockets. Membership in gangs is limited usually to a geographical area—the block or neighborhood. If gangs become distorted, as the boys grow into adolescence, this geographical base may become the "turf" upon which no other gang can trespass in safety.

Saroyan's *The Human Comedy* [4] is a delightfully accurate picture of this age. You may recall how the boys planned in March to steal into the old man's apricot orchard to snitch the green apricots from the trees, knowing full well that they could not be eaten. Mr. Henderson, the owner of the orchard, remembering his own boyhood days, "watched their

---

[3] William Allen White, *The Court of Boyville* (New York: McClure, Phillips & Co., 1906), p. 353.

[4] William Saroyan, *The Human Comedy* (New York: Harcourt, Brace and Company, 1943), pp. 164-171.

coming with fascination and delight—always satisfying the boys by appearing at the last minute and scaring them away." His sly aside that the boys would be disappointed if they were not discovered in their escapade rings so true!

The gang serves as the avenue for the exchange of whatever sex information the members may have accumulated. Their ribald stories are occasions for much secrecy and outbursts of boisterous laughter. The gangs of the eight-, nine-, and ten-year-olds (boys and girls) are likely to have elaborate rituals, constitutions that are highly prescriptive, and entrance examinations that would tax the ingenuity of an adult. After all, why have a club if you cannot thereby exclude someone! Often a premium is placed on sloppiness, toughness, being a good sport—which means sticking with the gang through thick and thin.

As the boys grow toward the sixth grade, their social life begins to take on an activity-oriented flavor. We find stamp clubs, riding clubs, swimming clubs, science and dramatic clubs; Little League, Boy Scouts, Girl Scouts, Camp Fire Girls. These clubs are formed of boys and girls who have like interests and wish to deepen their interests and improve their skills in association with their peers. Membership in the neighborhood gang may continue, but the group then becomes more activity minded.

In almost all situations, a few boys are excluded from all the peer gangs. The excluded boys seldom understand on a conscious level why they are excluded, nor do those who exclude know in any precise way why they don't include these others. Should you ask them, you would probably get a reply, "Ah, I dunno. He's just not like us," or "He's no fun!" Reasons for their exclusion may be that they are considered sissies; that they belong to a minority group—racially, economically, or religiously (especially if their religion demands that its members be different); that their parents have over-protected them; or that health has kept them from developing the skills prized by boys. Sometimes the newcomer is left out. Boys left out of gangs tend to be unhappy and poorly adjusted. This is a circular reaction. The teacher has the responsibility of helping them find an acceptable place in some groups. This may mean teaching them the skills they need, working with parents to help them understand the importance of gang activity for healthy development, or trying to create a climate in which *inclusiveness is a value to be cherished rather than exclusiveness.*

Because the gang is such a powerful force in the middle years, the teacher's role has to assume different proportions. These youngsters have outgrown their unquestioning faith that the teacher is always right. They do not hesitate to let an adult know how they feel. No adult—not even the best-loved ones—are beyond criticism. Jack's favorite Aunt Hannah may be referred to as Aunt Stinky or Old Tightwad. If Aunt Hannah understands these as terms of endearment, she is *in*. If she assumes that Jackie's most urgent task at age ten is to learn politeness, she will not remain a favorite aunt for long. Nor, incidentally, will she succeed in teaching Jack politeness.

The middle years are critical years in adult-child relationships. Frequently during these years a schism develops between parents and their offspring, between teachers and their pupils. Only by accepting, not necessarily approving, children's values can the adult expect to influence their behavior. If adults become alienated from children at this time, the gang's force has no counterbalance. It may come to be a stifling, crippling influence on independent thought and upon the process of identification. This phenomenon seems to explain in part the development in gangs that produces delinquency. Members of these gangs have become, somewhere in their development, alienated from all the decent adults that they have known. With alienation, identification weakens until it is meaningless. The emotional climate for the young humans is then that of a void. Into this void comes the gang with its soporific of a tight force to bind members together. Since the gang that we are describing is one in which leadership is obtained and held by a strong arm, gang members have to be submissive; they accept gang standards without critical thought. They exchange their individuality, or whatever potential they have for the development of individuality, for the great tranquilizer of gang loyalty and security.

If the teacher's role is not one of correction, of insisting upon the values held important in adult living, what then is his role? He has several constructive ways of working with these budding adults. First, he must accurately determine the current of their lives and be willing to *go with the current* rather than against it, except in those cases where the penalty of a mistake is too great to risk. In Section Three of this book, we suggest several ways of studying the currents of childhood and adolescence.

Second, the teacher tries to be an acceptable and accepting model to his pupils. He is there. He has the knack of showing up when he is likely to be needed. He overlooks the petty, insignificant infringements upon good taste and manners so that he may be heard when more important problems arise. He does not, however, condone these behaviors nor indulge himself by "joining in with the boys." Third, the teacher studies the school and the community to determine if the most promising circumstances are available for growth. If they are not, he acts as the child's agent to try to improve circumstances.

Boys make collections of a wide variety of things during these years. At nine they are likely to be collecting trading cards, or pictures of baseball players, or match folders. Of course, the major feature of this type of collection is the trading activity that goes with it. As they grow into more mature interests, their collections become more specialized and more central to their own life styles. The boy interested in natural science may start collections of fossils, rocks, snakes, bugs; the future explorer may become interested in stamps, coins, postmarks, or maps; the future musician may start a record collection that comes to be invaluable as the years roll by. On the other hand, these collections may be transitory.

The games of the middle-year boy are highly competitive. Our culture places a high value upon competition and since this is an age peculiarly sensitive to adult mores, the young endorse the types of activities that are rewarded in adult living. Some recent studies of youth indicate that highly organized, competitive team sports are not as appealing as we once assumed that they were. A national survey of representative adolescent boys between ages fourteen and sixteen showed that the three activities they enjoyed most are swimming, hunting, and working on cars and motorcycles. Of the ten activities they enjoyed most, only three are team sports.[5]

Social Development of Girls

The old rhyme, "Little girls are made of sugar and spice and everything nice," is the image that middle-year girls are urged to live up to.

Little girls don't speak in loud voices.
Girls don't fight. Girls don't tell dirty jokes.
Girls don't hang around in the street.

[5] Boy Scouts of America, A Study of Adolescent Boys (New Brunswick, N. J.: Boy Scouts of America, 1955), p. 52.

Girls don't play boisterously.
Girls don't swear.
Girls don't!

And what *do* girls do?

Girls must speak in sweet, low voices.
Girls must learn to be little ladies.
Girls walk gracefully.
Girls sew and cook and sweep and dust,
And keep the house clean and tidy!
That is what little *girls* do!

Girls are more concerned with form and verbal imagery than boys this age. Their gangs have elaborate constitutions that are masterpieces when it comes to solving the perplexing problems of by-laws, articles, dues, membership, club names, and the like. Their clubs exist more for the practice they afford the girls to exercise their verbal powers through the forms required by club life than for the sociability afforded. We recently ran across a club kept most meticulously by a middle-year girl. The officers in this club consist of two presidents and one vice-president. The club has eleven members; each one has a name that was selected from a list of approved fruits and vegetables. The members include: pea, orange, apple, grapes, pumpkin, carrots, corn, banana, peach, fruit, and vegetable. (Each of the two presidents is known as either fruit or vegetable.) The club record begins with a dramatic statement entitled: *The day the Club began.* It was declared that this day should be a holiday. "Club Ruls" were stated as follows:

Leaders meet on Monday. No Club meeting on Monday.
If fights, the person who fights will be out of the Club for a day.
The children [presumably the members] can make ruls for the Club too.
Some times the children can make up there minds where they want to do.
You have to be in the Club one day before you get your pin.

Next follows a club code in which the alphabet and the numbers one through nine are given symbols of dots and dashes so that a secret language is possible. A is one dot and a dash, B is one dash and a dot, C is a dash and a dot and a dash and dot, and so on. The "Club Promiss" reads: "I promiss to help other people every day and be kind to all people and love thy Mother and thy Father." The Club, which is unnamed in this case, has a song and very meticulous "attedenties" records.

Girls' clubs or gangs tend to be more exclusive, more autocratic, and more tightly knit than do boys' gangs. Adult attitudes of protectiveness toward girls encourage this, we believe. Girls between nine and twelve seem to react to the boys' indifference toward them by responding in kind, but somehow they fail to show much genuine intensity in their overlooking of boys. A few girls refuse to accept the female role and become known as tomboys. They participate in boys' games, in extreme cases they even become leaders of the gangs. As such, they seem bent on outdoing the masculinity of the boys themselves. Such a girl was Susan. We believe you'll enjoy the following description of her by her teacher, especially if you happened to have been a tomboy at one time.

> Susan is ten years old, average in height, athletically built, and engages in all types of sports. She is what we would call a real tomboy. I have yet to see Susan wear a dress. Her wardrobe consists of Bermuda shorts, dungarees, and man-tailored shirts. Susan refuses to conform to any behavior which is expected of her. Her parents have tried to get Sue to tone down a bit in her behavior, but they usually seek to influence her by promises of extravagant trips, toys, and other bribes. There seems to be a real lack of understanding between Sue and her parents.
>
> Susan is a storehouse of aggression. Evidence of this can be seen through her play. She will enter into wild and rough sports and must be reminded when the limit has been reached. Signs of aggression are also expressed verbally. One instance in particular stands out in my mind. The conversation had gotten around to homes. I asked her what she would do if she had her own home. She replied, "If I had my own home, I would wreck it." This desire to wreck a home may also be due to the fact that new furniture had just been purchased by her parents and Susan was informed that she must exercise extreme caution not to damage it. Susan is extremely competitive in every phase of work, always wanting to be "top man."

Most girls spend considerable time daydreaming about romantic notions of love. Barbara, age eleven, felt free enough to discuss her feelings with her teacher. He recounts them as follows:

> On Tuesday, I had the class write a short composition on their ideas of a perfect day. Barbara's composition told about her "sweet sixteen" birthday. She said she would have a date with a good-looking boy who would take her out dancing. She went on to tell about the beautiful gown that she would wear and said that she would stay out until 4 a.m. Barbara was really describing herself as a sort of Cinderella in modern times complete with champagne.

Girls in the middle grades go in for "gooey" movies and romantic serials on television. (It would seem that many middle-aged women do also.) They like books that have as their heroines sweet, feminine, courageous girls or women whose superior understanding brings them, after the usual amount of suffering, the reward of living happily ever after with a strong, virile man.

At the beginning of the middle years, girls usually eat as heartily as the boys. The rounded belly of the nine- or ten-year-old girl begins to disappear as puberty approaches and she may become quite finicky in her tastes. Her lusty liking for sweets diminishes. An invitation for an ice cream soda, that probably turned out to be a Super De Luxe Banana Split at nine (known in some regions as a "Belly Buster") is likely to become a hamburger by twelve. A part of the girl's reaction to food is undoubtedly her response to the cultural demands that an adolescent girl must be willowy, wear size ten, have an attractive figure and a smooth complexion.

Girls' collections are usually quite similar to boys' at nine. They go in for trading cards, match books, coins. As they grow older, they are likely to become interested in dolls from different countries, small animals or figurines, vases, shells, bells. Their collections tend more to the aesthetic than do typical boys' collections.

One behavior of the middle-year girl that teachers find most distressing is that of note-writing and passing. Frequently these notes are in a secret language so that if they fall into the hands of the teacher, as they usually do, he is baffled to understand their meaning. He may come to some horrendous conclusions if he takes the ones he *can* decipher too literally!

Gang Influences

We adults sometimes become quite concerned about the influences of gangs during the middle years. They are such powerful influences in the lives of boys and girls that we wonder if they can be wholesome for the child who is still relatively immature and easily influenced. As a matter of fact, gang influences can be so powerful that the individual may not be able to retain his ability to think for himself. No other cry is so frequently heard as, "Well, I don't see why I can't do so and so. All of the other kids do!" Yet our better judgment tells us that if the youngster follows his gang counter to his own values in important areas, some other factors are likely to be quite askew in his life. He may have no adults whom he trusts or he may have failed to develop an ego strong enough to carry him through the daily decisions that are his to make.

Another dilemma facing the middle-year group is that while ganging is a developmental characteristic, our modern culture makes little or no provision for its functioning. In an urban culture it is well-nigh impossible for a group of boys to cluster together without arousing the suspicion and disapproval of adults. Youngsters have little space especially designated for their unsupervised, informal use. Most modern housing projects are constructed as if their residents were expected to be sterile. Our older readers can remember the vacant lot, some space in the block unused by grownups where youngsters could gather to play "one-ole-cat," build huts, dig caves without adult direction or special purpose. There the extreme and important busyness of childhood could go on.

Not having a place where they can be, the youngsters get in the way. Being under foot, they are a nuisance. Once they smell that their behavior is bothersome to adults, it becomes infinitely more attractive to them. Modern urban communities have to find ways to provide for the normal developmental patterns of growing up if they expect to solve this youth problem. Neighborhoods must have tot-lots, swimming holes, places for "one ole cat," some decent dirt to play in, some hangouts for the middle year and older youth; places where the youngsters can be themselves and where they can be away from adults.

Gang membership does offer important learnings to the middle-year child. It provides a milieu in which boys and girls learn the skills of getting along with a small group of the same sex and learn the many social skills required of young men and women. They have an opportunity to learn a wide range of skills both social and physical, without the threat of adult sanction or withholding of approval. Up to this period in their lives, boys and girls have accepted the mores, values, and attitudes of their parents without too much questioning. The individual has developed an authoritarian conscience, as he has, through identification, accepted his parents as models. Through gang membership the individual has a chance to develop a rational conscience, since he must continuously make choices between following the gang or following his parents or following his own inclinations. This process of making independent choices is a necessary part of maturing. Since the gang is a group and is modeled after adult groups, the individual has a chance to experience cooperative endeavor, democratic procedures, self-control, fair play, and justice. We must be aware, however, that these qualities do not necessarily reside in gangs. The potential is there and with subtle, adult guidance in experiences outside the gang, the adult has a chance to encourage the emergence of these qualities in gang experience.

One phase of gang activity that requires careful thought is the extreme competitiveness of some gang activities. With the facility for greater organization, competition becomes more possible. The gang is parroting adult life in competing, as well as in many of its other forms. As is so often true with immature approaches, the urge of the youngsters to compete outdoes that of adults. Competition is less harmful if the sides are somewhat even. Youngsters have a way of caring for unfair competition if not influenced by adults. E. B. White describes such an incident as follows:

> Children have the gift of solving things directly, easily, and sometimes brilliantly. They do not refer questions back to dubious standards, and they ignore precedents. Something happened recently in Germantown, Pennsylvania, which perfectly illustrates this peculiar gift—we heard of it through a friend. In Germantown there are two schools, one predominantly colored, one predominantly white. The gangs of little boys from the two schools often play together. One day they invented a new game called Race Riot, but when they got assembled to play it they discovered that there were more white boys than colored boys. Clearly the thing was out of balance and unfair. What to do? Like a flash the children had the answer. The proper number of white boys promptly volunteered to play colored, and the race riot proceeded with even numbers, in perfect equality. Adults, we feel, would have had the devil's own time with a situation like that.[6]

One reason adults fear the influence of gangs is that they shudder at the thought of their children becoming aware of the sordidness of life.

[6] E. B. White. Reprinted by permission; © 1945 The New Yorker Magazine, Inc.; published in book form by Houghton Mifflin Company under the title The Wild Flag (1946).

Many upper- and middle-class families try to protect their children from contact with lower-class children for fear they will imitate their behavior. This theme was dealt with understandingly in the Broadway play, *Mrs. McThing*.[7] Since upper-middle-class children are more inclined to conform to adult standards than are lower-class children, the adult fears are not without cause. Parents are inclined to be more protective of girls than boys. A girl must not be exposed to the seamy side of life. A little "dirt" hurts a boy much less than a girl. Parents must ask themselves if growth and maturity come from conforming and from overprotectiveness. What happens when a youngster is subjected to the peer attitude of the following incident:

> "Come on, Mealy, and go swimmin'."
> "Aw, Mealy can't go. His ma won't let him."
> "Yes, I *kin*, too, if I want to," replied Mealy, stoutly—but alas! guiltily.
> "Then come on," said Piggy Pennington, "You don't dast. My ma don't care how often I go in . . ."[8]

Family Relationships

Two qualities characterize the relationships within the family. On the surface, the boys and girls seem bored with family affairs. Much of this is a cover-up for an intense need to be the center of the family picture. Recognizing the improbability of this, many youngsters seem to reject their immediate family, forming instead an intense attachment for an uncle, an aunt, an older cousin, or even a grandparent. These attachments are not necessarily formed with blood relatives. An understanding neighbor may become Aunt Sally or Uncle Tom in feeling-tone, even if not so designated.

This is an age in which an adult may be important in helping the young human to understand his feelings about himself, his relations with others, his growing-up processes. To be selected by an intermediate-age boy or girl for this relationship carries much responsibility. This age expects perfection from its adult models. A mistake not understood by the youngster may prove fatal to the relationship. The adult must help the

[7] Mary Ellen Chase, "Mrs. McThing," in *The Best Plays of 1951-1952*, ed., John Chapman (New York: Dodd, Mead, and Company, 1952).

[8] William Allen White, *The Court of Boyville* (New York: McClure, Phillips and Co., 1906), pp. 7-8.

youngster to understand that perfection is a goal not attainable in full measure.

The second characteristic of family relationships is the feuding among the siblings. If the children in the family are close together, by the time the oldest is ten or eleven, the home probably seems to an outsider to be a volcano threatening to erupt at any moment and frequently making good its threat. Children tend to treat each other as people regardless of their elders' conventions about "blood ties." If a few years separate the siblings, the older is likely to see the younger as a usurper of his position and the younger may look with envy upon the special privileges granted the older. Parents must plan ahead to make sure that special events involving the older child do not cast shadows upon the younger. The following perceptive themes of ten- and eleven-year-olds express these feelings most eloquently.

My Brother

I would like to tell you my feelings about my brother. We have many fights. When my parents scold me, I feel that they love him more than they love me, but I know that is not true. At the dinner table my brother is always in conversations, but I hardly ever get a word in, and I feel very left out. I guess when I get older I will be in the conversations. My brother is almost nine years older than I am. My brother and I call each other a lot of names. I call him Fatso because he is kind of fat, but he can't call me Fatso because I am skinny. I often wish I had the privileges he has, but my father always says I am too young. My brother usually lets me use his things, but when he is in a bad mood he doesn't.

Disturbance

I don't like my brother. When I'm reading, washing dishes, or even watching TV, it always seems to me he's trailing me. When I'm reading a book he jumps on me and makes lots of noise, so I can't read. To a summary of what I said, he bother's me a little too much.

Annoyance

My sister gets me so boiled up. She get in my things and messes up my drawer and siades she didn't. I don't like it when my mother makes me wear leggings. I hate to hear people file the nails in front of me. My mother makes me practed a half an hour and I do but when I come up she siaded I didn't. And I end up practicing for an hour. My sister turned on the lights when I went to sleep!

Language is an everlasting problem in the home at this age. The characteristic answers to questions are: "Huh? Yeah! Nope!" Sloppiness and what appears to be insolence, but often is really immature humor and an attempt to be tough, characterize the swagger of the middle years.

Relationships with Adults

Girls do not become as separated from adults as do boys. They retain their identification with mother and occasionally like to be companionable in sharing household duties. They take excellent care of younger brother or sister for brief periods of time. They enjoy getting dressed up for special occasions and seem not to have to exaggerate in their behavior to the extent that boys do. Doubtless this difference in behavior is culturally induced, since girls can identify more completely with adult females than boys can identify with adult males. The young boy seldom sees his father and his rearing is predominantly in the hands of women who are ambivalent about wanting him to develop into a real "he-man" and wanting to keep him "mama's sweet little boy."

We have implied much about boys' relations to adults during the nine- to twelve-year-old age. Probably we have tended to suggest that adults are of minor importance in their development. This is *not* the case. Adults are of inestimable worth to the middle-year boy, *but not adults on a pedestal.* These boys need grownups in their lives—grownups in whom they have confidence and trust, with whom they can feel at ease even in making a mistake or in behaving less acceptably than their own standards require. The middle-age child hates to make decisions contrary to the gang. He needs, and wants, adults to take responsibility for decisions. Few parents have missed hearing the child say, "Bill wants me to go to Coney Island tonight," and then whisper, "Say, 'no!'"

This is the age when the boy is learning a wide variety of new skills. He needs his parents and other skillful adults around whom he can observe and ask questions if he gets stuck. He likes to feel that he knows how, but given the right adult he will accept help in fixing an electric cord, hooking up a hi-fi set, putting on a roof, refinishing a piece of furniture, building a fire, doing a thousand and one things that a man needs to know.

The adult has many opportunities to influence the youngsters with whom he is associating if they accept him as a "regular guy" who isn't trying to make them over in his image, who is willing to accept them and their purposes as they now are, who will not treat them as if they were babies, and who has the capacity to see the relative unimportance of manners, orderliness, tidiness, and cleanliness. One of our teacher-students told us this story of Hank:

> The other day I noticed that Hank had a huge hole in the sole of his shoe. I brought it to his attention. He didn't even know it was there. Since his father is a millionaire, I know the hole represented boyhood rather than poverty. Hank said, "So what? It doesn't hurt my foot," and continued about his business.

The youngsters do not expect adults to condone some of their sloppy, irresponsible, helter-skelter ways, nor do they accept adults who insist upon their conforming to adult ways. This age takes quite as much *standing* as *understanding*. It takes adults who can be comfortable respecting the lines of privacy that the youngster establishes for himself. It takes adults who are not easily shocked or hurt, whose egos are strong enough for them to maintain a high degree of objectivity about themselves in relation to the youngsters with whom they are working. It takes adults who are skillful in keeping little habits and mannerisms from becoming blown up into major issues of conflict between themselves and the kids.

Development of Social Attitudes

In summary, the social thrust of the middle years results in the young human forming social attitudes that are quite clear and distinct and are likely to remain fixed during his entire life. He has learned to differentiate between what he sees as acceptable and unacceptable behavior. He has developed an image of the roles played by his peers and by adults and has identified rather clearly his feelings about these roles. He may reject the tattler, the sissy, the "mama's boy." Or, himself being a sissy, he may reject those tough guys he perceives out there.

His attitudes toward social groups are differentiated to the point that he identifies himself as a member of certain religious, political, racial, and national groups. As a Catholic, Democrat, second-generation Italian, he has certain feelings toward these groups, and others who belong to them, that are a part of himself and put him and the others belonging to these groups together, set them apart from others. These attitudes toward religion, race, and politics tend to fall on a continuum that describes degrees of flexibility, outgoingness, liberality, cooperativeness, acceptance of all peoples.

As he reads, lives, watches television, hears his folks discuss issues, he comes to identify himself as a psychological member of innumerable groups in our society and to reject others. This is a tremendous step in maturing that has its roots in this time span of life. As mentioned earlier, this identification with some groups and rejection of others is influenced directly by the home. Frequently, parents arrange their children's lives so that certain attitudes are incorporated into their personalities without their being aware of the process. Listen to the following incident reported in a parent conference:

> I asked Mrs. G. about Barbara's week-end visit to Smithville. She told me that Barbara goes to visit her grandmother and while there attends Sunday School. I asked if she knew anything about the boy-interest in Smithville. She said she did. It appears that Barbara did have a boy friend who used to call her almost every night. Mrs. G. told me she put a stop to that. Barbara would like to attend the Young People's Group at the church, but her mother won't let her because she gets home too late and because she doesn't like the people in the church. This is a Fundamentalist church and Mrs. G. would like Barbara to become a Unitarian.

The way in which social attitudes are learned from adults is well-illustrated by the following incident told by a student teacher who himself is a Jew:

> David got involved in a scrap outside of school last week. It seems that some boy from a nearby parochial school who was on vacation passed the school during dismissal time when David was on traffic duty. The boy was heckling David and said that only dirty Jews went to public schools. David punched him in the mouth. The principal of the school, a woman who seems to be afraid of her own shadow, told David that fighting on school grounds is against the law. I wonder what I would have said to him. David's defense against the boy seems to say a great deal about his character and faith in himself and his people. It is interesting to hear what one parochial-school boy's impression of public school is and to wonder about where he got his "information."

The Mental Thrust

The nine-to-twelve period seems to be the optimum time for humanizing; to many grownups it is the least human period of life. These children, unless severely handicapped or spoiled or deprived, have become literate. They accept a minimum of instruction. They want to know what *they* want to know; they have a dim view of what any adult wants to teach. They respect the somewhat older youngster who has desired knowledge and skills far more than the grownup who has a mania to teach. They think in the realm of spaceships and an early trip to the moon, unlimited by barriers of celestial mechanics and lack of oxygen and gravity. All wishes are attainable.

The individual has matured enough to be able to comprehend reality in physical and social relationships. He can distinguish between reality and fantasy. Few children in this age group believe that Santa Claus can visit every home in the world in one night. Few lack the perspicacity to allow parents to think that they believe in Kris Kringle for an advantageous year or two. Imaginary playmates no longer exist. The middle-year child knows that wishing alone does not make it so.

His sense of time and space has developed enough that his thinking reaches backward and forward, and near and far in rough perspective. He no longer inquires two hours after leaving Philadelphia for Yellowstone, "Are we almost there?" He is intensely *eager to learn.* His curiosity is insatiable, but he does not want to be told what he must learn. His capacity for wonder is too active to permit intrusion.

In his pioneer and classic volume, *Adolescence,* G. Stanley Hall with exceptional insight described the great mental activity of this age:

> The years from eight to twelve constitute an unique period of human life . . . the brain has acquired nearly its adult size and weight, health is almost at its best, activity is greater and more varied than ever before or than it will ever be again, and there is peculiar endurance, vitality, and resistance to fatigue. The child develops a life of his own outside the home circle, and its natural interests are never so independent of adult influence. Perception is very acute . . . Everything, in short, suggests the culmination of one stage of life as if it thus represented what was once . . . the age of maturity . . .[9]

The middle-year child is a collector of facts as well as of pictures of baseball players. Indeed, this is one reason he is interested in collecting their pictures. The typical nine- or ten-year-old can tell you more isolated facts about baseball than most adults know. He collects facts somewhat indiscriminately during the beginning years of this period of growth. He

---

[9] G. Stanley Hall, *Adolescence,* Vol. I (New York: D. Appleton and Company, 1904), p. ix.

asks a million questions, reads, listens, watches, talks to people—he is busy storing up these precious tidbits of knowledge. His interests are as broad as the universe. Here are some of the questions you hear these boys and girls posing:

> Why do planets twinkle and other stars do not?
> How far is up?
> What happens when a tadpole loses it tail?
> Where do turtles lay their eggs?
> Where does the plankton come from?
> Why does the pitcher always walk while the other players run as the sides change?
> Where does the color go when it gets dark?
> What do mosquitoes live on when there are no people or animals around?
> Who was Pasteur, Lister, Flexner . . . ?
> Would someone else have developed pasteurization if Pasteur had not lived?
> What is organic farming?
> Why do bees sting some people and not others?
> How do bees make their honey?
> What is a Catholic, a Jew, a Christian, a Mohammedan? Would I be a Mohammedan if I were born in Arabia?
> Were the Indians really the first people on this continent? Why did we treat them so bad?
> What is ju jitsu? How can they throw you like that?
> What is an illusionist? How does he keep the lady hanging in the air?
> Have you really been to Iwo Jima? Tell us about it. Could you talk to the people there? Do they have to go to school? What games do they play?
> Are there really people on the moon? How do you know?
> Is everybody's blood the same?
> Why do some people have blue eyes and others brown? Why do some people have brown skin and others white?
> Why is Mona Lisa such a great picture?

Look over these questions. Can you classify them as concerned with science, geography, history, anthropology, theology? We hope you won't find it necessary to teach as if you could do so.

Teachers of children in this period of development cannot possibly know the answers to a small fraction of their questions. Here, the teacher who is *afraid not to know all the answers* is sure to be dubbed a "drip" or a "dope," or whatever the popular epithet for an inadequate person currently may be. It is important that the teacher of middle-year youngsters have some knowledge and skills commonly sought by these children; of greater importance is the teacher's respect for children's concerns and questions and his ready access to resources for helping them learn what they wish to learn.

Speaking to a section of the National Education Association in the summer of 1958, Margaret Mead, among our most competent appraisers of culture, insisted that teachers seem preoccupied with teaching children what adults already know, a method "appropriate to the Stone Age. What we need now is a new conception of a teacher who, with students, is moving into a new and unknown country. This concept must recognize that the teacher is someone who lives in a moving society and must move along with it." [10]

The child's questions frequently seek the processes by which things happen, the properties of the things in which he becomes interested, and the beginnings of things: "Who was here first? What language did the first man speak? Who first thought of flying?" Just as he puts his collections in order every now and then classifying, organizing, listing, so he does with his knowledge, thus integrating to some extent his present state of knowingness. As he grows older, the youngster begins to become more selective in his explorations. He tends to find a few areas which he wishes to explore more deeply. He seems to begin to realize the statement made recently by Oppenheimer [11] that of the world's knowledge there is so little that any one man can know. The knowledge gained through interests explored between nine and twelve often serves as the foundation for lifelong pursuits. A Florence Nightingale discovers her keen interest in nursing; a Mendelssohn discovers the world of sound; a Picasso the world of form and color. As he puts his knowledge to use in everyday life, the child also searches for the more universal meanings of life. At this age his quest for purpose, for broader and deeper relationships to all of life, begins in earnest.

The Three R's

By the time the young human is nine, he usually has established enough skill in the academic processes to give him a solid base upon which to build. If his learning processes have not become blocked, if his

---

[10] Reported in *The New York Times*, June 28, 1958.
[11] *Conversation with Dr. Oppenheimer* (extended version of the Edward R. Murrow "See It Now" broadcast of January 4, 1955), 50 min., sound, distributed by New York University Film Library.

physical development has been normal up to this time, he has by nine come to use without effort the basic processes of reading; he can write legibly and communicate his thoughts through this medium; he has a vocabulary of between 35,000 and 50,000 words; and he is well on his way in understanding the fundamental processes of quantitative thinking. Primarily, growth in these areas from this point on is that of learning to apply these basic understandings to more and more complex situations, learning to see the interrelationships existing among all areas of knowledge, and learning to deal with abstractions.

The vigor of the middle-year youngster makes it imperative that the program be vital, dynamic, challenging, and elastic. These children are truly living on the growing edges of their own minds and of their culture. If they lack opportunities to apply their newly acquired skills to matters that concern *them,* they come to look upon school as a necessary evil where a person must put in his time, with little hope that anything important to him will happen there. What tragedies are revealed in statements like the one made by this lad:

> I do not like Hebrew school. I don't like public school. I can't stand arithmetic. I do not like art. . . . The best day in my life is when school is over. . . . I was almost late for school. Then I got a yelling at by my teacher. That was not too bad but when I was sent out of the class for five minutes and then had to stay after school for 75 minutes, I could have killed him.

How can we make the program vital? By taking our cues from the learners themselves. Given the slightest sincere invitation, they raise questions that lead to their own searchings. We recommend the film, *Learning Is Searching,*[12] as an excellent example of how this program evolves. The middle-year child is more interested in things than in people. Havighurst states: "He is still *feeling his way* in human relations while he is already *thinking his way* into the world of nature."[13] We do not imply a dichotomy between thinking and feeling. Rather the pupil has not yet differentiated his own self and his relations with others to the point that he can search verbally about human relations. He tends to accept people as they are. Schoolrooms must be filled with the things *he* wants to know about and learn how to use. If we can't get all the things

---

[12] *Learning Is Searching,* 30 min., sound, distributed by New York University Film Library.

[13] Robert J. Havighurst, *Human Development and Education* (New York: Longmans, Green and Co., 1953), p. 82.

themselves, we can get some second-hand information about them through books, movies, pictures, people who have been places and done things. And we can go to many of the things and places that we can't bring to our rooms.

Near the end of the middle-year period, children become fascinated by faraway places and distant time. This is an ideal time to study living in other parts of the world. These children also like to project themselves into future time.

Science fiction, spaceships, interplanetary developments are their meat. (Let's be sure we don't get in the way of their explorations because we feel insecure and of little faith in these areas.) The middle-year child has an intense interest in mass media. Most youngsters go to at least one movie a week; some go to three or four over the week-end. Comics are avidly devoured. The comic might be better called cartoon exposition. Radio and television consume many hours. In one suburban community studied by the authors, over half of a representative school sample spent more than ten hours per week watching TV or listening to the radio. Many spent as many as twenty hours per week watching TV.[14]

Boys between nine and twelve like adventure stories, animal stories, stories of explorers, stories depicting heroism—especially the brand of masculine heroism that requires the austerity of a lonely outpost, such as Sergeant Preston of the Yukon. They also like science fiction and factual stories. Boys' taste in books contrasts sharply with that of girls. While you may find many girls enjoying so-called boys' books, rare is the boy who admits liking girls' books.

Let us examine the characteristics of the mental thrust of the middle years by quoting Havighurst:

> Children are trying to find out the extent to which the larger world around them is predictable—how it behaves according to rules, how it follows a pattern that can be understood.
> Children are trying to establish boundaries to their world; not necessarily a single all-inclusive boundary, but rather a series of boundaries for each of the various areas of interest or concern.
> Children are working at finding or making some order in their world, at organizing its facts and incidents into a pattern that makes sense to them. At the same time children take avid interest in all kinds of collections of

---

[14] Mary Beauchamp and Howard Lane, *Survey of Interests, Needs, Concerns and Relationships of a Representative Sampling of School-Age Children in One Suburban Community* (New York: New York University, 1956).

data that have little in common with the intellectual preoccupations of intelligent adults, there are indications that children are trying to understand adults' processes of reasoning and of proof.[15]

Youngsters are working on widely differing levels of complexity during these years. They are learning through the utilization of varying media. Some require much more experience with first-hand materials and with one-to-one relationships than others. Some gain a "real boost" out of experimenting with abstract, conceptual thinking. Some are more dependent upon the use of the senses to integrate their knowledge than others are. Some need more experience in motor skill so that they actually get the feel of counting out fifteen and taking away seven. At this age, the unique ways in which each human learns about himself and his world become much more obvious. One of the functions of the teacher of these grades is to discern how each one of his pupils learns, what ways are most satisfying to him. Some will never employ the full range of conceptual possibility but may be more sensitive to stimuli coming from concreteness than are the ones who "take flight" in abstraction. All of these ways must be respected and held valid. Each individual must be considered of worth regardless of whether his way precisely fits the adult picture of the more intelligent way.

As children gain more experience, with the guidance of a teacher who knows where they are heading, we can expect that they will develop more understanding of cause and effect. They see that some things do cause others. They begin to look behind the process of the water dripping from the faucet to see what causes the water to drip. They begin to see that causality functions with people as much as with things. They recognize that some behaviors cause teacher approval and peer disapproval and vice versa. They are more capable of hypothesizing consequences of varying courses of action. They are able to figure out the causes for an individual's behavior. We recall the eleven-year-old who was promoted into Mrs. Jones' room. She had the reputation of being an old "battle-axe." When asked, "How are you getting along with Mrs. Jones?" his former teacher was delighted to hear the youngster say, "Aw, she isn't so bad. She's cross and mean sometimes, but you know her husband left her when her kids were little and she has to take care of them and see that they get through school. You can't blame her for being a sourpuss." This boy was

---

[15] Robert J. Havighurst, *Human Development and Education* (New York: Longmans, Green and Co., 1953), p. 88.

able to accept Mrs. Jones' bad temper because he understood the causes for it.

An interesting step in mental development of the middle years is the "as if" game. Let's act "as if" the boys are all gone and we shall plan what we would do if they were not here. The girls are able to project the situation mentally so that they can plan realistically. This process is challenging as mathematical concepts are worked with. We shall proceed "as if" Jane averaged fifty miles an hour on her trip to Chillicothe. She had two five-minute stops. The distance is 148 miles. How long does it take her? This interest in mental gymnastics is probably one reason riddles have such a universal appeal. (Don't plan to teach in the middle grades unless you are ready to be bombarded with riddles!) Most of the riddles have a ridiculous twist that appeals to the expanding mental capacity of this age and the mastery of mystery that the middle-year child revels in.

The child in the middle years begins to think abstractly. He can generalize in simple terms. He can see comparisons and differences in hypothetical situations. One boy we knew had fun tricking his buddies, and especially the adults in his life, by asking them, "How far is the farthest you have ever seen anything?" He invariably got replies such as the Rocky Mountains at a distance of fifty miles or the Empire State Building from New Jersey. Then he would spring his trap, "Haven't you ever seen the moon?" This appealed to him because of the mental gymnastics involved in leading people to think about sight of earthbound objects and comparing that to sight of objects not earthbound. We have listened to excited discussions of sixth graders on the concept of the earth hurtling through space at the rate of eighteen miles a second, comparing the earth with the man-made satellites that are now a part of the universe, differentiating between the natural laws governing the movement of the celestial bodies and the interjection of man-made satellites into the ordered "systems" of movement. In these discussions the youngsters show a grasp of the cosmos more akin to our most advanced abstract thinkers than most adults. They are able to admit into their thinking more hypothetical alternatives. To be specific, they find it easier to accept (and then to say, "What then?") the thesis of Harlow Shapley's *Of Stars and Men* [16] that there might be a hundred million planets capable of supporting our kind of life than are the authors of this book.

These middle years seem crucial in establishing an enduring life-style in various aspects of living. If the child then finds it necessary to disdain grownups in order to maintain his self-esteem, he is likely to carry always a dim view of constituted authority. If he feels inadequate in his world, he may deem himself inadequate or find his adequacy in other realms. If he finds acceptance and friendship only among persons disapproved by his elders, he is likely to become one who can find fun and significance only among people generally disapproved. If he remains interested in "snakes and snails and puppy-dogs' tails," when his elders expect him to flower into a scholar, he, as well as his elders, may be permanently disappointed in his academic achievements. If the elders value schoolbooks more than autograph books, penmanship more than lipstick and hairdos, it damages both those who accept and those who reject these values. If he finds his elders respectful of his uniqueness, mindful of his wishes and purposes, accepting of his deviations and occasional excesses and genuinely reverent toward human dignity, he grows beyond his present modes of behavior toward stability, respectfulness, acceptance of differences, and genuine regard for the dignity of man.

The school building and classroom of these middle-aged children must accommodate a great variety of life-styles, enterprises, experimentation and boisterous activity. It should abound in appropriate and useful cultural tools: typewriters, draftsman's tools, art materials in wide variety, many books on many topics, radios, TV sets, record-players, tape recorders. Important new tools and materials should find their way into schools early, rather than last of all, as is the common practice. (Most of the bars of America had TV sets before any substantial numbers of schools had them.)

These children require teachers who have genuine respect for them, who regard their development to be as normal as is the cuddly dependence of the earlier years. In general the adult world finds these years unattractive and annoying and seeks to insulate them through organized activities to keep them busy and out of sight. In school these "'tadpoles" must have advocates, authorities of competency, in matters which concern

---

[16] Harlow Shapley, *Of Stars and Men* (Boston: Beacon Press, 1958).

them, and agents to help them find significance in a world that has little use for them.

Recently we saw "buddying" between two classrooms—a sixth grade and a kindergarten. Life seemed transformed for the children, their teachers, and many neighbors as the two classes carried on many activities together. While on trips, singing and playing safely in the park, older children assumed genuine responsibility for the smaller ones. Boys as well as girls found real satisfaction in caring for the younger ones. Health materials which often seem quite silly when taught to sixth graders became alive and important when the eleven- and twelve-year-olds planned and prepared for using them with five- and six-year-olds. We believe more of this kind of activity could well be carried on in the elementary schools.

As children grow through the middle years, they seek to be fully in charge of their lives. They need and want adults. These adults must appreciate the fact, which the children don't recognize, that they represent a repressing and molding culture against which their earthy impulses must grow. This is an essential feature of the "good life" for children.

Suggestions for Further Exploration

▶ Spend several hours with a middle-year child. See if you can find some illustrations of the mental characteristics enumerated by Havighurst.

▶ Make a collection of riddles, either those that you hear middle-year youngsters use or those that you think they might enjoy.

▶ Collect examples of middle-year youngsters' trying to understand causality.

▶ Visit the upper grades of an elementary school and see if you can find some units of work in progress. Analyze these to see if they encompass the interests of the middle years discussed in this chapter.

▶ Ask yourself if you would like to teach this age. Write a short paragraph indicating your thoughts about this.

► Collect the questions you hear middle-year children asking.

► Try to observe a gang in session. Jot down your impressions. What can you add to the description given in this chapter?

► Continue your profile of the individual you are studying. Focus on his interests during the middle years as he recalls them or as he is now expressing them. (If you are studying a younger child, you cannot do this, obviously.)

► The following films will be helpful to you in understanding the middle years of childhood:

From Ten to Twelve (Ages and Stages Series), 28 min., sound, National Film Board of Canada.

> Depicts the characteristics of these ages, pointing out wide range of individual differences between individuals, between boys and girls, and the effects of these differences upon behavior.

Guiding the Growth of Children (Planning for Teaching Series), 18 min., sound, McGraw-Hill Book Company, Inc.

> Mrs. Carlton teaches fifth grade. The way she becomes acquainted with her pupils, their needs, drives, and differences is depicted in the film.

Sibling Relations and Personality (Child Development Series), 22 min., sound, McGraw-Hill Book Company, Inc.

Sibling Rivalries and Parents (Child Development Series), 11 min., sound, McGraw-Hill Book Company, Inc.

> The relations that siblings have as they grow up, the roles of the parents in the conflicts that arise are shown in these films. They deal with several quite common patterns of relationships: the more talented with the less talented; the more popular with the less popular; the one who feels his parents favor another sibling. The roles of the parents in sibling "squabbling" are handled in the film.

Additional Sources You May Find Helpful

> Willard Abraham, *Common Sense About Gifted Children.* New York: Harper and Brothers, 1958.
>
> *We include this book because at this age many adults begin to exert excessive pressure upon children with unusual gifts—often resulting in stunting and dwarfing their gifts. This book may be an antidote to this trend.*

> Arthur Witt Blair and William H. Burton, *Growth and Development of the Preadolescent.* New York: Appleton-Century-Crofts, Inc., 1951.
>
> *Especially strong and important book about the middle years. The discussion of cultural impositions of the period and their reinforcement by social-class structures is insightful.*

Alvina Burrows, *Teaching Children in the Middle Grades.* New York: D. C. Heath and Company, 1952.

This author understands the middle years. Her book is full of illuminating illustrations and sound insights.

Marie I. Rasey and J. W. Menge, *What We Learn from Children.* New York: Harper and Brothers, 1956.

This sensitive book tells the story of the insights gained from working intensively with children who are brain-damaged.

William Saroyan, *My Name is Aram.* New York: Harcourt, Brace and Company, 1937.

Saroyan knows boys. He writes with great charm and insight. This collection of stories about Aram are delightful. The wonderful quality that life has for boys this age makes the reader relive his own youthful days. (Girls will like the book, too.)

12

Early Adolescence

"YOUTH, the Period of Possibility, when Archimedes finds a fulcrum, Cassandra has a following and seven cities compete for the honor of endowing a living Homer." [1]

No sharp line separates the stages of growth between the middle years and early adolescence. The power of the peer group that was then noted continues to gather momentum until in this period of

[1] Ambrose Bierce, *The Devil's Dictionary* (Cleveland: World Publishing Co., 1911), p. 372.

life the individual demands the recognition of his independence from his parents. We consider in this chapter the years usually served by the junior high school—the twelve-to-fourteen age span or the seventh, eighth, and ninth grades in school. At no other time is there so much individuality and so much conformity. While the middle years are predominantly used to integrate and assimilate the learnings and perceptions of the primary years, early adolescence is a period of differentiation. The individual's personality structure loosens to permit the organization of a personality more appropriate for adulthood.

Individuals change rapidly with the onset of puberty. Puberty may occur any time during a four or five year period. One twelve- or fourteen-year-old may still be a middle-year human in his physique and behavior; another may be adolescent in his build, feelings, and perceptions. As you study the diagram below, note that each of these stages overlaps quite a bit

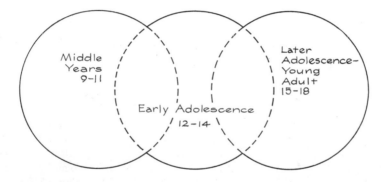

with the stage that precedes and follows it. Since early adolescence is in the middle of the time sequence during which the individual becomes a man or a woman, it is in reality an in-between period. In-between periods are usually unstable and perplexing; many new behaviors are "tried on," many ambivalent feelings are clarified.

This chapter on early adolescence and the following one on later adolescence should be read as a unit.[2] We look upon *early adolescence* as the time when the individual is *growing out of childhood; later adolescence* as the time when the individual is *growing into adulthood.* For each one of us this growth has been continuous, forming and reshaping

---

[2] The additional sources for both of these chapters are listed at the end of Chapter 13.

since life began. The dramatic and visible manifestations of the changes that occur during pubescence are climaxed by puberty, which occurs during the fifth, sixth, seventh, eighth, ninth, or tenth grades of school. For the large majority of girls puberty, marked by the menarche, or the onset of menstruation, occurs between eleven and fifteen. A range between ages nine and seventeen is considered normal, although individual cases occur much earlier and much later than the normal range. By seventeen most girls have reached their maximum growth. In terms of technical biology boys attain puberty when live sperm appear in the urine. On the average boys mature two to three years later than girls, thus they do not usually attain puberty until fourteen or fifteen. The average boy reaches his maximum growth in height, length of bones, by nineteen. The schematic arrangement below may help you to visualize the growth sequence during the period of adolescence:

ADOLESCENCE

Early Adolescence.................................Later Adolescence

(Ages 11-14)   (Ages 15-19)

Pubescence	*Puberty*	*Post-Pubescence*
Two years preceding puberty. Sometimes known as pre-adolescence. Beginning of physical growth, change in body proportions, maturing of primary and secondary sex characteristics.	Point at which biological changes reach a climax. In the girl, the menarche—normal range 9-17. In the boy, live sperm appear in the urine.	Girl continues to develop and grow. Menstrual regularity and fertility develop. Boy continues to develop and grow. Actual beginning of fertility in boy is not known precisely.

Puberty

a Mark of Adulthood

Puberty comes from a Latin word meaning adult; it marks the point at which the individual is physiologically capable of bearing or producing offspring. The attainment of puberty is a rather dramatic event for which the body has been preparing for about two years. This preparation involves processes that affect the total functioning—emotional, social, and mental—of the boy or girl as well as bringing about sharp anatomical and physiological changes.

Consistent with the principles of growth, the physical changes in the body give cues for other changes that are less apparent. We shall examine first the physical changes that occur during pubescence, puberty, and post-pubescence, and then discuss the ways in which these changes are perceived by adults and by the early adolescent himself.

Physical Changes in Boys

During pubescence the boy begins to grow more rapidly than he has for several years. Not infrequently the junior-high-school teacher fails in September to recognize the boy whom he knew in June. This growth spurt increases in tempo until the boy may gain as much as four or five inches of height during the peak year and twelve to fourteen pounds in weight. This is the time when parents just can't keep their youngsters in clothes that fit them. Most of the growth of both boys and girls occurs in the extremities—the neck, arms, and legs. The boy's shoulders broaden; his hips narrow; his legs become scrawny; his feet seem distressingly large. He becomes harder and more muscular than the girl. Dismaying to the early adolescent boy is his cracking voice, which is likely to burst out at the most inappropriate moments. While adults find the sudden breaks amusing, the boy is embarrassed because he has scant control over when and where his voice cracks. The boy's voice becomes lower and more masculine in texture as a result of the rapidly lengthening vocal cords.

Pubic hair begins to appear followed shortly by axillary (armpit) hair. A light fuzz appears on the upper lip and eventually the boy reaches the age when he has valid reason to shave—a real mark of manhood to him. Sometime later, probably during later adolescence, hair appears on his chest and continues to increase in area through young adulthood. The skin coarsens and becomes more oily due to the increased activity of the sebaceous glands. This frequently results in unsightly blackheads and acne about which the young adolescent is hypersensitive.

His sex organs are increasing in size. The penis grows in length and circumference and becomes pendulous. The testes and scrotum enlarge. The penis erects quite readily to a variety of stimuli including the sight of erotic pictures. Few pubescents know the specific causes of this phenomenon. Erection carries with it a strong urgency for sexual release, which is a new feeling for the young male. The increased activity of the pituitary gland results in these changes. Its activity stimulates the functioning of the endocrine glandular system which includes the thyroid, the adrenals, and the gonads (sex glands). Because of the increased activity of the endocrine glandular system all the growth sequences occur. Subnormal pituitrin causes some boys to be "breasty" and "hippy." These boys are embarrassed, often distressed, in communal showers. They are the victims of cruel teasing by their age-mates.

Physical Changes in Girls

The glandular functioning in girls follows the same general sequence as in boys during pubescence, but the outcomes are quite different. Like the boy, the girl has a peak year of growth during which she grows from two to four inches in height and gains from eight to eleven pounds. She develops a layer of subcutaneous fat that gives her body a round, soft contour. Her breasts begin to develop and continue to fill out for several years. Her hips broaden; consequently her walk becomes more seductive as viewed from the eyes of a male. Pubic and axillary hair appear. She may have some hair on the chest and around the nipples. The contours of the body, the quality of the skin, the gloss of the hair suggest a young woman.

During this change the menarche occurs, usually around thirteen. This represents an important event in the girl child's sexual life. If sex information has been either withheld or incorrectly given, menstruation may be a traumatic experience for her. Her attitudes toward sex and toward her own body may be definitely affected by her first experience with this universal mark of womanhood. It is noteworthy that in our folk culture menstruation is sometimes called "the curse." For about a year after the first menarche the young girl usually menstruates irregularly and is infertile. In some primitive cultures this is a period of approved sexual experimentation for the young girl.

Some Growth Problems

Both boys and girls are distressed about the asynchrony, or unevenness, of their growth. Since some organs grow faster than others, the adolescent may begin wondering whether or not he *is* normal. Since growth is so fast at this time, the imbalance causes poor coordination and leaves the individual more embarrassed than is necessary. This phenomenon accounts for the awkwardness of this age. The young girl's feet may suddenly reach adult size. Her size seven shoes look somewhat queer supported by spindly legs, and seem ever so much more queer to her because of her extreme sensitivity. The boy's voice change may start while he is still to all appearances a little boy. This early outward mark of manhood is a source of embarrassment to him. Present-day culture urges that adolescents be young men and women in dress, manners, and concerns. It values highly those who seem near-adult and tends to discredit those who persist in childish ways.

The wide range of years during which puberty is reached creates another problem for the young human. The early maturers not only start growing sooner but grow faster than the late maturers. We have discussed the problems that this brings to the overly tall girl of eleven. Her stooped shoulders, long feet, and unhappy expression bespeak her sad plight, as she sees it! The other extreme of this growth continuum is the late maturing boy who at age fourteen, even sixteen, is still a little boy—short, smooth-cheeked, while his classmates are growing out of their pants and caressing the fuzz on their faces. He begins to worry, "Will I ever begin to grow? Is something wrong with me? Am I going to be a runt all of my life?" He feels left out of the thought and feelings of those with whom he has been buddying for years, for there is no way he can share their present state—and he can't understand his erstwhile pals fooling around with the girls.

The rapidity of the growth he experiences during pubescence and puberty is confusing to the adolescent. So many changes are occurring all at one time that he has little chance to get used to them. These changes are attended by a complexity of emotions that often leave him feeling defeated and aggrieved. The awareness of conditions within the body are feelings. At this period new circumstances and new physical conditions are attended by unaccustomed feelings. Thus they urge immediate attention. The loves, hates, enthusiasms, and aversions of the moment seem eternal. Some parents and teachers become panicked by transitory excesses in feeling and behavior and prolong these excesses by strong opposition and strict regimentation.

**Who Is
the Early Adolescent?**

"Who am I?" is a consuming concern during the entire adolescent period. As the young person's body undergoes such rapid changes and as he experiences the baffling, confusing, often frustrating feelings of growing up, he is presented with a host of problems in establishing his identity. That identity which he had as a child has become disorganized. He is left wondering about himself, his future, his potentialities. We have progressed quite a distance since the youth of the authors when we were taught that there is one right way, one right mate for each of us, one right job for each to do. Today we are more likely to accept the notion that there are clusters of promising ways available to each one in terms of the answers derived from "Who am I? What do I seek from life?"

Teachers are able to help adolescents by discussing with them the clusters of potentialities that await them—taking into account their values, their temperaments, their interests, and their capabilities. This is quite important; for although many adults have intellectually discarded the concept of a one and only right decision about mates, jobs, colleges, and other important decision areas, they still cling emotionally in their subconscious to earlier teachings. How often do we hear: "I wonder if I made *the right* decision! Is this *the right* job for me? Did I marry the *right one?*" These are useless questions; they lead nowhere. We should like to see teachers help adolescents assess more accurately their own sources of gratification so that they may make their choices with greater chances of fulfillment.

Adult Perceptions of the Early Adolescent

"Who is the early adolescent?" As seen through most adults' eyes, the adolescent is a stranger to his parents. He becomes secretive and turns away from the sources of help that he has readily accepted for so long. Often he turns to an accepting adult outside his family for advice, sometimes to adults that the family is somewhat skeptical about. His failure to confide in his parents is a deep source of anxiety and sometimes hurt to them. The boy is rough in language, dress, and behavior. The girl retreats to silence or a secret language. The boy seldom walks into a room. He either runs in, tumbles in, or lounges in insolently. Girls are adept loungers at this age. Sprawling on the belly on the floor is a favorite position. The early adolescent is accident-prone, tripping over the furniture, breaking the legs off delicate chairs, dropping pieces of china and marring the surfaces of wood. The boy seldom sits in a chair. He uses it as an object to coil himself around. He scoffs at any expressions of sentiment. Boys and girls alike resist most behavior that parents urge upon them. A constant source of irritation is the adolescent's room. He refuses to keep it in any semblance of order. Clothes are left where they were flung when taken off. Shoes are mixed up with papers, candy, fishing tackle, bobby pins, and comic books.

The adolescent is vacillating. Most of the time he is highly resistive and then suddenly he becomes compliant. Mother remarks, "He's his old self again." She has spoken literally. It *is* his old self that he is trying to leave behind, but he has to return to it every once in a while because his doubts about the new self are great. He goes to extremes in clothes. His daily dress is likely to be a dirty sweat shirt, a comfortably wrinkled pair of slacks or levis, and loafers without socks. She is likely to wear an over-sized shirt or an under-sized sweater, a comfortable skirt, and dirty shoes. On occasion the adolescent can drive his folks "mad" with the fastidiousness he demands of himself and of them. You note that his behavior is similar to that attributed to the middle years. It is similar, only more unpredictable.

As pubescence continues, the youngster's erratic behavior intensifies. He becomes more and more disorganized. He becomes more egocentric. He sees the world revolving around him. If he needs to be picked up at school after the basketball game, it is unthinkable that mother should consider the conflict in her own evening schedule. He is demanding of money and special privileges. He wants these privileges without accepting the responsibilities attending them. To discuss responsibilities with him is an affront. His feelings are easily hurt. While this is written primarily in the masculine gender, the feelings discussed are as characteristic of the girl adolescent as of the boy.

Conflicting areas between the early adolescent and adults center around use of the telephone, table manners, dress, hours, readiness for assuming certain adult behaviors, money, homework, club activities, and disrespectful behavior. Many a family has had to stretch its budget to include two telephones because the adults gave up trying to control the amount of time the youngsters "hang on." The best adjustment is to develop a sense of humor about the situation. Telephone conversations during early adolescence are largely with the same sex. Their content consists of a superabundance of giggles and trivia which is highly important to the adolescent. Table manners and dress are topics that permeate adult-adolescent discussions since they are daily and constant. Continuous nagging over trivia in these areas weakens the adult's effectiveness when he attempts to make himself heard about something really important.

Hours are another source of conflict. The early adolescent feels that he has reached the age when he should decide for himself when he should go to bed, determined by when he is sleepy and tired, and what time he needs to be in the house after the evening meal. Unfortunately he is not so eager to accept responsibility for getting up in the morning. Getting the early adolescent to school in the morning often turns out to be a daily tug of war that leaves mother exhausted, father outraged, and Junior seething. Normal human perversity has reached its zenith. At about the same time that the question of hours arises, other behaviors create a furor. One morning Maria comes to breakfast with her mouth exaggerated with vivid lipstick, another day she may emerge from the bathroom with a white forelock. And so it goes!

As the early adolescent begins to participate in more school activities, his need for money increases rapidly. In most cities it takes thirty cents just for transportation. School activities requiring money have increased tremendously during the past fifteen years. (We give more details on this in the next chapter, page 334.) The youngster needs much money. He *feels* he needs much more than he does, certainly more than his parents feel he needs. Our culture, especially the urban culture, provides few opportunities for early adolescents to earn money.

In school, conflicts between pupils, parents, and teachers center around homework, club activities, manners, and disrespectful behavior. Teachers who have rigid standards of behavior have no place, nor peace, with the adolescent. The wise teacher of this age fails to pay attention to most of what he sees. He is able to interpret behavior that appears rude and inexcusable as a necessary part of trying out new relationships with adults. Remember the tendency to exaggerate or overact when new learnings are being ingested! If we can go back in memory to our own adolescence, we are better able to empathize with adolescent behavior. This is an advantage the young teacher has—he is not so far from his own adolescence. Once empathy has been established, a sense of humor has the power to turn many a potential conflict into one from which new understandings emerge.

We recall a teacher recounting an incident that occurred in her classroom when two boys (one about a foot taller than the other) had been building up hostility for some days. Finally, it broke out in the classroom. They angrily faced each other and were about to have it out when the teacher became aware of what was happening. She went up to the larger boy and said with a twinkle, "Wait, just a minute until I get you a stool." The ludicrousness of the situation became apparent to him. The boys had to laugh and the tension was broken.

Of course, the picture we have drawn is a stereotype of the early adolescent as seen through adult eyes. Like all stereotypes it does not fit all adolescents. Many grow through this stage with little apparent disruption. The expectations adults have of youngsters this age make a difference in the intensity of separateness felt. If the adolescent feels cut off, out of communication, with those he loves and has depended upon for so long, his behavior has to be more extreme for his emotional output is intensified in areas that are nonproductive. His problems are so consuming to him that he feels surely his parents, of all people, should understand how he feels and make allowances for him. He cannot verbalize these feelings for he himself does not understand them well enough to put them into words. In many cultures adolescence is not a period of concern either to the youngster or to society. These tend to be cultures in which the roles of both adolescents and adults are much more clearly defined and rigidly marked off than in our culture. Parents and teachers who find their appropriate roles with these emerging young adults meet less resistance and less rejection than we have described. In our culture, however, if the adolescent is too docile, too concerned with what adults think, too centered upon adult goals of orderliness, cleanliness, politeness, and studiousness, it is likely that the youngster is failing to achieve the emancipation that he must achieve to grow into mature adulthood.

Adolescent Perceptions of Himself

"Who is the early adolescent?" As seen through his own eyes, he is a "mixed-up, misunderstood kid." He is not sure of himself. His body is playing strange tricks upon him. Is he an adult or a child? One day or hour he feels like an adult and demands the recognition that adulthood brings. As suddenly, he becomes unsure and creeps back to childish ways, refusing to accept the responsibilities that he thought he wanted. He continues, however, to reach out toward adult work. Over half of the junior-high-school boys and girls interviewed in one school in New York City said that helping other members of the family with work was what made them feel grown up.[3]

The early adolescent is engrossed with his own self. He is introspective. As a corollary to this quality, the early adolescent is also engrossed with what other people think of him. He feels as if all eyes are upon him. He is painfully sensitive about his clothes, feeling that they are too tight or not modish, or too drab or too bright, or too extreme, or. . . . He worries (both boys and girls) about skin quality. Every little pimple becomes a full-blown case of acne in his mind. Girls are self-conscious about their shapes. They imagine that men are staring at them. Some develop a slump in seeking to hide their developing breasts. Boys question their own manliness. In short, adolescents feel as if they are out-of-step, and they would give everything they possess to be in step, if only they could find out how. This age youngster is likely to feel that his family and the world have it in for him. He projects a good many of his feelings onto others by being brutally frank in the perennial slam book that makes its appearance nearly every spring, by assuming heroic roles that he plays for a day, a week, or a month and then discards for more heroic ones, by idolizing

---

[3] Mary Beauchamp, *Building Neighborliness* (New York: Center for Human Relations and Community Studies, New York University, 1958), p. 24.

popular heroes of the day. Steffens in his autobiography describes the process of assuming a variety of roles which at the time seemed heroic and popular to him: "I became a drunkard as I had been a knight, a trapper, and a preacher, not for long and not exactly with my whole heart, but with a large part of my imagination." [4]

| **Developmental Tasks of Adolescents** | Now that we have a picture of the early adolescent and some of his needs, let's examine the developmental tasks that are unique to this age. |

During the total span of adolescence the individual is working harder than he has ever worked before on two all-consuming developmental tasks. They are: (1) *to achieve emancipation from home;* and (2) *to establish heterosexuality.* In accomplishing these tasks he is also attending to a number of related developmental tasks. These two, however, are fundamental life achievements which he must work on at this time if he is to become a mature adult. These are *his* tasks, anchored in his own self needs. The other developmental tasks are ones that society thrusts upon him. Frankwood Williams describes the transition that takes place as follows: "He begins life entirely dependent, egocentric, irresponsible; he should become fully independent, altruistic, responsible. He has to pass from the completely filial to the completely parental attitude." [5]

Achieving Emancipation from the Home

Anyone who has lived with young adolescents must have resounding in his ears expressions such as these:

I simply must have a pale blue Cashmere sweater for assembly Friday.

But, dad, you don't understand. All the other girls are going to have them.

I'll do the dishes in a minute.

Why can't I go on the trip? Everyone in our class is going.

[4] Lincoln Steffens, *The Autobiography of Lincoln Steffens,* abridged ed. (New York: Harcourt, Brace and Company, Inc., 1931), p. 87.
[5] From *Adolescence: Studies in Mental Hygiene* by Frankwood E. Williams. Copyright 1930 by Rinehart and Company, Inc., copyright 1958 by Marion E. Kenworthy. Reprinted by permission of Rinehart and Company, Inc., Publishers.

Mom, have you seen my shoes? I can't find them anywhere.

Oh, I forgot!

I'll take the garbage out when I come home from the game.

This is a *private* conversation.

You're absolutely impossible, dad.

Early adolescence is the period of the most intense rejection of adults. Parents are the recipients of the keenest rejection. They frequently are the last to accept the fact of their offspring's growing up and are the last to be accepted by their offspring. Redl describes this age as the "phase when the nicest children begin to behave in a most awful way." He also states that this is an age when "a child's personality is broken up or loosened, so that adolescent changes can be built into it and so that it can be modified into the personality of an adult." [6] This implies that a disorganization has to take place before the individual is able to integrate himself into an adult. The disorganization brings with it many types of behavior that are misunderstood by adults. The youngster really loses ground during this time, for he returns to many of the irritating ways of his early childhood. The carefully instilled habits, which he has never completely incorporated into his own self but has followed because of his identification with his parents, are now thrown overboard as his parents are displaced as models for behavior. Because these habits have not become integrated into his own self, they break down under the strain of the physical and emotional upheaval of adolescence.

The more resistance the adolescent meets from adults, the harder he must fight to emancipate himself. During pubescence, nail-biting, masturbation, tics, silly antics, carelessness, boisterousness, and disrespect are to-be-expected behaviors. Poor table manners, dramatic outbursts, insolent speech, and impudent dress (Jane's donning of dad's oversize shirt and dirty saddle shoes, and Sam's dirty sweatshirt and wrinkled slacks) are characteristic means that the adolescent adopts in order to assert his independence.

The adult's lack of understanding of early adolescence has an everlasting quality to it. Some ancient writings are concerned with the depravity of youth, and similar statements may be found for nearly every

---

[6] Fritz Redl, *Pre-Adolescents—What Makes Them Tick?* (New York: Child Study Association of America, pamphlet).

generation. Would you believe that the following statement was made in 1921?

> There is a good deal of anxiety throughout the world, apparently, over the adolescent. People are greatly worried about him and his antics, and there is a conviction on the part of some that what we need to do is to take him by the scruff of the neck and dance him along in the way he should go. The adolescent seems to have got out of bounds and coercion is advised to bring him back.[7]

Today, resentment against the adolescent has reached a new peak, and the cracking-down that Williams refers to is expressed in more virulent terms. Let's see if we can partially understand the phenomenon of the *separateness* of adolescents and adults. The early adolescent has to issue his declaration of independence. If he does not, he is likely to remain Mr. Milquetoast. Philip Wylie [8] has used strong words to describe the effects of "momism" in our culture. In trying to achieve independence, the young human seems to reject those whom he loves and who expect him to love them. A conflict situation with strong, but ambivalent, emotions is created which becomes demanding and insistent. While many parents today intellectually accept the necessity for the behavior of their adolescents, they find the "dailiness" of it impossible to accept with equanimity. Appeals are made to his sense of gratitude for all his parents have done for him. Quite obviously the adolescent sees the inconsistency of such appeals, since the parents voluntarily chose to do whatever they have done for him. Lacking appreciation, the parents decide they have reared a monster. And the gulf widens!

Then, too, we must remember the early adolescent has as much mental acuity as he will ever have or as we adults have. He has more vigor than we do. He is as big as we are. He has far more strength and more courage and more insistence. A flabby middle-aged father looks at his husky son and remarks mentally, "Why can't I make him realize that I am stronger than he is?" [9] The visual evidence that "our little girl or boy" has grown up is quite disarming to parents. The adolescent can no longer be expected to act like a child, but we are not quite sure what kind of man or woman he is going to be. Whenever ambivalent feelings are present, emo-

---

[7] Williams, *op. cit.*, p. 62.

[8] Philip Wylie, *Generation of Vipers* (New York: Rinehart and Company, Inc., 1942), pp. 184-204.

[9] Sally Smith, *A Child's Guide to a Parent's Mind* (New York: The National Committee for Mental Hygiene, Inc., film strip and recording).

tions are more difficult to understand and utilize constructively. For over a decade, parents have formed habits of "thinking for," "planning for," "doing for" a child, and suddenly before them stands a young man or young woman saying, "I shall go my own way now." He doesn't even add, "Thank you!" and that is the part that hurts. Wall expresses this sentiment as follows:

> Unhappily many parents have not themselves successfully passed through adolescence. They see the growing beauty of the girl, the increasing strength of the boy, the intellectual challenge that maturing intelligence brings, as threats to their privilege and authority, a cause of jealousy, or a reminder of hope and ambitions that time has defeated.[10]

We have to look at still another quality of this relationship which increases the ambivalence of the situation. Adults are continuously after adolescents to be like *they* are. Yet they know what a "sorry mess" our world is in. The discrepancy between the kind of behavior adults advocate for (sometimes demand of) adolescents and their own observable behavior creates such a chasm between the real and the ideal that adolescents are inclined to take admonitions with a tongue-in-cheek attitude. Recently we heard a group of adolescents agree that their parents really were envious of them and being envious had to keep them in their places. Since the parents are involved emotionally in this process of their offspring's emancipation to as great an extent as their children and since they feel somewhat at a disadvantage in the contest, the feelings that build up in both parents and youngsters at this time are largely ones of frustration, humiliation, resentment, and despair. Fantasy, born of despair, leads to thoughts of suicide at times. Sandburg describes this feeling in his life thus:

> I had my bitter and lonely hours moving out of boy years into a grown man. I can remember a winter when the thought came often that it might be best to step out of it all. The second thought came, "What would be the best way?" [11]

These feelings of frustration and resentment can be avoided if adults are mature enough to understand their own feelings and take the long view

---

10 W. D. Wall, *Education and Mental Health, Report Based on European Conference Called by UNESCO,* November-December 1952 (New York: Columbia University Press, 1955), p. 145.

11 Carl Sandburg, *Always the Young Strangers* (New York: Harcourt, Brace and Company, 1952), p. 375.

about their youngster's development. This is an age when the individual must be *stood*.

Home for the early adolescent comes to be a base of operations to which he returns when he needs to refuel—to get his meals, to change his clothes, to make his demands for money or privileges, and to sleep. Whatever additional time he spends there is likely to be in body only. A few homes serve as a meeting place for the gang, which by now is a small group of the same sex who have come to have emotional ties with each other. These are usually homes in which the parents, recognizing the adolescent need to be out-of-reach of adults, either make themselves scarce or have set aside a part of the house in which the adolescents may congregate. The rumpus room in the basement serves many adolescent groups in this way.

Establishing Heterosexuality

The early adolescent at the beginning of pubescence is still a homosexual individual. He rejects the opposite sex; he gets his major satisfactions from the same sex. During the two or three years that we are considering, he takes some important steps toward heterosexuality. Tryon sums up the process as it takes place:

> . . . Achieving mastery of one's sex role in adolescence is a process of reintegrating past experiences with new physical impulses, new expectations from the peer group and from adult society. Each individual's readiness depends upon the kinds of feelings he has about his father and mother which have accumulated through the years, his feelings about the "goodness" or "badness" of his own body, the way in which he has explored adult roles in fantasy play of early childhood, the successes or failures he has had in identifying with his own sex play-group in late childhood, and so on.[12]

The perception that the male adolescent develops of maleness in our culture is strength. Every boy wants to be tall and strong. Any "dope" can tell what a premium our culture places on size and strength. The boy wants to excel at sports; he is sometimes painfully aware that this is his dad's fondest dream. During early adolescence the boy is concerned about

---

[12] Caroline Tryon, "The Adolescent Peer Culture," *Adolescence, Forty-Third Yearbook,* Part I (Chicago: National Society for the Study of Education, 1944), pp. 231-232.

being a good athlete. He frequently takes as his model someone who excels in sports. He compares his size and strength with that of his peers. He must convince himself that he really *is* a man. The first step toward achieving heterosexuality is to establish one's sex as an undeniable fact with one's peers. The national studies carried on by the Boy Scouts and Girl Scouts of America conclude:

> Boys maintain their interest in sports and games and real skill activities longer than girls. When asked to suggest activities for a club, boys less often mention social activities of any kind, and in particular they *much* less frequently suggest dancing and parties (boys: 26%; girls of the same age: 57%).[13]

The study sponsored by the Boy Scouts indicated that 57 per cent of boys worry about areas of achievement, such as passing in school; 29 per cent worry about being accepted by others, and 29 per cent about reality pressures such as money.[14] These worries indicate what the boy adolescent holds important in his life.

The girl's perception of femininity is grace, charm, gentleness, social service, sociability, and beauty. She is concerned about the proportions of her figure. She recognizes that her feminine role is "to please." Her ideas of the perfect figure come from Hollywood. It is an advantage to be tall, but one must not be too tall and one must be thin. During the past few years oversize breasts have come to be the symbol of supreme feminine desirability. The early girl adolescent is excessively preoccupied with her dress and her appearance. She spends hours experimenting with coiffures. She is a "push-over" for all kinds of cosmetic fads and dress fads. Every detail of her dress is scrutinized and discussed endlessly with her girl friends.

The early adolescent girl is beginning to look ahead to her life after school and she sees this as a time when she will have a job and be independent. As the girl grows into later adolescence, she thinks more about marriage as a life career. The great *majority of girls today see themselves as married and holding a job.* This is quite a shift in perceptions from a generation ago. The adolescent girl shows an interest in social service. She perceives herself as ministering to humanity, is likely to believe that

---

[13] Girl Scouts of America, *Adolescent Girls* (Ann Arbor, Mich.: Survey Research Center, 1957), p. 238.
[14] Boy Scouts of America, *A Study of Adolescent Boys* (New Brunswick, N. J.: Boy Scouts of America, 1955), p. 14.

she wants to be a nurse. These impulses are countermanded by fantasies
of glamorous occupations such as movie actress, air line stewardess, oper-
atic singer.

The early adolescent years include numerous heterosexual activities.
These are usually group affairs. "Pairing off" is rare at this time. Three or
four girls and three or four boys go to a movie together or Hortense invites
a group of boys and girls to a party. Some of the more precocious ones
enjoy dancing and occasional "smooching" but, for the most part, parties
are times when one sits around, probably in dim light, if it can be managed, listening to records, laughing, giggling, eating, and from the adult
point of view doing nothing worthwhile. An occasional game of "post-
office" is enjoyed more because of its daring quality as "forbidden fruit"
than from any real satisfaction in kissing. Many boys are still smaller than
the girls and often express disdain for their social activities. They usually
participate because of the "eats" that are available, or so they say. Ham-
burgers disappear like magic.

The same type of social activity takes place in community centers,
settlements, and other agencies that serve this age. Some agencies have
a lounge program, which simply means that a lounge is available for
dancing and listening to records. The early adolescents invariably demand
to participate in the lounge program, but little heterosexual dancing takes
place. Girls dance with each other; boys watch and make remarks. They
are sizing up their own tastes and values. Girls practice their arts of
enticing while boys assess their inclinations for being enticed. This phase
of heterosexual development somehow reminds us of the dances some
animals perform prior to the mating season when elaborate rituals that
seem wholly meaningless, except to the participants, take place.

We have mentioned hero worship as a characteristic of this age. This
is a step toward heterosexuality. You may recall that the pre-schooler
developed a love affair with the parent of the opposite sex and how this
led to identification with the parent of the same sex. These are childhood
steps in developing a sex role. The early adolescent now must reject his
parents as objects of identification in order to emancipate himself from
his dependency upon them. He still needs a model. He seeks this model
in some member of his own sex, usually one whose sex role he admires
and wishes to imitate. Thus, girls seek models from Hollywood; after all,
society has placed its stamp of approval upon these reigning beauties.
Boys often select their models from the world of sports, since they epito-

mize society's approval of strength and virility. In imitating their heroes, they are "trying on" the sex roles of adults and gaining some assurance in the feelings of these roles. Some individuals who have developed distinctive life-styles before adolescence select their models from the area of endeavor which is to claim their life's energies. With one it may be a scientist, another an explorer, another a financier, another an artist or musician, another a teacher or minister.

Another form in which heterosexuality finds expression is in the selection of someone from one's own sex upon whom to lavish the feelings that are associated with heterosexuality. Deep, intense friendships—sometimes with another youngster one's own age, sometimes with a younger or older child, sometimes with an adult—are characteristic of this age. Into this friendship the early adolescent pours the feelings of tenderness, loyalty, sharing, and need that we associate with marriage. Farnham vividly describes the adolescent friendship:

> At its intense level, there is great fealty, great fondness and admiration. There is purpose in all this. Such a relationship acts as a sluiceway, a safety valve for all the unmanageable feelings with which the young person may be beset. Love his parent he may not. Love himself he must not. But to love another, a different parent, another, often a better self, may offer a compromise, a way out.[15]

These intense friendships are often disturbing to parents. Sometimes these friendships are homosexual in actuality as well as in spirit. Parents sense this and are opposed without verbalizing their fears. The adolescent senses the fear and frequently cannot understand it or counter it. Adolescent friendships may be precarious. They often become stronger if opposed even if the parent communicates only non-verbally that there is something sordid about the relationship. This is for the adolescent the most beautiful part of his emotional life. If we wish to help him grow beyond this friendship-love affair, we must respect it as a step toward real heterosexuality. We must identify with him and his feelings and *wait*. If the adolescent stays in this stage too long, then is the time to consider ways to help him grow beyond it or to seek more expert guidance if it seems necessary.

BLOCKS TO ESTABLISHING HETEROSEXUALITY. The natural development into heterosexuality is blocked often in our culture by some common and

---

[15] Marynia F. Farnham, *The Adolescent* (New York: Harper and Brothers, 1951), p. 27.

serious misconceptions. Adults place so high a value on earliness that they often arrange heterosexual experiences for early adolescents before they are ready. These leave the youngsters feeling confused and frustrated. We recently heard of an eighth-grade graduation in which the boys wore tuxedos and the girls evening dresses. Parties were arranged during graduation week so that "couples" attended. Dancing was the main social activity. Such affairs are usually sources of considerable tension to the adolescent. Girls this age are more mature than boys. They do not especially relish dancing partners a head shorter than they. Some girls and boys are inevitably left out in the process of pairing. For some the uncertainty of knowing the correct thing to do and say precludes the possibility of pleasure. We recommend *The Dark at the Top of the Stairs* [16] as a dramatic and sensitive picture of the suffering of a timid girl and a boy of a minority group in such adult-contrived parties. Such pushing of adolescents occurs side by side with the efforts of many parents to hold their children back by resisting the behaviors that come with growing up and denying them the right to grow as their own selves dictate. Finding both of these attitudes functioning in the parents of a single social group compounds the difficulties.

Another misconception of our culture is the emphasis placed on the importance of being popular. Many parents contribute to the early adolescent's insecurity by their drives to have popular children. This is particularly intensified with girls of middle-class parents whose social mobility is somewhat dependent upon the daughter's acceptability to higher class boys. Friends must be carefully chosen—not so much on the basis of enjoyment or compatibility as on the status of their parents. The drive for popularity leads to extreme conformity in behavior. It intensifies the emotional strain felt during these years and tends to pile up troubles that come to a head in later adolescence. The need to be popular motivates the youngster to be and to act in ways incompatible with his temperament and interests. Whenever genuineness is denied the human personality, confusion, frustration, and hostility build up and eventually must be expressed. Our culture is in the throes now of some aberrations resulting from hostility developed by adolescents as they reach toward

---

[16] William Inge, *The Dark at the Top of the Stairs* (New York: Random House, Inc., 1958).

adulthood. We refer you to *Must You Conform?* [17] as an eloquent statement of this point of view.

A third block to the natural development of heterosexuality that our
culture produces is that coming from our feelings about sex. We teach
that sex is something dirty, wrong, and degrading. We reinforce this
teaching by admonishing our young boys that they must treat women as
they would treat their mothers or sisters, must act in no way that they
would not act with their mothers or sisters. We have made a fetish of the
purity of femininity, trying to instill in the young the notion that all
women are frail, delicate, pure creatures, who must remain beyond human
touch. These ideas are unhealthy for both boys and girls. They force the
young male adolescent, who *must* make tentative moves toward girls, to

be guilty about the way he feels, and to carry on his sex activities in
secret. They may impel him to seek gratification from those women who
clearly have denied their purity. The girl feels that she has sinned if she
enjoys the first tentative outreaches of her young male friend. Such
thoughts, feelings, and actions can only stand in the way of healthy
heterosexual development.

On the other hand, many girls are taught that all men are depraved,
that their only thought is to conquer the female sexually. Many girls when
being admonished by mother before going on a date have protested, "But
don't you trust me, mother?" The typical reply to this query is, "I trust

---

[17] Robert Lindner, *Must You Conform?* (New York: Rinehart and Company, Inc.,
1956).

you implicitly, dear, but *no man can be trusted.*" The implanting of such fears, if accepted by the young girl, stands in the way of healthy social relationships. She finds herself anticipating that all heterosexual relationships must be sexual relationships. Even today some middle-aged women can conceive of no female-male relationships other than in sexual terms. These teachings encourage attitudes between the sexes of a contest instead of complementary relationships. If the girl does not accept these attitudes of the culture, she is likely to feel guilty in rejecting her parents or feel that "It's too bad mother is such an innocent." The adolescent has a difficult time achieving both of these important developmental tasks unless wise adults see them as important to achieve.

Perhaps a word should be said about the feelings which mother must control in herself as she watches another girl become the center of her son's universe, or as father must when he sees his daughter turn to another man. This has to be accepted by parents and it is well to recognize the displacement that occurs with the acceptance. The daughter blooming into beautiful adulthood may subconsciously rival her mother. Unless mother can welcome this development, unhappy situations occur, perhaps permanently damaging mother-daughter relationships. Mother may use many wiles to keep her son tied to her, to disparage the worth of other females. In so doing she stunts her boy. Father may react quite as violently to daughter's boy friends—causing her to be uncertain about all men. Parents often find themselves in opposition to each other about the daily behaviors of their adolescent children. While each may have logic-tight rationale for his attitudes, their subconscious wishes stem from their own feelings about each other and from their feelings about their children growing away from them.

Accepting Values to Live By

The youngster's world expands significantly in a physical sense during this period of his life. Then, most boys and girls enter junior high school, which is a larger school that frequently serves a more heterogeneous population than the elementary school. Here the adolescent is introduced not only to an increased number of relationships but also to an increased complexity of relationships. He has less supervision. He is out later. His activities involve more decisions. His peers come from many different value systems representing greater variety of social classes, religious groups, political affiliations, and individual differences that are acceptable in a democratic culture.

In this complex situation our young adolescent finds himself faced with decisions that are going to make differences in his entire life. For example, in many schools he has to choose whether he is going to become a member of an exclusive club and thus endorse exclusiveness; he has to decide to what extent and in what areas he is going to think independently, and how much he is willing to conform to the mores of the group; he has to decide to what extent he is willing to adhere to the standards that he believes he has accepted for his own. He has, in short, to begin to establish some values which are uniquely his own that he feels he has to live by regardless of "what other people think." The "other people" who concern him are his parents and his peers. In spite of the ostentatiousness of his revolt against parental authority, he *does* care how they feel about his behavior. He also cares how his gang feels. He is often in conflict with both, for like each of us, he has a unique cluster of values that he endorses in his daily living.

The adolescent has reached the stage in his value development in which he begins to see that rules were made for man, not man for rules. That rules can be applied to help men grow is a fairly new concept and one that many adults find some difficulty accepting. The utterance that "Man was not made for the Sabbath, but the Sabbath for man" has caused many heads to roll in the history of the world. We should not get too impatient with young adolescents when they fail to comprehend and apply this doctrine.

Roles of Adults in Lives of Young Adolescents

You may infer from this chapter that the authors counsel abandoning the young adolescents—letting them live their lives, make their mistakes, and take the consequences. Nothing could be farther from what is needed by young adolescents. Adults play key roles with adolescents. First, adolescents need to feel that it is all right to resist their parents, and to question and doubt other adults. The myth of the infallibility of adults should be shattered. We trust it has been well-exposed before the onset of adolescence. Adolescents need to feel that parents accept their behavior and can distinguish between the outward behavior and its inner meaning. They need to understand, too, just as they did in the middle years, that acceptance does not imply endorsement of behavior. It is just acceptance of what is, and probably must be, in our culture.

We mentioned earlier the need for a sense of humor. The best definition of humor is "the art of throwing perspective on a problem." During this phase of growth all details are so "terribly urgent" as to prevent seeing any problem in its real proportions. Often the adult can focus the situation with a wink or jest. The use of humor must be an accepting one, not one that rejects or alienates. It may have a touch of the ludicrous which usually appeals to adolescents. Currently, adolescents call it "whammy."

Parents need to sit and talk and plan calmly with their adolescents, treating them as adults if they behave as adults, respecting their urges toward responsible adulthood, but being sure that the youngsters have the security of knowing their parents are not going to run out on them or let them down. This implies some rather clear-cut lines of authority that are consistent, reasonable, just, understood, and mutually decided upon. Preventive planning avoids crises with adolescents just as surely as it avoids accidents with toddlers.

Parents need to clarify their own feelings about each other. The emotional investment in a child is a factor that must be reckoned with. If adolescence can be a time when mom and pop grow closer together in their mutual recognition of the imminence of Mike's leaving the nest, they probably can see Mike and his needs more clearly. They are sure of their own needs. Such a clarification tends to minimize the hurts that come from having Mike turn to the young minister or the athletic coach instead of turning to his parents for advice and counsel.

Role of the School

The young adolescent is no scholar. He is too restless, too self-centered, too confused, to be a logical, reasonable human being. He expends too much of his energy in fantasies to focus for long on imposed tasks. He responds very poorly to traditional methods of teaching. He is always late, always procrastinating.

The curriculum for the early adolescent has to take into account his feelings about himself and about adults. The physiological changes occurring within him make it undesirable and impossible for him to be a steady, concentrating student. The program, therefore, must be one in which his new powers of decision-making are employed. He should have a much larger share in helping to plan the activities which are to command his attention. If he does, the program will be far more active than it characteristically is today, more attention will be given to first-hand experiences, more small-group work will emerge, and the areas of biology, physiology, human relations, and psychology will be threads running throughout all the learnings.

This is the time for the teacher to let the curriculum grow out of the personal concerns of the pupils. They are curious and studious in learning about their bodies, what is happening to them and why. This is an excellent time to teach physiology, anatomy, and biology—if it is taught so that the pupils are aware that they are learning about themselves, are getting *their* questions answered—not just those in the textbook.

This is an excellent time to ponder about human motivation and come to some conclusions. History and literature taught with this focus can be understood and appreciated by the early adolescent. These subjects taught as a recounting of something that happened long ago, cherished by our culture, with emphasis on dates and events, emperors, generals, and presidents remain dead and rejected by the pupils.

The curriculum for the early adolescent must be focused directly on the fundamentals—by this we mean the fundamentals of the adolescent. These are: Why do I behave as I do? Why do I feel as I do? Do others feel like I do? This focus will hold young adolescents and lead them into profitable areas of learnings. A factual, logical presentation of content organized around subjects will leave them cold and unresponsive. Those who respond to the teacher's requests may appear to be "good" students, but their intellectual curiosity is being dulled rather than whetted. The trivia of form and style must wait until later years. Now is the time for an active curriculum, one with a flair for the dramatic, the novel, the fresh approach.

"Periods of intensive physical growth, whether in infancy or adolescence, are times of rapid emotional growth as well. Because of the stresses and strains accompanying rapid changes, these are hazardous periods of the growth process," [18] reported Blos in his study of the adolescent personality which was requested by the Commission on Secondary School Curriculum. At this hazardous period, the junior high

---

[18] Peter Blos, *The Adolescent Personality* (New York: Appleton-Century-Crofts, Inc., 1941), p. 276.

school, the most generally accepted structure for this age, weakens the relational content of its program by fragmenting the school day into small bits. As a result few of the students know any of the others very well and the teacher has so many pupils pass in and out of his room in any day that *he* cannot possibly know any of them in any *whole*some way.

The curriculum for the early adolescent must be one that has as its *first purpose* the establishing of firm, strong, friendly bonds between some knowing and well-qualified adults and a group of boys and girls who are searching for adults whom they can trust, with whom they can talk, with whom they feel comfortable in revealing themselves, and in being themselves. The UNESCO Conference, referred to on page 316, states in discussing problems of secondary education:

> ... A school system which leaves the child unaided in an impersonal world of specialists is, at best, not assisting healthy social, emotional and intellectual growth; at worst it is contributing to the incoherence of view which marks many young people.

> ... The first charge on his (the major teacher's) time and energy should be that of getting intimately to know each of his pupils and building up between himself and them an atmosphere of trust and confidence. He should be the principal contact between the school and the parents.... For all general matters affecting the child's life at school he alone should be responsible and should, as it were, occupy a half-way position between the adult friend and the aloof pedagogue. It is to such a person that the child should naturally turn when he finds himself in difficulties whether in his work or in his general life.[19]

This is the considered opinion of sixty experts from twenty different countries. Perhaps it would be wise to give our thoughtful attention to their counsel.

Suggestions for Further Exploration

► Select five twelve-year-old boys and five twelve-year-old girls (thirteen or eleven will do just as well). Make two kinds of studies of them:

> Compare the boys with the girls and then compare each of the five boys with the remainder of the boys. Do the same for the girls. As you make your comparisons note: height, weight, body proportions, rate of growth

---

[19] W. D. Wall, *Education and Mental Health, Report Based on European Conference Called by UNESCO,* November-December 1952 (New York: Columbia University Press, 1955), pp. 184-185.

during past six months, voice quality, muscle tone, interests, activities, size of feet.

Discuss your findings with your classmates.

► Interview the mothers of five seventh or eighth graders. See if you can discover their major concerns about their adolescent youngsters. What are points of conflict? How do the mothers show understanding or lack of it? How would you write the section "Adult Perceptions of Adolescents" if you were writing this book?

► Talk with a few junior-high-school teachers. Find out the major sources of conflict between teacher and pupils. Did the teachers show awareness of adolescent developmental tasks? If so, how? If not, explain. Write a paragraph stating your feelings about teaching in junior high school.

► Read a physiology book on changes occurring during pubescence.

► Attend a couple of mixed social affairs of junior-high-school youngsters. Jot down the tentative outreaches toward heterosexuality you observe. Discuss with your classmates.

► Talk with the individual you are studying and see how the content of this chapter applies or fails to apply to him—if he is as old as early adolescence. Add to your profile after your conversation with him.

► Some films depicting the early adolescent are as follows:

The Teens (Ages and Stages Series), 28 min., sound, National Film Board of Canada.

> The film deals with earlier and later adolescence. The frantic life of the family which has several teen-agers is vividly portrayed. The parents' roles in guiding the teen-ager are stressed.

High Wall, 32 min., sound, Anti-Defamation League.

> The effects of rearing upon prejudice and the consequences of encouraging young children to hate is shown in realistic terms in this film.

Physical Aspects of Puberty (Adolescent Development Series), 19 min., sound, McGraw-Hill Book Company, Inc.

> This film shows the physiological developments that occur during puberty. This process of growth is shown for the boy and for the girl and some of the usual growth problems, such as the underdeveloped boy, the fast-growing girl are dealt with.

13

The Adolescent- Young Adult

His body was rearranging itself toward manhood, and he was shaken by the veering winds of adolescence. One moment he was dedicated and pure and devoted; the next he wallowed in filth; and the next he groveled in shame and emerged rededicated.[1]

Even when I was a fairly precocious young man the nothingness of the hopes and strivings which chases most men relentlessly through life came to my consciousness with considerable

[1] John Steinbeck, *East of Eden*, (New York: Viking Press, 1953), p. 450.

vitality. Moreover I soon discovered the cruelty of that chase, which in those years was much more cleverly covered up by hypocrisy and glittering words than is the case today . . . the consequence was a positive fanatic (orgy) of free thinking coupled with the impression that youth is intentionally being deceived by the State through lies; it was a crushing impression.[2]

These paragraphs show in part the extreme range of perceptions and concerns to be found among normal near-adults. For most individuals the years between fifteen and eighteen are ones in which giant steps are taken toward integrating the adult roles that the early adolescent struggles so hard to secure and tries on in many guises. The older adolescent is still working on the developmental tasks of establishing his independence from his childhood home and achieving his heterosexuality. If his early adolescence has been wholesomely lived, he has developed the abilities and understandings necessary to achieve these tasks. In this chapter we describe the later adolescent, analyze his efforts toward becoming adult, comment on secondary schools, and discuss some of the problems peculiar to adolescence in our culture at this time.

Physical Growth

During these years the individual attains, or comes close to attaining, his maximum growth. He may continue to gain weight, but he probably has his full height. He has to integrate the functioning of his adult body. He has to learn to accept himself in whatever shape and size he has become. The young man must learn what to do with his new height, his added powers; the young woman must learn how to manage her greater charm and more seductive shape.

Older adolescents are highly aware of their bodies and some are hypersensitive about them. They are inclined to fear that they do not measure up to the basic criteria of maleness or femaleness. A small mole on a girl's cheek may loom so large in her view of herself that she sees it as a barrier between herself and the attainment of her femininity. Girls tend to worry about their figures, the size of their feet, their hairlines, the amount of hair on their faces and arms, and all slight blemishes of skin.

---

[2] Paul Schilpp, ed., *Albert Einstein: Philosopher-Scientist* (New York: Tudor Publishing Company, 1951), pp. 3-5.

They resent, often reject, the wearing of needed glasses. A shapely figure, dainty feet, smooth and flawless skin, shining eyes, a distinct hairline are to the girls symbols of beauty, grace, and charm. These assets must be achieved to make her desirable to the male.

Boys are concerned with size, strength, skill, and daring. In our culture these are symbols of manliness. The boy tends to wrestle, joust, take a great variety of perilous chances to find out how he measures up to his own standards and to those of his peers. He wants to know where he stands in muscle development, dexterity, stamina, virility. He is especially, and secretly, concerned about the size and adequacy of his sex organs, anxious lest they be considered inferior to a man's potential.

One of the more unhealthy developments in secondary and higher education is the disproportionate adulation accorded through interscholastic athletics to the unusually strong, tall, dexterous boy. In many schools he is sharply trained in otherwise useless skills to be used for the amusement and diversion of the adult population. More and more he is becoming a gaming-piece for gamblers. Only the most mature boys who possess a high degree of perspective can escape developing a lopsided view of themselves, which may plague them the remainder of their days. We trust that the time is not far off when the games originally intended for young people to play for fun will be returned to the youngsters to be enjoyed. We have no evidence that striving for championships, for praise in the press, for all-star selections builds health or character.

Concern for physical adequacy, to say nothing of superiority, tends to give the adolescent gnawing feelings of unworthiness. He tends to withdraw, to hide, or to compensate by exaggerated display of bravado, boastfulness, extravagant physical activity. This kind of behavior is more acceptable in boys than in girls, and offers a more healthful means of disposing of anxiety than is available to girls. Boys are disposed to joke about themselves, to tell exaggerated stories about themselves and their friends, and to boast about somebody they know who. . . .

Girls do not develop the same degree of openness displayed by boys. They are inclined to be excessively modest. They are more likely to withdraw into daydreams and fantasies and to join fan-clubs that indulge in mass devotion to the currently popular "glamour boy." They tend to display disdain for femininity by bizarre dress, to experiment with make-up, exaggerated hair-do's and costumes in order to divert attention from lamented and often imagined shortcomings in their features and shapes.

Achieving **Independence** **from Home**	Most of the older adolescents have learned to accept the adults in their lives and to understand that they may not be old-fashioned "sour-pusses" after all. If the young person has been allowed to grow

without undue restraint, he has begun to assume adult roles and to be comfortable in them. Tilly can afford now and then to ask mother's advice about which dress to wear or how to handle an ardent boy on a date; Tom can be quite chummy with Dad about the first time Dad wore a tuxedo. With the slowing down of growth and a fuller acceptance of himself as he is and is to be, the adolescent feels less necessity to assert his independence in extravagant forms. He is able, now that he has integrated some of his growth, to consider other people's feelings and needs. In this process, however, many mutual understandings have to be hammered out between the younger and older adults of a family. Frequently the oldest child has to bear the brunt of being a trail-blazer for younger brothers and sisters in developing relationships that are satisfying both to parents and their offspring.

Choice of Friends

One of the areas of conflict between parents and their adolescent youngsters has to do with choice of friends, especially friends of the other sex. Middle-class parents are inclined to expect their offspring to choose their friends from the same social class or higher. Since junior's choice of friends at this age suggests possible marriage, parents are disposed to be over-concerned. Parents from older cultures are inclined to be more protective of their young girls than is customary in American culture. This results in conflict between the generations as friendships are formed and new ways are adopted. Problems facing adolescents and their parents have to do with hours to be home after dates, appropriate places to go on dates or after dates, and frequency of dates. We recommend the play, *High Pressure Area*,[3] as a perceptive presentation of the problems that cluster about dating.

Since dating is a symbol of one's desirability and the adolescent *must*

[3] Nora Stirling, *High Pressure Area* (New York: The National Committee for Mental Hygiene, Inc., 1949).

feel himself desirable, the problems that are related to dating are fraught with tense and intense emotions. Rare is the adolescent who sees eye-to-eye with his parents about these matters. As he matures, becomes more sure of himself, he has less tendency to overact or exaggerate the importance of his position. If he has learned to perceive himself in a more nearly adult role, his approach will be less defensive; he will be able to talk through some of the problems and the likely consequences of the decisions he must make. If he perceives that his parents cannot see him as anything but a child, he is henceforth likely to go his own way without consulting them. If a girl is denied the right to go with a certain boy, for example, she may meet him at a friend's house, at the drugstore, or at the party.

Many parents are dismayed at the lack of communication between themselves and their teen-agers. The need of the older adolescent to be considered as a peer of parents who express an equalitarian attitude explains much of this lack of communication. Communication is an urgent necessity to the adolescent, yet he has so many confused feelings that he finds it difficult to express himself. If he finds that his parents cannot help him put his feelings into words or are judgmental in their relationships with him, he goes elsewhere to express what he has on his mind and in his heart. He has to talk to someone. Sad is the comment heard so often, "I couldn't tell my mother."

The play *Blue Denim* [4] has a line that expresses the feelings many adolescents have about their parents. The fifteen-year-old boy tells his pal that he has the feeling that every time his mother looks at him she is seeing "pink ribbons." Needless to say, his efforts to discuss with her the serious problem of his paternity of an unborn child are futile. Her first remark to him, regardless of what he has on his mind, is, "Take off that dirty sweatshirt. You've been wearing it all week."

Use of Car

Another problem area is the use of the family car. We live in a motorized age. The centralized high schools that are becoming more and more the pattern of secondary education are far from the homes of most of the students. Most states issue drivers' licenses at age sixteen or later. If the family has only one car, society has created a ready-made problem:

---

[4] James Leo Herlihy and William Noble, *Blue Denim* (New York: Random House, 1958).

"Who is to use the car tonight?" If Mac has been enterprising and lucky enough to purchase a jalopy for his own use, the area of conflict may be more extreme. Mac's inclination, supported and encouraged by the adult culture is to "soup up" his jalopy, to make a hot rod of it. Some parents look upon this activity as next door to delinquency. Mac's interpretation of his parents' opposition is, "They treat me like a baby. It's all right for the 'Big Three' to make motors of 400 horsepower, but I'm not trusted with 100 horsepower." Since, like all humans, he tends to live up to the perceptions that others have of him, Mac often begins to act like his parents have inferred to him they expect him to act—delinquent. If in his adolescent culture there is a pull for Mac to join a delinquent gang, his parents' anticipations certainly make it easier for Mac to answer the call.

If parents were to start from the premise that motorization is a fundamental part of the older adolescent's life, that the youngster should not have to be wholly dependent on his parents driving him to and from, we believe a balance of concern and necessity could be achieved without the sense of rejection that comes from a contest. Mac takes out of his experiences not that his parents are concerned about him, but that they don't trust him. Lack of trust means rejection, and rejection justifies defiance of the restraints imposed by those who reject. This is not a simple problem for parents who have outgrown their eagerness to take chances, who must pay bills for damages, and who must stand between their children and the demands of the law. The teacher is faced with a dilemma—he knows that "boys will be boys," but he knows too that the public is urgently demanding more discipline and regimentation in the schools.

Money

A third conflict area, mentioned briefly in the last chapter, is money. The expense of the last three years in most high schools is excessive. More and more emphasis is placed upon competitive athletic events; big, formal, expensive social affairs; extravagant social amenities before and after dances and parties. Consider some of the expenses that an average high-school youngster has. You probably recall them all too well from your own high-school days. There is an activity ticket to admit the student to standard extracurricular affairs that may cost as much as forty dollars; special clothing for special events—formal dress, dress for physical education classes, dress for glee club, the choir, cheer leaders' uniforms; contributions to innumerable drives; corsages for formal dances; treats after the social affairs—food and drink; books; transportation to and from school; special trips to watch the athletic teams play; the senior trip. In one school in a low economic area of a large city, the annual cost for ordinary school affairs averages $100 a year. In suburban schools, the costs are often three or four times this amount. These figures do not include cost of clothing and dating.

Many families just do not have the money that is required for Marge or Bill to be "one of the crowd" in a high school today. Some youngsters earn their own money by part-time jobs, but there are not enough available jobs to go around. So much of the adolescent's sense of well-being

depends upon his being in the stream of the social activities that he is willing to put up a vigorous fight for money to make this possible. Concern for money gets out of proportion to other values because prestige is at stake. The high school has a responsibility, it seems to us, to re-examine its purposes and to analyze its social structure realistically. We must ask ourselves what we do by allowing a large number of students to be rejected by the social structure because of financial inability to participate in it. By sponsoring a large number of expensive affairs, the high school solidifies social-class status lines and contributes immeasurably to the stresses and strains of family life. These strains are felt not only during the adolescent years. Many mothers accept jobs in order to stretch the family income to meet the needs of their adolescents, thus limiting their relationships with the younger children of the family.

We hypothesize that as many dropouts in high school are related to social-emotional factors experienced by the dropouts as by their lack of academic achievement. To isolate these factors is difficult. We do know that social relationships in school are of first importance to the student himself. If his feelings about his place in the social structure are negative, he is likely to have difficulty achieving academically. It seems quite likely that his lack of money may be a crucial factor in his failure to be an accepted member of the social structure. We believe that the school might wisely diminish the need for money in its program and its activities.

Establishing Heterosexuality

The fifteen-to-eighteen-year-old has developed rather specific perceptions of sex roles. These were discussed in the preceding chapter. He has had meager opportunities to play out these roles in adult ways. The older adolescent years are given over to projecting the sex roles one expects to assume as an adult. The boy for the first time becomes more interested in social activities than in sports. The high-school youngster begins to look upon himself not as a child but as a future wife, husband, parent, job-holder, and member of a community with civic responsibilities and opportunities. The hang-out—whether it be a candy store, the corner drugstore, the filling station, the girl's bedroom, or the rumpus room—becomes the hub from which many roles and perceptions are projected. The song that goes "Standing on the corner, watching all the girls go by" catches the spirit of the hang-out. We recall from our own youth that adults feared the pool hall would lure young lads away from their righteous upbringing. Winning a turkey, the prize for high score in bowling, created quite a dilemma to the sixteen-year-old who dared not take it home and announce how he had secured it. The cellar clubs that have developed in some cities are in many respects the modern counterpart of the pool hall of a former generation.

"Pairing Off"

From the heterosexual activities of early adolescence emerges "pairing off." This is followed by "going steady," which is the custom these days. Soon thereafter arises the question of "to pet or not to pet?" or perhaps it would be more accurate to say "How much to pet?" The current peer code determines the behavior that can be expected from the two members of a pair. The peer code today places more value on a non-competitive climate and rigid forms, once pairing occurs, than was true a decade or two ago. When the authors were young, the girl's goal was to get her dance card filled with as many interesting male dancers as she could attract. Certain dances were reserved for the girl's date; the remainder were available to the bidding of those who wished to dance with her. Today a couple go to a dance together, only occasionally trading partners with another couple of good friends. Today a girl and boy "go steady," even if it is for a week only. During that time, however, the girl or boy is not shopping around for other possibilities. The pattern of dating seems to have moved away from fluidity toward more rigidly conceived forms and rituals that require that one affair be ended before another one begins. What the explanation of this phenomenon is, we do not know. The places one goes on dates, the hours one keeps, the amount and kind of petting are all rather clearly understood by the members of one's social group. Adults know little of the actual details of the peer code. We live in a "paired" culture—adolescents and adults alike. Many wives expect to accompany their husbands on business trips. The stag party is now quite rare.

Much of the energy of the older adolescent is expended in making himself acceptable to the opposite sex. The individual who is left out of dating, who doesn't have a date for Saturday night, is indeed desolate. Tremendous anxiety is experienced about doing the wrong thing. This results in considerable moodiness during these years. It seems to the adolescent that one mistake may be fatal to his status in the group. Which is the right fork to use for salad? Will I have enough money to pay the supper check? How do I find out what color corsage she wants? What do I say to her parents? Shall I let him kiss me goodnight? How do I introduce him to my parents? Shall I invite him in after the party? How can I suggest a Dutch treat? How can I find out if he really wants to go to this movie?

Since woman's place in our culture has shifted to a freer, more equalitarian state, this anxiety is compounded, for the rituals are not as rigidly observed and vary from one group to the next. When does a girl treat her date as if she were his guest and when does he treat her as just another one of the crowd? When is a Dutch treat permissible in this peer culture and when isn't it? When is it permissible to use her car and when isn't it? This phase of our culture is particularly troublesome to first- and second-generation Americans who have been reared in homes where the courtesies between men and women are rigid and unbreakable. Today in New York, for example, many Puerto Rican adolescents can hardly bear to participate in Dutch treats. As the adolescent adds to his experiences, he gains more sureness in his relationships. The ability to establish successful relationships with individuals in various situations, which are affected by different mores and traditions, is another one of the lifelong tasks that confronts a human. As the adolescent moves out of his home into a college setting (as many of you probably remember vividly) or a work situation, he is faced with another batch of anxieties that entail his feeling out the acceptable patterns of the new situation.

At no time are these anxieties as intense as they are during adolescence; one of the major reasons for this is the quality of the social structure itself. The adolescent culture is composed of a number of groups to which individuals belong. The athletes and their satellites may comprise one group. Sometimes they have the highest status and are known as the "big wheels." In another school the "big wheels" may be the all-around students who are leaders in dramatics, music, school politics. The intellectuals, frequently called the "brains" or more recently the "egg heads" comprise another group. Some groups cohere because they are left out. Members of minority groups often come together from such a motive. If they are pushed around too much, they may become known as the troublemakers of the school. Nearly all adolescents are striving to belong to the groups carrying high prestige value; this means that each must watch his step carefully. We know of one school in which the girls begin to get their social lives completely organized as freshmen in order to qualify for the status organization in their senior year. To complicate the adolescent's problem, status changes rapidly in the adolescent culture. Tryon discovered in studying 200 children from fifth to twelfth grade that not one individual "managed to maintain top status in the group throughout the period; many individuals experienced marked changes in status positions." [5]

---

[5] Caroline Tryon, "The Adolescent Peer Culture," *Adolescence, Forty-Third Yearbook,* Part I (Chicago: National Society for the Study of Education, 1944), p. 229.

Validity of Deceitfulness?

One aspect of heterosexual relations that our culture promotes is that of the acceptance of the validity of deceitfulness. Much of what the adolescent absorbs from his environment is: How can I keep him or her from finding me out? *How can I hide my real self?* This, we dare say, accounts in part for the high divorce rate. Let's examine this phenomenon. If an individual must hide himself, must appear to be what he isn't, he is denying the worth of what he really is. This is an unhealthy attitude and leads to serious doubts about the possibility of establishing reciprocal relationships that can be mutually respected. On a superficial level, we find numerous appeals to deceitfulness in advertising. An examination of one teen-age magazine reveals these appeals:

Color your hair. Glorifies your hair with glamorous color highlights or adds thrilling new color.

Exotic look comes from sun-lit hair, splendidly artificial.

Reshape your bosom with a new twenties-ish bra.

Consider a major change, a new nose, say, or capped teeth, a new neat hairline via electrolysis.

Try false nails, if yours are stubby.

Change your shape, if you need to.

Change the color of your eyes. It's possible with tinted contact lenses.

De-ceit-ful: foundation controls trimness in tummy, waist and hips, builds in a bustle.

Now . . . extra high uplift.

These are only a few of the appeals made to young girls to be something which they are not. These appeals permeate our society. They function not only in areas of appearance but also in areas of social-class status. "Men of distinction . . . Woman of taste . . . Known by the company it keeps." We are inclined to smile, but maybe it is time to ask ourselves how much these appeals get inside us and have an influence on our values.

The acceptance of the validity of deceitfulness functions on deeper levels also. Much has been written during the past few years about the conformity of youth. An appropriate question seems to be: Conformity to what? Obviously, the youngsters are conforming to the values they sense in our adult culture. *Sham* is one of those values. Acceptance of sham is so interwoven with all we do and say that we are hardly aware of it. One area in which this value functions is in feelings about people.

Many high-school youngsters feel that they must appear to like, to dislike, approve or disapprove, of certain people because this is what the "crowd" does. They are so concerned with watching the crowd that they forget the crowd is watching them. Listen to this senior who was asked what he thought about the student who doesn't go along with the crowd. His reply was:

> If I were talking to the "crowd" I would call him a "fag" because he is different; but I really envy a person who has the ambition to do things differently and not lead the same dull life every day of the year. Let's face it. The rest of us are in a rut and they are not.

The sad fact is that this fellow cannot "face it" with his peers. He pretends to like activities that he doesn't like. For instance, one boy said, "There are only one or two places where it is all right to go on a date—movies and dancing. To go bowling or to a ball game would be considered a sin." One pretends to want to go to college whether he is interested in advanced study or not. As one boy said, "People who don't want to go to college are sometimes forced to take preparatory courses because of social pressure. Many times the person would rather work with his hands, but he doesn't say so because he dare not risk the opinions of his crowd."

This lack of genuineness in many of the social relationships developed in high school and later in college carries over to adult life, making possible a generation that responds to the kind of motivation described in *The Hidden Persuaders*.[6] The older adolescent is busy contriving how he can convince the "crowd" that he likes what the crowd says he should like rather than realizing *himself*—his own needs, interests, and feelings. Because of this he sometimes fails to discover and value himself as a real human being who is about to face many major issues of life—finding a life's work, mating, and becoming a parent. The task of knowing "who am I?" is, of course, a lifelong quest. The waste results from the false feelings and premises that are developed during the years that count for so much in shaping permanent attitudes. If one's goal is to date the most popular girl, one may find himself married to the most popular girl, who is a total stranger once the sham is exposed. We discuss this as a part of heterosexual relationships because so much emphasis in our culture is placed on fooling the opposite sex.

---

[6] Vance Packard, *The Hidden Persuaders* (New York: David McKay Company, 1957. New York: Pocket Books, Inc., 1958).

In developing heterosexual relationships, the school serves as a social laboratory in which these relationships are tried out and solidified. The curriculum that is recognized by a board of education and a teaching staff may be history, English, science, and mathematics. The curriculum that the youngsters are committed wholeheartedly to learning is how to carry on their social relationships with a maximum of satisfaction. They converse before and after school, as they pass from room to room, at lunch, not about the Russian Revolution but about who is asking whom to the dance, what the gang is going to do tonight, how to earn ten bucks to pay for Rachel's corsage and treats after the dance, who is going steady with whom, and where can a fellow get the best deal on a hot rod? The school staff that understands this social structure and takes it into account has more opportunities to relate in meaningful ways to adolescents. Note the next chapter on "Study of Group Situations."

The replies of several different groups of teen-agers indicate an urgent need for teachers to be more aware of the problems adolescents face. One group of teen-agers was asked to reply to the question: "Do young people feel that teachers know how to deal with them?" The youngsters' responses varied, but a strong thread similar to this response ran throughout:

> No, to a certain degree no . . . because there's only a very small fraction of the teachers who we really do like and appreciate and want to learn from. The other teachers—either feel that they aren't teaching us enough or that they don't know how to teach. I think they are trying awfully hard. They want to, but about all they can do in 45 minutes is just try to get the work covered, and they don't have time for any, oh, specific personal problems. You can't really get to know the teacher as a person. They're just someone put at the head of the class to be in authority.

In a survey of one city school 57 per cent of a group of high-school students responded that they liked teachers who took time to talk with them and taught well; about the same percentage indicated that they disliked teachers who yelled at them and talked too much.[7]

Gordon's study of *The Social System of the High School* [8] is one that we recommend for secondary-school teachers. He poses the hypothesis that "the dominant motivation of the high school student is to achieve

---

[7] Mary Beauchamp, *Building Neighborliness* (New York: Center for Human Relations and Community Studies, New York University, 1958).

[8] C. Wayne Gordon, *The Social System of the High School* (Glencoe, Ill.: The Free Press, 1957), pp. 1-25.

and maintain a general social status within the organization of the school."
The roles he accepts are consistent with his perceptions of the demands
of the social structure and of his relative standing in the social system.
For example, if he perceives that he is likely to be labeled a "brain" if he
answers too many questions in science, he modifies his participation to
be consistent with the peer code relative to "brains." Gordon found, for
instance, that "grade achievement was least significantly related to general
status," and that the "prestige values of the informal sphere were found
to be friendships, dress, grade-level, clique incorporation, dating, and
morally approved behavior. Money, leisure, car, and kindred possessions
were highly relevant." [9] With this in mind, listen to the statements of a
few high-school seniors relative to these factors. These statements are
from an upper-middle class suburban community.

> I usually conform to everyone's ideas of what girls I should take out,
> whether I think they're right or wrong. The biggest problem here is drink-
> ing and also smoking. People have taken up drinking to conform with those
> about them. Smoking by the girls is purely something started in order to
> conform with the gang. Going steady is in some cases a result of conforming,
> too. This is proved by how short a time (sometimes only a week) some
> people go steady.

> If a girl doesn't have a certain amount of new clothes each year and
> isn't able to show off a certain amount of cashmere sweaters, she is not "in
> with the crowd." The majority of girls are in with a clique. Within this
> group each girl conforms with the rest.

> As far as dating goes, we all have different hours, but they are in the
> same vicinity. This is usually about 1:00 for movie dates and 2:00 or 2:30
> for dances and the like. I guess one reason for the kids' drinking is to go
> along with everyone else.

> It is true that unless you behave somewhat as your group, you will not
> be accepted. Anyone who deviates from the ordinary format is thought of
> as an "odd ball" and is more often than not rejected by his classmates.

> It rules the way I dress, the kids I hang around with, the parties I go to.
> I think that conformity rules most of the daily lives in our high school. I
> would like to give an example of a high-school dance. About a week before
> the dance you'll find what to wear is usually the center of attraction. I know
> if one girl decides to wear a sheath, other girls will abruptly change their
> minds, if they planned to wear full dresses, immediately to a sheath. P. S. I
> think it's awful that women don't have any backbone.

---

[9] *Ibid.*

The youngsters who wrote these anonymous statements were asked to state how they felt about the social situation (with all its implied conformity) in their school. The following are representative of the replies that were received:

> I don't particularly like it, and I think in the senior year kids start to break away from the crowd. However, since no one wishes to be left alone, especially me, there is no one who is brave enough to try and change things. I, for one, don't think it's worth the time and energy.

> There would be twice as much creative acting, thinking, and even dress if the amount of conformity was cut down on considerably.

> I do not respect those who don't conform just for the sake of not conforming. I do respect those who don't conform to the bad standards that have been set.

> I have always felt that a certain amount of non-conformists are absolutely necessary in any field just to keep society on its toes ... but I feel that I get more accomplished if I don't consciously try to be one of them.

> I think conformity is a good thing although it may be looked down upon by some because it leads to a more tightly knit group where friendships flourish.

> I feel it doesn't make any difference to what extent a person conforms so long as he is honest with himself and happy in what he is doing.

> I feel sorry for the people who do not follow the set patterns. The usual reason is financial or self-expression. We conform because we want to, not because we are forced. I would never wear some of the odd clothes those so-called artistic people wear.

> Those who don't conform are for the most part fags or actors. They could be popular if they wanted to, but most of them think they're exotic or sophisticated or something else. Most of them think they're superior. I am more than sure that all the conformists have a lot more fun than those who don't conform.

We could go on. These excerpts give a vivid picture of how powerful the social structure of the school is and how its activities revolve around heterosexual development. What this means to the adolescent as he seeks to declare his independence from home and how the school needs to recognize these developmental tasks is discussed at the end of this chapter. It seems to us that many adolescents do not grow out of their consuming concern about "what other people think." As one reads *The Organization*

Man,[10] one has the feeling that the structure of the high school has been transplanted to the business firm and is functioning with a similar scale of values and motivations. We have much to do in helping adolescents evaluate their responses to their social structure.

Achieving Means for Economic Independence

Rare is the adolescent today who achieves economic independence. The percentage who achieve it immediately after high-school graduation becomes smaller each year, although adolescents do look forward to it and take some active steps toward readying themselves for jobs in which they feel some competency and interest. Thoughts about "what they want to be" consume a considerable part of their time. Today this is true of almost as many girls as boys.

The adolescent requires careful adult guidance with this developmental task. Too often he does not get the kind of help that he can use, for we have failed to incorporate this task into the secondary curriculum in any meaningful way. Sometimes he cannot use the help that is available to him because of adult pressures. If father has decided that Tim must follow in *his* footsteps and become a lawyer, doctor, or merchant, while Tim has other plans, he is "really on the spot." Suppose he has the ability but not the interest. His refusal to comply with dad's expectations is interpreted by dad as rejection. In his hostility toward his son, dad may cut off opportunities for any further education. Tim may receive an ultimatum—business administration, or nothing! Far more likely, Tim will be subjected to innumerable subtle pressures inducing him to accept the fact that it is his filial duty to carry on the family business as well as the family name. If he fails to do so, he may suffer guilt, which he carries without knowing its source and without receiving any help in understanding it. If he capitulates to his father's wishes, he may do so at the cost of the development of his own uniqueness. He is likely either to overcompensate and become a stickler for every little detail of the business being kept as father now has it or to adjust to the situation by flunking out of college or even high school. Of course, he may discover, too, that he really likes the work once he gets into it.

---

[10] Wm. H. Whyte, Jr., *The Organization Man* (Garden City, New York: Doubleday Anchor Books, 1956).

Suppose Tim is willing but really lacks the ability to follow in his father's footsteps? His dad is so informed by the school. He finds it hard to hear the words, let alone to accept the facts. He is more likely to blame the school for his son's lack of success, thus making it easier for Tim to continue deceiving himself. He may try "influence" to get Tim accepted in a college; he may have Tim change schools. If Tim cooperates with his father in these endeavors, he may find himself trained to be a second-rate doctor, lawyer, financier. He is faced with living life in an uneasy feeling of incompetency on the job. In addition, society is forced to put up with his second-rateness. His sense of inadequacy spills over into other areas of living and affects the kind of human being he is becoming.

What about the youngster who is not going on to college because he lacks money? First, we must say that in our opinion, it makes no sense for the richest country in the world to spend millions for defense and pennies for education, to utter sanctimonious words about the need for educated manpower and to refuse to appropriate funds to make that manpower available. The nation is still failing to educate at least ten per cent of the adolescent population who are able to do college work but cannot afford a college education, in spite of the fact that this condition was called to the public's attention in 1946 by the book, *Who Shall Be Educated?* [11] The alarming number who are shortchanged by quota systems, segregated schools, poorly staffed schools, double sessions, and inadequate facilities is a matter for serious conjecture. Nor can the problem be totally solved by a system of tuition scholarships. A student has to participate in the whole life of the college community if he is to develop fully. This takes money these days.

What of the youngsters who are not capable of continuing their education or who do not wish to go to college? What is the secondary school doing to help them achieve economic independence? In a comprehensive way, very little! Some city schools have guidance counselors who try to locate employment opportunities. Their student load is rarely less than from 600 to 900 individuals. Many schools lack even this token of help. Each spring as we graduate thousands of young people, we literally say to them, "It is a tough job market you are facing. Now it is up to you!" Usually they apply for work to someone they know. Then their jobs are

---

[11] W. L. Warner, R. J. Havighurst, and M. B. Loeb, *Who Shall Be Educated?* (New York: Harper and Brothers, 1946).

only accidentally related to their competencies and interests. Many get into blind-alley jobs or spend their lives floating from one job to the next. Many get work that uses only a fraction of their capabilities. They settle down into these jobs to become robots; they have little initiative to seek better jobs because the economic system is too complicated for one person to fathom by himself. They feel helpless and unsuccessful. A few become so resentful as to take out their resentments in behavior that society terms delinquent. We often wryly reflect, "Who is being delinquent?" This situation exists not because we don't know how to help young people find themselves in the world of work but because we don't consider it important to provide money for trained staff to help them. Herein lies the tragedy.

A great many of our youth are exploited by the culture which proclaims to need them. Many young people become so resentful and bitter that they form dissident minority groups to oppose any outlay of money in order to improve the quality of secondary education. The human being has a strange capacity to "pass on" to other people the treatment he has received himself. We call this the sophomore complex. Lillian Smith says, "What a sad and true thing that when we hate someone a great deal we borrow from him the qualities that gave him power to harm us, and wear them like a crown!" [12]

We have cited the problems that confront an adolescent as he tries to build his economic cornerstone to show that giving vocational guidance alone is not enough. As teachers work with youth in high school, at least three additional processes must be carried on.

---

[12] Lillian Smith, *The Journey* (New York: World Publishing Company, 1954), p. 36.

School's Role in Helping Youth Achieve Economic Independence

First, the teacher and other adults must help the adolescent *understand himself as a whole individual in relation to work*. This is not accomplished by giving him a battery of tests and informing him of the results. A person does not learn about himself by being *told*. He must experience relationships and have ample opportunities to discuss these relationships with people whom he trusts. Kubie says:

> As a result of the failure to consider the sources of error in the human being himself, when our academic disciplines assemble together in our educational institutions, they re-enforce the tacit, fallacious assumption that man can understand the world that lies outside of himself without concurrently understanding himself.[13]

Our secondary schools will not improve markedly, regardless of the trifling experimentation that is done with the curriculum, until they are organized in ways that students may experience continuing, trustful relationships with teachers who assume that a part of their task in teaching is to be helpful to each individual as *he himself* decides he needs help. This implies a greater knowledge of motivations and processes of human development. "Without self-knowledge 'in depth' the master of any field will be a child in human wisdom."[14] We must help our youth to acquire self-knowledge in depth and toward this end we must train our teachers to develop self-knowledge in depth.

The second process in helping the adolescent reach toward economic independence is a much *expanded concept of* the necessity for *first-hand experiences in the economic world*. A "career day" once a year is hardly sufficient! These first-hand experiences should be of two types: (1) *actual participation* in the world of work; (2) extensive first-hand *knowledge about the world of work*. The authors believe that we stunt youth by delaying the time when they can participate in *useful work*. At present, we have a "kept" population of several million who are adult physically and who almost universally *want* to work. One cannot know whether he wants to be a lawyer, until he has "felt" a law office, preferably many law offices. He cannot know that he wants to join the Merchant Marine until

[13] Lawrence S. Kubie, "The Forgotten Man of Education," *Harvard Alumni Bulletin,* February 6, 1954, pp. 349-353.
[14] *Ibid.*

he has been on the high seas in rough weather. A girl cannot know whether she wants to be a nurse until she has emptied a few bedpans, made a few beds with patients in them. An individual cannot know whether he wants to teach until he has worked with groups of children of varied ages in different situations. The diversified work program of a few high schools is making a small beginning toward helping youngsters to "feel" a job. It is usually limited to those who are not going to college. The secondary schools need a systematic approach to work experiences so that every pupil has many chances to experiment, to try out, to "feel" a variety of jobs.

Another part of experiencing jobs is to *learn about* the world of work, through an organized program, not limited to one year, to one unit, but continuing throughout the high-school years. In addition to acquainting the student with a wealth of factual material about jobs, this program would include trips to industries, hospitals, colleges, business schools, studios, shops, offices, laboratories; it would include first-hand contact with people from a variety of occupations. We would hope the contacts might have a continuous quality to them, so that, if a youngster got interested in a given area, he might go back again and again to someone he knew and wanted to talk with. A program like this would acquaint students with the kinds of things they must learn and the abilities they must develop. Such a program would do much to penetrate the fantasy that many adolescents have built about work. A more realistic view of work is urgently needed. Finding oneself in work is not easy; it is often painfully difficult—repeatedly discouraging. The realities of family finance, of individual abilities, of work opportunities, of necessities for training must all be faced with candor.

The third step in this process of achieving economic independence is to make available to the student a *wide variety of tests* that *measure specific* aptitudes, weaknesses, and interests; that give insight into personality and maturity; that help the youngster to "size up" himself as a whole and to understand the potentials, as well as the hazards, in his interests and budding plans. A significant part of this interpretation is in helping the youngster understand the likelihood of placement in his occupational choices. We believe these tests should be interpreted by someone who knows the individual and who has had a continuous relationship with him long enough to have developed a climate of trust and honesty and searching for individual meaning.

In our culture there is a strong pull on the adolescent to decide early what he wants to be. This pull is confused with his drive for prestige among his peers, his ignorance of what he *can* be, and his impatience to get at his life's work. This impatience is operative particularly with youngsters who plan to enter the professions and who see from five to ten years of training ahead of them. All these factors must be considered by the teacher who is working with the adolescent in the area of economic independence. Use of vocational interest tests seems to indicate that "patterns of interests are often remarkably persistent throughout the school years." [15] In a footnote, Carter says that "the vocational interests of high-school boys and girls as measured by the Strong blanks are almost but not quite as stable over a period of years as are the interests of college men." [16] This documentation seems to justify spending considerable time and energy helping the youngster understand himself as a future wage-earner and job-holder.

You are doubtless saying that such a program requires more time than is available. We believe it is about time that schools for adolescents put first things first. We visualize a secondary-school program that has at its core the developmental tasks of adolescence with the other areas falling around these concerns. Today high-school teachers waste countless hours drilling dead, meaningless, isolated, unwanted facts into the live, questing minds of young people. Nearly every survey shows that pupils do not remember or use these facts. Their behavior indicates that we are not succeeding in making educated men and women out of our teen-agers. All the knowledge of the world has meaning if it is understood and accepted by the individual, but he has to discover the meaning in relation to his unique needs. We believe a realistic consideration of the adolescent's needs in his thrust toward economic independence would help return work to the importance it can have and once did have in a person's fulfillment. Our present-day attitude toward work as something distasteful, but to be endured, is dangerous to mental health. We urge you to consider the words of *The Prophet,* "Work is love made visible!" [17]

---

[15] Harold D. Carter, "The Development of Interest in Vocations," *Adolescence, Forty-Third Yearbook,* Part I (Chicago: National Society for the Study of Education, 1944), pp. 259-260.

[16] *Ibid.*

[17] Kahlil Gibran, *The Prophet* (New York: Alfred A. Knopf, Inc., 1923), pp. 30-34.

Accepting Values	A careful reading of the preced-
to Live By	ing pages reveals many values that
	the authors infer are motivating

forces in the adolescent culture. We shall try now to be more specific in understanding the nature of some of the value situations that face adolescents. We assume that a person's values are more dependably revealed in what he does than in what he says. All of us have learned the correct, the ideal thing, to say in many situations, and we respond somewhat parrot-like without an assessment of how consistent our actions are with our verbalization. One way of discovering values is to find out how the individual spends his time and money. If he professes to love beautiful pictures but never goes near an art museum, he may be saying, "I believe that you believe that I *should* love beautiful pictures."

If we examine the ways adolescents spend their time, we discover that they value peer relationships very highly. To many of them these relationships are more vital than any other of the virtues they have experienced. The goal in peer relationships is to attain a high-level prestige in a social group or to be identified with a high prestige group. The question immediately arises as to how inclusive or exclusive the individual wishes to be. Some groups are open to everyone, but these frequently are not the high prestige groups. This issue reaches a climax for the individual when he is invited to join a fraternity or sorority. Choice is made more difficult by the clauses in many constitutions which discriminate against certain groups. That these societies are secret and are banned officially by the school further complicates the value decisions. As you read this, it may seem that everything is stacked against joining secret societies. Yet thousands of adolescents belong to them. Doubtless many of you belonged in the past and do now belong; many others may have felt left out because they were not asked to join. The prestige value of belonging to a status social group has tremendous pull with young and old alike.

Perhaps the most deplorable part of the situation is that adolescents seldom have an opportunity to discuss this issue in a setting that stimulates critical thinking. They are told that secret societies are banned, and they are forbidden to belong. The societies go underground, and the adolescent makes his choice in terms of a forced situation, often without adequate information or clarification. A dramatic example of high-school students being given opportunities to discuss issues relating to the acceptance or rejection of people occurred in the Clinton, Tennessee, high school which was integrated in the fall of 1956. Five years earlier the high-school principal and staff led the student body in thinking through their own basic feelings about integration and about complying with the Supreme Court mandate when it came. At the peak of the resistance, after Negro pupils had been admitted to the school in 1956, the principal was threatened by rabid segregationists and told that the people of Clinton were all against him. He immediately called an assembly, stated the issue to the students, and left them to decide whether to stand their ground or capitulate to the rabble-rousers. In fifteen minutes the student president reported a unanimous decision to stand firm for integration and the next morning all except forty of the students' parents had signed statements to that effect.[18] These students had some rigorous experience and training in value formation which has most probably made them stronger individuals.

Another troublesome area in which adolescents have to make value decisions is that of sex. Modern living provides boys and girls situations in which promiscuity is possible and inviting. Many studies show that adults are unwilling to consider realistically the degree and kinds of problems that are posed by modern living, or the manner in which their children respond to these problems. Susie has a cute figure, but she just has not "clicked" with the status groups in school. Perhaps she comes from the wrong side of town. Maybe she "can't keep up" financially with the crowd. She has felt left out and hurt for three years during high school. She wonders what's wrong with her. She tries to wear the approved clothes and to be one of the "crowd." Then one of the "big wheels" asks her for a date. She begins to feel desirable; she has been noticed. She is wild with excitement. They go to a drive-in movie and afterwards he finds a private place to park. He begins feeding her a line about how cute she is—"Where have you been all of my life?" They begin petting.

Susie's dilemma may seem a simple one to someone who does not have Susie's need to be popular. If she refuses to pet and to go as far as the fellow wants to go, she knows she will be labeled a "prude," a "wet blanket." Once again she will have failed to make the grade with those whose friendship she wants so much. Because she hasn't been a member of a social group, she has not acquired the skills of verbally parrying with

---

[18] Told to authors in conversation with David Britton, principal of Clinton High School, at the time of its integration.

"big wheel." She feels awkward and unworthy in maintaining a position she really values. In social relationships she is a novice. If she goes along and plays the game as "big wheel" urges her to do, she may soon find

herself with a reputation for promiscuity and a heavy load of anxiety and guilt to carry by herself. An individual has to be quite secure in order to respond maturely to the invitations inherent in our motorized adolescent culture.

Some adolescent groups consciously make a decision to indulge in sexual experimentation. This poses another kind of problem to the youngster (boy or girl) who has belonged to the group for a long time and values his membership in it, but who cannot feel comfortable in this activity. Adolescents recognize the explosive quality of the situations in which they find themselves. They are concerned with the whole area of sex. Many have intense fear and avoid situations in which they will be expected to behave in ways incompatible with their own values. The adolescent boy who will have nothing to do with girls is an illustration. But this is really no solution. One does not learn how to cope with one's problems by avoiding them.

Youngsters need help in clarifying their values. The kind of help needed is well expressed by Farnham:

> What the adolescent wants is neither blind opposition nor equally senseless permission; he wants sympathetic understanding and help where he needs it and an open door between himself and his parents. All these can be supplied by facing the facts with him clearly—the facts as they are, *not* as the parent wishes them to be . . . the parent will have to be the one to point

up the immense responsibilities that are also involved, the need for control and thought, the danger of unhappiness if there is nothing but a helpless giving way to impulse. Finally, the parent must make it clear that he intends to go to the youngster's help and supply the lacking control through his own firmness if he thinks it is necessary. Many a youngster wants to know that.[19]

Parents are not the only adults who share the responsibility for giving young people chances to talk out their concerns in a climate of frank consideration rather than one of condemnation. Teachers, church workers, agency workers, all have to be sensitive to youth's need for honest and friendly advice and must seek opportunities to give such advice.

Perhaps it is the age of the authors that leads us to state that present-day youth seem to us less concerned with altruism than the youth we knew a couple of decades ago. Perhaps altruism is a value that appears incongruous with the state of the world today. Never, we believe, have we needed more drastically a pervading spirit of willingness to accept the other person at his best and to help him function in that way.

Developing values to live by these days is one of the toughest developmental tasks all of us have. We keep working at it throughout our lives. If our values do not grow as we spend time on this planet, we are living static lives. The formation of values is especially difficult today because we are living at a point in time when the tried and true absolutes (which are largely restraints upon behavior, the "thou shalt not's") have been challenged successfully enough to diminish their power as restraining forces in behavior. While absolutes are tottering, we have not developed satisfactory ways of evaluating our decisions with our young or within ourselves. We often say values are relative. This means little to the kid who needs a car to take his girl to the dance and knows where he can borrow his uncle's (without his permission) for the evening. *Relative* to what and by what criteria? And how can one tell whether a course of action is sane or unsane, selfish or altruistic, wise or unwise?

The Scout studies [20, 21] give us hope about young people's values. They indicate that adolescents value adults who can do things that the

[19] Marynia F. Farnham, *The Adolescent* (New York: Harper and Brothers, 1951), p. 125.

[20] Boy Scouts of America, *A Study of Adolescent Boys* (New Brunswick, N. J.: Boy Scouts of America, 1955).

[21] Girl Scouts of America, *Adolescent Girls* (Ann Arbor, Mich.: Survey Research Center, 1957).

young people want to have done, who have the personal qualities of generosity, kindness, and zestfulness, and whose character and judgment are positive. A much larger percentage of girls mentioned superficial qualities which they value than did boys. Girls placed more emphasis upon personal qualities than did boys. In a study made of lower-class youth, when asked what are the most important things a friend should be, nearly half responded, "Someone nice, good, and friendly." Loyalty was a very high value with these youngsters. Nearly a fifth of them mentioned "someone to stand by you." [22]

What School for Adolescents? The older adolescent is in an integrative growth period. He is highly motivated toward finding himself as an adult citizen and toward getting himself lined up vocationally. He has matured enough, has had enough experiences, to be able to handle abstractions. He can solve complicated problems. He is called upon to make many decisions that tax his mental capacity. He can generalize on a conceptual level. He takes time firmly in hand and can realistically consider the historical past and project himself through long term goals into the future. He has learned to distinguish fairly well between his fantasy world and the world of hard, cold reality.

He is ready to integrate his knowledge for his own use. He is stretching toward greater depth and wider scope in his mental development. He is beginning to perceive that soon the fate of the world will be in his hands. His will be the decisions that make a difference in whether the children of India have bread to eat, how the resources of America are to be conserved, what kind of educational opportunities the oncoming generation of children will have, how honest our public officials shall be, and how well the basic freedoms of our land are kept intact. The older youth is an idealist. He believes ways can be found to make life better than we have ever known. He seems to have a predisposition to favor the underdog. He searches for final causes, trying to establish for himself the moral and ethical principles he wishes to live by. He is searching intensely for the motivations of human behavior. "What makes people behave as they do?" is a persistent query.

[22] Mary Beauchamp, *Building Neighborliness* (New York: Center for Human Relations and Community Studies, New York University, 1958).

All these qualities should lead to a dynamic, vital, challenging learning situation. What do we have? As we have observed secondary-school students and as we study the investigations that have been made, we find a small percentage of students who seem to have their goals well-established and who are intently working on them. Another small percentage, which is larger in some schools, explicitly, by their own statements and behavior, are just "putting in their time," waiting for the day to come when they can drop out legally. Psychologically, they dropped out a long time ago. The vast majority between these two extremes are, as mentioned earlier, much concerned about their social relationships, but bored and listless with the academic program of the school. They comply with the teacher's requests in a superficial way, treading the line of least resistance. Some of them "keep score" quite closely to be sure that they are meeting the standards necessary to go on to the college of their choice. This commonly involves sharing of homework and themes, pressing mom and dad into helping with the homework, and considerable cheating on tests. We seldom hear an adolescent discuss animatedly a homework assignment; we listen often to many excited conversations about the development of jazz in America and what it means in our culture. We don't find youngsters catching fire about the chemistry experiments they perform, but we observe them working meticulously, strenuously, and with dogged persistence to hook up a hi-fi set, to make a "ham" sending set, to tear down and rebuild a jalopy, and recently to put a rocket into the stratosphere. We hear them groan about *Silas Marner* but go into ectastic discussion of Lawrence Olivier's performance in *Mark Antony and Cleopatra* or Marlon Brando's in *Julius Caesar*. Why?

The basic explanation, as we see it, is that the pressing problems, the developmental tasks of youth, have been sharply separated from school. We say to the adolescent, "Park your interests, your social life, your feelings about your body and about your sex and the opposite sex, your vague ambitions on the doorstep as you come in. We will teach you about the world—as it was when *we* first saw it." Of course, this is preposterous. We get ludicrous, sometimes disastrous results, including an emphasis on so-called extracurricular activities that many times completely overshadow the academic program.

The authors take a clear-cut critical position about the program of the American secondary school as it is generally experienced by adolescent

ADOLESCENT-YOUNG ADULT

youth. Enough bright spots exist to point the way to more intelligent approaches, but the vast majority of present-day youth have not experienced such programs. We believe that much of the current criticism is justified. The solutions generally proposed are *not* in agreement with available knowledge about how people grow and how learning takes place. Our young people are poorly prepared to assume adult roles. Teaching more of the same, administering it in stiffer and stiffer doses is not going to cure the patient. He needs a different medicine. It is not a question of *how much* our young people are learning. The question is *what!*

We make the following proposals. We cannot spell them out in detail since this is not a curriculum book. We think your imagination will be able to fill in the skeleton herein presented.

Every pupil must have an opportunity to be known well by one teacher who sees the pupil *whole,* who has associations with him during his high-school life. The teacher has the responsibility of being the liaison between the home and the school—not to discuss the pupil's shortcomings behind his back, but to confer with him and his folks at intervals frequent enough to keep in close touch with his needs and progress. Every effort should be made to establish this relationship so that it is mutually perceived as a friendly, honest sharing of responsibility in helping the youngster grow. Fundamental qualifications of these teachers should be that they have a scientific understanding of adolescence as a short period in a person's life, and a "feeling with" this age.

The daily schedule of the school must be reorganized so that a pupil's life has some unity and coherence. Six fifty-minute periods with a new group of thirty individuals entering the room every period is too much of a merry-go-round even for a sturdy New Yorker to keep up with. Little integration of learning can take place as long as we persist in chopping up time in medicine dropper portions.

The school must be organized so that the adolescents have opportunities to practice democratic citizenship in a realistic setting. For the most part, the students should be responsible for running the school. They should be held responsible for such activities as publishing the school newspaper, organizing the social life, holding elections, developing rules and regulations, managing lunchrooms, ordering and distributing supplies. This, we believe, would necessitate considerable simplification in school-keeping. And that would be all to the good!

The content of the curriculum must have as its organizing threads the developmental tasks of youth. These will run throughout the program and be interwoven with all content. This is for the purpose of helping youth understand the purposes and goals of their own lives in relation to the culture in which they live. We might think of the curriculum as divided into four subject matter areas: the humanities, the arts, the sciences, and mathematics. Running through these studies are the themes for all the learnings: establishing heterosexuality, accepting values to live by, achieving means for economic independence, achieving independence from the home, learning to come to terms with one's own body. Schematically, the curriculum might look like this:

	Humanities	Arts	Sciences	Mathematics
Establishing heterosexuality				
Accepting values to live by				
Achieving economic independence				
Achieving independence from home				
Coming to terms with one's body				

Utilizing Developmental Tasks

Are you saying, "What difference would it make to organize the curriculum this way?" We will illustrate. It is rather easy to see how the developmental tasks would serve as organizing themes in the humanities, so let us take a difficult example, mathematics. If we were to follow through on the plans discussed earlier for achieving economic independence, we would have to make some judgments about the functional mathematics needed by various occupations. A minimum amount is needed by all. This would be taught in such a manner that its applications would be immediately available to the learners. Simple problems—such as making and living within a budget, finances involved in time payments, income tax matters, consumer research, keeping a bank account, using simple statistical concepts—would serve as the content. These items might become quite complex when applied by some individuals to their own affairs.

Differentiation in content would be necessary as the student progresses in school and becomes more clear about his needs. The mechanically inclined youngsters would need certain procedures and applications that the future doctors would not need. Mathematics would be taught as a tool—which it is, not as an esoteric discipline. Mathematicians have long recognized and discussed at their annual meetings the fallacy of teaching geometry as if it were separated from algebra and calculus, as if it had little affinity for either. We propose, therefore, that mathematics, which has functional use in solving problems, be taught, drawing from all the branches of mathematics as required. You can readily see that as this is done many *scientific* learnings are also accruing. In this way, integration has a chance to take place. The teacher loses his preoccupation with labeling something as algebra or physics or geometry. Einstein said he was grown before he saw the relation between physics and mathematics.

At the same time that the thread of economic independence is being woven into the teaching of mathematical concepts, other developmental tasks come into focus. The details of growth from pubescence to adulthood provide a fascinating study in mathematics and science—one the adolescent is eager to learn. As he learns the use of mathematics in various jobs, he also develops a picture of himself as an individual in the world of work or in the home. The self-image of maleness and femaleness is being filled in. Values, of course, permeate all discussions.

The spirit of this school would be a searching one. The students would be seeking answers to their questions, developing processes for their search, evaluating their progress. Teachers would be wise adults who see teaching as "leading one to the threshold of his own mind." [23] The methods used would be discussions, small-group work, individual conferences, lectures (when the search demands lectures), demonstrations, constructing sessions, and laboratory methods. Mock-ups would be used to simulate reality whenever reality could not be had.

We believe such an approach in our secondary schools would be a challenging experiment. We would like some foundation to be daring enough to underwrite a high school committed to such a plan for a period of ten to fifteen years, with careful evaluation in terms of up-to-date purposes written into the plan so that we would have more than our most intelligent hunches as guides for the future. Blos expressed this need in 1941. So far we have turned our backs on an obvious error in our secondary instructional program. We alibi out of it by protesting that most teachers would not be able to teach in this creative way, that it would cost too much, and that it sounds radical. We wonder what our world

---

[23] Kahlil Gibran, *The Prophet* (New York: Alfred A. Knopf, Inc., 1923), p. 64.

position would be today had we applied that same line of reasoning to our missile program. Listen to Blos (italics ours):

> In the light of the tasks to be accomplished at adolescence, education must acknowledge the adolescent as distinct from either the child or the adult and must realize that the most important contribution toward his growth lies in social experiences, community participation, vocational planning and exploration; in status-giving activities, privileges, and responsibilities; in thinking through the potentialities, needs, and aspirations which he possesses as a sexually mature person, as a family member, as a citizen, and as an individual with inner resources; in searching with him for values and standards acceptable by society yet distinctly his own. *In these terms each aspect of the curriculum can be utilized to greatest advantage and the prolongation of youth relieved of some of the devastating consequences. Experiences of all kinds, then, are to be related to the young person's growth; to the adjustments which he is called upon to make during his adolescent years.*[24]

**The Meaning
of Youthful Disorder**

This is written in the midst of several years of grossly misplaced concerns about the teen-ager. He has been lazy, and has thus permitted the Russians to beat the U.S.A. in putting a man-made object into the Earth's orbit. He has been ill-disciplined and is now responsible for a vast increase in crime and public disorder. The increase of disorder among the near-adult male population is a clearly established fact. Common among adult responses to this condition are anger, dismay, demand for more regimentation, threat of reprisal, and a great variety of diverting "youth programs." The gloomy critics of youth today might ponder the following paragraph written in 1904, by America's pioneer and greatly distinguished authority on adolescence:

> In all civilized lands, criminal statistics show two sad and significant facts: First, that there is a marked increase of crime at the age of twelve to fourteen, not in crimes of one, but of all kinds, and that this increase continues for a number of years. While the percentages of certain grave crimes increase to mature manhood, adolescence is pre-eminently the criminal age when most first commitments occur and most vicious careers are begun. The

---

[24] Peter Blos, *The Adolescent Personality*, p. 498. (New York: D. Appleton-Century Co., Inc., 1941. Reprinted by permission of Appleton-Century-Crofts, Inc.)

second fact is that the proportion of juvenile delinquents seems to be everywhere increasing and crime is more and more precocious.[25]

A mature society looks upon defects in its human "products" as objectively as does a manufacturer, and seeks ways to lower to a minimum its rejects. A community which says, "We have many bad children," is really saying, "We do a bad job of raising our children." We have stated earlier that a malnourished personality grows crookedly. The "bad-man" theory of human degradation is now discredited. We cannot prevent disorder and delinquency merely by locking up or giving therapy to damaged people.

We offer here a few observations derived from our own study and experience in dealing with delinquent youth.

> Delinquency covers a vast variety of behaviors. Technically a juvenile delinquent is one who has been "booked" and dealt with by the authorities. Hence, a community's delinquency rate is the percentage of youngsters its policemen arrest.
>
> It appears that the most important incident in the confirmation of a delinquent career is that of the *first arrest*. From this incident on, the youngster and his neighbors picture him as a criminal. He has "tangled" with the law.
>
> The great bulk of delinquents come from "poor" homes. This means, in part, that these homes have provided inferior rearing; in larger part it means that a community's good homes are more likely to be accorded the right and responsibility for "straightening out" their erring children.

Virtually all delinquents present a history of rejection. They were not wanted by their parents—or misfortune and adversity in their families led to neglect and hostility. The neighbors did not want them to play with their children because they used bad language. They were placed in the "woodpecker group" in first grade because they were not as literate as teachers like their pupils to be. In secondary schools they were placed in "X-classes," were dubbed non-academic. Most of them have rejected grownups in order to maintain their own self-respect. They are the children who have *struck out, not back* in response to wholesale rejection.

A goodly number of delinquent careers began in simple quest for fun. A few have found it exciting to play "cops and robbers" with real police-

---

[25] G. Stanley Hall, *Adolescence*, Vol. I (New York: D. Appleton and Company, 1904), p. 325.

men. Exuberant physical activity is not readily accommodated in the city. Some of our authorities are dismayed by the fact that more than half of the car thefts are committed by teen-agers. This seems to us not surprising, since we live in a motorized country; kids have always liked a "hard ride." In most of our families the youngster cannot own his own car. The state will not permit him to drive. The great bulk of car thefts are, in reality, unauthorized borrowings. (We do not imply approval of this practice.) Our large cities now are making it illegal to leave a vacant car unlocked. More important, it is becoming increasingly illegal to be young in the modern, complex, hurried, adult-owned world.

We offer a few proposals for reducing the amount of disorder among youth and diminishing the amount and severity of conflict between the generations.

> Widen neighborhood and community concern for well-being and good living of all children. A few years ago in informal discussion, Margaret Mead expressed the idea somewhat like this: "We shall make no more progress in rearing children until a community is as much ashamed of rearing bad children as we now expect a family to be."
>
> Find really important use for children during the growing years. No amount of diversion, dances, and sports will satisfy this urge of the human spirit to be needed. We doubt that the home alone can find adequate use for youngsters in these times.
>
> Accord to the young full citizenship in their spheres of concern. They must be included in planning and managing enterprises meant for their good.
>
> Increase neighborhood and community tolerance for varieties of youthful behavior. There must be space and time for accommodating the ways of both youth and their elders. Often youth are penalized for indulging in disturbing behavior, when the only one disturbed is the adult teacher or parent. Compare the number of bars in your neighborhood with the number of places youngsters can go to be with their pals.

Minimize competitive activities—those in which the goal of the activity is to defeat someone. Numerous youngsters take this motive literally and move directly to accomplish it.

Study and correct administrative practices in schools and other social organizations in order to reduce the amount of rejection now practiced under a variety of names.

Organize community activities to increase satisfying person-to-person contacts between youngsters and grownups. Move away from activities in which grownups use children as puppets, trained seals; find genuinely satisfying human relationships in common activities. The only adult contacts many youngsters have are with their parents and teachers, none of whom they had any part in choosing.

Maintain statistical perspective on the incidence of disorder. A small percentage of "bad boys" can seem like an insurrection in a huge high school. A slight percentage of vandalism appears to be impending catastrophe when reported in the large city press.

Give pupils and teachers more time just to visit together. We cannot supply the urgent need for adults other than relatives by setting up systems of counseling. Surely the high schools and colleges of America will do something to reduce the complexity and disintegrating forces of competing, divergent activities which prevent friendly, challenging relationships between teachers and pupils.

Crucial Problems of Modern Youth

As this book is written the writers have assumed that most of its readers are in their late teens or shortly out of them. We trust that we have not said, nor implied, that "youth is a mess." It seems to us that youth today are more knowing, more realistic than they were a generation ago. However, it seems that unsolved problems have accumulated into a dangerously top-heavy pile. We entertain the hope that the youth of today will not, as have earlier generations, become so preoccupied with establishing homes, launching careers, and rearing children as to abdicate their personal and collective responsibility for recognizing stresses in the circumstances of young people and for taking appropriate action to reduce these strains. Social as well as individual strains break into violence unless resolved by intelligent action. We present here in capsule form some observations of certain common circumstances which seem to demand thoughtful, constructive action.

During the later part of the growing years persons are inclined to engage in exaggerated, unreliable, hostile, unpredictable behavior. Their parents and teachers are disposed to fear that these patterns will persist forever unless curbed. Adults are reluctant to give responsibilities to young people in this state. Thus they encourage the attitude that one does only what authority demands. All too often, even among middle-aged graduate students, we find the attitude that one works only when he is watched.

While the adolescent is biologically and socially mature enough to be a mate and a parent, his culture urges him to postpone these roles until the completion of his education and the establishment of his economic competency. Of late, the possession of money has become essential to day-by-day living. Youngsters today have no money of their own; they are dependent upon the generosity and earning ability of parents. Money is no longer real "stuff of wealth" to be exchanged for some other "stuff of value." It is, in terms expressed by Justice Brandeis, "liquid claim to wealth," an assigned amount of purchasing power, the amount and value and availability of which is always determined by somebody else. Youth, being for the most part without power to earn, has little independent power to convert wants into realizations.

Our youth have grown in a culture that pays eloquent tribute to freedom. Valuing freedom, they find themselves in highly regimented high schools in which their opportunity for choice and self-direction, if they are "good" boys and girls, is limited to such things as choosing between ice cream and fruit cup for dessert. It seems clear that the teenager looks upon late hours as time he can be free from adult monitoring. This accounts for the value he places upon them.

Many of our children live in a success-driven culture. Surveys indicate that at all social levels people believe that they need twenty-five per cent more income than they have. The adolescent lives among anxious grown-ups. What is to be the ultimate result of the atomic weapons race? If I should become ill or lose my job what of the mortgage, the car payments, the monthly insurance premium? Suppose the boss' wife should find my home untidy?

All too many parents are disappointed in their own careers. Results of vocational surveys made through two generations show that more than 60 per cent of the teen-agers expect to work in one of the professions, the creative arts, or in business management. As economic life is now constituted, fewer than 10 per cent can so work. We like Mr. New Fist's [26] definition of an educated man to the effect that he knows what his community needs to have done; he knows how to do some of those things. Few mental tests reveal increase in mental power and acuity after age sixteen to eighteen. Yet persons of this age have little occasion to "use their brains" for appropriate purposes. Quite commonly, high school and college students testify that school has provided scant occasion for contriving and planning apart from problems such as, "How to circumvent the rules? How to get credit without doing the work?"

Notes on Maturity

This chapter completes our description of the growth of the human toward maturity. We have not meant to say that human beings are more alike at any one period of growth than at any other. In recent years, however, the term *teen-ager* has become a stereotype carrying negative meanings that result in clouded thinking. It seems to us that at no period of life are differences given more attention, nor do they seem more important to the individual himself and to his older associates than during the later teen years.

During the growing years the person has stretched toward maturity. He has accomplished a long and intricate series of developmental tasks as he has sought to become a member of the culture and to accept and foster his own uniqueness. Of late many books have been written on being mature. Here are some criteria by which to judge the maturity of the person who is growing out of his teens:

> The mature individual strives for long-range goals without losing sight of the importance of the gratification of day-by-day living. He retains his capacity for hearty enjoyment.
> He cannot find happiness at the expense of others. He judges the validity of his behavior in terms of its effects upon other people.
> He is able to see others in his life as people, not merely in terms of status (parent, professor, principal, boss, adversary). He denies to them the right to control his "human life." He accords to them the right to be human. He is dissatisfied with maintaining the status quo. He seeks ways to make creative changes by hopeful means.

---

[26] Harold Benjamin, *The Saber-Tooth Curriculum* (New York: McGraw-Hill Book Company, Inc., 1939).

He is in charge of his own life; he lives life, does not merely let life happen to him. He maintains control of his whole life allowing no part of it to become more important than all of it. (He does not put all of his emotional eggs in one basket.)

He assumes his obligation to do his share of the world's work. He will not be a "kept" person.

He asks for himself no gratification which he does not seek to make possible for others.

He solves his problems by the method of intelligence: he accepts conflicts that cannot be resolved, plans effective solutions for those that can be solved.

He maintains statistical perspective. He knows that with every move he makes he takes chances. He calculates and accepts his "odds."

He has solid self-respect, genuine regard for his own feelings, preferences, aversions. He doesn't have to read the reviews to know whether or not he likes a movie.

He is able to engage in effective compromise seeking the greater good for the greater number and at the same time seeking more creative solutions.

He knows and accepts himself; he engages in a minimum of sham.

He expects his world to be no better than he strives to make it.

Summary

Now that we have watched the infant grow to a mature personality, let us reflect upon the meaning of the changes and constancies we have observed. When he was but a few pounds of rather low-grade animal life, baby displayed definite personality. He was alive; he expressed his wants forthrightly, made his discomforts clearly known. He demanded satisfactions now, on the spot. What has become of his hearty zest in gratification as he has learned to forego and hide his feelings? Why are so many older children so bored in home and at school?

Many of our current patterns of child-rearing go back to the delusion that an infant is a wad of clay to be molded to whatever pattern the molder desires. This gloomy doctrine implies that the child lacks urge to grow, to be—that whatever the child becomes results from adult directing, pushing, and shaping. One has only to reflect upon the many complicated skills a two-year-old has mastered to discredit this notion and gain some humility in his role as parent and teacher.

Too much do modern ways of life restrict really dynamic growth. Excessive regimentation by clocks and rigidly organized living is the rule.

Clubs, music lessons, supervised play, doing the correct thing with the right people leave little time for the child to go and grow on his own steam.

Increased emphasis upon schooling delays for years behaving as the body is built to behave. An essential feature of mental health is independence appropriate to the ability to manage one's life. Modern living and schooling delays genuine independence. Rarely in school has the young man or woman occasion to function on his own, to use his own judgment, to do anything of genuine worth to other people. A notable quality of a recent interview held by a well-known TV commentator with a group of college students was their wish when they completed college to have some responsibility, to be needed by society. Most of them seemed to imply that they must wait until they finish college to acquire these opportunities. Perhaps we should reflect seriously why they must wait until after college for these goods of life.

Everyone loves a baby despite his being noisy, messy, bothersome. His compulsions to grow, to reach out, to test and inspect are expected and welcome. Dynamic independence in adults is commonly approved. But what happens during the growing years when the child is awkward, impudent, perverse? Then children especially need tolerance, opportunity to stretch, to err, to gloat in achievement. Teachers, parents, and neighbors must hurry to foster ways and means and to provide freedom for dynamic growth for our young in all their stages and phases.

Suggestions for Further Exploration

▶ Try some role-playing with a small group of older adolescents. Encourage them to role-play some of the conflicts they are having with their parents. Lead them in a discussion about their feelings and their parents' feelings. (See Chapter 15, "Tools for Child Study," for suggestions on role-playing).

▶ Lead a discussion with a group of teen-agers about any of the problems they want to talk about. What did you learn about them and their problems as you listened?

▶ Find out as much as you can about the social structure of the high school of your community. See if you can identify the high-prestige groups. Ask the youngsters why they value their memberships in these groups.

▶ Discover the kinds of decisions that students make within the school structure. Compare these with decisions they make outside of school.

► Listen carefully to as many teen-agers as you can for one week. Collect illustrations of:

Efforts to deceive	Expenses
Conformity	Parental conflicts
Enthusiasms	Awareness of roles

► As you read about youthful disorder, see what part rejection plays in delinquency. Can you illustrate from your own experiences?

► If you are studying an adolescent, talk with him about some of the things we have discussed in this chapter to see what his ideas are about his school, his life ambitions, his conflicts, and the like.

► The following films depict the adolescent of high school age:

Discipline During Adolescence (Adolescent Development Series), 16 min., sound, McGraw-Hill Book Company, Inc.
Depicts the problems facing parents of adolescents as to how much discipline to impose upon their teen-agers. The effects of too much and too little are considered. The audience is asked to participate in coming to a sound decision about the problems presented in the film.

Emotional Maturity (Adolescent Development Series), 20 min., sound, McGraw-Hill Book Company, Inc.
The film shows the effects of lack of control in an adolescent boy who is entrusted with valuable property and who is confronted with many adult-like decisions to make. Traces his behavior back to parental treatment as a child.

Social Acceptability (Adolescent Development Series), 20 min., sound, McGraw-Hill Book Company, Inc.
The problems that come to a high-school girl who is not accepted by her classmates in school and the effects this rejection has upon her personality are depicted.

Additional Sources You May Find Helpful

Harold Alberty, *Reorganizing the High School Curriculum*. New York: The Macmillan Company, 1947.
An insightful presentation of the need to sharply change the kind of secondary-school education program.

Association for Supervision and Curriculum Development, *What Shall the High Schools Teach?* 1956 Yearbook. Washington, D. C.: National Education Association.
A discussion of some of the theoretical issues that need to be resolved before secondary education can be effective in a modern, industrialized, global culture.

Peter Blos, *The Adolescent Personality*. New York: D. Appleton-Century Co., Inc., 1941. Reprinted by permission of Appleton-Century-Crofts, Inc.
An invaluable book dealing with the adolescent period of growth. This book is authoritative, insightful, and comprehensive. We strongly recommend it to anyone who is planning to teach in the secondary schools.

Roland C. Faunce and Nelson L. Bossing, *Developing the Core Curriculum*. Englewood Cliffs, N. J.: Prentice-Hall, Inc., 1951.
An excellent discussion of one way to vitalize the secondary-school program.

Arthur J. Jersild, *The Psychology of Adolescence*. New York: The Macmillan Company, 1957.
An approach to an understanding of the adolescent by merging the overt, descriptive phases of behavior and the inner, subjective dimensions of self. The discussion of self is most perceptive.

Earl C. Kelley, *Education for What Is Real*. New York: Harper and Brothers, 1947.
In this profoundly simple book Dr. Kelley shows that each human sees what is behind his own eyes. It describes and interprets demonstrations of the principles of perceiving which give unique meaning to the experiences of each individual.

Robert Lindner, *Must You Conform?* New York: Rinehart and Company, Inc., 1956.
An angry, insightful account of youth's state of mind in today's world. This book will challenge you to think seriously about the values of our day. His discussion of conformity raises many questions.

Agnes E. Meyer, *Education for a New Morality*. New York: The Macmillan Company, 1957.
This Kappa Delta Pi lecture by a noted journalist "charts the new morality which the public schools must develop."

How
to Study Children
and Youth

The three chapters in this section express our deep belief that *means* cannot be separated from *ends,* that the student in training to be a teacher cannot attain a mastery of his profession merely by reading about children and youth. He must ever thoughtfully apply the concepts and understandings he gains as he continues learning to become a teacher.

We have urged you as you have read this book to study an individual child, to make group studies, and to take frequent soundings of your own responses while you have pursued your studies. This section presents some concrete aids for you to utilize as you move along. You will find yourself turning to this section frequently as you continue to learn to teach.

14

Study
of Group
Situations

In this chapter [1] we take an analytical look at the organization and functioning of groups. Our purpose is to learn what we must look for as we study groups so that we may be able to respond more accurately to the many conflicting situations that arise in the classroom. Human behavior takes place

[1] The authors are indebted to Dr. Stella Gervasio, University of Wisconsin at Milwaukee, for her insightful reading and help with this chapter.

in groups. The individual is never "in orbit," circling around this lonely universe by himself. Even when he is alone, he carries within himself the groups of which he is a part. As you drive along in a car by yourself, for instance, you imagine many group situations and role-play yourself and others. You say, "I'm just going for a little spin to think something out."

Because we are human, we can talk with others even though they are not present. As we talk, we project a variety of situations out of which we refine our purposes, clarify our attitudes and values, and rehearse the roles we would like to assume. From such imaginary role-playing, we develop our capacities for self-criticism. Mead in *Mind, Self and Society* [2] indicates that this process of self-criticism is a social control that helps the individual to integrate himself and his actions to the processes and experiences of the groups in which he has membership. As the individual becomes aware of the attitudes of others and perceives how his own actions affect their attitudes, he consciously criticizes himself as a group member.

Each of us reveals our human qualities in groups. We express empathy for each other. We communicate. We perceive ourselves, others, situations, and the complex relationships inherent in all of these. We respond to rules, limitations, authority. We accept responsibility or fail to do so. We develop friendships. We fall in love and establish homes, produce children. We work in groups. The quality of all these relationships is tested and realized in group situations. This makes it imperative that as teachers we become discerning about what happens in groups; that we learn the necessary skills to work in groups in constructive, challenging ways; that we learn how to help children and youth become effective group members.

A group is difficult to study because of its complexity and because it is more than a sum of its parts. Furthermore, it does not stand still; moving objects create illusions and confusions. Most authorities agree today that groups do have some predictable developmental patterns; that while groups vary tremendously—depending upon their membership and their purposes—they also seem to grow through various stages. Group development depends to a great extent upon the leader's willingness to give members freedom to grow. A large percentage of groups cannot in a

---

[2] George H. Mead, *Mind, Self and Society* (Chicago: University of Chicago Press, 1934).

psychological sense be termed groups because their members are not free to exercise the functions that characterize group activity.[3]

Developmental Stages of Group Growth

When a number of people come together for a purpose, a degree of uncertainty pervades the situation. If there is an appointed leader (in the classroom the teacher), the members look to him for direction and clarification. *Dependency is the most noticeable quality of a beginning group.* Accompanying this air of uncertainty is a certain amount of jockeying for position and testing of the leader. Group members explore their limits, test the authority, and assess methods that may work to influence the group and the leader. (Every beginning teacher has to live through this stage as he takes over a class on his own. This is one reason why student teaching is so unlike "real" teaching. The pupils have gone through the testing process with the regular teacher and have progressed to another stage of development.) Members expect to be told during this stage. Communication is extensively two-way, between the leader and an individual member or the group as a whole, rather than multi-directional. Learning is limited to the information given by the leader and to his interpretations. Speaking figuratively, we could say that this is the infant stage of the group.

The second stage of group development may be likened to the toddler age when the favorite words are "No! No!" A negativistic attitude prevails. Decisions are hard to come by. Bickering, hair-splitting, and special pleading come to the fore. This happens because as individual members become more sure of themselves and know what to expect of each other and of the leader, they begin to assert more independence. Some develop this independence much more readily than others. This results in subgroup formation and unevenness of procedure. Three people, for example, are united in their feelings that the group should ask Teacher Brown if they can have a picnic Friday afternoon. Four others feel as strongly that this is being presumptuous; another group proposes having the picnic after school without Mr. Brown. In other words, some members are much more ready to move ahead on their own in decision-making than others are; some are more inclined to treat the leader (teacher) as an absolute

---

[3] William G. Hollister, "The Risks of Freedom-Giving Group Leadership," *Mental Hygiene*, Vol. 41, No. 2, April 1947.

authority than others are. Perceptions of appropriate group behavior vary with individuals.

Because individuals bring to groups such a wide variety of internalized feelings and needs growing out of their own experiences, the formation of sub-groups is a necessary part of group development. Even small children have varying degrees of need for dependence. If you observe a nursery-school group, you discover some children able to make choices of activities and playmates without asking teacher while others must have teacher's approval for every move. The older the group—until adulthood is reached—the wider becomes the range of dependence among the members. This becomes clear when we realize that some adolescents are still as dependent as some nursery-school children while others function as mature adults. As we work with groups, we expect that a basic need around which sub-groups form and differ will be that of *dependence*. It helps to think of these sub-groups falling someplace along a dependence-independence continuum with extreme dependence representing one end of the continuum and extreme independence the other, as follows:

Dependence   *Independence*

The wider the range along this continuum, the more difficult it is for the group to move out of the second stage of development. This dependence is expressed by reliance upon absolute authority. A corollary to the dependence-independence is the authority continuum:

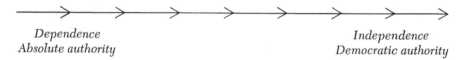

Dependence   *Independence*
Absolute authority   *Democratic authority*

Two other closely related individualized needs that serve as forces for sub-group formation are members' predispositions about inhibiting or expressing feelings, and conforming or individualizing behavior. Expressed on a continuum these attitudes look like this:

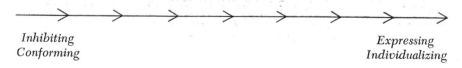

Inhibiting   *Expressing*
Conforming   *Individualizing*

The attitudes of inhibiting feelings and conforming are expressed in groups by such expressions as: "You mustn't say that.... Miss Jones wouldn't like that.... We must all wear white shirts and ties in this class. ... Let's all go to the dance in slacks.... Nice people don't lose their tempers.... Nice people sit up straight and keep their feet on the floor.... We line up to go to the bathroom in this school.... Oh, we always have a festival in April; we have done that for twenty-five years." Quite obviously not all individuals in a group feel the same about inhibiting feelings or conforming. Sub-groups then form around these issues.

One other quality of group living that functions as a nucleus for subgroup formation is the continuum of competition—cooperation. The internalized needs of individuals to compete vary greatly. Those who *must* compete tend to approach the tasks of group endeavor differently from those who have internalized cooperation. "Let's see who can have the best group and do this in the shortest amount of time," is a motivation that will be grabbed with alacrity by some and ignored or resented by others. This quality functions in many, many different ways. A fifth grade gets in an argument about whether to give prizes for the best exhibit in the science fair; a junior class in high school debates whether they shall have a queen for their prom; contests are organized in elementary grades with the boys pitted against the girls; the room that has the most parents attending parent meetings is given a record or a geranium.

As we observe emotions becoming crystallized around issues that have to do with internalized needs relating to dependence-independence, absolute authority-democratic authority, inhibition-freedom of expression, conformity-individuality, competition-cooperation, it becomes obvious that the second stage of group development requires consummate skill, creative listening and planning on the part of the teacher-leader. The group has to be maintenance-centered during this phase of its development. If it is not, it will disintegrate or regress to the infant stage. This is the period of development in which members complain about "waste of time." Many members are insistent upon the leader's making decisions so that "we can get on with our task." Learnings need to be focused upon human relations rather than content.

The third stage of group development may be called the adolescent period. The group by this time has cast aside much of its childish squabbling. Much of the dependent behavior has matured to the point that decisions may be reached on many matters without consulting the teacher. Implicit agreements have been reached about inhibitions, competition, and conformity. As with individuals, however, in times of crises the group may be thrown back to an earlier period of development. Ambivalence exists between wanting to be independent and luxuriate in the warmth of the leader's approval. A new emergent of interdependence is obvious at this stage. More decisions are reached by consensus. It takes less time to come to decisions. More give-and-take and sharing of responsibility exists. Attempts are made to resolve sub-group conflict and to bring about group harmony in ways that generate healthy feelings and make possible the completion of tasks. The group is more goal-centered, more purposive. Sub-groups complement each other rather than compete for ascendancy. The leader is more dispensable because the group has a greater awareness of it own powers, motives, and goals.

Finally, a few groups exist long enough and give enough attention to the ways in which they function to mature into the kinds of groups that may be described as adult. They tackle tough problems with an assurance that the challenge of the task and the respect of each for all will carry them through successfully. An interdependent, cooperative approach is assumed, with decisions being tested in terms of consequences and commitment. Individual differences are accepted and used so that less time is required to work with intermember conflict. Sub-group membership tends to shift with the need for specific competencies. The functioning of all sub-groups overlaps, giving the total group structure cohesion and strength. Intergroup relations tend to be constructive and enriching rather than threatening.

Perhaps it is a mark of our lack of knowledge about groups that causes us to see so few really mature groups. Few leaders are ready to give a group the freedom it must have to grow. We must recognize, too, that the growth line of a group is not *even*, any more than the growth line of an individual is. Regression followed by spurts of progress characterizes groups. Being mature as a group has little to do with the age of the members of the group. Some ten-year-olds conduct themselves more maturely in their group operations than do some fifty-year-olds. A group comprised of mature individuals is able to grow more rapidly and with less growing pains than one comprised of less mature people.

Description
of Group Functioning

All groups have certain common factors and characteristics. To analyze the functioning of groups is difficult because all aspects are so interrelated; yet we cannot talk about all phases of a group at once. To establish some relationships among the various aspects of a group, we use a schematic approach. Imagine that you are looking at the cross-section of a ball which represents the inner workings of a group. The parts you see in the cross-section look as they do in the diagram below, but should you look a few seconds later, these inner workings may have shifted just as when you look through a kaleidoscope. You remember a group does not stay put. It is not static nor rigid. The only stable element to the phases of group life is that they all emanate from the nucleus of interaction-relationships.

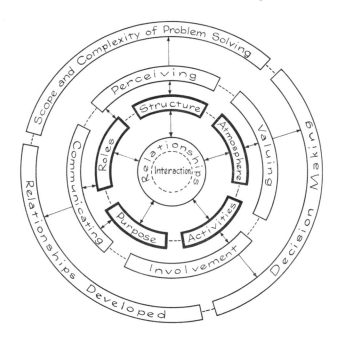

Interaction the Heart

The heart of every group's functioning is interaction. This word does not have much specific meaning unless we see what is involved in interaction. Interaction leads to relationships which lead to new interactions.

It is estimated that a teacher averages between three and four hundred interactions per hour in the classroom. Out of these interactions are built teacher-pupil relationships. Interaction and relationships are so much a part of each other that we show them separated only by a dotted line.

Group Factors

The nucleus of interaction-relationships functions in a group that has certain factors. These factors affect the quality of interaction and are also affected by the interaction themselves. They are described in a variety of ways in the literature about groups. We choose to think of them as being five in number—each intimately bound to all the rest; each a determiner as well as a determinant. They are *structure, roles, atmosphere* or *climate, purpose,* and *activities.* All of these are dynamic. They do not stay put. All of these factors affect the interaction-relationships and are affected in return. Each is interrelated with all. For example, structure helps create atmosphere; atmosphere encourages certain types of structure; purposes of the group affect both; roles vary as structure and atmosphere change; and activities change with purposes.

Group Characteristics

The third concentric circle in our diagram shows the group charac-teristics that emerge from the group factors. Each group comes to be characterized by the quality of its *communicating, perceiving, valuing,* and *involvement.* In one sense these characteristics are ends or results of the functioning of the various factors of the group. The structure of the group, for example, affects the involvement of the members, the kinds and degrees of communication, the ways of perceiving, and the valuing of group members, as do all the other group factors. If we had a readable way to show it, we would have an arrow running both ways from each of the factors to each of the characteristics.

Group Goals

Finally, in the outer circle we come to the generalized goals of all group functioning, that is to learn how to solve problems effectively, to have opportunities for decision-making in wider and more complex areas, and to have opportunities for developing solid, challenging relationships with ever more inclusiveness. Our circle has come full around now, for we started with relationships as the nucleus of groups and we come to relationships as one of the dynamic goals of groups.

To be sure you understand the movable quality of what we are trying to picture, look at the diagram below:

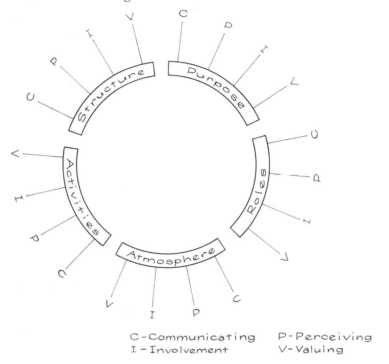

C–Communicating   P–Perceiving
I–Involvement   V–Valuing

In this second diagram we have attempted to correct the false impression of our first diagram by showing the manner in which each of the five factors is related to the four characteristics that it helps to produce. You may want to experiment with illustrating these concepts by constructing a three-dimensional model of a group so that you can move the parts to demonstrate the infinite possibilities of dynamic situations, or you may find it interesting to construct and experiment with some movable parts on a flannel board.

Analysis of

Group Functioning

We are now ready to analyze each of the factors and characteristics of a group so that we can perceive the critical points in the functioning of each.

Group Structure

Every group has a hierarchy of statuses within it; even small, informal, social groups tend to award certain members more and other members less status. This is known as group structure. In a mature group, that has as its goal the growth and development of individuals within the group, the status awarded an individual is the result of his ability to contribute to the purposes of the group. Thus, as activities change and different abilities are required, the status of individuals shifts. In a group that functions maturely, the hierarchy of status is flexible and is related directly to the purposes and activities of the group.

Since the concept of a mature group is more a figure of speech than a reality (remember we bring all our individual and immature needs to the group with us), status within a group often is determined by sex, age, wealth, social-class, number of years in the community or in the group, as well as by one's contribution to the group. In some groups of children and youth, status may be determined by size, or by the possession of the one baseball and bat on the block, or by owning the one hot rod, or perhaps by having the loudest voice. An illustration of size and newness affecting status comes from a study made by a student teacher of her class.

> Larry's status in the classroom is influenced by many factors. He and one other boy (J. B.) were taken out of their respective classes and put in with this group which has been together for three years and is consequently tightly knit and well used to one another. Larry's position is made more difficult because he is the smallest and the youngest in the class—a fact of which he is aware and which is something tangible for the class to pick on. For example, when Miss Agnew asked him to write something a little higher on the board, a few of the boys laughingly called out that he couldn't reach higher. Larry is able to laugh off and clown away these slights, but it comes out in other ways that these things do hurt him. For example, he once told Miss Goldstein that he feels very big in his bulky winter things, but when he takes them off he's still his same, skinny, small self!
>
> However, I do feel that the main reason for his partial rejection is his newness rather than his size. I say this because the other new boy who is large, athletic, and an all-around boy is also rejected to about the same degree as Larry. For example, when Neil, the largest boy in the class, had a birthday party, they were the only two boys in the class who were not invited. Inevitably, these two boys are drawn together, although they are

by no means a tight little clique. Both, but particularly Larry, seem to be reaching out and striving to be more friendly with others. Larry often seems to be trying to relate to the much larger boys.

TEACHER INFLUENTIAL FACTOR IN STRUCTURE. In the classroom the teacher is a determining factor in group structure. This is clearly demonstrated as we watch the same group of youngsters with different teachers. In one classroom a well-defined clique covertly may be making life miserable for the teacher, whereas in another classroom this same clique

may be so actively involved in their own learning that they cease for the duration of the period to function as a clique. Perhaps you have heard a teacher reply to the remark, "I just can't seem to say anything that doesn't set Tom, Randy, and Bill into gales of laughter," with "I have never noticed them ganging up in my room."

One student teacher describes the way she perceives her cooperating teacher affecting the structure of the classroom as follows:

> As I see the group, it is a status-centered one. The teacher is the group leader and they follow her direction whenever she is present. This, I believe, is what makes her feel that they are a "good group." When she is present, she can control the group tempo without much trouble. When she is not in a friendly mood, they feel it and stay out of the way (or else). At other times they know that they can relax a little more without having her get too upset about it. All in all I think they know just what they can and just what they cannot get away with, and when.

The teacher influences the structure of the group in at least four ways: (1) the controls he uses; (2) the rewards and punishments he uses; (3) the content of the learning situations; and (4) his perceptions of peer structure. We shall examine each of these ways briefly.

CONTROLS USED. Pupils expect teachers to define the limitations which the classroom situation places upon them. In this process the teacher begins to shape the structure of the group. The teacher has many choices available to him. The thoughtful teacher raises questions about controls, and examines the many alternatives; through self-criticism he comes to some tentative decisions about the degree of independence which the controls encourage. He recognizes, as he works to establish controls with boys and girls, that they are expert parrots. They soon become adept at repeating back to adults the admonitions they have heard so often. With solemn faces, they insist that they must not fight, or talk out-of-turn, or tease—only to go on participating in these acts so recently proclaimed nefarious. Discussions have little meaning unless the teacher leads the group to cut through the adult language which connotes imposed adult standards. The teacher can judge his success in cutting through the parroting by noting if youngsters talk about: *When* do we *have* to fight? *What* do we do about teasing? *How* can we keep from talking-out? As the teacher thinks about controls, he asks himself:

What is the proper *source* of controls: the teacher, the class, or both in serious consultation?

If controls are imposed by me (the teacher), what will this do to the structure of the group? Will there be a greater or lesser tendency for the peer structure to be used effectively in our classroom?

If controls are worked out together by teacher and pupils, who then *interprets* the appropriate manner to respond to controls? Who *administers* the regulations agreed upon?

Are these children with their limited experience able to help set their own controls?

How much formal control is necessary and desirable in this group?

Should the *same controls function* for all alike or should we recognize *individual needs and uniqueness* in our system of controls?

As he contemplates these questions, the teacher recognizes that he has to consider his own temperament, the former experiences of the members of the class, and their expectations. He has also to recognize that the manner in which these questions are raised with the class is of vital importance and affects the responses of the pupils. Youngsters soon "catch on" to the inner responses of the teacher and know whether it is safe to "hoist the storm flag" as one sixth-grade class did when teacher was in a bad mood. Past experiences and present expectations function in the social structure of the classroom because from these come our perceptions about the ways groups ought to function. The groups we have belonged to before serve as reference groups in helping us decide how we feel about the behavior of the present group. These reference groups function often on an unconscious level. For example, we may be completely unaware of having accepted the dogma of a group that insists that children should obey adults implicitly until an incident occurs in which this value is challenged. Then we insist with great tenacity that "these kids just have to learn who is boss around here." Thelen [4] refers to this type of reference group as a *relic* group for we seldom identify its members. The sources of authority in this group reach back to early childhood and frequently remain on an unconscious level.

Each individual brings different reference groups to the classroom with him. He perceives the social structure of the classroom through the veils of these reference groups. If he has learned through his membership in other groups that controls are automatic, authoritarian, and overpowering, he may be greatly confused to discover that the present situation is different. If he has learned that the structure of the classroom encourages a pretense of obedience with an undercurrent of "let's see how much we can get by with," his feelings about a structure that encourages an open, frank, facing of problems as they arise are not likely to be noted for clarity or genuine understanding. The teacher must recognize that, while he is a potent factor in the social structure of the classroom and that while the way he uses controls inevitably affects this structure, his own expectations of outcomes are more realistic if he understands his pupils' perceptions.

REWARDS AND PUNISHMENTS USED. As the status leader in the classroom, the teacher has much power and pull. Almost every behavior of his may be interpreted as having reward or punishment significance—a tone of voice, failure to see a hand waving, looking over a child's shoulder, using his book. A thousand thoughtless acts add up to a perception on the part

---

[4] Herbert A. Thelen, *Dynamics of Groups at Work* (Chicago: University of Chicago Press, 1954), pp. 231-241.

of the child that "He likes me, or he doesn't like me." Much of the reward or punishment value in a situation is communicated non-verbally. The warmth of voice, the twinkle in the eyes, the slight gesture of restraint or acceptance, the extra second teacher lingers by the desk—all are felt as denoting rejection or acceptance. They are expressions of empathy that the pupils interpret, usually with a great deal of validity. The teacher molds the structure by his distribution of rewards and punishments and by the manner in which they are administered. Numerous studies have shown that teachers tend to reinforce the social structure existing in the community; that middle- and upper-class pupils receive a disproportionate amount of rewards and lower-class pupils receive a disproportionate amount of punishments.[5] Observe in classrooms or Sunday Schools or other structured situations and see how rewards are distributed. Here are some of the ways a teacher rewards or punishes a pupil:

Rewards

Asking pupil to run an errand
Appointing him for any special kind of duty
Giving him some of the teacher's authority and responsibility to teach, to give special help, to administer punishments, to make records
Calling on him when visitors are present
Pointing him out to other adults in a favorable light
Appointing him to represent the class
Praising him
Giving him superior or excellent marks
Entrusting him with special honors or giving him special privileges
Suggesting him for class or club officer
Giving him, his possessions, or his clothes special notice

Punishments

Keeping the pupil in after school
Pointing him out to adults or peers in an unfavorable light (ridicule or sarcasm)
Giving him poor or failing marks
Nagging him about his work
Ignoring him when visitors are present
Anticipating that he will not do his assignments or will get into trouble
Depriving him of privileges that other pupils have
Failing to notice him, his possessions, his clothes

[5] Louis E. Raths and Stephen Abrahamson, *Student Status and Social Class* (Bronxville, N. Y.: Modern Education Service, Box 26), 1950.

As the teacher attempts to build a social structure that has qualities stimulating for growth, he asks himself these questions about his use of rewards and punishments:

Am I aware of what factors influence my distribution of rewards and punishments?

Am I aware of how the pupils see my distribution of rewards and punishments?

How much do I appeal to extraneous motivation for the accomplishment of goals?

Are the rewards given within the reach of all or only a select few?

Are the norms established as worthy of reward consistent with democratic values, or do they tend to set people against each other, or to depreciate a variety of competencies and creativities?

Many classrooms, reflecting all too accurately the success theme of American culture, place such a high value upon being successful that deviant behavior is actually encouraged. Let's see how this works. If success is interpreted as reading unusually well or receiving high marks, as it is in many classes, and only a small percentage can by definition attain these goals, then the remainder have two alternatives: to seek success by any means or to reject the goal as one worthy of attainment. Much of the deviant behavior of youth that our culture is coping with at the present time doubtless has its roots in this phenomenon. The success value is expressed all too well by Andrew Carnegie: "Be a king in your dreams. Say to yourself, 'My place is at the top.'" There's only room for one at the top—a precarious perch. When we motivate for this type of success, we motivate nearly everyone to seek the unattainable. The newcomer to our culture, the dark-skinned youth, the street boy of our city slums, the slowly developing child of ambitious parents, the handicapped youngster soon sees that the only way he can get to the top is by some devious means not sanctioned by society. A dilemma confronts him: "Shall I turn my back on the American dream or seek it by fair means or foul? What matters as long as I get to the top?" So we get cheating at West Point, scoffing at learning, derision of adults who are associated with schooling, and a mutinous attitude toward authority. If we are to obtain desirable types of behavior, we must study the social structure in our classrooms to see how compatible the means and ends we use are with the realizable goals of those we teach.

ACCEPTABLE CONTENT. In addition to the controls used and the rewards and punishments given out by the teacher, the *content* of the classroom has a vital effect upon structure. The teacher, in cooperation with his pupils, attempts to design a challenging, growth-giving program. He asks himself and the learners questions such as these: What activities are acceptable as a part of our learning experiences? How do we decide how we shall spend our time together, what we shall work on, what we need to learn? How wide is the variety of activity that is rewarded? Is the girl who makes pretty pictures rewarded as respectably as the one who reads *Atlantic Monthly?* Are the stage-hands considered as important to the show as the actors? Does Georgia feel free to admit without loss of respect that she can't read that fifth-grade book? All these considerations affect the structure that is constantly changing and evolving. Whatever its form, it is pushing, shaping, and affecting the pupils and what they learn. If the content is boring, limited, not related to the interests of the learners, we can expect extraneous facts to influence the structure.

AWARENESS OF PEER STRUCTURE. In every classroom, growing in strength as the pupils grow, a peer structure exists which is functioning alongside, in conflict with, or in harmony with the structure that we have been discussing. The teacher can never know this structure completely, for he is outside it. To the degree that he understands its existence, its sanctions and non-sanctions, its patterns and practices, he will be able to communicate effectively with those he teaches.

You recall we defined structure as the hierarchy of statuses within the group. To discover the statuses that boys and girls ascribe to each other, the teacher has to know their choice patterns in a wide variety of situations. This is known as sociometry; it is employed by asking pupils to make choices of the three or five people whom they would select for a given task or a given occasion. To learn the techniques of sociometry, we refer you to *Sociometry and Group Relations.*[6] The teacher may also give the pupils a chance to express their dislikes by choosing anyone whom they especially would not want to work or be with.

From the data secured from the sociogram (a picture of choices, developed by the teacher), the teacher learns in a rather precise way about the peer social structure. For instance, he finds out which children have

[6] Helen Hall Jennings, *Sociometry and Group Relations* (Washington, D. C.: American Council on Education, 1951).

been chosen most frequently. These are called (unfortunately, we believe) the "stars." Some discreetly put questions, a lot of attentive listening, and sound reflection by the teacher usually makes clear the reasons why these people have been so frequently chosen.

Likewise the teacher finds out which children have not been chosen by anyone. These are called the "isolates." They are usually people who,

if absent, would not be missed. One cannot keep from reflecting what their feelings are in a social climate of this type! If dislikes have been sought, the teacher learns which of the pupils are actively and vigorously rejected by enough of the class that they live in a negative climate. Again, the teacher is not content to know *who;* he searches in all the ways at his command to discover *why.* Some research seems to indicate that the mental health of the rejectees is more positive than that of the isolates. At least in being rejected they have succeeded in being felt.

A fourth characteristic that the teacher looks for as he studies choice patterns are the mutual choices. One of the principles that applies here is that the more mutuals in a group the greater the cohesiveness of the group. The teacher also examines the other choices of mutuals to see how alike or different they are.

Another important characteristic of the structure of the group that sociometry yields is the sub-group formation. Some sub-groups are so rigidly structured that they become cliques; that is, no one chooses anyone outside the membership of the sub-group, and an outsider has little chance of getting into the group. Other sub-groups are composed of a much-chosen individual and the three or four people to whom he is the center of choice. Sometimes the sub-groups are formed by neighborhood patterns; in some instances they cluster around two rival boys or girls or a rival boy and girl; sometimes participants in a very popular out-of-school activity form the basis for sub-group membership. For instance, in some suburban communities the youngsters who take dancing lessons at "Madame Dubarry's Salon" may form one group who tend to "stick together" and exclude those who don't. Children who ride the bus to a city school may be a sub-group. Sometimes you find all the small boys forming a clique. "In numbers there is strength," they seem to be saying. Whatever the causes for the sub-group formation, it is helpful for the teacher to know the membership of sub-groups, the reasons for the sub-groups existing, and the degree of rigidity of the groups; the youngsters themselves know these facts and function in relation to them. Timothy, for instance, was working on sub-group membership in this case:

> There are times when you can actually see that Timothy is trying to break into one of the sub-groups. One particular incident was very revealing. The class had asked if they could make stuffed animals for Easter. The teacher agreed to allow them to do this if I agreed to cut out the patterns. This is the first time that they had done anything like this and there was quite a lot of excitement in the room. The group broke into sub-groups as they worked. Many of the children were having trouble handling a needle. Timothy had no trouble at all. He was always one step ahead of the rest of the group. As soon as the children noticed his work and started to comment that he was ahead of them, he slowed down and tried to help them. He went from group to group and offered to thread needles, turn the animals inside out or stuff them as needed. His animal was the first one to be finished and the teacher put it up as a sample until the others were also completed. You could just see Timothy beam as different teachers or students who came into the room noticed his stuffed animal. I had not seen him so happy since I had come to the class. He had finally found something he could do well. The rest of the group looked up to him and yet felt good about him for hadn't he helped them, too?

The teacher's goal in studying peer structure is to develop a fluid climate in which choices tend to become more inclusive and are made for purposes compatible with growth. This goal is never accomplished by ignoring or fighting the peer structure as it is known and felt by the pupils. It is accomplished by consciously building a climate in which a more appropriate structure emerges.

Although other means are available to the teacher in learning about the peer structure, sociometry gives the most complete and precise picture.

The knowledge gained by sociometry should be supplemented by careful observation, parent conferences, interviews with pupils, and any other creative ways of learning what makes these boys and girls tick. Many of these tools are discussed in the following chapter.

By understanding the structure, the teacher learns the quality and flow of communication in the group. One of the studies made of the sociometric data is the chains of communication that exist in the group. Have you ever worked with a group in which everything seemed to become known and was clearly understood almost instantly? Contrast this to the group in which, after much discussion of a plan, first one and then another pupil comes up with a question that has been answered many times before. We now know that youngsters receive much of their information from each other. If important links in communication are missing, the teacher may anticipate difficulty in having information understood.

Let's illustrate: Out of ten boys, we find that all communicate or would like to communicate with Elliot, but Elliot only communicates with four. We then have a two-way communication system between Elliot and four of the ten, which looks like the diagram below. The four boys also com-

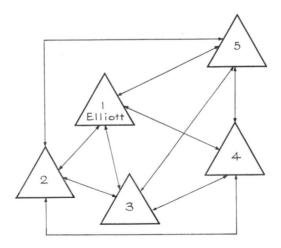

municate with each other. The remainder are not only out of communication with Elliot, but with the other four. Here then is a definite break in our link. If even one of these four communicated with one of the other five, the flow could get around without a break.

Let us suppose that of the five, two talk with each other, one talks to no one, and the remaining two talk with each other. We have a picture like the following diagram. Now we have five additional breaks in our com-

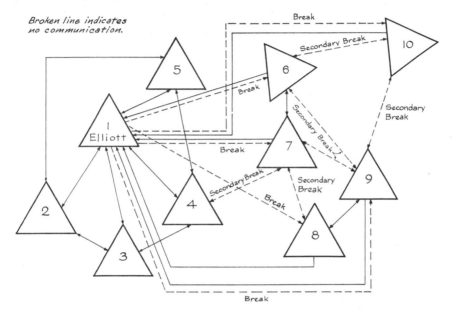

munication link. We have six primary breaks in communication among the ten people, and a number of secondary breaks. The teacher is going to have to make sure that each sub-group understands its responsibilities, or contrive a kind of grouping that cuts across sub-group lines, if he is to prevent a breakdown in communication.

Perception is also affected by structure. If the structure imposes social isolation upon a member of the group, he will doubtless come to see himself as an isolate and begin to behave like one. If the structure is a punitive one in which pupils learn to fear teachers, the pupils' perceptions of all adults in authority tend to take on this feeling of fear. Some interesting studies reveal the effects of structure upon peer relationships. Individuals tend to change their judgments to conform to the judgments of peer leaders, even when the evidence is clearly contrary to the judgments of the peer leaders.[7]

Obviously, the quality of valuing and of involvement change as structure changes. A group dominated by a well-intentioned but strong clique,

---

[7] Ruth W. Berenda, *The Influence of the Group on the Judgments of Children* (New York: King's Crown Press, 1950).

sanctioned even unconsciously by the teacher, results in a different hierarchy of status than one in which the teacher is aware of the structure and is contriving to keep it fluid and compatible with the greatest growth of the largest number.

STUDY OF TEACHER'S EFFECTS UPON STRUCTURE. In "Group Emotion and Leadership," [8] Redl describes ten types of central persons who exert enough influence upon the group to be instrumental in group formation because of the emotions they are able to evoke. Four of these types, as he describes them, are teachers; the types are applicable to any adult-child relationship. A teacher serves to evoke emotions by becoming an object of identification on the basis of either love or fear. Clearly a different social structure exists in these two situations. The teacher with whom the children identify on the basis of love, by recognizing the drives of the children, secures the desire of the children to be like him. Outward pressure is seldom necessary to maintain order and a work atmosphere. The teacher with whom the children identify on the basis of fear secures easy submission and unquestioning obedience. Now and then a youngster dares to rebel at which time he finds everyone against him for these pupils have truly identified with and incorporated the teacher's values into their own personalities.

Another basis for becoming a central person in a group is as an object for either love drives or aggressive drives. Doubtless the reader recalls some attractive young teacher he has had who served as the focal emotional release for a group of students, much as Liberace serves for audiences of middle-aged women. All of us have observed the teacher who was such an object of hatred that whenever pupils came together, Mrs. _____ was hung from a limb in effigy. She was serving as an object of aggressive drives. Each of these types of teachers has a major role in establishing and maintaining the structure of the classroom. The reader might try to analyze the structure he observes in classrooms and identify the teacher's role in its development.

Group Roles

The roles one plays in a given situation are the dynamic aspects of one's status. Trudy is the class president. As she carries out this status

---

[8] Fritz Redl, "Group Emotion and Leadership," in *Small Groups*, eds., Hare, Borgatta, and Bales (New York: Alfred A. Knopf, 1955), pp. 71-86.

position, she assumes a variety of roles that give her status its dynamic quality. Every human being has the capacity to play more roles than he ordinarily does. One of the goals of group living is to release each individual to feel competent to play a variety of roles, and to structure the situation so that he has opportunities to play these roles. We often hear teachers remark that Susie, Linda, and Chuck do everything so well. They are so dependable. These three are counted on to carry out a wide variety of roles—often at the expense of others who need the experience of trying out what they can do. Sometimes we forget that school is a place to learn, not a place to perform already learned roles. When we fail to give the less competent a chance to learn new roles, we also short-change the more competent, for they might well be learning the roles of encourager, facilitator, and expeditor—roles denied them as long as they are the doers, the initiators. The roles we play differ from one situation to another. I am a different *me* when I am giving a lecture to an unknown audience than when I am teaching my own classes. I am a still different me when entertaining friends in my home or hunting wild flowers in the spring.

ROLE COMPATIBILITY NECESSARY FOR MENTAL HEALTH. The roles we play may be compatible or incompatible with each other. Sad is the plight of one who feels he must play a role not in tune with his life-style! If the roles are too incompatible and are required too frequently, the strain on mental health is considerable. The unity of personality is eaten away and broken up. The discerning teacher studies the compatibility of roles sanctioned by the school. One common incompatibility of role occurs when we admonish pupils to love one another, to be unselfish, to share with others, and in the next breath we urge defeating one's friends and playmates by winning first prize or making the highest marks.

CLARITY OF ROLE EXPECTATION NECESSARY. Another factor the teacher must study is how clearly the boys and girls with whom we work understand the demands of the roles they are expected to assume. Lack of clarity in role expectation leads to frustration and anxiety. Indeed, teachers have considerable difficulty in clarifying their own roles. Some teachers assume that they cannot teach and become involved in controversial questions. Some teachers assume that they can, and they do, only to discover that the community (or some vocal part of it) has a different expectation of the roles of teachers. Teachers have to help their pupils think through carefully what is expected of the different roles they assume. A prior step, of course, is to make sure that the classroom experience gives ample opportunity for "trying-on" a variety of roles in circumstances where the pupils can afford to make mistakes.

A well-established practice in schools is to have someone in the classroom responsible for helping visitors to enjoy their visit and to understand the procedures of the class. The possible interpretations of this role leave a wide margin of uncertainty for the inexperienced host. The designated pupil may interpret his role as one of isolating the visitor from the rest of the class. Has he not been assigned the task of caring for the visitor's wants? He may interpret his role as just seating the visitor and introducing him to someone close by who would then carry on. He may contrive so that the visitor is limited to becoming acquainted with his special friends only. He may interpret his role as one of planning the visitor's entire time. Just what is expected of the individual who has the responsibility of host or hostess? Unless the individual understands what others expect of his role, he stands a good chance of carrying out his role in such a way that others are dissatisfied. He may develop anxiety and a sense of failure because he does not know what is expected of him.

The ways we perceive our roles depend upon our own individual needs and our ability to put ourselves in the other's place accurately enough to gain an added dimension to the perceptions of our own individual needs. To return to our host, let us suppose that the pupil designated for this role needed much attention. Acting only on his own needs, he might be led to "hog" the visitor's time and attention. If he has had some chance to build a self-other perception, his individual needs have a chance of being diluted by the process of self-criticism so that he knows he must share the visitor.

One teacher describes how she helped one shy child to understand her role as follows:

> I decided to help Barbara come out of her shell by putting her into a position where she could help her classmates in something she was capable of doing. It is now Barbara's turn to be in charge of the paint corner. We stayed after school one afternoon and went over all the details of running the paint corner. It was important that Barbara should feel confident about every detail of the job. Barbara sets up the paint corner every day, calls the children who paint that day, gets them the materials they want, helps them mix paints, and cleans up, and hangs their pictures to dry. I think the children sense they can depend on her. I can tell because they

go to her with their problems about the paint corner or their needs for more materials. She is now in a position to talk to all children in the class—a few weeks ago she spoke to no one.

Barbara was not only learning the roles expected of one who is in charge of the paints, but she was also gaining necessary skill and confidence to assume other roles that up to this time had been outside the realm of possibility for her.

NECESSARY TO STUDY REWARDS GIVEN ROLES. The rewards given roles assumed—if narrowly conceived—lead to frustration. Wise teachers analyze what they reward in their classrooms. If rewards are limited to a narrow range of role-taking activities, a major part of the group is being frustrated. The most common "prize" role in the elementary school is to be a "good reader." Now if all or the majority of the children read as well as the "good reader," he is no longer *the* good reader and the role has lost its significance. If only the good readers, who by definition must be few, receive rewards in the form of added prestige from the teacher, those who cannot be good readers must necessarily feel inferior. Today we seem to be bent upon rewarding above all others those who have unusual scientific ability. This seems to be a sure way to direct many individuals into science who will be mediocre scientists, but who might be superb social workers, teachers, artists, musicians, or....

GROUP ROLES AS SEEN BY PEERS. A teacher has little knowledge of a group until he perceives the roles that boys and girls assign to each other in various situations and understands the probable responses of each of his pupils to the emergents that develop from the functioning of these roles. Many social psychologists have built categories of roles that are usually found in groups. You will probably attach more meaning to any categorization if you try developing one of your own as you study a group. For some interesting categories, we refer you to Benne and Sheats,[9] Cunningham,[10] and Redl.[11] In most groups, we find individuals who may be designated as leaders, clowns, attention-getters, hair-splitters, organiz-

[9] Kenneth Benne and Paul Sheats, "Functional Roles of Group Members," *The Journal of Social Issues*, Spring 1948, pp. 41-49.

[10] Ruth Cunningham, *Understanding Group Behavior of Boys and Girls* (New York: Bureau of Publications, Columbia University, 1951).

[11] Fritz Redl, "Group Function and Leadership," in *Small Groups*, eds., Hare, Borgatta, Bales (New York: Alfred A. Knopf, 1955), pp. 71-86.

ers, idea people, bullies, model pupils, harmonizers, information-seekers and givers, opinion-seekers and givers, clarifiers, elaborators, evaluators, monopolizers, blockers.

One teacher's analysis of some of the roles she found in her group gives an idea of how a role analysis of a class is made:

Freddy in my fifth-grade class is an easily detected leader. He is a boy who takes the initiative in the group and who leads the entire group. Even in smaller groups, he is the aggressor and often carries the whole group toward its goal. Yet, he is also helpful in maintaining the group, for he takes everyone's suggestions into consideration and keeps them from straying off the topic. He offers constructive criticisms concerning the suggestions of his classmates and does his job so well that he does not seem to dominate the group or monopolize the situation.

Billy is another boy who plays an important role, but of a different type. He is the maintainer and staunch worker, the dependable type who can work successfully with any of his classmates. Ruthie joins Billy in his role of maintenance. Bobby B., on the other hand, is the "inspiration man." He has lots of ideas, but has very poor carrying-through powers. He leaves this to the "old dependables" in the group such as Billy and Ruthie.

Jeffry is a leader sometimes, such as in the area of maps, animals, and current events. However, most of the time he enjoys working on his own without cooperating with anyone.

Then there is Jim, the attention-getter. He will do anything to gain recognition . . . walks around all day, sharpening pencils, going outside, looking at displays around the room, getting up to talk to his friends, and the like. Last Thursday, I timed him . . . he did not sit in his seat for five consecutive minutes. In group work, he must always have a title such as vice-chairman, secretary . . . anything to get attention. Most people in the group do not like to work with Jim.

The role of the class clown goes to Bobby R. with Jonny S. a close runner-up. This boy can make a joke out of anything, and the class recognizes him as a comedian. This is a device he uses to get attention. In committee work, Bobby usually can coerce someone in the group to do his work for him. Everyone likes Bobby because of his jokes.

Jerilyn is one of those people who must have everything perfect and neat. She recopies and recopies page after page. As far as directions are concerned, she, as well as Jeff, must have everything spelled out for her so that she knows, without hesitation, what she must do. All day her questions concern detail. Jerilyn and Jeff are real hair-splitters. Yet, you can count on Jerilyn working well in a group and producing satisfactory results. Jerry is a follower. He must have approval of his work constantly, "Is this right? What should I do next?" Jerry needs a group situation for guidance. He does not work very steadily alone.

A somewhat more dynamic description of roles was made by this student teacher:

> When they are not being closely supervised, one can easily pick out the indigenous group leaders. This leadership shifts from time to time and from activity to activity. There are two group leaders in the class. A girl (Melanie) and a boy (Warren). Both of these children are older than most of the others, and they are both larger. They sit in the back of the room (not near each other). It is interesting to note that these two do not like each other, and they never do things together. They dislike each other and are very quick to tell anyone about it. (This is a sixth-grade class. The boy-girl rivalry is not uncommon at this age.)
>
> There are also other leaders in the group, but they are activity-group leaders. Leslie is the group leader on the playground. He is a very active child and is good in all the games and dances. He is always chosen (by the children as well as by the teacher) to lead their games. Monieva is the group leader whenever the activity centers around music. These children, and others, are task-oriented leaders. Their purpose is to see that a certain activity is carried out. There is only one child in the group that I would say is maintenance-oriented. She will do all she can to keep the group together. She often speaks out of turn to let us know that it is time to do one thing or another. The teacher calls this child the class mother. As in all groups, we have some children who are individually oriented. These children can be the most disruptive influences in the group when the teacher is trying to teach a lesson or when the group is trying to accomplish a purpose.
>
> If I were asked to classify Hezekiah's role in the group I would have to say that he is individually oriented. He is what one might call an attention-seeker. He is not a class leader nor have I ever seen him play the role of a sub-group leader. At times he will try to help me maintain the group, but these times are rare. Hezekiah seems to be trying to become part of the group, and up to this time he has been unable to do so. As a result he has become aggressive, belligerent, and sometimes sulky.
>
> One morning when the group was outside on the playground, Hezekiah was standing by the fence looking at the group. He would run his feet along the fence, turn around, swing his arms, or just stand and look at the children playing. The teacher asked him why he didn't join the rest of the group and he just looked at her and said, "Cause I don't feel like it." All she could do was shake her head and say, "That's a terrible way for a little boy to act. No wonder no one likes you." I wondered how this teacher could see so little of what was going on inside Hezekiah.

Teachers sometimes place a different value on the playing of certain roles than do pupils. We are inclined to place a positive value on the

398

STUDY OF GROUP SITUATIONS

model boy or girl, on the organizer, on the idea man, but pupils may see these roles as quite negative. What teacher does not long for a goodly number of serious-minded, work-inclined, obedient pupils! Yet, if we reward the roles demanding these qualities to the exclusion of those who seek another way to solve the problem, or who have an alternate suggestion as to how we should spend our class day, or who come to school with a favorite gag they wish to try out on their classmates, we do an injustice to those we teach. We make it easy for youngsters to label their classmates, who are playing some highly constructive roles, as teacher's pet, sissy, apple-polisher, and the like.

To secure additional information about roles in any group, try your hand at writing some general descriptions of the roles you find in a group, and then ask each pupil to list the names, including his own name, of the individuals who fit each description. If you, too, carry out the activity, you will discover how your perceptions of roles differ from the pictures the pupils have. For instance, a description of a clown might read: "Here is someone who is always 'cutting up.' He likes to play jokes on people. He wants people to think he is funny and to laugh at the things he does and says." A number of such descriptive paragraphs of the most obvious roles in the group furnishes the material to which the pupils and you respond. As you study these responses, you get three kinds of perceptions: the roles classmates assign to each other; each individual's perceptions of his roles; the teacher's perceptions of roles assumed by class members. Interesting comparisons of perceptions can be made.

Here are some questions we think important for teachers to ask themselves as they study roles in their groups:

What roles do I find represented in this group?
What roles does this group lack?
Who tends to play what roles?
How much flexibility is there among the youngsters in role assumption; that is, do I tend to find the same individuals assuming the same roles regardless of what we are doing?
What kinds of activities tend to produce flexibility in role assumption?
How does each of the group act when the role he has assumed is challenged? Suppose Theresa volunteers to referee the ball game and the group turns down her offer. What does she do—pout, protest to the group, seek the teacher's help, or . . . ?
How does each act when the group accepts the role he assumes, or pressures him to change his role?

How jealous is each individual of the roles he tends to accept in the group? Is he willing to relinquish his place on the room committee to someone who has not yet served, for instance?

How much feeling for the group (pride, joy, acceptance, rejection, indifference, ambition) do his roles reveal?

How are the boys and girls working on their own needs by the roles they assume? One student gives an excellent illustration of this as follows:

Most of Larry's efforts this term have been fixed on "belonging." With him the effort has been so determined and consistent that it was impossible to miss. With other children it is far less apparent and unless I was deliberately looking for it, I think that I might not have noticed how universal this goal is. I can see now how this drive reacts differently in children and how it explains much of their behavior. It accounts for the seemingly vicious and irrational act of filling a lavatory knee-deep with toilet paper on the part of a wealthy but isolated child. It explains the silent withdrawal of another, or the malicious destruction of a neighbor's property by still another. It can account for the creation of a scapegoat, and conversely for a hero. Every child is striving to belong —one by buying his friends with rides in his junior Thunderbird, another by making a clown of himself for the class' entertainment, and still another by always being the "good guy." The teacher's responsibility is to help the child find a place in his social milieu by creating an atmosphere which is accepting of all children and of all kinds of ability. If the teacher can really help the children to see that this is possible, and then if he can create situations that illustrate his belief, I think it will help children to believe and act upon the idea in their own peer relations.

Answers to these questions give the teacher the kind of information he needs to understand the ways in which group roles are functioning and how he can improve the learning environment. The teacher uses this information in these ways:

If necessary roles are missing, he works with group members to help them realize that the group needs an evaluator, an information-giver, or whatever roles are lacking. The lack of roles is not always apparent until one begins to look for this information.

If pupils are confining themselves to a narrow range of roles, the teacher tries to set the stage for wider role assumption. He may find that the types of activities in the classroom require only a narrow range of roles; that to help boys and girls learn to assume other roles, other types of activities are required. Or perhaps the group has come to depend upon a few of their classmates to carry the ball and the others have developed the habit of sitting back with the attitude of, "Let George do it."

If individual pupils reveal difficulty in handling such matters as sharing, taking turns, being rejected, challenged or pressured, the teacher works with the particular individual. Certain of these problems may be endemic to certain groups and need to be tackled as group problems.

Group Atmosphere

The atmosphere or climate of a group in many ways seems to be a product of the structure and roles found in a group; yet it is so definable a factor that we consider it separately. Groups develop distinctive atmospheres. We often speak of a group that gets things done, a group that finds it hard to settle down to business, a group that is easily upset, a group that is argumentative. If you spend any amount of time in a group day after day, you come to expect a certain quality in the climate or atmosphere of that group. This is a factor that helps us to recognize one group from another.

The atmosphere in the same group varies. Sometimes we step inside a classroom and we know immediately that this is the wrong day to visit that room just as we sometimes sense this in families when we drop in. We feel the tenseness in the air, although we would be hard put to identify what causes it.

As we are learning about human behavior, we want to develop some understanding about what produces certain types of atmosphere. As we mentioned earlier, structure and roles are certainly important aspects of group atmosphere. If the structure is rigidly controlled, we usually get an atmosphere that has slight toleration for the unexpected. If the control used is fear, we get an atmosphere that feels different from that in which the control is love. That the distribution and flexibility of role assumption affects the atmosphere is obvious. Watch for typical atmospheres in classrooms and try to discover what creates certain moods in groups. See if you can find out what kinds of moods are associated with certain activities. Do you hear the group saying, "Oh, do we *have* to have spelling today?" or acting as if they were saying it? Or do you hear, "Teacher, it's time for spelling!" How does the group respond to clean-up? Does it put them in a mutinous mood, a horseplaying mood, or is it done matter-of-factly? The following moods are frequently observed in a group: restless, disorganized, tense, morose, punitive, silly, peaceful, quiet, reflective, appreciative, good-humored, overly-active, active, curious.

Another aspect of group atmosphere that requires study is group manageability. Some groups are much easier to handle than others. Doubtless the personality structure of the members makes a great difference. One individual may infect the entire group with a certain mood and make it unmanageable. Such a boy was Auroro:

> One morning in particular I noticed that things were starting off very well. Some of the more industrious children had come in first and started to work on their logs while some of the so-called trouble-makers had not yet arrived. At 8:55 most of the group was working quietly and I was smiling to myself. This was going to be a good day for all, or so I thought. At 8:59 Auroro came in. It didn't take me long to find out that this was going to be one of his bad days. He didn't have his notebook with him, so I gave him some paper to do his log on. He sat and looked at the paper, then he said, "I can't do my log. I have no pencil." I gave him a pencil. Again he just sat there. I thought that I had better leave well enough alone and said nothing. But Auroro was not satisfied with my reaction. He shouted, "I can't remember anything we done yesterday." By this time the group was beginning to get restless, so I asked several children to read their logs. Auroro was angry and shouted out, "I ain't done mine yet."

Within a half hour the group was almost as restless and out of humor as Auroro. They could not do any independent work, nor could they sit still for any length of time. That morning during recess nothing was right. Neither the teacher nor I could keep them controlled. By now Auroro had calmed down a little, but the group had caught the fever and they had it all the long day.

Some of the facets to explore as you study the manageability of groups are:

How manageable is this group as compared with other groups I have known?

How easily are they thrown into a panic or upset?

How much can they do independently, and what activities can they manage by themselves?

What activities seem to leave the group in an unmanageable state?

What do they do when they become unmanageable?

How do they relate to me, the adult, when they become unmanageable? Do they argue, fight, call names? Do they stick together in their defiance of authority?

Many of these questions are "touched on" in this analysis of group atmosphere:

Certain attitudes or moods are apparent when certain activities occur. The children are calmer in the morning and more able to concentrate on such subjects as arithmetic and science or anything else which requires their attention. After lunch, they are a bit unruly and are less controllable. Knowing this, we usually schedule a light curriculum for the afternoon. Just before recess the class gets a bit jumpy. After they have let off steam at recess, they are able to sit and concentrate better. They are also less controllable on rainy days as compared with sunny ones. This may well be because they are indoors so much. If the class must sit for a period of forty-five minutes, they require an activity that lets them walk around, otherwise they are restless. Special periods often create excitement in my class. The boys are better behaved when they have something concrete and definite to work on than when they have music or creative writing.

A further facet of group atmosphere is to study the group's toleration for deviant behavior. Peer groups have their own code. It may or may not coincide with the adult standards which are generally seen as imposed. This code covers such areas of behavior as tattling, helping the teacher, conforming to teacher demands, conforming to peer rituals, acceptance and rejection of items of dress, speech, manners, and other similar things.

We think the following analysis shows an insightful understanding of peer codes.

> The "teacher's pet" in my class is not considered one of the gang. If a child called another the "teacher's pet," that child would consider it an insult. However, I've noticed that no one criticizes Mary when she brings apples or candy to the teacher. They all accept her as a child who does exactly as she pleases, and lives inside herself. In fact, they are generally kind to Mary, except at dancing time when the boys have to choose partners. They generally consider themselves "stuck" when they get Mary as a partner, although she is a good dancer. They make the best of it. If you are intelligent or clever in this group, you are admired and respected. The children who do their work well are very popular.
>
> According to the code, you are not supposed to give too much time or attention to the teacher, that is, to converse very often on your own time. Very often Freddy or one of the others will stall fixing his books or desk at dismissal time, and when the class leaves, he comes up to me for a discussion of some subject or problem. However, disrespect to the teacher is not accepted. On one occasion, one of the boys answered very fresh to me before the entire class and another boy said, "You should have more respect for Miss Angelo." You might also hear, "Don't you understand the teacher wants quiet!" or "Let's stop the hacking around."
>
> No one is supposed to tattle on another, although you are not an outcast if you do. If you create a discipline problem, you are not in much demand with the others. The steady, hard worker and very often the one who is not the top student is liked the most.
>
> To be accepted and popular, you should also like a member of the opposite sex so that your classmates can joke with you about it. It is good-natured razzing and the one concerned pretends to be embarrassed. However, if you have no girl or boy friend, you are left out of the fun.
>
> If you want to be rejected by the group, just try being selfish with your possessions or a "bragger" about everything you've got. The ones who share are respected for it.

The teacher may be quite in the dark about the peer code unless he adopts the kids' perspective as he watches them. We like Redl's term here, "The teacher has to get the worm's view." His first task is to learn in what areas the code operates and what its specifics are. Then he studies how rigidly the code is enforced by the peer group. Some questions the teacher asks himself are:

> What gives a pupil the most prestige among his peers in this group?
> What makes him lose face or be labelled a sissy, mamma's boy, teacher's pet?

What kinds of behavior are ruled out as completely unacceptable? For instance, is it all right for a boy to knit or to bring his baby sister to visit his class or to hold the door open for the teacher?

To what degree does the peer code recognize individual differences? For instance, is the little boy expected to be as good a ball player as the large boy? Is he ridiculed or isolated if he isn't, or are allowances made for his size? One delightful story we heard was of the boys moving the pitcher's box closer to the batter when the small boys came up to bat.

How does the group enforce its code? Is it punitive, rejective, or does it work out ways by which nearly all can have some satisfaction in the activities of the group?

Need we remind ourselves that whatever the peer code is and whatever the means of enforcing the code, they have been learned. If we wish to find out why some groups are punitive toward their members who don't quite measure up, we must examine the types of adult leadership they have known. A classic study revealing the effects of atmosphere upon the behavior of the members of a group was made by Lewin, Lippitt, and White.[12] In order to find out the effects that the leader had upon the atmosphere of the group, individuals were trained to assume the behaviors of a laissez-faire, a democratic, and an autocratic leader. They then studied the behaviors of the same groups with each of these different types of leaders. The group with a laissez-faire leader was least effective, both in work produced and in satisfied feelings. The group with an autocratic leader produced as much as the group with a democratic leader, but their products were less creative and they had little personal pride in their work. During the course of the autocrat's "regime," scapegoating was a common occurrence, and much aggression that could not be directed toward the leader was taken out on the other club members. The group with a democratic leader produced as much as the one with an autocratic leader, but their work was much more creative, and the members had a sense of pride and accomplishment in their work. The feelings in this group were such that work went on while the leader was out of the room, everyone helped in clean-up, plans were shared with all members, members sought help from one another as well as from the leader, and no organized aggression was directed toward any member. This experiment, which was repeated in a number of settings and which was filmed

---

[12] Kurt Lewin, "Experiments in Social Space," *Harvard Educational Review*, 9, January 1939, p. 31.

by the University of Iowa,[13] clearly demonstrates the teacher's effect upon atmosphere.

Group Purpose

Perhaps you wonder that purpose is included as a factor that needs studying as we work with groups. After all, isn't the purpose in the classroom to learn the "three R's"? If this were true, teaching would be one of the easiest professions instead of one of the most demanding. Today the purposes of education are broad enough to encompass the totality of the pupil's life within school. This requires the teacher to think through his purposes, to see if they really do promote, encourage, and stimulate growth so as to create a life-style uniquely suited to each individual.

The crucial question we must ask ourselves about purpose is: "Whose purposes are each of the pupils working on?" Obviously each teacher has purposes in his teaching process, but they have little meaning to the learners (pupils) until they see the relationship between their purposes and the teacher's. Establishing and working with purpose in a classroom is further complicated by the fact that boys and girls come to school involuntarily. With this involuntary group, we cannot assume that all boys and girls are in school because they want to be nor in a certain teacher's room because they want to be with that teacher or with those boys and girls. We can assume, however, that all children do have purposes. Sinnot[14] expresses this theory from a biological viewpoint and Allport[15] from a psychological one.

The teacher's role in working with the purposes of his pupils is twofold: to discover the purposes of each of his pupils, and to help these boys and girls establish relationships between their own purposes and the school program. Section Two of this book includes much data about the purposes that can be expected of children and youth at various ages. Knowing children's purposes, the teacher is ready to incorporate those purposes into the school program and to extend them into deeper, more complicated applications.

---

[13] *Experimental Climates in Social Space*, 30 min., silent, University of Iowa Film Library.

[14] Edmund W. Sinnott, *Cell and Psyche* (Chapel Hill: University of North Carolina Press, 1950).

[15] Gordon Allport, *Becoming* (New Haven: Yale University Press, 1955).

This we do know: no man grows by applying himself to someone else's purposes. We must attend to those things which have importance for us, or we begin the process of withering and dying. Yet the teacher must lead his pupils into deeper channels of knowledge and insight. To accomplish this is not as difficult as it may at first appear—if we understand what we are doing. Young, immature human beings usually have a wide, wide range of interests, and they also are easy to interest. They become absorbed in those areas of learning in which adults whom they like and respect are interested. The number one task of the teacher is to lead, not coerce, his pupils into challenging areas of endeavor by utilizing the interests of his pupils and himself. *Liking you, your pupils will want to be like you.* As we lead, we ask ourselves:

Am I giving my pupils a chance to express themselves freely so that I may discover their deeper purposes and concerns?

Is the program flexible enough to incorporate the pupils' purposes as group goals?

Am I prepared to keep the school program flexible enough that it has room for the highly personal, idiosyncratic purposes that emerge? Am I giving each pupil a chance to develop his life-style, in other words?

Do I understand the process of planning with pupils so that purposes are translated into challenging activities?

Does the structure of the group encourage creative, challenging purposes? (Let's not become mere gadgeteers just because we live in an age of gadgets.)

Involvement in group enterprises comes about as a result of the teacher's working with the purposes of his pupils so that they become their goals. If one is working on his own purposes, he is involved. If we are skillful in the way we work with groups, no insoluble conflict arises between individual and group goals. Individual goals are enhancements of the group, rather than threats to the group.

Group Activities

The activities in the group furnish the means by which much of the structure, roles, atmosphere, and purposes become real. We have stated a number of principles relating to group activities as we have discussed these other factors. Let us summarize them at this point:

Activities must be varied enough to utilize the range of individual differences in the group.

The prestige value of activities is related to the pupils' purposes more directly than to the teacher's standards.

Every member of a group has something to contribute. It is the teacher's role to discover the competencies of each pupil and then give him a chance to use them for the benefit, not at the expense, of his classmates.

Activities organized with a full knowledge of group structure, roles, purposes, and atmosphere have greater learning potential than those that lack such knowledge.

Activities must take into account the principles of variety, timing, appropriateness, relevancy, pacing.

Analysis of Group Characteristics
As stated earlier, all the factors of a group give it the characteristics by which it comes to be known. The four characteristics of communicating, perceiving, valuing, and involvement are identifiable in all groups. We have noted how the various factors help determine these characteristics; how structure, for example, directly affects who talks to whom about what; and how purposes determine the degree and quality of involvement. As we try to assess the effectiveness of a group, we apply certain criteria to determine the quality of the four characteristics, and thus the quality of group functioning.

Criteria for Effectiveness of Communicating

Are the breaks in communication links at a minimum?

Does communicating flow freely between teacher and all pupils? Does it flow among pupils without going through the teacher?

Does communicating cut across narrow group lines determined by neighborhood, social-class, religion, minority groups, academic snobbishness?

Is the responsibility for formal communicating (reporting, entertaining, investigating, evaluating) well-distributed among class members?

Are the members of the group becoming familiar with modern methods of communicating: tape-recording, television, voice writers, feed-backs, radio, films, other visual means?

Is the group learning to respect the necessity of communicating *feelings* as well as factual data?

Is the group recognizing the importance of knowing *who* said it as well as *what* was said?

Are pupils learning to handle effectively more difficult and complex ideas and feelings as they grow?

Criteria for Effectiveness of Perceiving

Are pupils given many opportunities to develop perceptions of others' feelings?

Do group activities give opportunities for developing self-criticism?

Does the group function so as to help pupils develop accurate perceptions of the roles they assume in a variety of situations?

Are pupils developing the kinds of perceptions that give them healthy respect for authority?

Are pupils developing expanding perceptions of how sound decisions are made?

Are pupils perceiving how individual uniqueness may be utilized in the achievement of group goals?

Are pupils learning to perceive adults as friendly, helpful guides who can be relied upon to aid them?

Are pupils perceiving expanding relationships as one of the major goals of group functioning?

Are pupils perceiving self-direction as a major developmental task of maturing?

Are we helping pupils to become consciously aware of *why* they perceive *what* they perceive?

Are pupils becoming more sensitive about the effects of their actions and attitudes upon others?

Criteria for Effectiveness of Involvement

Are pupils involved in their own processes of learning to the extent that they are active in:

Setting their own goals
Trying out a variety of means to achieve goals
Evaluating their own purposes and results
Developing their own controls
Developing their own rewards and punishments
Choosing their own activities for learning

Are pupils involved in a wide variety of decision-making situations, the outcomes of which matter to them?

Is involvement in class activities distributed among all members?

Are all types of involvement rewarded with respect from the teacher and pupils?

Is there sufficient involvement so that the group can handle conflict and differences without being weakened?

Is there an allowance for differences in feeling concerning the degree of involvement desirable? Are pupils allowed to be alone, to be non-participators, and yet merit as much respect as the participators?

Are the range and depth of involvement expanding with age?

Criteria for Effectiveness of Valuing

Are values a conscious part of the school program?

Are pupils helped daily to examine their own values in a variety of situations?

Are value discussions directed toward human values?

Are pupils led to perceive their own values against a backdrop of values of other cultures?

Are pupils helped to examine their own feelings in real situations in such ways as to understand others' feelings?

Are pupils taught to think about consequences to others and to themselves as they make decisions?

Is there a consistent examination of activities, decisions, structure, and purposes in terms of democratic values?

Do we examine the conflicts that arise in values in such ways that pupils learn alternative solutions to problems?

Is the range and depth of value application continuously expanding and deepening with age and experience?

Are values examined in terms of inclusiveness of human beings, long-term goals, recognition of individual uniqueness, and individual need and growth toward altruism?

Group Goals

If groups function so that these criteria of effectiveness are consciously applied, we believe that the goals of groups (developing healthy relationships, making sound decisions, and solving complex problems) will be achieved. To achieve such functioning, the teacher needs to know how to study group situations and how to interpret what he perceives in his studies. The teacher's skill increases as he studies groups. Since all of us are members of groups, we have ready-made laboratories. To become sensitive to group interaction, try charting it; to learn about roles, actually make some role identification analyses; to discover how people perceive, test it out. All these are functions you can carry out inconspicuously and without formal arrangements. We have made a number of suggestions at the end of this chapter for studying groups that we hope you will try out. There's no time like now to start!

Suggestions for Further Exploration

► Select a group that you are with rather frequently but for which you are not responsible, and try making these analyses of its functioning:

Make a sociogram of the group. Identify the stars, isolates, mutuals, cliques. Analyze the communication patterns. See if you can arrange some working groups that may help to make the structure more democratic.

Write a description of the atmosphere you feel in this group on three different occasions. Try to analyze the causes for differences perceived and identify the common elements in the atmosphere.

Make a role identification analysis (see pages 395-398) of the members of the group. Ask the members to do likewise. Compare your perceptions with those of the group members.

Make a list of all appeals that are made over a period of a few weeks to group loyalty. Analyze the causes and effects of such appeals.

Interview three or four members of the group to see what they consider the purposes of the group are. Interview the adult leader and compare the statements of the adult with those of the members.

Try to find out what these youngsters expect an adult leader to do (if it is an out-of-school group). How do they perceive the leader's role?

See if you can observe the peer behavior code at work. Jot down all the situations in which it seems to operate. Find out how aware the adult leader is of the peer code.

Select one person in the group and keep track of all the roles he plays as activities change.

Make a role distribution chart by jotting down all the roles taken by group members for a period of twenty or thirty minutes. Analyze this to see how widely roles are distributed and who takes what roles in particular situations. This is called a role distribution chart.

► If possible, view the following films and discuss them with your classmates:

Our Invisible Committees, 30 min., sound, distributed by National Education Association and New York University Film Library.

This is a stimulating film showing how members of a group are influenced by the pressures and forces in their lives; these pressures serve as invisible committees that direct one's action in groups.

Role-Playing in Human Relations Training, 30 min., sound, distributed by National Education Association and New York University Film Library.

An excellent teaching device to show how role-playing may be used to stimulate discussion and bring about solutions to problems.

Additional Sources You May Find Helpful

Adult Education Association, *Leadership Pamphlet Series*. Washington, D. C.: National Education Association.
Each pamphlet in this continuing series is about fifty pages in length. Titles of some of the most valuable to date are: How to Lead Discussions, Understanding How Groups Work, How to Use Role-Playing. *Sound and readable material.*

Kenneth D. Benne and Bozidar Muntyan, *Human Relations in Curriculum Change*. New York: Dryden Press, 1951.
An excellent source to develop a basic understanding of how groups work in the classroom situation.

Dorwin Cartwright and Alvin Zander, *Group Dynamics: Research and Theory*. Evanston, Ill.: Row, Peterson and Company, 1953.
This is an excellent reference book to consult as questions arise about the functioning of groups. Contains important research on group cohesiveness, group pressures and group standards, group goals and group locomotion, the structural properties of groups, and leadership.

Ned Flanders, *Teaching with Groups*. Minneapolis, Minn.: Burgess Publishing Co., 1954.
An excellent little paper-back that teachers find most useful as they try to use group methods in the classroom.

D. M. Hall, *Dynamics of Group Discussion*. Danville, Ill.: Interstate Printers, 1950.
Another paper-back that explains simply and clearly the roles played by group members, group goals, and methods of evaluating group activities.

A. Paul Hare, Edgar F. Borgatta, and Robert Bales, *Small Groups*. New York: Alfred A. Knopf, 1955.
This is another important reference book on the study of groups. This volume has collected most of the research on small groups and presents it in an organized scheme. Part I, entitled, "Historical and Theoretical Background," is of great value to the student who wishes to delve deeply into the functioning of groups. Also has a most excellent annotated bibliography.

Herbert A. Thelen, *Dynamics of Groups at Work*. Chicago: University of Chicago Press, 1954.
This is a readable, stimulating book. Chapters two and three deal with the methods of group work in classroom situations.

15

Tools for Child and Adolescent Study

How can I tell whether a child's deviant behavior is just a phase or a more serious symptom that needs attention?

How much value is there in teachers' keeping anecdotal records?

How can I help a child learn to work in a group, or to become more self-directive?

What are some ways of discovering deep needs?

What does a test score mean?

How can I be sure I'm objectively seeing a child—not just reading in my needs, interests, and motivations?

Teachers often find themselves in a dilemma similar to that of the mother who, holding her howling infant in one arm and clutching Dr. Spock's Baby Book in the other, queries: "Does he want the bottle or cuddling?" This chapter will not give you any definitive answers, for we believe there are none. It will give you a tool-kit to which you can go for help as you apply the theories you learn. It should be read in conjunction with Chapter 16, keeping in mind that an essential quality in using the social science tools is to know, understand, and accept oneself.

Just a word about tools and tool-kits. All of you have doubtless used your hands enough to know that no tool is sharper, more effective for the purposes for which it was designed, more capable of producing satisfying results than the skill of the hands that hold the tool. Tools, then, cannot be evaluated apart from the skill of the user nor apart from the purpose for which they were meant. We would shout in derision to see an adult trying to chop down a giant oak with a child's hatchet. This same hatchet might be most suitable to cut away some surplus shoots. In like manner we would be concerned to see a deadly ax in the hands of one unconcerned about where the chips would fly or how the tree might fall. The appropriate question to ask concerning a tool is: "Can it do the job for which it was designed?" not, "Is it dangerous?" Any tool is dangerous in the wrong hands—even a blunt pair of scissors or a kitchen knife. Every tool is useful when handled by someone who knows what he is doing and has acquired the skill to do it well. The tool must be appropriate for the task at hand. We believe we are past the day when teachers can excuse themselves for not using certain tools because they do not know enough about them. If we do not know, our business is to learn. The desire to know and understand one's motivations is the key to the usefulness of all other skills. This is a never-ending quest.

Teachers need to have not one tool, or two or three, but a kit that includes the necessary means for studying each individual as a whole. An accessory to the kit is knowing where you can borrow the tools that are not available to you. The tools described in this chapter are, for the most part, ones that help a teacher see behavior as an individual matter. Too much of our study of human behavior has been based on a normative concept which obscures the really significant, important uniquenesses. Some simple examples expose the ludicrousness of averages as telling anything significant about an individual. If a child had four fingers on one hand and six on the other, he would average five fingers per hand and have the correct total of ten fingers. Not one of us would consider him an average child in hand formation. If a child has a reading comprehension score of 2.6 and a reading rate score of 6.4, his average reading score is 4.5. But what do we know of the child's skill in reading by the score of 4.5? If this is a fourth-grade child, he is exactly average, yet he comprehends what he has read as a second grader. No group test score throws much light upon understanding an individual.

Many of the tools discussed in this chapter have been mentioned earlier in the book. We shall try here to summarize and extend the information. We cannot discuss any tool in as much detail as we would like. We hope you will feel impelled to consult the sources mentioned to gain additional help in your quest to use tools wisely and creatively.

School Records

Some individuals call records "canned gossip." They are that only in untrained hands. Nearly all schools today systematically keep at least three types of records on all children: cumulative records, health records, and anecdotal records. These are an invaluable source of information. We shall discuss the *keeping* and *using* of these records.

Accuracy, completeness, and up-to-dateness are prime essentials in record keeping. The information on records varies with the form used by a particular school system. Most cumulative records include name, address, family constellation, occupation of parents, language spoken in home, schools attended, attendance, tardiness, and test scores. Many include space for teachers' remarks and some guidance and personality data. Health records include data on vision, hearing, dental health, height, weight, record of school examinations and special health information such as diseases the individual has had, hospital experiences, allergies, heart ailments, and the like. Anecdotal records consist of a series of anecdotes or incidents that the teacher considers significant in the pupil's life. These are written in descriptive form and often are filed with the cumulative record and considered a part of it.

Keeping Anecdotal Records

Since an anecdotal record is a subjective thing, the writer needs help in learning how to record so that incidents carry a high degree of validity. Some authorities discount anecdotal records as being too subjective to be of value. Many years of training teachers lead us to conclude that anecdotal records have many values: (1) teachers can be trained to observe with a highly sensitive ear and eye and sense for selecting what is significant; (2) writing anecdotes over a period of time, about even one child, increases one's ability to observe significant items of behavior and to interpret their meaning; (3) keeping anecdotal records increases the teacher's own self-awareness and self-understanding; (4) keeping anecdotal records, especially if they are used as a basis for group discussion in child and adolescent study groups, tends to highlight weaknesses in the school program.

We have had the most success in training students to write anecdoctal records by asking them to begin their study with a *running account* describing the person selected. You will recall we asked you to do this in Chapter 2. We feel the study has more meaning and wider application if a so-called normal pupil is chosen. In this description, the writer seeks to make the individual come alive so that we recognize him as he comes into the room. In doing this, the observer may wish to present the person in a characteristic situation or type of behavior. Try to be specific, to use words that particularly fit this person. Avoid generalizations. This we have to reiterate and reiterate and reiterate. Avoid generalizations!

A couple of examples of early descriptions that we feel have vitality and authenticity follow:

> Alex is not very conscious about neatness and order. He is usually uncombed and half-washed. His finger nails have a half-moon of grit and grime under them. His shirt is usually half way out of his trousers and his shoes are never polished. His desk is in a state of chaos. He is wearing shoes with two big holes in the soles. He seems completely unaware of their existence. This child sems so wrapped up in what he is doing or what he is thinking that he finds little time to be concerned with the physical environment. Alexander is all boy. He's the first one out of the room at recess and with a whoop and a holler he has a ball game organized in nothing flat. Would that he applied himself as diligently to long-division!

> When we first met, Charles was silent and retired to the safety of his mother's side. He didn't speak for the first fifteen minutes; nevertheless, he was very active. He watched his mother's face and mine carefully as we talked. He smiled, nodded, and several times silently repeated things his mother said. During a lull in the conversation he quietly approached my chair and stood directly in front of me watching me most intently all the while. I smiled at him but he suddenly darted back to his mother's side again. I noticed that his face flushed slightly and that he hung his head and put his fingers slowly to his mouth. When his mother spoke again he was at once alert. Suddenly he leaned over to his mother and urgently whispered in her ear. She nodded and he dashed out of the room. Charles was back in a few seconds with a rather battered toy truck. He came up to my chair and said, "Here is what I got for Christmas when I was a little baby. I was two or one, or was I 'lest' than one, Mommy?" His mother answered that he was about two. Turning to me, he said quickly, "I was two; sometimes I forget about things." Once more he returned to his mother's side but this time he smiled at me and nodded at his truck.

> Charles is about five years old, he is small and wiry. He moves quickly and gracefully. Many of his movements are somewhat "darting" and rapid. When he is unsure or worried he is inclined to put his fingers in his mouth or clench his fists and thrust them quickly into his pockets.

As the observer continues his study of the boy or girl he has selected, he tries to build a moving picture of him. Just as a movie presents only fragments of behavior, so do anecdotal records. The fragments must be chosen so the reader may know the pupil as a whole. This means that the anecdotes often stand for or symbolize recurring patterns or trends of behavior. Some of the helps students have found useful are as follows:

Observe the individual, if at all possible, in free play.
Observe him in as wide a variety of situations as possible:
Using different kind of materials
With his peers only
With adults only
With both peers and adults
In large and small groups
In structured and non-structured activities
Observe for a very short span of time (5 minutes) and record everything that happens, all the bodily action by the participants, the conversation, gestures, use of materials.
Be sure to note others' responses to him as well as his responses to others.
Note his special areas of strength and his special weaknesses.
Be sure to note the body action—muscle tension, gestures, flushing, hand movements, manifestations of nervousness, pitch of voice. This may be called non-verbal communication. Often it tells us more about the person than what he says.

If we wish to know another, we must be able to tune in with his feelings. In some areas attitudes are quite significant for they represent critical phases of growth. We need to be particularly sensitive in observing and recording in these areas.[1]

ATTITUDES TOWARD ADULTS. Adults represent authority. Most of us have some difficulty as we grow up in clarifying our attitudes toward authority. We observe to see if behavior indicates fear of adults, withdrawal from adults, trust and confidence in adults, a feeling of outward compliance and inward rejection, unawareness of adults, resentment of adults.

As we try to determine a child's attitudes, we ask ourselves: How much do adults seem to influence him and in what areas of living? Is he able to share adults whom he loves with others? How does he behave when he is reprimanded or praised by adults? Does he see adults realistically or does he tend to act as if they were someone else (a mother, father, uncle, aunt)? Does he tend to idealize adults he loves so much that he does not realistically see them?

---

[1] We are indebted to Fritz Redl for suggestions secured from unpublished training material in this treatment of what to record.

Here is an interesting anecdote that illustrates an eleven-year-old boy's attitude toward the adult who was studying him:

> I met Michael in the hall Saturday morning as he was on his way to a music lesson. As always he asked me how the cat was and then where I had been. I had my arms full of groceries and another adult resident of the house who was in the hall said, "Why don't you help Miss J. with her packages?," to which Michael replied he had to go to his music lesson. With that he kissed me warmly and departed. It is perhaps significant that he was willing to kiss me in a public hall, and in fact is always demonstrative in his affections with people who show any affection for him. Eleven-year-old boys are not noted for this particular trait. To other boys of his age, and to many adults, this perhaps seems "sissy." I'm not sure that it means anything except that he has an affectionate nature and is willing to express it in accordance with his wishes. In many ways he shows an indifference to what he is "supposed" to be like. I don't know for sure, but I suspect that in an Italian boy, for example, such behavior would be considered quite normal. It is only in our culture, as well as in certain others, that a show of affection by boys is considered abnormal.

ATTITUDES TOWARD ROUTINES. Youngsters identify insistence upon carrying out routines with adults. Does the individual respond readily to routines, does he do his share, does he find ways to involve others, is he always the last one to get his notebook and pencil ready, does he help others even though it isn't his job? Which routines are easier for him? Which ones bring much friction, delay, and perhaps outbursts? Does he tend to respond better to more flexible or more highly structured routines?

ATTITUDES TOWARD PEERS. A person's selection of friends tells much about him. Whom does this individual tend to buddy with? Can you figure out why he selects a certain person as his buddy? Does he tend to like and keep one special friend; does he tend to like to be a member of a group; or both? Can he share his friends with others? How do his peers see him? What roles does he play in his peer group? Is he is a "loner"; if so, does this seem to give him concern? How constant or changeable is he in his friendship patterns? What is his appeal to his peers or why does he appeal? Does he share his possessions with his friends or does he tend to hoard them? Have you ever seen him try to buy friendship with gifts or favors? How loyal is he to the group code? What kind of ethics does he bring to his peer relationships?

These few snatches from anecdotal records illustrate how attitudes toward peers are revealed and recorded:

> Laurie seems not to care what the others think of her. In "Show-and-Tell" she spoke about her Sunday trip and the children made no attempt to be polite. They were squirming and looking around the room. Laurie noticed this, and said very sarcastically, "I hope I'm not boring you." She persisted in talking on until stopped by the teacher, although fully aware of this lack of interest. . . . One of the children brought her pet kitten to school and showed it to each pupil. It was quite obvious that she was extremely fond of the pet and everyone admired it except Laurie who said she didn't like it. One of the children in the class has difficulty in keeping up with the group and Laurie actually laughs aloud with obvious relish when he is unable to answer correctly.

> When I took a sociogram two weeks ago, David's first choice was Roger, one of the less well-liked boys. The reasons for Roger's low position on the sociogram scale is obvious. He is a boy who gives of himself only when he is sure he will get a good return. I have my own suspicions as to why David's first choice was Roger. Roger's father owns a bowling alley. I overheard the two boys talking one afternoon. It seems that Roger took David bowling free of charge. This was the price Roger was paying for David's friendship.

ATTITUDES TOWARD DISCIPLINE. What kinds of discipline has the individual become accustomed to? Can you discover how he feels about the discipline he receives at home? How does he respond to reasoning? Can you tell when he's going to "blow up"? How susceptible is he to appeals—by whom and in what areas? What kinds of punishments is he most afraid of? How does he respond when he is punished—does he get sulky, defiant, remorseful, mean? What kinds of activities or situations or what types of youngsters seem to cause him to get into trouble? Does he have to be punished often?

FANTASY LIFE. Every youngster has a fantasy life, and in too many instances this phase of development remains unknown to the teacher. We need to train ourselves to listen most sensitively to the wishes revealed in conversation, in play acting, in creative work of all kinds. Some of the aspects of fantasy we are searching for are the content of his daydreams, the degree of realism in what he says and does, the functioning of fear and anxiety in his fantasies, and the functioning of withdrawal into "a better world" of his imagination. We expect fantasy in young children. We should seek to keep the expression of fantasy free and open so it may be communicated. In this way the teacher may understand better the inner feelings of his pupils. We discuss this at greater length when we talk about the tool of creative work and play.

After the teacher has written anecdotes for several days, he is ready to study the record he has accumulated and apply some systematic interpretation to it. Prescott,[2] who has been encouraging and training teachers to keep and use anecdotal records for nearly thirty years, recommends that teachers develop multiple hypotheses from the material they have accumulated. This is simply a process of stating all the hypotheses or hunches you can about causes for the individual's behavior. To accomplish this, the observer relies on his knowledge of human development in general, and his knowledge of the individual being studied. You study the anecdotes recorded and ask yourself, "Wonder what caused Jerry to do that? What was he trying to say? Why was he so intense about this?" After the hypotheses are developed, the observer makes judgments about the validity of each one. We have always liked the retort that Adler gave Marie Rasey when discussing hypotheses, "Miss Rasey, it is not the guess that is wicked. It is to leave it unchecked that is wicked." [3] If you are a member of a study group, this whole process of developing multiple hypotheses and validating them becomes a group procedure. Space prevents us from presenting a complete study of a child and the multiple hypotheses that might be developed from it. Studies such as these are available in references noted at the end of this chapter. A list of multiple hypotheses might look something like this:

> Tom is secure in his mother's love for him, but ambivalent in his feelings about his father. Sometimes the father and son seem to have a

---

[2] Daniel A. Prescott, *The Child in the Educative Process* (New York: McGraw-Hill Book Company, Inc., 1957), pp. 99-150.
[3] Reported by Marie Rasey to authors in a conversation.

relatively close relationship and other times a complete lack of rapport. Hypothesis: Tom's father's attitude toward marriage and his children is ambivalent; Tom senses this and reacts to both attitudes with much uncertainty.

Tom's unusual awareness of "how to get around" adults is the result of this same uncertainty about his father's attitude toward him at any given moment. This, in combination with his personal attractiveness and intelligence, has made him unusually adept at getting his own way by indirection.

Tom's attitude toward his brother at this point is more of a reaction to John's attitude toward him rather than a spontaneous feeling originating with Tom. John seems jealous of Tom, and because of it is inclined to push him around a little. Tom seems to admire and want to imitate his brother but John's attitude makes this difficult to do.

Tom's unusual concern about money is the result of a scarcity of money in the family.

Tom's failure to paint many pictures, to sing, to model in clay, or do other creative and imaginative handwork is more a result of lack of art materials in the home (and school) than from lack of interest or ability.

Tom's relative lack of aggressiveness with his peers is probably the result of trying to compete with John and John's friends who are a few years older and bigger. He has apparently found that his only advantage over them with adults is being "cute," so he competes on another level than physical strength.

Tom's behavior is more cautious and he clings to the familiar more than one would expect at his age because of: (a) his position in the family as the younger boy; (b) his uncertainty in his relation with his father.

The two incidents where Tom changed his mood about wanting to go with me on a trip were a reaction to John's jealousy of Tom's being chosen to go and a way of appeasing John.

After you have observed enough to develop some multiple hypotheses, you then begin to realize that your observations fall into certain categories. These categories bring more organization into your thinking and observations. Prescott [4] suggests six aspects of an individual's life which yield significant insight into his behavior. They are the physical, the affectional (home and family relationships), the self-developmental (including areas of mental, language, attitude, and value development), the cultural (forces in society having an impact on him), the peer-group, and the emotional (the feelings which the meanings of his experiences give to him). As you continue to study an individual's behavior, you tap all the sources available to you for additional insight and under-

---

[4] *Helping Teachers Understand Children*, 16 mm., 40 min., sound, distributed by New York University Film Library.

standing about these aspects of development. From this procedure some hypotheses emerge as more valid than others. Once causes are ascertained in a relatively accurate manner, we may hope to find ways to guide pupils toward a more complete realization of their own potentialities.

To summarize the procedures for keeping of anecdotal records, we quote the characteristics of a good anecdote as perceived by Prescott:

> It gives the date, the place, and the situation in which the action occurred. We call this the setting.
>
> It describes the actions of the child, the reactions of the other people involved, and the response of the child to these reactions.
>
> It quotes what is said to the child and by the child during the action.
>
> It supplies "mood cues"—postures, gestures, voice qualities, and facial expressions that give cues to how the child felt. It does not provide interpretations of his feelings, but only the cues by which a reader may judge what they were.
>
> The description is extensive enough to cover the episode. The action or conversation is not left incomplete and unfinished but is followed through to the point where a little vignette of a behavioral moment in the life of the child is supplied.[5]

Using Records

If we expect teachers to consult records, they must be kept easily accessible. Some schools permit the records to be kept in the teacher's classroom. If they are kept there, they should be in a locked file and should be treated as the personal property of the teacher. Wherever the records are, they should be so arranged that they can be consolidated in a hurry. If a teacher has to spend an hour going to two or three offices just to locate the complete record of one pupil, he is not likely to retain his enthusiasm for record keeping or record use regardless of how devoted to teaching he is.

Each record tells as much about the recorder as it does about the individual whose record it is. We must remember that whatever is recorded filters through the recorder's own perceptions. His fears, anxieties, biases, and expectations influence what he selects to record. It is important to keep this in mind as one makes recordings or tries to interpret the recordings of others. As we come to know our own anxieties and

---

[5] Daniel A. Prescott, *The Child in the Educative Process* (New York: McGraw-Hill Book Company, Inc., 1957), pp. 153-154.

hopes, we are more likely to understand why we respond to different types of behavior and give the kinds of interpretations to them that we do give.

To interpret and evaluate records, then, it is important to know the person who made the recording, if at all possible. It frequently is possible in a school in which teachers stay in their positions over many years. We once knew a kindergarten teacher who made no positive recordings about any of the boys in her class. To have accepted her judgments about the children in her class (and her records were judgments) would have been most misleading. Such incompetence is not too hard to discern if one has been trained to be aware of how it can be spotted. If you cannot know the recorder, here are some evaluative criteria to help you decide how much stock to take in what you find on the record.

Examine a set of records kept by one individual to see if you find the same types of values or biases being applied to each child. The teacher mentioned earlier was obviously set against boys. The bias might be focused upon individuals from a minority group, a certain religion, or a certain part of town. Unfortunately, we do have prejudiced teachers who are not aware of their prejudices and how they cause them to exclude certain people.

Note the degree of specificity of the anecdote. An anecdote is a happening. If the record deals in generalities not documented by specific instances, it has little merit. For example: Wilbur feels at home and good in our class. He is even trying some of the things that were taken out of him by former discipline. He has a need to protect himself from the home-factions, but no need for protection in school now. I think we are getting someplace.

Note the degree to which the teacher's perceptions color the anecdote. For example: We have one problem child in the class. He has been a nuisance ever since his entrance last September. He never gets his work in on time and constantly has to stay in after three to complete his work. He spends most of his time annoying the rest of the children. Many of the other mothers have complained about him and the children are constantly reporting his aggravating behavior. He seems to be getting worse.

Note the degree to which the records of individuals in one class are similar to each other. If generalities are used, teachers often find themselves repeating the same phrases about three-fourths of the class. For example, "He adjusted to his classmates easily; he is a well-adjusted lad; he makes friends easily; he takes directions well and follows through on assignments." Such phrases hide all the uniqueness of individuals and tell only that the teacher got along with his pupils. This tells more about the teacher than the pupils.

Note the extent of negativism in the recordings. If a teacher sees most pupils as problems, has an unhappy, gloomy attitude toward living, his recordings may reflect his state of mind, and may be quite different from the actual behavior of the pupils. Then, too, such a teacher may evoke behavior that is not characteristic.

Home Visits

I knocked on the door and Mrs. Flannagan appeared. She only opened the door at an angle and peered at me in a startled manner, for I was paying her a surprise visit. I introduced myself and told her Hope was coming along nicely in school. Mrs. Flannagan had stringy brown hair and no make-up. She had a cigarette in her hand. Her eyes were large and seemed wildish looking, although her face, basically, seemed rather attractive. She was wearing some kind of unattractive summer dress with no sleeves. Through the partly-opened door I could see a man sleeping on what appeared to be a couch. I heard music playing from a radio. Her four-year-old boy also came to the door. He was very cute looking, but extremely dirty. He wasn't wearing shoes and his bare feet were black. We talked about Hope's work, but Mrs. Flannagan never asked me to come into her house. In a short time our conversation about Hope seemed over, and I began to realize that Mrs. Flannagan didn't want to ask me in. I tried to prolong the conversation by asking her about her other children and her husband. She told me a few things about her children and said that she had to scold her little boy a lot. He, meanwhile, was running in and out of the doorway. She said her husband was sleeping since he worked nights.

This episode illustrates the need for sensing whether a home visit will increase or decrease the teacher's chance to get closer to the pupil. This teacher learned much about Hope's family life that could not be gleaned in any other way, but we wonder if Hope wanted to have her teacher think well of her how she felt about having her family exposed to teacher's view. We believe that teachers should be most sensitive in "feeling out" the degree of privacy the pupil wishes to maintain and the family's feelings about a home visit.

If you have decided to make a home visit, you will learn more if you walk the last two or three blocks. In this walk you will note the number of children or youth in the immediate neighborhood (we are assuming that you will go after school hours), the activities of the younger set, and the kinds of homes in the area. You will make some comparisons about the relative status of this family in the neighborhood. You will assess such qualities as: Do the residents seem to take pride in their homes and yards? What else comprises the neighborhood? Is the neighborhood friendly or cold or actually hostile? Are the inhabitants homogeneous or do they include varying groups? Are there aspects of the neighborhood that are threatening to the healthy growth of young human beings, such as traffic hazards, saloons, dives, or hang-outs for street characters? Try as you walk along to see all this as your pupil sees it. What would he notice? What would he pass without noticing?

After you get inside the home, observe the family relationships: the way the mother and father seem to feel about each other, the feelings about siblings, the differences in feelings of parents for the respective siblings, the kinds of control used, the degree of independence allowed, the other adults (if any) living with the family and their roles. Observe, too, the space this boy or girl has for himself, and how much freedom he has to use that space (his room, if he has one) as he wants to use it. Again let us caution against being too sure that the perceptions we gain from a home visit are the ones shared by the parents or the child. The teacher's perceptions are used as *another* means of assessing how the child himself feels about his home. Human beings build their defenses slowly and carefully guard against revealing even to themselves those areas that are of most concern to them.

Remember as you make home visits that it is in the home that the child develops a sense of security, a sense of being part of a family, not because of what he can do or how cute he is, but just because he *is*. Home visits give you a chance to assess the quality of this security or lack of it.

Parent Conferences

We should like to urge an expansion of our concepts of the functions of parent conferences. For years, effective schools have been having parents come to school once or twice a year or more often to discuss the progress Billy or Sally is making in school. That is fine. Certainly a team relationship needs to be developed between the teacher and parent of every child, just as it is between the pediatrician and the parent. The teacher is the professional who can advise, counsel, and teach the parent those things he needs to know concerning the schooling of his young.

The yearly shift in Billy's teacher makes this most difficult, and we hope the day may come when this practice will be examined critically. But that's another story.

Conferring with parents is useful and necessary for purposes other than to report progress. We advocate that teachers develop *parent group conferences*. Nearly all parents are anxious about their children's development. This anxiety is actually produced by feelings of guilt by some parents. Many of our practices today tend to increase this anxiety. Every woman's magazine is peddling advice about child rearing, and much of it is conflicting. What to do, whom to believe when one does not know are serious quandries.

Teachers who call together the parents of their pupils find that parents are relieved to discover that other five-year-olds, ten-year-olds, fifteen-year-olds are going through similar developmental stages. Teachers have a chance to help parents understand what is to be expected at a given age, what behavior is considered a red light suggesting danger ahead unless handled now, and how to deal with certain troubling phases of growth. As parents learn more about human development, they tend to support each other in the kinds of expectations they have about their offspring. This reduces the amount of home friction resulting from one youngster using another one as a lever to get what he wants. You doubtless recall, perhaps you still use the line, "Why can't I have the car? Tony's dad lets him have his!"

Parent group conferences are helpful to the teacher in studying his pupils for in a group parental attitudes and values are focused upon specific practices. Frequently, one parent's ideas are challenged by another. In such situations, the teacher has a chance to observe the ways individuals handle conflicting situations. This yields valuable insight into one's pupils and their behavior.

A further extension of parent conferences that we urge is to include gradually and at specified times the boy or girl about whom the conference is being held. As youngsters grow, they come to resent "mother going to school to talk about me." It's a kind of "sneaky" thing to do! Yet we need to retain the relationship with parents. Some conferences are more successful if the pupil is present. This practice might result in more serious attitudes by both parents and pupils. We suggest bringing the pupil in as soon as he is mature enough to understand the reason for it. This might be when he is nine, ten, or eleven. Certainly, the junior-

and senior-high-school pupil should be considered and encouraged to be independent enough to merit the dignity of being included in conferences in which he is concerned.

A third extension of parent conferences that yields better relationships between parents and teachers and more pertinent information is for the parent to see the teacher outside his professional role and the teacher to see the parent other than as Rebecca's mother. If parents and teachers work together as interested adults and citizens on matters of consequence to the community, many problems that formerly loomed large turn out to be picayune. We strongly urge teachers to contrive ways to see parents socially, to encourage conversation about styles, prices, current headlines, hobbies, home furnishings, and the like. Many parents need to discover that teachers are human, too; and maybe we teachers need to discover that parents are all sorts—most of them "pretty fine human beings."

We wonder, for example, if the following episode would have taken place (as it really did) if the teacher had known Richard's parents socially or if his parents had been present when this exchange occurred:

Teacher: Richard, have you been cooperating with the rest of the class?
Richard: Nope.
Teacher: Suppose Richard accidentally bumps into someone or pushes someone but doesn't hurt him, what should the person do?
Tina: Ignore him.
Teacher: How do the rest of you feel?
Children: Yes, we should ignore him.
Teacher: I think that's a very good idea. Suppose Richard deliberately hurts someone, what should the person do?
Clemens: Sock him hard.
Teacher: Yes, if I were you and Richard pinched me or deliberately started a fight, I would beat him up so hard that he would never fight again.

Free Play

No teacher knows a child well unless he has seen him in free play. No teacher knows an adolescent well unless he has seen him when he is just "foolin' around with the gang." By free play we mean *time which the individual is free to use as he wishes.* The variety of activities of free play may include the whole span of individual and group pursuits, active and passive endeavors, momentary and continuing interests. Ronald may choose to read a book in time that is not structured by someone else; Gordon may seek his playmates on the block for a ball game; while Eloise may find her satisfaction by pouring "a pitcher of water down the mail chute." What an individual does during free play, how he does it, and with whom all help to tell the story of his satisfactions and needs.

Play is the small child's business. It is also his language, for his language is action. Long before a child can put his thoughts and feelings into words, he can act them out; and if we remain attuned to people, we continue to be able to say more in our free non-verbal expression than can be put into language. Who can say all that Van Gogh was feeling in "The Starry Night"? Play is important. Through it we learn to free ourselves from the conflicts, the frustrations, and the anxieties that we experience. Play is a safe way of expressing these feelings. If we allow them to pile up in a child, or force them underground, we are creating trouble of a serious nature at a later date. The body is an instrument for expression and we have our most satisfying modes of expression in that which we call play. Play is as natural as breathing and as necessary as milk to the proper nourishing of the body.

Children and youth at play express their attitudes toward themselves and their world. Some children fight, some take flight, and some seek compensation. To play it out is autotherapeutic. To talk it out is good. To play it out is better. One fertile source of the content of play is imitating adult activities. An individual is selective in what he imitates, however. Those roles he chooses to assume have emotional overtones of love, hope, fear, anxiety, security. To fathom the meaning of play we have to understand the principles of choice in play.

Meaning of Play

In play, a youngster can be anything he wishes. He can have whatever his imagination creates. In this way he has a kind of omnipotence. Miss Elliott discovered this when she interrupted a five-year-old who was zooming around the kindergarten in a scooter with: "Don't you know if you make a right turn, you're supposed to make an arm signal?" The response she received was: "Don't you know if you put your arm out a space ship, it will be blown right off?" As we watch children and youth at play, we *wonder* about what they admire and why. Why did he choose to act out the role of a lonely little boy when he could have been a knight?

Why did she choose to be a father when she might have been a mother while playing in the doll house?

One characteristic of the play of small children that needs careful study is their assigning a role to an inanimate object. Sometimes this seems to be done so that a doll or stuffed animal can do things which are denied to the child. Bill can have a dog bite the doctor who has just given him a shot, but he would never have the brashness to do this himself, or he may have his teddy bear "tell off" his mother. In this manner he achieves his wish while still keeping his superego intact.

Another interesting form of play occurs when the child takes the role of the defeated, the underdog. Some children in their play seem to be saying, "See, I can't succeed." This individual has to take the nasty medicine in his fantasy, is defeated in his make-believe combat, loses his favorite toy, doesn't get invited to the party.

The function of play seems to be to dissemble reality in some way. Thus, a happy ending to a play episode may be a reversal of the real ending. The playing out of a tender, solicitous mother may be a wish for such a mother. A blundering clown in play may be the individual's way of expressing his mastery of the situation. One's real identity is hidden in play, and this is the very quality that makes play so significant.

One must be cautious in interpreting the meaning of play. The child may be saying this is how mother treats me; this is how I wish she would treat me; this is how she feels toward me; this is how I wish she felt toward me when she finds out what I've done. Play, then, may be expressing genuine conflicts and hostilities; it may be disguising genuine conflicts; it may be a means for releasing anxiety; it may be an imitation of intriguing adult activities; it may be a means for releasing unacceptable impulses; it may be a playing out of wishes. One cannot interpret the meaning of play by analyzing its content. Murphy states:

> The healthiest, best-adjusted children I have seen over the years have destroyed babies, mothers, all female authorities, wrenched the sides of cribs off, torn off tigers' tails or other appendages, and otherwise acted out strong feelings of jealousy, hostility, or fear. Such incidents tell us that the child is coming to terms with what are the basic problems of the young child in our culture: his resentment of adult pressures and of competition from babies and the opposite sex. They do not tell us whether the child needs help.[6]

---

[6] Lois Murphy and Associates, *Personality in Young Children*, Vol. I (New York: Basic Books, Inc., 1956), p. 15.

Murphy continues by pointing out that the structural aspect of play has to be analyzed to tell anything significant about the child. One seeks to discern whether the content represents clarity or confusion, order or disorder, organization or disorganization, flexibility or rigidity, coherence or incoherence, originality or stereotypy, idiosyncrasy or conventionality.[7]

The child uses objects to project his purposes in play. They may be means for solving problems or they may be endowed with qualities that bring them to life. The teacher notes whether there is a progression in the child's use of materials. If a child re-  peats the same structure in block building or draws rockets every day for several weeks, he is giving us a signal that something needs attention in his life; or if he regresses to patterns of play and use of materials long ago put away, he speaks of some disorganization within himself. We often see this happen at pre-adolescence when the individual returns to playing with dolls long ago forgotten, or other toys that appealed when he was six or seven. At this time we expect such disorganization because the entire personality is being "shook up" so that it may be restructured into the young adult that is emerging. Regression occurs when the individual is greatly disturbed about something.

The teacher notes how active or passive the child is in his play; how overtly he plays out the emotions that he ascribes to the situation, or how covertly he expresses unacceptable feelings; how engrossed he is with people, or if things seem of greater importance to him. Play gives us many insights into the life-space of the child. If he is playing house, the way he sets the table, the language he uses to the members of the family, the materials he uses, all spell out many of the details of the child's life. One little girl, after making elabo-

---

[7] *Ibid.*, pp. 15-16.

rate preparations for breakfast, kissing her husband good-by as he took his lunch bucket and left for work, went to the telephone, dialed, and said, "It's all right, Joe; you can come over now." In one of our city schools, the girls in the doll house suddenly drew back screaming at the sight of a cockroach, whereupon Pat spoke up, "Shucks, my place is loaded with them." One can scarcely imagine this information coming out in a report or a written composition.

As we watch the child at play, we note the expressiveness of his body. Is he free, spontaneous, enthusiastic, or does he inhibit himself, withdraw from new materials or new situations? We note verbal expression. The way the child talks to himself reveals his picture of himself. We note his relation to the adults in the situation. Some children at play do not notice the adults present. Some look to them for help and are dependent upon them—beseeching an adult to make choices for them. We note the content of the fantasy that the child reveals. We note how much the child observes, how well he organizes, how intense his emotions are, how skilled he is in manipulating materials and in leading people. In group situations we note the quality of social relationships that develop, the roles each child assumes, who takes the leadership, whom he includes and excludes, the originality of the play, and the manner in which roles and activities shift. Try analyzing the following bit of play.

Janet, Danny, and Peter, all age five, were jumping from a low chest onto several pillows which they had piled on the floor:

Janet:	Jump, Peter!
Peter:	Put the pillows in one big pile.
Danny:	No, let's make a big circle.
Peter:	But it's softer when the pile is high.
Danny:	O. K., crime doesn't pay.
Peter:	Let's don't jump! Let's swim.
Danny:	O. K. Let's swim.
Janet:	The pillows are a river.
Peter:	Oh, I'm going to take off my shoes. I can jump better.
Janet:	Yes, me too. My shoes are heavy.
Peter:	Watch out, Janet. I am going to jump on the pillows. Oh, you moved the pillows, Janet. I hurt myself. (Janet had not moved the pillows.)
Janet:	I didn't move them.
Peter:	Well, I hurt my feet.

Janet: Well, anyway I didn't move them.
Peter: The pillows are nice now. Don't jump on them anymore.
Danny: I won't mess them up.
Janet: Come on, let's jump.
Peter: Don't jump.
Danny: Why?
Peter: I'm tired and we need a rest.

The three children threw themselves on the pillows and pretended that they were sleeping.

The teacher has a responsibility, if he is to use play effectively, to make available those play materials that evoke the most creative responses in children—blocks, finger paints, water play, clay, dolls of a variety of shapes, sizes, and materials. Murphy advocates the use of miniature life toys, which are sets of toys one might use in playing house—dolls, dishes, furniture, animals, clothes. In using these, children are able to project their own feelings into the play. We like the commentary in the film *Finger Painting*,[8] which accompanies a pre-school child's delight in squashing the paint through her fingers: "She is not making a painting. She is using paints."

In observing the play of adolescents, our focus is primarily on social relationships and attitudes toward authority. These have been discussed in considerable detail elsewhere in the book. One phase of play that consumes much adolescent attention is "trying on" new, exciting adult roles. These cluster around boy-girl relationships and behavior in situations that carry over into adult life such as party manners, appropriate dress, correct behavior around adults, and learning the skills of adulthood.

Our patience may wear thin with a young adolescent who hangs onto the telephone for an hour as she recounts in detail to her girl friend, whom she left all of an hour ago, Jack's remarks to her as he walked her home; but we understand that she is really learning the social grace of using the telephone for adult purposes. We may be discouraged at breakfast as we greet our teen-age daughter, her eyes heavily pencilled and mouth shape exaggerated beyond recognition; but again we know that such behavior is the expression of a reaching toward adulthood. The boy driving his hot rod, his sneaking of cigarettes and an occasional beer, are his way of saying, "See, I am a man now."

---

[8] *Finger Painting*, 22 min., silent, color, distributed by New York University Film Library.

As with the play of little children, we examine the play of adolescents to see what it expresses about the individual's internal organization, his coherence, his flexibility, his clarity, and his ability to express *himself* even within the narrow confines of group conformity that is to be expected at this age. Wise teachers understand that opposition at this age is likely to stamp in the behavior we seek to eradicate or ameliorate.

One of the most telling phases of the adolescent's play is his choice of friends. The scope for choosing friends usually expands overnight as the young boy or girl leaves a small elementary school and enters a larger junior high school. The value system of the individual comes to the fore at this time as he has to decide how inclusive to be in his friendship patterns, how altruistic in sharing himself with those who wish his association. Girls tend to have a bit of mothering impulse to befriend those who need friends which they confuse with genuine affection. Perhaps you recall some very attractive girls who have extended their friendship to individuals who are unattractive and uninteresting but who are obviously in need of friends. Attitudes and values solidified at this time are most powerful and are likely to remain with the individual for the remainder of his life.

Play reveals the mores and cultural values of certain groups. For example, a group worker in a settlement house was baffled when one of the adolescent boys in his group refused to help clean up the kitchen and wash the dishes. The boy's behavior not only indicated an indifference to the sharing that was one of the group's accepted goals, but the feeling was expressed in such violent terms that the group worker concluded the boy was highly disturbed. Only later, when he discovered that he had asked the boy to defy his own cultural norms (the boy had recently come from Puerto Rico) which decree that males must not help in the kitchen clean-up, could the group worker make an adequate interpretation of this boy's behavior.

Creativity

Each human being has the urge to create, to extend himself beyond his skin. He is a questing animal and his quest takes many forms. Having conquered many of the dimensions of his space-time world, his opportunities for questing are becoming more and more infinite—using infinite in a literal sense. Throughout this book we have urged teachers to get out of the way of the questing of their pupils. Let's take a few minutes to summarize what is meant by creativity, to discuss conditions which encourage it, and to find out how the creative work of children and youth helps the teacher understand the *why's* of human behavior.

Meaning of Creativity

Our culture has endowed the word creativity with a vague, omnipotent meaning. Many of us have been trained to believe that only a few of any generation are creative. This is a myth, the acceptance of which tends to produce individuals who have walled off a part of their lives from full development—thus resulting in tight, narrow, inhibited lives. What then is creativity? It is the stuff of dreams. It is the functioning of the unconscious. It is the emergence of wishes, fears, anxieties, hopes, joys. Nisbet and Blitsten state:

> The stuff of the creative process . . . is composed of dreams and reverie, as well as conscious reflection or study, of hates as well as loves, of idleness as well as the sternest discipline, of pricks of conscience or the buffets of fate as much as the hope of reward. The unconscious is as deeply involved as is the conscious mind, and no act of creation can be separated from the emotional, as well as the intellectual, character of the creator. Whether his work can be great or small, there is always at work some unique concentration of purpose, need, and knowledge that is the product of the many elements which compose his own distinctive being.[9]

---

[9] Robert A. Nisbet and Dorothy Blitsten, "The Creative Context: A Preface," *Autonomous Groups*, Vol. XII, Nos. 3 and 4, Spring and Summer 1957, p. 2.

The first thing we can say about creativity then is that it is of the deeper self. We can say, too, that creativity is a part of the common discourse. It is rooted in the community of language, of feelings, of symbolism that is common to all of us. Maslow has this to say about it:

> This kind of primary creativeness is very probably a heritage of every human being. It is a common and universal kind of thing. Certainly it is found in all healthy children. It is the kind of creativeness that any healthy child had and which is then lost by most people as they grow up. It is universal in another sense, that if you dig . . . into the unconscious layers of the person, you find it there. . . . You know that in our dreams, we can be an awful lot more creative than we are in waking life. We can be more clever, and wittier, and bolder, and more original, and so on and on.[10]

Conditions for Encouraging Creativity

Since creativity is of the deeper self, no one can force it, develop it, or correct it except the human being himself. What then is the role of the teacher in encouraging creativity? Marie Rasey delightfully describes this role as one of *creating the habitat in which creativity flourishes*. Habitat means "the state of nature in which a species is at home." Now if one is at home in his culture, he does not have to suppress his creative processes. These processes, according to Rasey, are "selection, ingestion, assimilation, and rejection." These processes are described as follows:

> The habitat for the young of human kind must provide scope for his questing, opportunity to search out what he wants, and to make his own selection from what he finds. It implies, as well, freedom to reject even "what is good for him" in the judgment of another. . . . It (the habitat) must be sufficiently complex as to furnish him both with problems needing to be solved and the stuff of their solution. . . . Any habitat in which a young human can move in the direction of becoming more perfectly that which he already is, must, in potential furnish scope and facility for the culture of deep feeling. He is created the purveyor and the releaser of his own energy. No one can do it *to* him. It is his own value, set by his own feeling which can trigger the output of himself. . . . His budding pride of creation may not flourish if it meet too brusque or too insistent criticism.[11]

---

[10] A. H. Maslow, "Emotional Blocks to Creativity" (lecture given before Creative Engineering Seminar, April 24, 1957).

[11] Marie I. Rasey and J. W. Menge, "The Educative Process in Terms of Habitat" (a mimeographed statement).

If the teacher attempts to create a habitat that allows the pupil to express himself, he encourages the non-conformist, as did the teacher who received this bit of writing:

> But it feels good
> To say everything
> And not worry about
> What other people think.
> And maybe from all these words
> One or two lines will be pretty.
> And I can feel proud
> About what I've said
> About what I've felt
> Without worrying how
> Anybody else feels
> About what I've felt.

He sees that the classroom program is concerned with problems that are complex enough to challenge the young, problems that are on the growing edges of our culture, problems that are broad enough in scope to have appeal to individual uniquenesses. The teacher who wishes creative work refrains from using the red pencil on products of the creative spirit. What a loss, had the teacher corrected this bit of self-expression: "The cow has a fine sense of smell; one can smell it far away. This is the reason for the fresh air in the country." [12]

Study of Creative Work

Creative work takes many forms. It may be a piece of sculpture, a painting, a blob of paint on a piece of newsprint, a short story or poem, a bit of acting out, a song or dance. We observe the creation to see what it tells us about the child or adolescent. As in play, creative work tells about the individual's inner self, how he feels about life, and the way he perceives himself in his world. We accept the creation as it is proffered; that is, in confidence that it will be appreciated. Without such a spirit, no creative work flourishes. Love is the most creative of all emotions. The personality permeated and motivated by love takes into account the needs, ambitions, desires, problems, griefs, and successes of those around him. Man's needs change, but not his love, nor his desire that his love should

---

[12] H. Allen Smith, *Write Me a Poem, Baby* (Boston: Little, Brown and Company, 1956), p. 44.

satisfy his needs. Since the creator endows his creation with some of his own spirit, the teacher must be tender and loving in his attitude toward the creative product.

As we study the creative work of our pupils, we also watch the process of their creating just as we do when we observe play. One teacher describes Ronnie's contortions while writing a story.

> Ronnie sits with his pencil in his hand staring at the paper. He has one hand on his head, the other in his pocket. He suddenly jumps up, draws his feet up to his seat and sits on them as he scribbles frantically. He breaks the lead on his pencil. He throws his pencil down in disgust, reaches for it, goes to the pencil sharpener and grinds vigorously. Back to his seat, feet up on his seat again. In this half-standing, half-sitting position he writes steadily for a few minutes. Then he looks up at the ceiling, relaxes, and sits in normal position.

The teacher is in a key role to encourage creative work in a wide variety of media. In arts and crafts, the teacher finds many, many ways in which art enriches the program. He has a plethora of materials around including quantities of "found" materials. He quietly notes the interests expressed by pupils. Some draw only horses; some get "caught up" in space ships; others are drawn to and draw the mechanical gadgets of 1965. The teacher notes what the child or youth seems to be saying in his creation and then observes for behavior that confirms or denies the hunches he has formed. He may see tiny inhibited lines, an abundance of detail, or wide sweeps— thus expressing feeling about space. The teacher may see an individual who finds it possible to get out of himself and express that which is usually repressed; such a child is Jane.

> Jane loves to work with her hands. Often during art periods she will use clay and mold a variety of shapes, most of which are quite humorous in form. She makes animals out of wool and is also in the process of building a cage to house our rabbits. She seems to derive

a great deal of pleasure from this type of activity. Perhaps this helps Jane gain some sort of emotional release. I have stated before that Jane is a perfectionist. When Jane is involved in her crafts, she is oblivious to everything except her own artistry. Her need for perfection is lessened and she doesn't remain the neat little girl in the classroom. Her hands get full of clay, even her face gets dirty, but she doesn't seem to mind it as she does when she is in a structured atmosphere.

As a contrast to Jane, consider Nathan, a six-year-old:

> During the days that followed, when Nathan drew pictures they were usually of boats and fish. He began folding these papers and drawings into the tiniest pieces of paper and stuffing them in his pocket. He also threw several in the garbage pail. After our relationship developed, I asked him if he would like to learn how to make an envelope for his work. He was intrigued by the envelope. I did all the work and he wrote his name on the outside. During that week he made several envelopes of varying sizes. One was for the fish that he drew and cut out and wanted to save. I wrote "fish" on the outside. I believe he really knows this word now. I watched him measure an envelope to be sure his drawing would fit it—he traced it and left room for folds. It was precisely done and every motion seemed to indicate that it was a special thing for him.
>
> His drawings led us into many conversations—one fascinated me so much I asked him if I could write his story down. He continued and then he would say, "Read what you have!" The stories were about his father's boat and about fish he had caught. I did this story idea for several days. I wanted to use them as a way to get him to tell the story to the group. He, however, wanted to take them home in his envelope. One day I had him look at a picture of children in a classroom. There were fish tanks and a group painting and a small toy boat. He said, "Let's make believe this is really a cabin cruiser," and proceeded to tell me about advanced boating. He mentioned his father was away and that he mailed one of his stories to his father. I suggested he write a letter to his father. He said, "O. K., but I tell you stories. You write this one." I wrote how much I liked Nathan and he began smiling cautiously.

This experience illustrates how a sensitive teacher can open up new possibilities in creative work. Not only was Nathan expressing a part of his life, he was gaining confidence in his teacher; he was learning how to put his ideas and feelings into words as well as into paints. Later on the teacher made a paper fishing game which she brought to the class. She reports: "Nathan played with it during free activity. He was wild with excitement, his voice reaching a high squeaky soprano. I never saw him jump or giggle so much." What a different approach from this one: "David came to my desk and asked if he could draw a picture. I told him he could if he would write a story about it."

Three-dimensional work, group work, work that calls for much freedom of movement are all superior ways of evoking creativity. The creative teacher has clay or plasticine handy; he sees possibilities for development of large group projects such as murals, puppet shows, making of large paper-maché figures, mobiles, masks, and the like. A word about puppets— they are an excellent means for the projection of feelings that are not acceptable when one acknowledges them as one's own. A projective use of painting is to suggest that pupils draw their families at work, at play, at dinner, and in other situations. One eight-year-old drew her father eating alone while the family enjoyed a picnic. Her remark was, "My pappa's having a picnic by himself. He doesn't like to eat with people."

Creative writing cannot be assigned, but the teacher can cherish and nurture the feelings Nathan had as he wrote his story about the fish. Whenever we request all to write on the same subject we are likely to get much chaff in the writing. Children and youth, like all of us, must write out of their own experiences, and when they do we often get eloquent expressions. The following story written by a city adolescent is one such example:

> Yes, I can tell you about my block. In fact I can probably tell you a storry about every house in my block, and even tell you a storry about the houses which are no longer standing and are not a refuge for garbage. I don't intend telling you a storry for every house, but I'll outline my block and its conditions and of course its people and people who live in streets or blocks like mine.
>
> The houses in my block are old and delapoted, about to crumble down. The halls are so dark at night and during the day very little sunlight enters the houses and even some apartments in order to make it gay and pleasant. The dirt and filth in the hallways and the way some of the people live its not fit for a dog to live.
>
> The streets are always filthy even on Saundays, ash cans overflooded with garbage, broken glass all over the streets. And only one's to blame for all of this, is the people. Yes, I said the people if some people only new the facts, that they have to live in that dirt and filth. There are all kinds of people who live in my block. You will find good and bad. But lets not put the blame on them. Its the landlords who want to raise the rent every month and can't afford to spend a little money trying to improve the conditions of his house. I also blame the Department of Sanatitition. Why neglect to pick up the garbage. You can go downtown and the streets are so clean you can almost eat off them but not in my block. And who cares, no

one. Some people wonder why they catch all kinds of diseases. Some say he gave it to me, I caught it from her instead of looking around at the surroundings in which he or she live in.

Not all the people in my block are like this. We have some wonderful folks who live there also. My house is old and warn out, but my apartment is always clean and thats how we try to keep it. We all have our up's and down's and hope to make the best of it. Some people who live in my block or anyone who has lived in blocks like mine turn out to be some of Americas best citizens. And yet some turn out to be dope peddlers, bookies, reefer smokers, all goes along where I live.

Please believe me I am not proud to say I live in my block. The streets are so dirty it even makes me feel bad to walk into them. I do hope when I am a man and have kids there wont be anymore slums, the word would not have to be used again.

Some suggestions that other teachers have found useful in stimulating creative writing are:

Develop a portfolio about each child in which he places samples of his writing. One teacher started this project by asking each individual to write about himself and then his pet peeves, and later his likes. Such a wealth of material she unearthed! The children also drew pictures to illustrate their writings.

Develop a list of projective subjects to write about and let the children choose those that are appealing to them. Some suggested topics are: If I Were Principal of This School, If I Were Mayor, If I Were My Father (Mother), If I Were Teacher of This Class, If I Had Three Wishes, If I Could Take a Long Trip, If I Had to Choose Three People to Work With, My Kid Sister, When I Grow Up, Pet Peeves, When I Turn the Light Out at Night . . .

Encourage pupils to hand in "Scraps." Whenever they have a thought they want to get down in a hurry, jot it down on a scrap of paper and put it in a box. Later these scraps are read and talked about in an informal manner.

Develop the habit of spending some time each week in having oral reading of writing with positive acceptance of the writing. For creativity to be complete, it must be shared.

Develop a class paper that is functional.

Devise as many real needs for writing as you and the pupils can think of. When you write letters, for instance, write them to real people for a needed purpose and mail them. Have a class emphasis upon communicating ideas.

We quote a few samples that came from the portfolio idea—which also included pictures—that the class made of situations in their families. These are uncorrected. They are ten- and eleven-year-olds speaking:

My Family

My family is pretty big. There are 6 people in it. My mother, father, big brother, little brother, grandfather and me. My big brother, Bob, is 19½ years old. He's 6 ft. 1 in. tall. He weighs about 160 lbs. He has brown hair, blue eyes, and he goes to N. Y. University. My little brother Tom is 7 years old. He's kind of plump, he's about 4 ft. 4 in. tall, blond and blue eyes.

You know what I look like. My grandfather is 80 years old. My father is about 6 ft. tall and he has green eyes. My mother has dirty blond hair, has blue eyes, and is about 5 ft. 7 in. tall. That's all.

Disturbance

The thing that disturbs me most is school. Its that blasted work. Its all work and no play. You do arithmetic then mintists leater its spelling. School berns me up.

My Pet Peeves

I think my pet peeves happen when I am out with my mother and father. For instance when I go bowling with my parents. They always tell me to hold the ball one way and if I don't they yell at me. I really do better if I am left alone. Other times my mother yells at me for something I couldn't help. After all what are mothers for. I agree with her sometimes but other times it really isn't my fault.

Pet Peeves

The things that really disturb me are my sister. She always screams at me a lot! And she sucks her thumb and that really gets me! ! !

Next is my brother. Even though he is only three years old he really bosses me around! He wouldn't even let me sit on a chair. He takes it all for himself!

My mother is half okay! But she wouldn't even let me stay in my room when my sister is doing her homework.

My father is okay.

And that is all the thing that really disturb me! ! ! ! ! ! ! ! !

Pet Peeves

One of the things that distrubs me is my Sunday School teacher also annoys me is chalk skreeching on the black board. I also dislike aunts and uncles and other reilitives to pinch me. I don't like my sister to feel and talk like I just can't understand anything. I dislike to be called anything. I dislike to be called a baby. Also I hate relitives to say "do you remember me? I saw you when you were five months old." (as if I was soposed too.)

Enjoyments

When I receive money it makes my happy. When my brother tells my parents something on me but doesn't no the real thing and gets in trouble I am again happy. I also enjoy when I'm in some sort of game but can't be in it because I have to go somewhere and then find out I don't have to go to that somewhere. To me school doesn't disturb me at the slitest. I think it's just a thing you have to go through in life. But when I get through with school on Friday I'm happy and I look forward to the weekend.

Things I Like, Like Like Like Like Like etc.

I like to have chicken for dinner. I like to live. I like to go to sports attractions. I like to read the paper. I like to stay home from school. I like gym.

The thing I like like like like like like like like like like like best is . . . . P. S. I like my brothers and parents.

The creative field is a place where children and adults meet as equals. The most creative people are often the most childlike. "Lest you be as little children you shall not enter the Kingdom of Heaven" seems to apply in this connection. The same principles which apply to studying samples of arts and crafts and writing also apply to any creative expression: music, dance, creative dramatics, creative discussion. Each is a means of developing interpersonal relations in which the pupil feels secure, safe, the recipient of adult understanding and appreciation. Each media gives the individual a chance to project himself, to try-out, to build an identification with people and with materials, to experience a wholeness.

Perhaps we should stop here, but being school teachers we must utter a few words of advice. We live in an age in which we have a tendency to believe that some people should tell others what to like. We live in an age of ready-made art. Gadgets are numerous and temptingly clever. Being human, teachers are often tempted to use kids to make themselves look good in the eyes of the public. (Need we mention operettas, bands, tediously rehearsed dramatic shows?) We are still struggling with the pioneer concept of climbing to the top over the shoulders of others. We must caution specifically here against the teacher's drawing lessons, moralizing, blaming, correcting—all of which quench creative expression. In observing the obscure language of self-expression, the teacher seeks to receive unspoken revelations of the child's inner self. Thus he must stifle all impulse to criticize or compare. *These are all sure ways to kill creativity.*

Role-Playing

"You be the mama and I'll be the daddy," speaks the five-year-old as she goes about her busy way playing house. At five, children are delightfully open and free in their role-playing. We call it creative play and learn about the players by listening and observing. As the child grows, frequently something happens. He begins to pull down the blinds to his inner self—thus hiding many of his thoughts and feelings from the adults who might be able to understand these feelings. His experience teaches him that adults cannot always be trusted and do not always understand. We introduce role-playing to children and youth to try to get back to that openness and freeness of little children, so that we may know more completely what we are working with, and so pupils may have a chance to make conscious many of the unconscious anxieties that they do not understand or know what to do about.

We are discussing role-playing as a spontaneous enactment of a social situation. We call this sociodrama. This tool is most effective beginning with children about nine or ten and extending throughout the life span. Industry as well as the social sciences have found sociodrama to be an unusually powerful and effective method for learning. The teacher may use role-playing for a variety of purposes. Suppose the class is having a party for their parents and they need to learn how to manage this new situation. The role-playing calls for some children to be mothers and fathers, for someone to be the teacher. As the play-parents and the play-teacher assume their roles, the teacher has a rich opportunity to observe the pictures that the role-players have of these particular adults. Role-playing in this instance is used to rehearse a new experience. School is replete with situations that can be better played out than talked about. You can have an interesting time imagining all the situations and relating the kinds of insights about the pupils that the teachers might get from these situations.

Another use of role-playing which reveals more of the individual's own feelings and attitudes is the playing out of conflict situations that arise or are incipient in the group. Suppose that this is an American history class or a core class and the pupils are discussing the Supreme Court decision making segregated schools illegal, or the influx of Puerto Ricans to the Mainland, or the migration of Southern Negroes to Northern cities. These are all current happenings that are loaded with individual perceptions that run the gamut in feelings and attitudes. To talk about these situations without having an opportunity to examine one's own feelings and others' feelings about them is just "covering material." Little is uncovered that has personal meaning and little is generated to act upon in future living. Role-playing gives the teacher a tool through which feelings can be explored and recognized as the real generators of our behavior. The person who believes that "Niggers should know their place and stay in it," by playing a Negro, has the chance to *feel* how it feels to be treated as an inferior. We do not assume, of course, that a lifetime of feelings are going to crumble through one such experience, but frequent examination of one's feelings may lead one to understand *why* he has come to have these feelings. He may then become more susceptible to change and more insightful in his understanding about how others feel. The same situation may reveal to another person feelings that he has been unaware of until he started to play out the role. Much in our culture has "carefully taught" us to give the proper, the accepted right response no matter how we really feel. Using role-playing to identify feelings and to work with feelings leads to more flexibility of personality as well as more thoughtfulness about the meaning of human rights.

Some teachers have examined the content areas of the subjects they teach to see how they can be personalized, individualized, and endowed with living emotions through the use of role-playing.

One of the developmental tasks of adolescents is becoming an independent, mature person. We often refer to this as "untying the apron strings." Role-playing is one way to help the girl or boy understand the problems his parents face in this process. And if you are working with parents (as we hope you will be), it is equally effective in helping parents realize the adolescent's feelings and needs.

Because we are working with feelings in this use of role-playing, the teacher discovers some of the most important data about his pupils. He learns, if he listens wisely, the degree of flexibility the individual has in putting himself into someone else's role, the quality of openness he is able to reach as he plays a role, the depth of his understanding of human motivation, the blocks he has to understanding the feelings of others, and in what areas these blocks occur. He learns a host of attitudes which the individual has that he may deny or be unaware of—particularly attitudes toward authority; toward conformity; toward differences in race, religion, intelligence, social-class status; toward codes of behavior that govern when no one is looking; toward himself—his own worth and needs and hopes. He observes those areas in which verbalizations and behavior are in conflict and knows that the pupil needs help in understanding his conflict. We hope you will learn to use this tool with skill, for it is one of the more difficult to use, yet one of the most useful in your kit. One small caution in using role-playing, never assign roles to be played. The response must be *voluntary* if it is to be valid.

Sociometric Tools

The knowledge gained from sociometric devices has been discussed fully in the previous chapter, "Study of Group Situations." This is an important tool—one that you will need to learn how to handle effectively. With this tool you will have a better knowledge of the friendship patterns in your class. (See sociograms on pages 390-391.) This knowledge is invaluable in assessing feelings. No teacher knows what he teaches unless he senses the feelings of his pupils.

Samples of Work

You will find it helpful as you begin your teaching to make a folder for each of your pupils in which samples of work may be kept. Keep some of the pupil's writing, some of his art work, his own evaluations of his progress, records of what he has read. We believe you will want to discuss with each pupil just what he would like to have included in his folder. Now and then you and the pupil will look over the samples and make some decisions about the pupil's progress and what skills his future work needs to emphasize. These occasions may be enviable moments when the pupil has the undivided attention of his teacher, or they may be moments to be dreaded. It all depends on the teacher's attitude about his role in learning. If he assumes his role is to *make* the pupils learn, this tool may turn into a weapon.

| **Life-Space** | One of the more important tools is to become familiar with the pupil's life-space. Take a walk home with the pupil and try to see his |

environment through his eyes. Note the things he passes that would be of interest to him. If you are lucky enough to have him accompany you, take note of what he chooses to point out to you. Note those phases of his life-space that might be negative to a child's development. Note the feelings he has about his home, his toys, his family, his friends. We like the story in *Heaven in My Hand* when the school teacher, smelling the odors from the kitchen of a meager home, said, "Thy mother must be a wonderful cook." Her answer from the child was, "My mother is no cook. She is the Lady What Cooks!" [13] Such a distinction indeed reveals a world of difference in feelings about one's home. This is what one attempts to sense as he tries to understand the life-space of another.[14]

| **Informal Associations** | Try to see your pupils outside of school if you can. They have a different picture of you seen away from the classroom. This often leads to a freer exchange of feelings, and |

you will see them differently when you are not responsible for them. If you teach in a community where many of the children go to a settlement house, or community center after school, drop in some afternoon and watch them at play. If they are in a play or a program away from school and invite you (and they will if they have an inkling you'd like to be invited), accept and see what your pupils attend to when not busy with school. If you see the pupil outside school, you are less likely to respond as did this teacher: "The next day Bill brought in a whole album of Rock 'n Roll records. Fortunately, we were very busy and did not have time to

---

[13] Alice Lee Humphreys, *Heaven in My Hand* (Richmond: The John Knox Press, 1950), p. 28.
[14] See earlier discussion of life-space, pp. 146-150.

play them." In those school systems that have school camping, teachers come back from a week with their pupils with changed perceptions of the boys and girls. We dare say the pupils' perceptions of teachers are changed considerably, too! At adolescence teachers have more chance to develop the kind of relationship that de-emphasizes status. Secondary teachers have the best chance of coming to know their pupils through extracurricular activities. These activities (if we allow them to be run by the pupils) enrich the classroom relationship far more than we would expect, judging by the time they require from the sponsor.

Specialists'
Help

Nearly all schools today have some specialists whose job it is to help the classroom teacher in diagnosing and working through problems that are too severe for him to handle by himself. The elementary school has a school nurse, perhaps a psychologist, a helping teacher, a supervisor, and a principal. Some schools have remedial teachers for reading and speech. Some have special teachers for art, music, physical education. Nearly all secondary teachers have guidance personnel as well as the other categories of specialists. The classroom teacher then does not have to be the "be-all and know-all." We urgently insist that the classroom teacher is in a better position to know the child in depth than any other person on the staff. The classroom teacher, therefore, must be accepted as a vital, equal member of a team when special help is required.

Fortunately, teaching is moving toward becoming a profession, and teachers are more frequently accorded the respect of professional status in discussing records and materials collected about a pupil's behavior. We believe the more effective way for specialists to use their competencies is to work with teachers in helping them understand the signs of trouble, the kinds of blocks to mental health which some practices engender, and the channels for securing help when the school's resources are exhausted. One of the great wastes of our day is the psychological data collected by some school psychologists and filed neatly away because the teacher does not understand the recommendations or has so little confidence in them that they are not implemented. The teacher-psychologist relationship must be one of equals who respect each other, but who have different tools with which to help the pupil. We believe the psychologist should see the pupil in the classroom before making judgments about him. The teacher's use of the specialist is as effective as his understanding of what services the specialist has to offer and his confidence in the effectiveness of these services. Today many tests are available to the teacher in helping him gain a more complete picture of a child's mental, physical, and social development. While it is outside the scope of this book to discuss these tests, we note here that often the teacher needs the help of a specialist in interpreting these tests.

Creative

Listening

Perhaps you wonder that we include this as a tool. If you do, set up a tape recorder in a classroom some day for an hour and then play it back. Record the amount of time the teacher was talking and compare it with the time the pupils talked. Now, you can't be listening if you are talking. Most of us school teachers are big talkers. We know so much that we want to pass on. We have so much material to cover. We forget that we miss so much by not listening attentively—trying hard to hear what the individual is saying between the lines as well as on the lines. So much of our effort in school is to keep people quiet, but pupils who are really quiet, who are "shut up" are inaccessible to learning.

Creative listening is a tool that permeates all we do. You use it in sociometrics as you interview the pupils about their choices, in role-playing, in home visits, and don't (whatever you do) fail to listen creatively in parent conferences. Somebody once said that we need three ears; one to listen to the words, a second to listen for meaning and a third to listen for feelings—what is not said. We are aware of the great lengths to which some of us go on occasion to use words to conceal our feelings. We must train ourselves to become sensitive to what is behind the verbal screen. What was she really trying to say? What did that expression in his eyes mean when he said he couldn't see me this afternoon after school? Some of the cues to watch for as you attempt to listen creatively are:

Is the language simple, direct, concrete, or is it stilted, vague, obscure, euphemistic?
Does the individual come straight to the point or is there verbal hedging?
Does the language he uses and the non-verbal communication convey the same message? If there's a conflict, better trust the non-verbal.

As you teach, each of you will learn to handle these tools with skill. You'll learn just what model seems to fit your personality and your ways of working. You will undoubtedly discover many more that you will want to add to your personalized tool kit. We have not mentioned test data, or projective techniques, for example. Many of the tools discussed are projective, and the variations and adaptations available in their use are multiple. You will be working with test data in many of your courses. The sources that follow indicate many of the helps available for you. As a person beginning teaching, remember that teaching is not the performing of tricks nor the application of formulae. Teaching is an art. The most basic characteristic of an art is that it must flow out of the life experiences of the creator. The joy and challenge of teaching is that opportunities to be creative never run out. You have an inexhaustible supply of creative means waiting to be fashioned by your hands, your thoughts, and your feelings into a work of art—the art of teaching.

Additional Sources You May Find Helpful

You'll need to read more about the tools we have discussed in this chapter. We hope you'll try using these tools as you continue your training as a teacher. Consult the following sources. You'll find them helpful.

READINGS ON ANECDOTAL RECORDS

Association for Supervision and Curriculum Development, "Using Anecdotal Records," *Fostering Mental Health in Our Schools.* Washington, D. C.: National Education Association, 1950, pp. 184-202.

Roger Barker and Herbert F. Wright, *One Boy's Day: A Specimen Record of Behavior.* New York: Harper and Brothers, 1951.

Peter Blos, *The Adolescent Personality.* New York: Appleton-Century-Crofts, Inc., 1941.

Daniel A. Prescott, *Helping Teachers Understand Children.* Washington, D. C.: American Council on Education, 1946.

————, *The Child in the Educative Process.* New York: McGraw-Hill Book Company, Inc., 1957.

Marie I. Rasey and J. W. Menge, *What We Learn from Children.* New York: Harper and Brothers, 1956.

Arthur E. Traxler, *The Nature and Use of Anecdotal Records.* New York: Educational Records Bureau, 1939.

450

READINGS ON HOME VISITS

Association for Supervision and Curriculum Development, "Children Bring Their Families to School," *Fostering Mental Health in Our Schools*. Washington, D. C.: National Education Association, 1950, pp. 18-31.

Allison Davis, *Social-Class Influences Upon Learning*. Cambridge, Mass.: Harvard University Press, 1948.

James Hymes, *Effective Home-School Relations*. Englewood Cliffs, N. J.: Prentice-Hall, Inc., 1953.

Fritz Redl and William W. Wattenberg, *Mental Hygiene in Teaching*. New York: Harcourt, Brace and Company, 1951, pp. 377-379.

Ruby H. Warner, *The Child and His Elementary School World*. Englewood Cliffs, N. J.: Prentice-Hall, Inc., 1957, pp. 379-381.

READINGS ON PARENT CONFERENCES

Dorothy W. Baruch, *Parents and Children Go to School*. Chicago: Scott, Foresman and Company, 1939.

————, *Parents Can Be People*. New York: Appleton-Century-Crofts, 1944.

Katherine E. D'Evelyn, *Individual Parent-Teacher Conferences*. New York: Bureau of Publications, Teachers College, Columbia University, 1950, pamphlet.

Eva H. Grant, *Parents and Teachers as Parents*. Chicago: Science Research Associates, pamphlet.

Grace Langdon and I. Stout, *Teacher-Parent Interviews*. Englewood Cliffs, N. J.: Prentice-Hall, Inc., 1954.

J. Murray Lee and Dorris May Lee, *The Child and His Development*. New York: Appleton-Century-Crofts, Inc., 1958, pp. 575-593.

Fritz Redl and William W. Wattenberg, *Mental Hygiene in Teaching*. New York: Harcourt, Brace and Company, 1951, pp. 360-376.

G. Wesley Sowards, "Three Way Conferences, Child-Parent-Teacher," *Childhood Education*, Vol. 30 (January 1954), pp. 216-219.

Ruby H. Warner, *The Child and His Elementary School World*. Englewood Cliffs, N. J.: Prentice-Hall, Inc., 1957, pp. 390-393.

READINGS ON FREE PLAY

Virginia Axline, *Play Therapy: The Inner Dynamics of Childhood*. New York: Houghton Mifflin, 1947.

Lawrence K. Frank, *Projective Methods*. New York: Charles C. Thomas Publishing Company, 1948.

————, "Therapeutic Play Techniques, Symposium, 1954," *The American Journal of Orthopsychiatry*, Vol. XXV, No. 3, July 1955, pp. 576-590.

Clara Lambert, *Play; A Child's Way of Growing Up*. New York: Play School Association, Inc.

Mildred Celia Letton, *Your Child's Leisure Time*. New York: Bureau of Publications, Teachers College, Columbia University, pamphlet.

C. E. Moustakes, *Children in Play Therapy*. New York: McGraw-Hill Book Company, Inc., 1953.

Jerome M. Seidman, *The Child: A Book of Readings*. New York: Rinehart and Company, Inc., 1958, pp. 328-355, 547-583.

Joseph C. Soloman, *Therapeutic Use of Play: An Introduction to Projective Techniques*. Englewood Cliffs, N. J.: Prentice-Hall, Inc., 1951.

FILMS ON FREE PLAY

Balloons: Aggression and Destruction Games (Studies of Normal Personality Development Series), 17 min., sound, New York University Film Library.

Finger Painting (Studies of Normal Personality Development Series), 22 min., silent, color. Distributed by New York University Film Library.

Play Is Our Business, 20 minutes, sound, Sundial Films.

Understanding Children's Play (Studies of Normal Personality Development Series), 11 min., sound, New York University Film Library.

READINGS ON CREATIVE WORK

Rose Alschuler and La Berta Hattwick, *Painting and Personality*. Chicago: University of Chicago Press, 1948.

Gladys Andrews, *Creative Rhythmic Movement for Children*. Englewood Cliffs, N. J.: Prentice-Hall, Inc., 1954.

Alvina Burrows and Others, *They All Want to Write*. Englewood Cliffs, N. J.: Prentice-Hall, Inc., 1952.

Natalie Cole, *The Arts in the Classroom*. New York: John Day Company, Inc., 1940.

Victor D'Amico, *Creative Teaching in Art*. Scranton, Pa.: International Textbook Company, 1942.

Margaret Heaton, *Feelings Are Facts*. New York: National Conference of Christians and Jews, pamphlet.

Viktor Lowenfeld, *Creative and Mental Growth*. New York: The Macmillan Company, 1952.

A. H. Maslow, "Emotional Blocks to Creativity," *Journal of Individual Psychology*, Vol. 14, No. 1, May 1958, pp. 51-56.

Hughes Mearns, *Creative Youth*. New York: Doubleday and Company, Inc., 1929.

James L. Mursell, *Music and the Classroom Teacher*. New York: Silver Burdett Company, 1951.

Caroline Pratt, *I Learn from Children*. New York: Simon and Schuster, Inc., 1956.

Ruby H. Warner, *The Child and His Elementary School World*. Englewood Cliffs, N. J.: Prentice-Hall, Inc., 1957, pp. 93-135, 180-225, 349-375.

READINGS ON ROLE-PLAYING

Association for Supervision and Curriculum Development, "Sociodrama as Educative Process," *Fostering Mental Health in Our Schools*. Washington, D. C.: National Education Association, 1950, pp. 260-285.

Alex Bavelas, "Some Comments on the Uses of Role Playing," *Sociatry*, June 1947.

Arthur Katona, "Sociodrama," *Social Education*, January 1955, pp. 19-26.

Howard Lane and Mary Beauchamp, *Human Relations in Teaching*. Englewood Cliffs, N. J.: Prentice-Hall, Inc., 1955, pp. 266-279.

George and Fannie R. Shaftel, *Role Playing the Problem Story*. New York: National Conference of Christians and Jews, pamphlet.

READINGS ON SOCIOMETRY

Helen Hall Jennings, *Sociometry in Group Relations*. Washington, D. C.: American Council on Education, 1948.

Howard Lane and Mary Beauchamp, *Human Relations in Teaching*. Englewood Cliffs, N. J.: Prentice-Hall, Inc., 1955, pp. 312-316.

Horace Mann Lincoln Institute of School Experimentation, *How to Construct a Sociogram*. New York: Bureau of Publications, Teachers College, Columbia University, 1947.

J. L. Moreno, ed., *Sociometry and the Science of Man*. New York: Beacon House, 1956.

READINGS ON USE OF SPECIALISTS

Robert Felix, *How a Child Guidance Clinic Can Help the Troubled Child.* Bethseda, Md.: National Institute of Mental Health.

Fritz Redl and William W. Wattenberg, *Mental Hygiene in Teaching.* New York: Harcourt, Brace and Company, 1951, pp. 339-359.

Carl Rogers, *Client-Centered Therapy.* Boston: Houghton Mifflin, 1951.

Ann Marie Walsh, *Self-Concept of Bright Boys with Learning Difficulties.* New York: Bureau of Publications, Teachers College, Columbia University, 1956.

FILMS ON WAYS SPECIAL COMMUNITY SERVICES HELP CHILDREN

Angry Boy, 33 min., sound, Mental Health Film Board.

Head of the House, 37 min., sound, Mental Health Film Board.

Problem of Pupil Adjustment: Part I—The Dropout: A Case Study (Educational Psychology Series), 20 min., sound, McGraw-Hill Book Company, Inc.

The Quiet One, 67 min., sound, Film Documents.

16

Know Thyself

As we come to the writing of the closing pages of this book, we note an article in *The New York Times* [1] stating that a world-wide shortage of teachers exists. This is not surprising, for the task of teaching is indeed a difficult one calling for an inordinate amount of commitment and high purpose. Teaching, however, calls for *something in addition to the will to teach*

[1] Paul Hofmann, "Lack of Teachers Held World-Wide," *The New York Times,* August 5, 1958, p. 29L.

well. It calls for a sensitive ability to work constructively with the intricate fabric of human relations. The great teacher is a consummate artist.

The purpose of this chapter is to make more explicit one of the underlying themes that runs throughout the book: the necessity to "know thyself," and to use this insight to enrich your own teaching. We have inferred throughout the book that the teacher teaches no better than the accuracy and sensitivity of his perceptions of the feelings that are generated in the classroom. An important aim of all education is self-understanding and self-acceptance. This chapter indicates some ways to work toward these aims in one's life and in one's teaching.

With so much of modern business and social success depending upon the impressions one makes upon other people, much of child training at home and in school results in hiding and repressing feelings and urgent personal wishes. In many of us, particularly those who have succeeded in high school and college, this motive has become so deeply ingrained that we dare not trust our own perceptions of our feelings and wishes nor accept their validity. The diversity and intensity of the conflicting pressures of modern life have convinced many thoughtful persons that disinterested professional help of trained diagnosticians and therapists is necessary to enable us to see ourselves clearly and to determine for ourselves appropriate courses of action. The reliance upon psychotherapy as a means for solving personal conflicts is particularly strong in many cities—in those areas, in other words, where relationships are more impersonal, life moves more rapidly, and roots tend to be less well anchored.

We are unwilling to accept the idea that the conditions that cause personal confusion and widespread reliance upon a profession of "listening" must continue to exist. We deem it important to train those who work with the young to create and maintain conditions which help children and youth to see themselves ever more clearly, and to accept the validity of their own preferences as developed from respect for the quality of living of their associates as well as of themselves.

Certainly no sharp line can be drawn between therapy and education. We believe that teachers must look upon the two functions as interrelated processes which occur in daily associations with people; that being a teacher carries with it responsibility for being an individual from whom the young may receive effective non-technical therapy. Probably you have not had much help in gaining self-understanding as you have gone through school. As you guide the directions of education for those you teach, you have the opportunity to help your students develop self-understanding.

Necessity for Knowing Yourself

You cannot know another in ways *you* have not known, consciously or unconsciously. You are able to help children work with their feelings constructively to the extent that you are able to understand and resolve, to a tolerable level, your own conflicts. How true in the classroom is the saying, "You know not what you do," if you are unaware of the feelings that are continuously interplaying with the content and structure of the class.

We believe the days are gone when a teacher at any level (including college) dare be unconcerned with the total development of the human beings he says he is teaching. Re-read Elmo Roper's statement on page 99 in which he discusses this thesis. Skills are too easy to come by and too easily used, either consciously or unconsciously, for destructive purposes unless insights and values are nurtured most carefully. Mankind has gone to war every fifteen or twenty years throughout recorded history; often the warring peoples have been the most schooled. When one gets to bedrock causes, wars are caused by neurotic people, immature people, people with great skill whose values are warped. Our time demands a generation of mature people. We should like to quote several statements made by Chisholm as he spoke about this need most succinctly at a gathering of psychiatrists for the second series of William Alanson White Memorial Lectures held in New York in October 1945:

> The training of children is making a thousand neurotics for every one that psychiatrists can hope to help with psychotherapy . . .
> In whatever direction we explore . . . we come back inevitably to the

necessity of having in every country large numbers of mature, reasonable
people, free of guilt and inferiorities . . .

The government of a country cannot organize and impose any social developments or external relations which are too far ahead of the state of
maturity of its citizens . . .

The most important thing in the world today is the bringing up of children. . . . To be allowed to teach children should be the sign of the final
approval of society . . .

Can such a program of re-education or of a new kind of education be
charted? I would not presume to go so far, except to suggest that psychology and sociology and simple psychopathology, the sciences of living,
should be made available to all the people by being taught to all children in primary and secondary schools . . .[2]

Since most of us were not taught "the sciences of living" in primary
or secondary schools, we have the obligation to become well-informed in
these areas during college days or later. We suggest a few ways for developing self-understanding that have proved helpful to us.

Ways

for Developing

Self-Understanding

One way to develop self-understanding is to become *familiar on
a reading level* with the thought of
those who have analyzed human
behavior, the "sciences of living"
as Chisholm calls them. You have
had a taste of this method as you have studied this book. Much of the
content of psychotherapy is now being written in language that is understandable to the layman who wishes to be thoughtful about human motivation. Psychology seems to be taking a turn which emphasizes the
personal, subjective streams of human interaction in contrast to the
normative approaches of the past generation or so. These newer approaches are rich fields to explore in your reading. At the end of this
chapter we annotate a few of these references. These will lead you to
others.

Another process for coming to understand yourself is to cultivate the
habit of self-analysis. We use the word advisedly, knowing that some of
our colleagues will cringe before it. Such cringing, the authors believe, is
a reaction to the idea that anyone can be an analyst, even an untrained

---

[2] G. B. Chisholm, "The Psychiatry of Enduring Peace and Social Progress," The
William Alanson White Memorial Lectures, *Psychiatry*, Vol. IX, No. 1, February, 1946,
pp. 1-44.

person. However, to be critical, aware, thoughtful, and self-analytical, about one's behavior is a necessity for a teacher. Unconscious processes must be raised to the conscious level. A part of an analytical attitude, of course, is to be aware of areas and times when more specialized help is needed, to know how to secure it, and to accept the wisdom of seeking such help.

Much insight comes to one who forms the habit of asking: "Why did this happen this way? Why did I feel like that? Why did I feel I had to do or say that? Wonder what *he heard* me say that I was unaware of saying when he flushed like that?" Helpful in understanding human motivation is the process of mental role-playing through which you can anticipate probable responses to alternate ways of handling a situation that is fraught with potential conflict.

Another step closely related to mental role-playing is to learn to talk about your feelings rather freely in a group composed of individuals in whom you have confidence and with whom you have a peer relationship. The dianetic [3] movement that swept the country a decade ago was probably exaggerated in its claims and uses, but a seed of helpfulness resides in the general idea of "talking out" one's feelings in a systematic way with individuals who respect and accept us as we are. As has been said so many times in this book, repression of feelings is unhealthy. Yet all of us, especially teachers, have to repress in our daily lives. We need a safety valve to counteract the frustration that builds up as repression continues. A group of colleagues with whom you talk freely and feel free to be yourself, even if it is sometimes a rather bruised self that emerges, is of great help as a safety valve.

The "talking out" process has another purpose that is of even greater value, for it helps the individual to point toward the future with deeper, more inclusive insights. If the group values a searching atmosphere (if it doesn't, it has little function), many questions are raised that may not have posed themselves to the individual at the time of his conflict. From a consideration of these questions come additional explanations of *why* the individual behaves as he does, additional alternatives to play out mentally in order to determine consequences of action. This process leads to deeper analyses of human behavior.

Another way to develop more self-understanding is consciously to discover some means whereby you feel released, and then give yourself

---

[3] L. Ron Hubbard, *Dianetics* (New York: Hermitage House, 1950).

an opportunity to spend some time in this activity. We recall a doctoral student who had been quite concerned about some of the conflicting relationships that had arisen during her advanced study. She had occasion to drive a friend's car on a trip (hers had long ago been traded in for tuition), and returned with her old assurance and poise restored. When she got behind the wheel, familiar muscle patterns and nerve reactions began to function. She found herself able to think more clearly. The way she put it was, "The world is mine again!"

Most of us respond in a similar manner to a variety of activities. Maybe a vigorous swim or a long, solitary walk is what releases you. We believe that there are many ways individuals have found to release their feelings. It is especially helpful to the teacher to identify his areas of release so he consciously may seek them out as he feels the need for them, for he has more than the usual demand to hold his feelings in check.

If we are to be insightful about ourselves, we must seek not only to release but also to *clarify* our feelings. Trying to put our feelings into words, or pictures, or forms, or movement so that they make sense to us, will help us to develop more critical self-awareness. As we clarify, we ask *why*. We examine that which has been released to ask ourselves the personal, private meaning of it.

If you like to hold a pencil, stream-of-consciousness writing may afford you the clarification of feelings that you seek. If you like to paint, water colors or oils may serve to release your tenseness and give you perspective on your conflicts. Working with clay or marble, creating a musical composition, or interpreting one created by another may be the activities satisfying to you.

The teacher's own life-style is expressed, among other ways, in the choices he makes for spending his leisure-time, for *gratifying himself* by doing the things *he* wants and needs to do. The teacher's life-style is an important ingredient in the teaching process. We urge teachers to take note of their own life-styles and to utilize these creative interests in their classrooms. Too often we find teachers trying to keep their own inner concerns and interests separated from what happens in the classroom. We think of Mr. Jeremiah who is a "whiz" with hi-fi. He is continuously experimenting with sound production and his wife gets "tangled up" with endless feet of wiring. At school no one knows this about Mr. Jeremiah. He teaches world history from the text and is considered a drone by his pupils. The creative teacher shares himself. He explores with his pupils the meanings and joys that he has wrested from life and endows them with personal significance, giving them personality.

With mixed amusement and sadness we have observed promising young teachers trying to assume the life-style of teachers whom they found valuable in their own lives. No teacher attains full effectiveness as long as he attempts to copy someone else. It makes a real difference to the pupils to have you with your own life-style as the teacher—not that you are better than one with another life-style, but that *you* are *you*, bringing your joys and ways of doing things to the classroom.

We have found it helpful in seeking self-understanding to develop associations with individuals who are older, more experienced, who seem mature and self-directive, and who express social concern in a devoted spirit and with assurance. A really mature person is able to accept you as you are. Such acceptance leads a person to new vistas in self-exploration. Having gone through school with others our own age, we tend to avoid the companionship of older people. Thus we miss exposure to much earthy wisdom that comes only from experiencing deeply and over a long enough period of time to bring perspective to the joys and sorrows of life. Be sure you have some older friends.

Rogers expresses the values that come from relationships that are accepting of individuals as they are as follows:

> ... it seems reasonable to hypothesize that if the parent creates with his child a psychological climate such as we have described, then the child will become more self-directing, socialized and mature. To the extent that the teacher creates such a relationship with his class, the student will become a self-initiated learner, more original, more self-disciplined, less anxious and other-directed. . . . It appears possible to me that we are seeing the emergence of a new field of human relationships, in which we may specify that if certain attitudinal conditions exist, then certain definable changes will occur . . .

> If I can create a relationship characterized on my part:
>   by a genuineness and transparency, in which I am my real feelings;
>   by a warm acceptance of and liking for the other person as a separate individual;
>   by a sensitive ability to see his world and himself as he sees them;

> Then the other individual in the relationship:
>   will experience and understand aspects of himself which previously he has repressed;
>   will find himself becoming better integrated, more able to function effectively;

will become more similar to the person he would like to be;

will be more self-directing and self-confident;

will become more of a person, more unique and more self-expressive;

will be able to cope with the problems of life more adequately and more comfortably.

I believe that this statement holds whether I am speaking of my relationships with a client, with a group of students or staff members, with my family or children. It seems to me that we have here a general hypothesis which offers exciting possibilities for the development of creative, adaptive, inner-directed persons.[4]

The ways, discussed briefly in the preceding paragraphs, are those that the authors have found helpful in their lives. You will find others that suit your particular needs, temperaments, and interests to add to this list. Out of this exploration of yourself, you'll be seeking answers to questions like these:

Why do I get tongue-tied around older people, when I am such a glib talker with my own group?

About what subjects do I find myself talking in louder and louder tones when someone disagrees with my point of view?

Why can I tolerate "smart-alecky" behavior in a girl and not in a boy? Or the other way around?

Why do I sometimes feel so alone in a crowd?

What causes me to "blow my top" without due reason?

What kinds of temperaments make me feel comfortable, at home? What kinds irritate me? What kinds do I fail to respond to? Why do certain temperaments affect me as they do?

What sources of authority do I find acceptable and what sources do I reject?

Why do I listen and heed advice coming from _____ and resent the same advice coming from _____?

What mannerisms do I have that pupils might find annoying, amusing, distracting?

For what concerns will I go the second mile?

Can I anticipate my own breaking points of fatigue, anger, uncertainty? Have I found ways to handle constructively situations in which I reach the breaking point?

Do I understand the strengths and fallacies of my attitudes toward authority? Am I aware of their origins?

Am I irrational or illogical in my attitudes about certain areas? Which ones?

Does the discussion of some topics cause a lump to come into my throat? Which topics? Under what circumstances?

---

[4] Carl R. Rogers, *Becoming a Person*, Nellie Heldt Lectures, Oberlin College, Oberlin, Ohio. 1953, pp. 6-7.

Am I aware of my inner purposes when I overexpend my energy, when I procrastinate unduly, when I insist upon being exactly punctual, when I am extravagant in any one form of behavior?

Use of

Self-Understanding

in Teaching

Process

This brings us to a consideration of how the teacher uses his self-understanding in the teaching process itself. We should like to present a point of view that may create considerable differences of opinion. If it stimulates additional thought, we shall be satisfied to close the book with it. We believe that in our world today—laden as it is with such tremendous conflicts, such acceleration of time and diminution of space, such centralization of communication facilities—the teacher must be a non-technical therapist if he is to *help develop the kind of mature people the world needs.*

Before rejecting or accepting the concept, let's examine what we mean by therapy and why so many people withdraw from any connotation of the teacher's using therapy. We use the phrase "non-technical therapist" to distinguish the encouraging, challenging, caring-for processes of teaching as distinct from the concept of therapy administered by one trained in psychoanalysis or psychotherapy. We believe that the negative attitudes expressed about teachers as non-technical therapists belong to the same time-span as the concept that people who were mentally ill were clearly definable. Now with greater understanding of mental health, we recognize that normal and abnormal are not clear-cut points on a continuum of mental health; that all of us are abnormal in some ways about some things and at some times. Kubie describes behavior thus: "Behavior is normal or abnormal because of the nature of the inner forces which produce it."[5] Most children successfully grow through most of the symptoms which are ascribed to severe disturbances. Yet we do not consider this behavior of children abnormal because the inner forces which produced the behavior were not disturbed. The greater the influence of unconscious forces upon any particular act, the more likely the act is to be neurotic. This principle is easy to recognize in a psychotic person—he is

---

[5] Lawrence S. Kubie, "The Nature of Psychotherapy," *Bulletin of the New York Academy of Medicine,* Vol. 19, No. 3, March 1943, pp. 183-194.

pushed into behavior that makes no sense to him but he cannot keep himself from acting in that way.

Although literally the word therapist means "an attendant or servant," through usage it has come to mean "to take care of or to serve." This function the teacher must assume with each of his pupils. Since feelings are present in every group situation, the insight with which we assume this function determines the quality of the therapy which we give. We *do* affect behavior. As teachers, whether we like it or not, we do have *power over* and *power with*. Since we have power and since we are working with feelings, we must know what we do and learn how to do it with skill and understanding if we are truly "to serve." One distinction that might be made between education and therapy is that while the two are one and the same in methods and purpose, they deal with different data.

All of us are in need of a therapeutic climate or atmosphere to keep from letting the abnormal phases of our personality become the ascendant forces within us. The movie, *Gaslight,* is an interesting illustration of an individual's attempt to induce abnormality in another by creating a climate for it. The ways in which we assume our roles as non-technical therapists depend upon our self-understanding and our understandings of the needs of the individuals within our classrooms. As stated earlier, these two cannot be separated. For example, it may be therapy to see to it that Helen gets to feed the rabbits every morning for a few weeks if she is grieving about the loss of her mother, or that Joe has a task that is just a bit too difficult for him to accomplish with perfection if Joe is beginning to form a picture of himself as infallible. It may be therapy to let Ed sit apart from the group for a few days if he seems to need this apartness before he can make the effort to accept the belongingness that is being offered by the group. It may be therapy to listen to Sue read to you, the teacher, until she knows that you are not ashamed of her because she can't read as well as her mother thinks she ought to. Maslow says: "We must learn to think of it (therapy) more as a technique for fostering growth and general improvement of the human being, for encouraging self-actualization." [6]

We accept our role as therapists when we accept the responsibility for assuming a vital part in making life "good" for the children we teach. We refuse the role when we refer pupils to a specialist and assume no

---

[6] A. H. Maslow, "A Philosophy of Psychology" (lecture to lay audience, Cooper Union, New York, N. Y., March 7, 1956).

responsibility thereafter. Our profession will make little progress, it seems to us, in arranging healthy therapeutic environments for living as long as we assume that the specialist can know children's needs and interests apart from close and continuous consultation with the teacher who lives with them day-by-day.

As the teacher works with groups of boys and girls, he has many levels of relatedness available to him. Powell describes these levels as, "ranging from that of intellectual alignment, which is nearest the surface, to that of individual drives such as love and hate, wish and dread, dominance and submission, with all their conflicts, which is deepest hidden." [7] The deepest level should be left to the analyst. Teachers often limit their relatedness to the surface level of "intellectual alignment." At this level we feel safe. In between these two extremes is a vast area of intrarelatedness which gives a sensitive, insightful teacher opportunities to affect behavior in positive directions. One quality needed by the teacher is to be able to listen creatively. Everyone is able to listen, but to listen effectively one has to *hear what the talker wants us to hear.* Many important communications are not put into words, but these communications are likely to give us important data in understanding feelings. One teacher says, "I have learned to say less and allow my children to think for themselves." Anna Freud's book, *Psychoanalysis for Teachers and Parents,*[8] is a helpful source for extending one's thinking about how one relates on deeper levels of meaningfulness to children.

We shall discuss five aspects of the therapeutic processes involved in teaching: (1) giving of support and encouragement; (2) preventive planning; (3) working with emotions so as to raise problems to awareness; (4) extending oneself to the parents of one's pupils; (5) knowing when specialized help is needed.

Giving Support and Encouragement

The teacher serves as a therapist in giving *support* to the boys and girls he teaches. This is nothing new. Wise, understanding teachers have always used encouragement, love, and empathy as they have related to

---

[7] John W. Powell, "Process Analysis as Content: A Suggested Basis for Group Classification," *The Journal of Social Issues,* Vol. VIII, No. 2, 1952, pp. 54-66.

[8] Anna Freud, *Psychoanalysis for Teachers and Parents* (New York: Emerson Books, Inc., 1954).

their pupils. Grandmothers have traditionally assumed this role in many cultures. Two differences exist between grandmother's role and the modern teacher's role. The teacher is not relying completely on his intuition. He knows what he is doing and why. Second, the teacher usually is supporting and encouraging the individual in a group situation. This makes the task much more complex. We assume grandmother's success might be attributed to the strong bond of love and kinship which sharpened her intuitions and helped her see each of her grandchildren as an individual. Maslow describes eloquently the difference between grandmother and today's teacher when he says, "This is the triumph of science, that ultimately it can take the innate wisdom of the great intuitors, correct it, test it, winnow it, and come out with a better product with more certain and reliable knowledge." [9]

To give support and encouragement intelligently the teacher has to know a great deal about each individual in his group. He has to know much the same kinds of things which grandmother knew just because she was grandmother. That is, he needs to know as much as possible about the affectional life of this child, his interests and concerns, with whom he plays or relaxes, what he does when he is alone, if he is ever alone, the pressure he feels from the adults in his life, his temperament, his health record, his major achievements and failures, and something of his fantasy life, if possible.

We have no difficulty supporting and encouraging children and youth who behave as we think they ought to behave. The naughty, defiant, sullen, impudent pupil may need support and encouragement more than the well-behaved. Most of the discussion on this point is concerned, therefore, with support and encouragement of the pupil whose behavior seems negative to us. Support and encouragement are given by refraining from ridicule, sarcasm, blaming, and shaming. These have no place in the classroom. Youngsters reject not only these behaviors but the one who uses them. As soon as threat is introduced into a situation, distortions occur and perceptions narrow. If we wish learning to be positive, we will refrain from producing threatening climates. To be subjected "to anger-producing situations" without release is destructive of mental health.

---

[9] A. H. Maslow, "A Philosophy of Psychology" (lecture to lay audience, Cooper Union, New York, N. Y., March 7, 1956).

Dorothy Baruch [10] counts this as one of the major cultural stresses to which children are subjected. Especially is this true of children of middle-class culture.

Knowing this about children and youth, we may find it feasible to give support in the classroom by allowing the release of anger. This is hard for us teachers to take, especially if the anger is directed against us. To feel comfortable with anger or hostile feelings, we have to understand the sources of our own hostile feelings. The film, *Angry Boy*,[11] shows the effects of anger upon a boy who has not been allowed to release it. Thoughtful teachers try to find many ways that anger may be released and rechanneled in an atmosphere that is supporting of the individual. Some nursery school and primary grades have a punching bag for this purpose. Creative activities, especially those requiring large movements, help the individual to release his feelings into materials or forms. In this process, a pupil begins to sense the ways in which feelings become a part of something outside of himself and how they may be communicated to others. Clay, building materials, dancing, swinging, and painting are excellent media for releasing hostility.

A direct handling of anger, through acting out, role-playing, or counseling, is preferable to the enforced submission that is required of many children. Situations that arise in the classroom between class members may be acted out by the involved individuals without harm resulting. Suppose two boys are having a fight about who gets to use the basketball for practice shooting. To refrain from stepping in with an admonition, "Now let's be nice boys or neither of you may use the ball," may be a wise act of support. The teacher makes some quick calculations about the need of these two to settle their dispute in their own way, the likelihood of either one getting hurt physically, and the requirements of their total life situation to repress their angry feelings. Allowing children and youth to act hostilely toward each other is one way of supporting them.

If a direct acting out is too dangerous, role-playing the situation may result in a release of feelings that is almost as therapeutic to the participants (see Chapter 15 for a discussion of this method). In all situations in which the teacher encourages the release of anger and hostility, he tries to find many ways to reflect to the pupils the feelings they are expressing,

---

[10] Dorothy Baruch, "Therapeutic Procedures as Part of the Educative Process," *Journal of Consulting Psychology*, 1940, Vol. IV, No. 5, pp. 165-172.

[11] *Angry Boy* (Mental Health Film Board), 33 min., sound, distributed by New York University Film Library.

and to communicate to them his acceptance of their feelings as ordinary, to-be-expected in the process of living. We have tried to say so far that the teacher encourages and supports by recognizing the need of many children to release anger and hostility in school because they are not free to express it at home. The teacher searches for wholesome ways for anger to be released. The film, *Anger at Work*,[12] shows some interesting approaches to the constructive use of anger. The teacher refrains from creating anger-producing situations. He works with all children to help them understand the angry, hostile feelings that they have, and to understand anger as a human emotion that has positive values as well as negative ones. The great reformers are frequently angry humans.

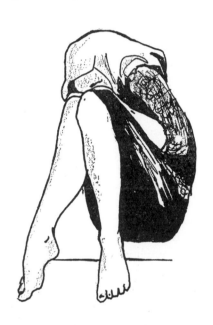

Support and encouragement is needed also by those children who are withdrawn. Frequently the withdrawn ones are suspicious of adults, and need large doses of support and encouragement before it is possible to break through the barriers that have been erected, so that they become trusting enough of adults to be willing to reveal themselves. This may be a slow, tedious process. The older the child, the more difficulty the teacher probably will have in establishing a contact. With little children, the process may begin by actual, physical contact—extra cuddling, time to be with the teacher alone, to sit on his lap, to walk around the room or playground with him. For some little children, physical contact is too threatening. The first step then may be judicious leaving alone, observing what the child shows interest in and seeing that this is available. He may choose a special toy with which to play. The teacher makes sure the child has the toy, and tries to be nearby when the child shows signs of wanting to relate to her.

---

[12] *Anger at Work*, black and white, sound, 21 min., International Film Bureau. May be secured without charge from state health departments.

With older children, the relationship may begin through a common interest. If the teacher can find a way to make the withdrawn child necessary to him, this serves as an effective means to begin communicating. The teacher aims also to create the kind of atmosphere that encourages the withdrawn child to relate affectionately to the group. He studies his group astutely to see what temperaments and interests promise to produce satisfying results if teamed together for a project or an assignment. He observes the non-verbal communication that is so powerful in a classroom. He interprets silences; he watches for cliques; and then he makes judgments about the withdrawn person's chance to make his way in the group and arranges the most favorable atmosphere possible to help him. It is a mistake to allow the withdrawn child to become dependent upon the teacher's approval and acceptance. He needs to be taken into the group. Too close identification with the teacher blocks this process.

The wise and understanding teacher does a multitude of supporting, encouraging things every day that are therapy for some of the pupils in his classroom. He laughs and jokes with his pupils. He notices each one as an individual. He takes time to know the important happenings (and this includes feelings) in his pupils' lives. He spends more time with those pupils who are needful of him; he provides many chances for acting out feelings. He reflects to his pupils the feelings they find troublesome or satisfying and lets them know these are feelings we all have. He plans activities in the classroom that give release to feelings. He is judicious in "letting children alone." He maintains a non-critical attitude toward the expression of feelings that are frequently looked upon by adults as negative or destructive. The therapy is effective and dynamic to the degree that the teacher understands these acts as significant in the growing processes of his pupils. In the words of Maslow, ". . . then therapy should be taken out of the office, and spread to many other areas of life. . . . Support, reassurance, acceptance, love, respect, the giving of safety, all of these are therapeutic." [13]

Preventive Planning

The teacher serves as a non-technical therapist by engaging in preventive planning for therapeutic ends. As we plan what is to be done in

---

[13] A. H. Maslow, "A Philosophy of Psychology" (lecture to lay audience, Cooper Union, New York, N. Y., March 7, 1956).

the classroom, with what materials and experiences, by what methods and for what purposes, we are not only considering what content shall be included in the curriculum, we are also making judgments about the interests, needs, concerns, fears, hopes of each of our pupils. This is therapeutic. If we accept as one of our ends the full development of each individual's uniqueness, we shall avoid standardization of procedures and materials as much as is feasible with group activity. If we accept respect for oneself as a vital, necessary ingredient of mental health, we shall avoid managing our classrooms on a competitive, "better than" basis. If we accept readiness as one of the sound psychological principles in learning, we shall not expect all of our pupils to respond today to that which was introduced to them. Nor shall we penalize them when they don't. If we accept growth as an inner force that emerges as circumstances are right, we shall not use rewards and punishments as extraneous motivations to force growth.

In other words, preventive planning as a process of therapy is taking into account the principles of growth and development that have been established as sound and then arranging circumstances that are consonant with these principles. The demands made upon human beings by the stresses of modern living are so great that major attention must be given to preventive maladjustments, disturbances, and disequilibriums. The statement by Chisholm that the training of children is creating neurotics by the thousands must be seriously considered. A teacher consciously accepting his role as therapist and skilled in it studies his pupils and their circumstances for growth to see how preventive therapy will help to see a pupil through a minor disturbance. Growing up is a difficult process at best. The teacher can help by thoughtfully considering an individual's problems and by anticipating the rough spots of the developmental stage with which he is working. How joyous are the child's words: "I can handle this myself!" Our aim as teachers is to plan in such a way that the feeling expressed by these words may be an assured part of every pupil's life every school day.

The implementation of preventive planning must include a penetrating, thoughtful examination of present school practices. We have a strong hunch and considerable evidence that many of the accepted practices of our schools—grading; grouping; labeling as non-readers, late-developers, retarded, gifted; punishing; promoting on a yearly basis—do contribute markedly to the neuroses of our day. The concepts of levels, of absolute norms, of materials to be covered seem to smother the creative and expressive needs of many individuals and result in serious emotional damage for them. Read *The Story of a School* [14] to see how a school may be organized around the creative and expressive needs of children.

Redl [15] considers preventive planning as one of the notches in maintaining an atmosphere of permissiveness. Just as we don't give a baby fire to play with or turn a toddler loose in an unfenced yard, so we don't

impose psychological decisions upon immature individuals that are beyond their capabilities for handling with some discretion. A healthy atmosphere for growth is one that stretches one's decision-making capacity, but also keeps it in good working order by not demanding more of it than it can possibly deliver. Every individual requires well-defined limits within which behaving occurs. The teacher plans preventively by establishing limits clearly in consultation with his pupils, keeping them to a

---

[14] Central Office of Information, *The Story of a School* (London: His Majesty's Stationery Office, 1949).

[15] Fritz Redl, "Notches of Permissiveness" (notes from a speech made to a class in child development in Washington, D. C., 1954).

minimum, and working with the group to achieve an understanding of them.

Another aspect of preventive planning is to learn how to recognize the beginnings of deviant behavior. These symptoms, though mild, often lead to serious consequences, unless worked with in their early stages. The child who is too good to be real, the withdrawn child, the perfectionist, the child who gets too much satisfaction from hurting—these are some of the ones to give us concern. We have attempted throughout this book to be suggestive about how the teacher learns to recognize early the severely deviant.

Working with Emotions
to Raise Problems to Awareness

In a report of the Committee on Preventive Psychiatry this statement is made:

> As a result of this slow evolutionary process, the educational system is ready now to include programs for the promotion of healthy emotional development as part of the regular curriculum, and to accept further responsibilities for the preparation of its students for adaptation to the problems of stressful life.[16]

The teacher accepts therapeutic functions as he works directly with emotions. The manner in which he does this determines the value of the therapy and is affected greatly by the insightfulness of his understanding and acceptance of his own emotions.

The teacher accepts as criteria these guidelines: he does not assume the role of judge to categorize emotions as "good" or "bad"; he does not become shocked at the expression of antisocial feelings; he does not pry nor probe—rather he takes his cue for sharing of emotions from the manner in which the individual readily reveals himself; he accepts the individual as he is; he realizes that sometimes he has to withdraw from the pupil's revelation of feelings because, in retrospect, the pupil may regret his "spilling over," and resent the teacher for having listened.

With these criteria in mind, the teacher works with the emotions that inevitably come forth if living is challenging. He encourages a certain

---

[16] Committee on Preventive Psychiatry of the Group for the Advancement of Psychiatry, *Promotion of Mental Health in the Primary and Secondary Schools: An Evaluation of Four Projects*, Report No. 18, January 1951.

amount of acting out of feelings. He tries to read between the lines to determine what is not being said because it is felt so strongly. He becomes skilled in the area of non-verbal communications, for he realizes that the strongest feelings can seldom be put into words. So he watches gestures, postures, facial expressions, muscle tension, activity, and passivity. Since he is working with groups most of the time, he searches for meaning in friendship choices, in activities that produce disorganization, in leadership patterns, and other forms of group functioning.

The report of the Committee on Preventive Psychiatry describes four curriculum approaches to working with emotions. These approaches are designed to influence the "mental health of the child through the child's direct experience in the classroom." [17] All of these projects utilize discussion of personal experiences as a means for helping boys and girls to develop insight into their own motivations, drives, and needs. Perhaps the most comprehensive of the projects is that of Ralph H. Ojemann [18] who is revising materials used in the curriculum in a few schools in Iowa so that the dynamics of human behavior are integrated into the teaching process. Thus the why's and how's of human behavior are being taught. To insure the wise use of materials, teachers are being taught how their attitudes toward children are significant and influential in determining what children learn. Teachers are learning how to encourage and help pupils as they discuss causes of human behavior and how to develop an accepting atmosphere for discussion.

The discussing of interpersonal relations often leads to a consideration of situations that can be role-played. Through this method, we have not only a reliving of the situation, but an opportunity to reverse roles so that individuals gain an inkling of the other's feelings and an opportunity to play out situations in more than one way. Using role-playing enables the teacher to guide the pupils to an examination of the consequences of behavior. This process gives teacher and pupils many opportunities to consider limits that are a necessary part of any group situation, and to consider the consequences of ignoring established limits.

As the teacher works with the emotions of his pupils, he becomes increasingly aware of the importance of having clarified his own feelings. As he seeks opportunities to help the individual pupil become aware of his own feelings, the teacher reflects back to the pupil the feelings he

[17] *Ibid*, p. 2
[18] *Ibid*, pp. 8-10

seems to be expressing. The teacher's accuracy in reflecting is obviously dependent upon how insightfully he hears. As the pupil becomes more and more aware of his own emotions, he learns his own processes of rationalization and distortion. He learns much about what threatens him, what gratifies him, and he senses many of the why's, although he may not have words for them. As the teacher attempts to help his pupils to work constructively with their emotions, he realizes how necessary his own self-understanding is in the teaching process. He meets situations daily that are devastating to him unless he recognizes the sources of the emotional currents in his own life. Many teacher-education programs today are encouraging teacher trainees to seek the services of counseling centers or to participate in therapy in order to develop more insight about their own deep-seated conflicts. Certainly many teachers today have opportunities to establish relationships with professional groups that can aid them in their search for self-knowledge in depth. Jersild has been a great force in teacher education in exploring this area with teachers and in developing ways to help teachers face themselves.[19, 20] As has been stated previously in this book, the quest for self-understanding and self-acceptance is a lifelong search and one that involves at times pain and uncertainty as well as yielding moments of great satisfaction.

Extending Oneself
to the Parents of One's Pupils

When a teacher was asked recently, "What have you done today that was therapy?" she replied, "I had a long discussion with Jack's mother who has just moved to our town from the South. I tried to help interpret some of our Jewish culture to her." This teacher recognized the importance of what she did. We cannot limit our efforts to the pupils we teach. We must go beyond the walls of the classroom and become interpreters of child behavior and cultural demands to the parents and other adults of our communities.

One of the most direct ways in which the teacher acts in a therapeutic role with parents is to assess insightfully the climate in which the child

---

[19] Arthur T. Jersild, *When Teachers Face Themselves* (New York: Bureau of Publications, Teachers College, Columbia University, 1955).

[20] ———, "Understanding Others Through Facing Ourselves," *Childhood Education,* May 1954.

or young person lives at home. Knowing this, the teacher not only knows a good deal about the kinds of climate needed at school, but also is in a position to make sounder judgments about how much of the child's behavior should be shared with the parents. For example, if Jim's father is going to give him a beating after he learns that Jim is inattentive in school, the wise teacher may refrain from mentioning Jim's inattentiveness to the parents. Teachers often have to stand between the child and his home. Because he was unwise in selecting his parents is no reason to hold the youngster responsible for his parents nor to intensify his problems by "tattling" on him.

With the large majority of parents such an attitude is neither necessary nor desirable. Whenever feasible, the pupil's education should be looked upon as a mutual enterprise by home and school. In these cases, the teacher's therapeutic role is to interpret to parents the professional insights and knowledges available to teachers, but frequently not within the experience of most parents. Teachers counsel parents about punishment, extrinsic motivation, pressure, health needs, and psychological services; they inform parents of developmental stages and tasks; they help parents refocus (if that is necessary) on positive aspects of growth; they keep in close communication with parents so they may know causes for sudden changes in behavior. These are all therapeutic. They particularly help parents avoid over-anxiety about those areas of development that are a part of the growth process.

Circumstances Requiring Specialized Help

We have no intent to communicate the idea that the teacher is the "be-all and end-all" for all his pupils. We do believe the teacher must be the nerve center for all the other services, and that one of his primary roles as a therapist is to know when he needs additional help, what kind of help he needs, where he can get it, and how his job as teacher is related to the special help he secures.

A teacher needs help when he finds a pupil who does not respond over a period of time to any of the processes discussed in this chapter. These times will be rare in most schools. Let's remember, however, that in working with feelings and perceptions, we must give enough time for a process to be accepted and tried out. This may mean weeks or months. One teacher states her understandings about the time it takes thus: "I've learned everything isn't solved in a short while. You have to be patient. You must watch and wait. The child is going along at his own pace. Each day you learn to know him better. Each day brings a better understanding and the pieces of the puzzle begin to fall into place."

A teacher needs specialized help when he finds a pupil who has such a harmful effect upon the group that the teacher is not justified in subjecting the group to this effect. How can he tell what kind of help the pupil needs? He recognizes that many psychological hazards first manifest themselves through a disturbance in the body. If the teacher has a hunch he needs help, one of the first sources to consult is the school doctor or nurse. The teacher begins his search for help by learning thoroughly the functioning of the child's body; he is wise if he reads the health record with great care. Many events are foreshadowed by the child's health history. Any sharp deviation from the individual's own normal patterns is an important diagnostic symptom of danger. In almost all cases where the teacher must request specialized help, a thorough medical examination is recommended. Medicine is tracing more and more emotional imbalances to physical causes. The medical examination needs to be a detailed one, probably including a basal metabolism, urinalysis, blood tests, neurological examinations, electrocardiogram, and any other special tests that seem to be indicated.

After a thorough picture of the individual's physical condition has been obtained, the psychologist, helping teacher, or visiting teacher (or whatever similar type of service the school affords) is probably the next most useful source of help available to the teacher. If at all possible, encourage the psychologist to observe the child or youth unannounced in his group, so he gets a perception of the youngster's relationships within the group when he is not trying to "put on a show." The physician and the psychologist will have other sources of help to recommend to the teacher.

After help has been secured, it seems to us that the classroom teacher should try to assimilate all the data obtained and hypothesize the effects of any recommended course of action upon the child as *he* knows him. This kind of analysis should be part of the psychologist-teacher relationship. But too often the relationship flows in the opposite direction: the psychologist writes up a report, discusses it with Miss Brown, and tells her what to do as a result of his testing. For example, we recommend that if the psychologist is considering the feasibility of a remedial reading program for the child, the classroom teacher's opinion about the effects of such a program should be considered before the recommendation is made. Then, if the teacher and psychologist agree that the recommendation is advisable, the remedial teacher and the classroom teacher work closely together to design a program that promises to have wholesome effects upon the child.

Some youngsters have special competencies that demand nurturing which the teacher cannot provide. The child with unusual musical or art ability, the one whose quantitative thinking extends far beyond that of the teacher, the one who has a gift for languages, may need to be guided into relationships with older boys and girls or with adults who can help the youngster secure real satisfactions from his competency.

In this chapter we have tried to develop a concept of therapy that seems more appropriate for our age than the one frequently held today, that therapy is a process of "caring for," and that all of us, young and old alike, seek therapy from our relationships. We all *do.* If we receive adequate caring for, we feel good, we trust others, and we are able to respond by sharing ourselves with others. As we care for, we learn to care; when we care, we want to share. A teacher who is an artist in his profession accepts the challenge of assuming the role of non-technical therapist by making a vigorous and disciplined study of human behavior that includes the understandings available from many related arts and sciences.

"Love Thyself"

Man has long recognized the ease with which we love and cherish those who promise us protection and advantage. How to love those who menace and threaten us is an ancient, and as yet, unresolved problem. In this book we have stressed the need for love in the healthy development and wholesome being of every human. Teachers persistently inquire, "How can we love the unlovely child? Are we to love the naughty, the smutty, the hostile? Do they deserve our affection, even our acceptance?"

Teachers are the professional growers of human beings. They must keep in mind that people have become more and more civilized as they have employed intelligence to guide the expression of raw, creature impulse. Poets and philosophers have proclaimed the value of love. Yet we seem more and more to live in an atmosphere of contention, suspicion, and threat of violence. Perhaps this is due to our perceiving love to be a commodity to be passed out sparingly to those on our side, to those legally entitled to it, or as payment for those who have earned (deserve) it.

The great moral admonitions of our culture are "Know thyself" and "Love thy neighbor as thyself." Modern psychotherapy operates on the principle that only as you know and like yourself are you able to love your neighbor. The only abnormality among human beings which is not an exaggeration of a normal tendency is dislike for self. The person who really hates himself is sick indeed. Thus, the crucial aspect of "Love thy neighbor as thyself" is the perception of self. Among those who feel inferior, unworthy, guilty of evil doing, this perception is most perilous.

Much of current school practice developed when religion and the prevalent power structure belittled the individual and required self-depreciation. Very few centuries ago to love another meant to despise one's self, to love mankind more meant to love God less. Many teachers now active were trained to avoid friendship with pupils, to guard against intrusion of their feelings into their relationships with pupils.

Love is the emotion of acceptance. The primary need of every baby is constant, reliable love of the mother or mother substitute. While the source and expression of this love changes as we move along through life, the basic need for acceptance remains constant. Love begins in the warm, secure acceptance of the womb and grows to the genuine appreciation of the aged. Convincing evidence indicates that the neonate "knows" whether he is wanted and accepted.

To love another does not imply enthusiastic acceptance of him as he is. We love an infant, yet would be dismayed should he long remain unchanged. Likely the natural function of love is to foster development. The love of a child is acceptance of responsibility for his human well-being and *becoming*. The child who has no guidance or restraint in avoiding costly mistakes and perilous behavior is a loveless child. Learning to forego immediate gratifications today for better and more lasting ones tomorrow requires loving attention. The child with no fences, no limitations upon expression of transitory impulse is an uncared for, lonely child. The child must feel supported rather than restrained by the individual exercising the restraint.

Love does not imply complete, unwavering approval. It is not a spiritual lollipop. A child needs to know that his behavior has consequences for others, that some of his behaviors result in harm and hurt and inconvenience. This he can learn only in an atmosphere of respect for his rights and satisfactions. But love is not harsh, nor punitive, nor repayment in kind—vengeful. To allow the loved one to reap the harvest of the behavioral seeds he has sown is not to team up with the natural laws of cause and effect.

Since the need to think well of, to love one's self is fundamental to the love of others, we tend to erect strong and enduring defenses against rejection. When frustrated in our quest for acceptance and love, we tend to become quite unlovable, proclaiming in our behavior, "I don't care if you don't love me." In trying to understand the unlearning, unruly child, we must look and feel deeply into his feelings of acceptance and rejection.

Agreeing that to love means to care for, we might profitably reflect upon what love is not. Love does not impose indignity upon the loved one; it does not inflict pain or hurt. Love does not demand nor expect exclusive attention nor possession. It does not demand conformity to the lover's ways nor preferences, nor find gratification in the subjection and deference of the loved one. It is not offered as a reward for favors or devotion. It maintains no system of credits and debits.

All too often to love means to satisfy an appetite as expressed in "I just love strawberry jam." In these terms one may love those who satisfy his appetite for power, or worship, or amusement. One engages in no human love for another in using him for his own gratification whether in exhibiting him to the PTA or making him a willing slave.

We cannot accept the all-too-common notion that any trace of love can be found in punishment, ridicule, brain-washing. As this is written we sense a regression to those unloving times when men commonly believed that valuable learning and wholesome developments resulted from the child's reluctant compliance with the harsh demands of his elders.

A most destructive abberation of the ideal of love is held to be the near-ideal in romance. It is expressed in terms such as, "If you really loved me, you wouldn't want to be with your old friends, go fishing with the boys, go to the theater with the girls." Numerous children are made to feel unloving whenever they prefer to be elsewhere than at home. We have known teachers to express marked jealousy of students whose interests wandered away from their special offerings.

Many persons who have been reared in an atmosphere of good-bad, naughty-nice have become quite distrustful of their preferences and distastes. We were good (loved) when we refrained from doing what we wanted to do and bad (unloved) when we followed our own impulses.

As grownups these people have little basic moral sense and scant self-respect. Some cannot tell whether they like a book or a picture until they have read the opinions of the critics. Love requires a fundamental respect for the validity of the tastes of the loved one. It need not imply the obligation of the lover to share those tastes.

A common threat to the development of love is the atmosphere of comparison, the implication of striving for rationed acceptance. Comparisons must be avoided in areas of endeavor in which competency is expected of all. Few men feel threatened by their inability to sing soprano. Many children feel quite unlovely and unloved as a result of unfavorable comparison in reading. Hatred is the fundamental emotion of rejection. Its natural expression is to destroy. We have known of no teacher slaying a pupil. Yet, destruction persists all too much in common school practice. Without constant, intelligent loving the teacher can destroy self-respect, capacity for growth, hopes and joys. Not uncommonly do we destroy a child's gratification in a story he has written, a picture he has painted, an idea he has conceived. We are dismayed at the current re-emphasis of the notion that schools maintain high standards by rejection and elimination of human beings rather than by improved guidance and teaching.

We learn only from those we love. As reading can be learned only among those who read, loving can be learned only among those who love. We believe that this emerging generation of teachers will join more intimately the great leaders and prophets of mankind in promoting love as the primary good of human life. Medical men have sought deeply and widely to reduce unavoidable pain and to eliminate disease of the body through sanitation, therapy, vaccination and anaesthetics. The teacher's most urgent tasks are to discern the threats to wholesome child life and eliminate them from our culture, to search deeply for those positive ways of living that promise long-term gratifications for the human race, and to continue the quest for understanding the wondrous meaning of being human.

Additional Sources You May Find Helpful

Dorothy M. Baruch, *One Little Boy*. New York: Julian Press, Inc., 1952.
  In her statement about "Why This Book Was Written," Baruch states, "All children's intimate thoughts about life and sex and love and hate are basically similar." In reading this detailed, intimate study of Kenneth,

the reader gains many understandings about the unspoken feelings and thoughts of children as they seek to grow toward their own best selves in the complex, strange world they experience.

Lawrence K. Frank, *Society as the Patient.* New Brunswick, N. J.: Rutgers University Press, 1948.

A collection of essays of one of the wise minds of our generation. Mr. Frank states, "they are offered not as pronouncements but as invitations to new ways of thinking. . . . If we can see ourselves as carrying on the endless endeavor to develop a human way of life, we will not shrink from accepting the great privilege and immense responsibility of renewing our culture and reorientating our social order, as the task we and our children must undertake."

Anna Freud, *Psychoanalysis for Teachers and Parents.* New York: Emerson Books, Inc., 1954.

In simple, clear language Anna Freud gives the psychodynamics of behavior and helps adults working with the young to understand the deep effects of their ways of handling various behaviors.

Howard Lane and Mary Beauchamp, *Human Relations in Teaching.* Englewood Cliffs, N. J.: Prentice-Hall, Inc., 1955.

The authors delineate the dimensions of what it means to be human in the mid-twentieth century and suggest ways the sensitive teacher may help the young to grow into wholesome human beings capable of handling the human problems facing us today.

Rollo May, *Man's Search for Himself.* New York: W. W. Norton and Company, Inc., 1953.

The hope of Mr. May is that in reading this book the reader may see himself and his own experiences reflected in the book, and in so doing, may gain "new light on his own problems of personal integration." We found the book fulfills its author's hope.

Karl Menninger, *Love Against Hate.* New York: Harcourt, Brace and Company, 1942.

The content of this book, presented in a form understandable to thoughtful laymen, is the substance of Menninger's teaching to his students. The title of the book carries its main thesis. We recommend the book to students seeking greater self-knowledge.

Ashley Montagu, ed., *The Meaning of Love.* New York: Julian Press, Inc., 1953.

This book is a collection of essays by distinguished psychologists, biologists, anthropologists, and psychiatrists on the subject of love. Love in its many forms and its power in the affairs of humans is presented in a scholarly, insightful, and appealing manner. Don't miss Alvin Johnson's essay on "Love of Friends."

Patrick Mullahy, *A Study in Interpersonal Relations*. New York: Hermitage Press, Inc., 1949.

An excellent collection of essays designed to illuminate the complex factors affecting interpersonal relations.

Harry and Bonaro Overstreet, *The Mature Mind*. New York: W. W. Norton and Company, Inc., 1949.

The Overstreets have made a major contribution through their lectures and writings to clarify the concept of maturity as we see it function in everyday behavior.

Carl Rogers, *Client-Centered Therapy*. Boston: Houghton Mifflin Company, 1951.

The concept developed by Rogers is that individuals with emotional problems are able to work out their own solutions if they are given an accepting atmosphere in which to develop relationships. The far-reaching significance of this assumption in the teacher-pupil relationship is an area you will want to explore as you continue your study and as you associate with children and youth.

Jurgen Ruesch and Weldon Kees, *Nonverbal Communication*. Berkeley, Calif.: University of California Press, 1956.

The book illuminates the ways in which individuals communicate nonverbally, the characteristics of nonverbal communication in various cultures, and the meaning of nonverbal communication in role and status analysis.

Leon J. Saul, *Emotional Maturity*. Philadelphia: J. B. Lippincott Company, 1947.

This book consists of Dr. Saul's teaching materials. Part of the book was written to help families of emotionally disturbed patients to understand the meaning of emotional disturbance and the ideal of emotional maturity. You will find "spot reading" most valuable. Saul states: "There are no problem children, only problem environments . . ."

Lillian Smith, *The Journey*. New York: World Publishing Company, 1954.

A beautifully written account of the nature of the human qualities that set us apart from other creatures. The defenses that man builds within himself; his capacity for love, hope, faith, and courage; his need for something to believe in, to accept are written about with understanding, insight, and creative beauty.

Edward Steichen, *The Family of Man*. New York: Simon and Schuster in collaboration with the Maco Magazine Corporation, 1955.

This unusual collection of photographs was brought together for an exhibit at the Museum of Modern Art in New York. From a three-year search and an examination of over two million photographs from all over the world, Mr. Steichen selected 503 photographs from 68 countries to tell the story of mankind. The exhibit which toured the country was "conceived as a mirror of the universal elements and emotions in the everydayness of life—as a mirror of the essential oneness of mankind throughout the world." The "Prologue" by Carl Sandburg is a beautiful statement that closes with these words: "A camera testament, a drama of the grand canyon of humanity, an epic woven of fun, mystery, and holiness, here is the Family of Man!"

W. D. Wall, ed., *Education and Mental Health*, a report of a UNESCO conference held in Paris, November-December 1952. New York: Columbia University Press, 1953.

The content of this book, presenting the consensus of thinking as it emerged from some of the wisest educators and psychologists of our day who spent a month discussing with each other the problems of education, might well serve as a means for evaluating current educational practice. The contributors to this report stress the "general evil of overstrain at school ... (which) gives rise to maladjustment which must militate against the ideals pursued, or which should be pursued, by the school."

Sources of Materials in the Area of Mental Health

American Orthopsychiatric Association
1790 Broadway, New York 19, N. Y.

Child Study Association of America
132 East 74th Street, New York, N. Y.

Child Welfare League of America, Inc.
24 West 40th Street, New York 18, N. Y.

The Hogg Foundation
University of Texas, Austin, Texas

Mental Health Materials Association
1790 Broadway, New York 19, N. Y.

New York Committee on Mental Hygiene
105 East 22nd Street, New York 10, N. Y.

Index

C

Cannon, W. B., 57, 70
Capacities, 46, 99
Car, use of 333-334
Carmichael, L., 200, 211
Carter, Harold D., 349
Cartwright, Dorwin, 411
Challenge, 38-39
Change, 209
Character:
  as educational goal, 157-158
  changing concepts of, 165-169
  determined by motives, 161-165
  meaning of, 155-175
Chase, Mary Ellen, 286
Chess, Stella, 135
Child, I. L., 139
Child study, 17-20, 24, 42-43
Child Study Assoc. of America, 482
Child Welfare League of America, 482
Chisholm, Brock, 175, 220, 225-226, 457
Chromosomes, 185-186
Church, Joseph, 212
Coghill, G. E., 189
Cole, Natalie, 451
Combs, A. W., 138
Communication:
  beginnings of, 198-202
  breaks in, 390-391
  criteria for, 407
  in early childhood, 251-261
  in groups, 373, 379, 387-392
  teen-agers lack, with adults, 333
Comparisons, 88, 122-123, 479
Competition, 55, 88, 280, 285, 362, 376
Conception, 185-186
Conformity, 113-114, 158-161, 321, 339-344
Congenial pace, 46
Conscience, 165-169, 225-226, 264-265
Cooperation, 101-103, 233, 242, 245-246, 289, 376
Creative listening, 448-449
Creativity, 39-40, 77-78, 434-442
Cretinism, 58
Culture:
  Balinese, 125

Culture (*cont.*):
  common likenesses, 109
  dominant themes, 110-118
  effect on behavior, 27-28
  expectations, 111
  roadblocks, 118-123
  school, 124-125
  sex-linked behavioral differences, 51
  unique to individual, 110
Cunningham, Ruth, 395

D

D'Amico, Victor, 451, 452
David, Henry P., 153
Davie, James S., 121
Davis, Adelle, 63
Davis, Allison, 87, 120, 129, 217, 450
Davis, Clara M., 196
Dawe, H. C., 228
Delinquency, 111, 243, 279, 314-315, 359-364
Democracy, 19, 101, 285, 324, 350-351, 356, 359, 361, 375, 404
Deprivation, 109
Development:
  early, 50, 54
  late, 51, 54
  oral stage, 197
  phallic stage, 219
  sensory, 196-198
Developmental tasks, 179, 195, 215, 238, 272, 313, 330, 357-359
D'Evelyn, Katherine E., 450
Dewey, John, 43, 106
Differences:
  in babies, 194
  in pre-school children, 215
  to be cherished, 19, 54
  used in groups, 377
Differentiation, 180, 195, 201, 207-208, 218-221, 303, 357
Discipline, 126, 134-135, 383-384, 419
Dobzhansky, Theodosius, 185
Drill, 182
Dullness, 33, 48
Dunbar, Flanders, 70
Dwarfism, 59

H

I

Ruby and Helen sit side by side in their s
feels she faces the world alone. One beats th
other cringes from her world. Each needs yo
stand securely upon it.

Sam keeps t
ing? Sam will
discover what l

very difficult for Ellen her first day in school.
unable to face us; she can't meet our eyes or
s. Is she afraid; is she grieving for her former
mething hurt her this morning? How can we
onfidence without pushing her farther away?

Understanding
Human Development

Understanding Human Development

Professor of Psychology and Education
Howard Lane, *San Francisco State College*

and **Mary Beauchamp**
Professor of Education
Alameda County State College